RAILROAD LABOR DISPUTES

RAILROAD
LABOR DISPUTES

The Beginnings

of

Federal Strike Policy

• • •

GERALD G. EGGERT

Ann Arbor
The University of Michigan Press

Preface

HISTORICAL ACCOUNTS of public policymaking are often written as if the process were simply the unfolding of an orderly, rational, predestined scheme. Somehow what happened seems to have had to happen just as it did. If there were real choices or alternatives to the courses pursued, they do not appear. Public officials tend to lose their identity as men and become indistinguishable from the offices they fill. The decisions they made and the actions they took seem but mere functions of their official positions, as if any person holding the same office under like circumstances would have made the same decisions or acted in precisely the same manner. Such accounts can be very misleading.

Three observations that recurred frequently during my research considerably shaped my point of view in writing this study of federal railway strike policy in the late nineteenth century. None of the three was particularly original or startling; I list them only to emphasize what is too often overlooked, forgotten, or taken for granted. The first was that chance and accident played as large a part in the government's handling of railway labor disputes as did careful deliberation, planning, or forethought. Policy often was made during crises, at times axiomatically unsuited for handing down decisions of far-reaching consequence. The second observation was that ultimately individuals made policy. Although policymakers spoke and acted through such institutions as courts, laws, and legislatures, in the end it was the men themselves, not the institutions, that decided what would be done and how. The ideal of government by laws rather than by men is, at best, imperfect. Because all government, of necessity, is administered by men, even government by law cannot rise much above the limitations of the men involved. Finally, public officials, when making decisions, were influenced to a significant degree by their own pasts, their positions in private life, their continuing ties with that past, and their personal ambitions and economic interests.

In the present study I have, so far as possible, traced policy decisions back to the individuals who actually made them. I have also attempted to reconstruct in detail the pressures and circumstances under which decisions were made, including evidences of private ties between public policymakers and parties to the events.

It would be naive, of course, to assume that a simple one-to-one relationship existed between policy decisions and the economic interests of the policymakers—as if judges who owned railroad securities, for example, handed down injunctions against strikers in order to protect their own interests, or government officials who were also in the employ of railroad companies were thereby induced to order out troops to suppress railway strikes. There was, however, a high correlation between judges and other public officials with long, intimate ties to the railroad community and antilabor decisions and actions during railway strikes. On the basis of the available evidence it would seem more than naive to suppose that these economic considerations were without consequence or that they played no role in the decision-making process. Men who spent most of their lives as railway officials, railway lawyers, or owners of large blocks of railroad stocks did not shed their prejudices about railroads or strikers simply because they entered public life. Their conduct during strikes bore ample evidence of their leanings.

It can be argued, on the other hand, that the pro-business, pro-railroad bias of public officials in the nineteenth century is an old and well-known truism. The objection to the proposition, however, is that as a generalization it is imprecise, too all-inclusive, and unfair to public officials who did not share the bias. It fails to discriminate between officials with railroad connections who attacked and those who befriended labor, or between officials without such ties who sided with the companies and those who did not. This study will attempt to make those distinctions. It will also demonstrate that public officials, some with and some without the general bias, proposed apparently reasonable alternatives to the repression of railway strikes during the era under consideration.

Other personal biases have helped to shape this work. I do not regard preservation of the status quo as the primary objective of government in a free society nor the perpetuation of any particular private property relationships as the distinguishing characteristic of the capitalistic order. During the closing decades of the nineteenth century, American workingmen were frequently subjected to exploitation. It was often necessary for them to strike out against prevailing conditions. To protect the public at large, the government was forced from time to time to intervene and to restrain those disorders. It is my contention that such intervention should have been as completely neutral as possible with respect to the parties at dispute. Further, to the degree that the government deprived laborers of their right to strike in order to alter their working conditions, it was obliged to provide other lawful channels through which the struggle could be continued. In my opinion the rise of labor to a share of power in determining the course of the American economy has strengthened both capitalism and democracy. I have, therefore, tended to deplore those acts of the federal government in nineteenth-century railway strikes that retarded labor's advance.

I wish to acknowledge my gratitude to the Scholarly Advancement Fund of Bowling Green (Ohio) State University and to the Central Fund for Research of The Pennsylvania State University for financial assistance in preparing the manuscript of this study for publication. I am especially indebted to my teacher and friend, Professor Sidney Fine of The University of Michigan, who kindly read and carefully criticized the entire work. My former colleagues of the Department of History at Bowling Green State University, particularly Professor James Q. Graham, were most helpful in the early stages of my writing; they patiently listened as I expounded my theories and then gently exploded the poorest of them. The staff of the Rutherford B. Hayes Library in Fremont, Ohio, was most generous in assistance. The news clippings which Robert V. Bruce collected for his book *1877, Year of Violence* and placed on file in the Hayes library greatly facilitated my newspaper research for the 1877 strikes. I am also grateful for permission to reprint in slightly different form in Chapters III, V, and VIII, materials that were first published as an article, "A Missed Alternative: Federal Court Arbitration of Railway Labor Disputes, 1877–1895," in *Labor History*, VII (1966), 287–306.

Finally, for excusing me for hours at a time from family activities and for giving me encouragement and understanding, I wish to thank my wife Jean and my children Michael, Susan, and Christine.

Contents

I. The Problem *1*

II. First Crisis: The Railway Strikes of 1877 *24*

III. Decade of Drifting *54*

IV. New Directions: The Burlington Strike *81*

V. Appeal to the Courts *108*

VI. Dress Rehearsal: Coxey's Army and the
Great Northern Strike *136*

VII. Climax: The Chicago Railway Strike of 1894 *152*

VIII. Vindication and Change *192*

IX. Conclusions *226*

NOTES *243*

BIBLIOGRAPHY *285*

INDEX *297*

CHAPTER I

• • •

The Problem

BEFORE 1877 THE UNITED STATES GOVERNMENT had neither a
labor policy nor established procedures for dealing with major
labor disputes. Even railway strikes—which involved interstate
commerce—seemed to lay beyond its province. The doctrines
of laissez-faire, as then practiced, theoretically precluded governmental interference with labor problems that were purely
economic. To the extent that labor disputes involved lawlessness and disorder, local and state governments were responsible
for quelling them. The great railway strikes of 1877, however,
launched a new era. Never before in America had labor disputes, even on the railroads, been so widespread, so damaging
to commerce, or so marked by violence. Between the onset of
the strikes of 1877 and the close of the Chicago railway (or
Pullman) strike seventeen years later, railroad strikes, boycotts,
and strike threats became common. At least two, the opening
and closing strikes of that era, took on many of the characteristics of the modern national emergency strike.

In spite of the simpler, less interdependent economic structure of late nineteenth-century America, serious disruption of
the transportation system could not be long ignored or long
tolerated. The inconvenience and hardship, not to mention
outright danger to the public, was too great. Almost inevitably
the halting of important railroad services by labor disputes
provoked federal intervention in one form or another. In coping
with these troubles, the federal government slowly evolved
machinery for suppressing strikes and to a degree formulated
the beginnings of a labor policy. The lessons learned and the

1

machinery created at that time continued to be used and modified through the decades that followed. Some remain in use even today.

When the government crushed the Chicago strike in 1894, it became clear to all, especially to the railroads and to their employees, that nationwide blockages would no longer be tolerated. Other means for resolving disputes of that scope had to be worked out. In 1898 the government offered guidance in the form of the Erdman Act, which provided for the voluntary arbitration of railway labor disputes. But more important, collective bargaining increasingly became the accepted procedure by which railroads resolved differences with their employees. Whenever direct negotiations broke down, the government turned to mediation, arbitration, and sometimes to legislation to prevent serious strikes. The nation did not experience another major railroad strike for nearly thirty years and never again did it suffer a rash of rail tie-ups comparable to those that took place between 1877 and 1894.

Unfortunately, other industries having considerable impact on the economy were slow to grasp the significance of the railroad experience or its implications for them. As a result, much of the twentieth century has been devoted to relearning the lesson of the railway strikes, namely that means must be found for settling labor disputes without tying up industries vital to the nation's health, safety, and welfare.

The purpose of this study is to review the first, or "railroad," phase of the federal government's strike policy. Specifically, how did the government become involved in those early strikes on the railroads? What were the grounds for intervention? How did the government meet the various problems posed by the strikes? What purposes lay behind the courses of action pursued? And, to what extent did the private interests of the policymakers shape the role taken by the government?

That the first strikes to involve federal intervention took place on the railroads was to be expected; railroads were this country's first "big businesses." From the 1850's well into the twentieth century they set the pace of modern industrial development. They were perhaps "the most powerful single initiator" of the "take-off" stage of American industrialization, just as later they sparked similar developments in Germany, Russia, and to a lesser degree in Sweden and Japan.[1] Certainly railroads opened vast tracts of the Old Northwest, the Great Plains, and the Far

West to settlement and brought commercial agriculture to areas not already served by canals and natural waterways. In the wake of the railroads came towns and cities with new industries. "[H]istorically the very existence of most American communities and regions, of particular farms and industrial firms and aggregates, was made possible by the railroad."[2] The railway network provided the transportation base upon which America's modern, specialized, interdependent, urban, industrial society rested.

Railroads also played a vital role in capital formation throughout the last half of the nineteenth century. Railroad promoters pioneered in the arts of amassing, administering, and manipulating the immense sums of money needed to construct and operate railroad systems. In the process they developed techniques ranging from the prudent, conservative methods of a John Murray Forbes to the brash, even reprehensible innovations of a Jay Gould. Railways led the way to ever greater business combinations by experimenting with pools, mergers, and holding companies in order to increase efficiency and profits and to escape the ravages of unrestricted "cutthroat" competition. The marketing of nearly $10 billion worth of railroad securities by 1889 contributed greatly to the rise of investment banking. Eventually, railroads were among the first to fall victim to finance capitalism when control passed from the builders and owners of the lines to the masters of finance who furnished the capital for expansion and consolidation.[3]

The large-scale production of iron and steel, upon which a major portion of America's industrial might in the post-Civil War era was based, owed much to the railroads. Although the iron industry long antedated railroads, mass production of steel was made possible in many instances only after rails brought together the raw materials. Frequently, railroad companies owned the coal fields and the iron mines and used their capital to develop these resources. Consumption of coal and steel by the railroads was probably even more important to the growth of those industries than either railroad transportation or capital. Steam locomotives were largely powered by coal throughout the late nineteenth and early twentieth centuries, and as late as 1880 three-fourths of all the steel produced in the United States went into the manufacture of rails.[4]

Railroads had become the bellwether of the nation's economy by the close of the Civil War. When railroad construction boomed, the economy as a whole boomed too. When rail-road securities dropped in value and construction slowed, the entire economy sagged. Though by no means the cause of depressions in the post-Civil War era, overexpansion of railroads in the early 1870's and 1890's helped to stimulate the speculative fevers of those years; halts in railroad construction and railway receiverships were marked features of the Panics of 1873, 1884, and 1893.[5]

By 1877 the railroad network consisted of over 79,000 miles of line. Overall the industry represented an investment of almost $5 billion, nearly half of which ($2.26 billion) was bonded debt; the national debt that same year, for purposes of comparison, stood at $2.1 billion. In spite of depression conditions the railroads in 1877 netted over $170 million; total receipts of the federal government from all sources were just under $281.5 million.[6] About fifty corporations, each operating between two hundred and a thousand miles of road, made up the bulk of the nation's railway system. Of the fifty, the Pennsylvania stood first and was the nation's greatest single private enterprise. Capitalized at $398 million (in 1873), it owned, operated, or otherwise controlled 6600 miles of line and employed probably 20,000 men.[7] No other industry in the country approached this scale of operation.

But railroads were not only the country's economic pacesetters and its largest businesses; by 1877 they were fast becoming economically indispensable.[8] All land transportation of persons and goods, save that of a purely local nature, went by rail. By the 1870's railroads had overtaken canals and natural waterways as carriers of the nation's freight. As early as 1871 only 34 percent of the total freight tonnage passing through St. Louis was carried on the great river; by 1877 only 10 percent. In 1872 the 10 million tons of freight carried by the Erie and New York Central railroads to New York City was nearly triple the 3.7 million tons borne there over the Erie Canal. Four-fifths of all the grain received at Eastern seaports in 1876 came by rail and in 1878 freight received in New York City by way of the Erie, New York Central, and Pennsylvania railroads was five times by volume that brought to the port city by way of the Erie Canal.[9] Nearly all passengers, the mail, troops and their supplies, perhaps from two-thirds to three-fourths of all freight—indeed most of the nation's commerce—moved over the railroad network.

The reasons are clear. Canals, though offering cheap transportation, were slow. Perishables required speed in transit. Rails, because they were more flexible, could serve communities that canals could not reach. They were also easier to maintain; canals were plagued by erosion and silting. Trains operated the year around while springtime flooding, summer drought, and heavy autumn rains all interfered with regular operation of canals. From November to April, moreover, freezing blocked waterways except in the South. Increasingly, canals carried only bulky, low-value cargo such as lumber, coal, ore, gravel, stone, and cement.[10]

Railroad growth between 1877 and 1894 was phenomenal. Road mileage reached 230,000, nearly tripling. Water transportation, already lagging in 1877, continued to fall behind. Rails carried 640 million tons of freight in 1889 as compared with 129 million tons moved over all canals, the Great Lakes and St. Lawrence River, and the Ohio-Mississippi river systems combined. Capitalization of the railroad network stood at $8.6 billion in 1894, of which $5.36 billion was bonded debt; the national debt that year was slightly over $1 billion. Because of economic depression, net income for railroads in 1894 was only $60 million (down from $114 million in 1893), though $95.5 million were paid out in dividends. Federal government receipts from all sources amounted to $386 million in 1894. The railroads in 1889 employed 750,000 men, of whom 323,000 worked for the sixteen largest companies. The Pennsylvania maintained its leadership with nearly 65,000 employees. By contrast, the entire federal bureaucracy in 1891 consisted of but 157,000 civilians.[11]

Matching the economic power of the railroads was their political influence. In some states they seemed to control the political machinery completely and their rapport with high federal officials was impressive. Railroad promoters and lobbyists swarmed in the state houses and in the halls of Congress, seeking charters, franchises, subsidies, and land grants while fighting against investigations, regulation, and new taxes. When not at war with the farmers and small town merchants who were trying to bring them under control, they struggled with one another for legislative favors. The inducements they offered were the free pass, the political contribution, influence, and on occasion the outright bribe. They also held out such considerations as legal fees to be paid, construction contracts to be let, and a wide variety of positions to be filled.[12]

The courts, too, devoted much time to railroad affairs. Litigation involving personal damage suits, controversies over contracts, leases, and rights-of-way, claims to be paid or collected, receiverships, reorganizations, and bankruptcies provided much work for lawyers both in small county seat towns in the South and West and in the major cities of the East. Talented attorneys in almost every community at one time or another were hired by the railroads and many of them became "railroad lawyers" in every sense of the word. When these men later became judges, legislators, governors, senators, or cabinet members, they often maintained friendly ties with their former clients and carried a pro-railroad point of view to their new positions.

The other principals to railway strikes, the workmen, had little economic or political power in the late nineteenth century. At best they were only partially organized. Membership in unions generally swelled or shrank with changes in the business climate, the size of a particular union at any given time often being directly related to whether it had recently won or lost a strike. No single union or group of unions spoke for railway labor throughout the years between 1877 and 1894, so each major upheaval found the workers fighting under new banners. Recognition of the unions by the companies for purposes of collective bargaining was not common. Sometimes companies negotiated wages and work rules with unions for the sake of convenience, or out of necessity, but never as a matter of right.[13]

At the time of the strikes in 1877, organized labor was in considerable disarray. The Panic of 1873 and the ensuing depression slashed total union membership in the United States from about 300,000 in the early 1870's to probably no more than 50,000 by 1878.[14] Among railwaymen a minority of the skilled workmen were organized, by function, into three brotherhoods, the Brotherhood of Locomotive Engineers (BLE), the Brotherhood of Locomotive Firemen, and the Order of Railway Conductors. The BLE, oldest and most powerful of the three, from its beginning in 1863, had tried to win concessions from the railroads by stressing the importance of competency among its members and by insisting upon loyalty to the companies. This nonstriking policy met only limited success and the BLE abandoned it briefly during the winter of 1876–77. Defeat in a few strikes, however, quickly convinced the leadership to return to its former nonmilitant stance. Thereafter, the BLE, like the other brotherhoods, scrupulously avoided conflict with the companies. During the strikes of the summer of 1877 the brotherhoods provided no leadership whatsoever.[15]

The rise of the Knights of Labor in the following decade offered the brotherhoods some competition. The Knights, however, drew their strength among railway workers primarily from the unskilled. In their battles with organized labor, the companies were able to exploit jealousy among the brotherhoods and had little trouble inducing the Knights and the brotherhoods to "scab" on one another.[16]

From time to time attempts were made to unite railway workmen into a solid front to face their employers. These attempts sometimes took the form of simple federations of the brotherhoods; sometimes they produced new, aggressive unions that undertook to bring together all railway labor, skilled and unskilled.[17] Of the latter type, the Trainmen's Union, formed in June 1877, offered promise of uniting railwaymen on the eve of the great strikes. The organization began to fall apart just as the strikes started, however, and the strikes and union died together. Another, the American Railway Union, formed in 1893, won a significant victory against the Great Northern Railway before being smashed by the Pullman strike.[18] The railway workers, their organizations denied recognition by the companies and often at odds with one another, lacked institutionalized channels through which to secure redress of their grievances. Sometimes in frustration they struck out against their employers; when they did, they usually lost.

Exception might be taken to considering late nineteenth-century railway labor disputes as serious enough to warrant federal intervention or to compare the more severe of them to modern national emergency strikes. Such matters are always subject to differing opinions, of course. The theorist may argue, for example, that capital and labor should be left free to battle one another without governmental interference unless or until the nation's transportation, industry, and commerce are paralyzed and a large part of the population is reduced to actual suffering. But these questions are usually resolved more pragmatically. That portion of the public directly inconvenienced or injured by a strike rarely sees any benefits from its suffering. At the first sign of hardship the cry goes up for governmental intervention to halt the disorders. The demands of an outraged public, particularly when widespread, are not often ignored by public officials. In a very real sense, whether or not a strike constitutes a national emer-

gency or is sufficiently serious to justify federal action is largely
determined by the reaction of the public and of public officials
to its consequences.

That the public may be mistaken in its demands is always
possible. That public officials may panic too easily and use their
powers to intervene unreasonably or unjustly is also always
possible. Prudence dictates that public officials act with discretion in these matters; but it also demands that they act while
injury may yet be averted. Neither their contemporaries nor
history is apt to forgive officials who are so cautious that they
allow threats to materialize into realities that do serious harm
to individuals or to society at large.

Turning more specifically to the strikes in question, could
it not be argued that the United States in the late nineteenth
century was still relatively primitive in its economic and industrial development? Industries engaged in the mass production
of consumer goods were virtually unknown and the economic
specialization and interdependence so typical today had scarcely begun by 1877 or even 1894. Labor, moreover, was too poorly
organized and undisciplined to sustain strikes of long duration.
Finally, the argument might run, the United States was still
basically rural. No strike, not even a railroad strike of whatever magnitude, could possibly imperil any substantial part
of the nation. Most towns and cities were small and close enough
to farming areas to live off the neighboring countryside. The
few very large cities could probably survive on goods brought to
them over the canals, rivers, and Great Lakes. In other words,
economically, strikes threatening to the nation's welfare were
not yet possible.[19]

These objections bear the markings of hindsight. Today
the railroads carry but 43.68 percent of the nation's freight,
2.52 percent of its passengers, and only a portion of its mail.
Motor trucks, busses, automobiles, and airplanes offer convenient substitute means of transportation. Yet, a major railway strike would be regarded as a national emergency which,
if allowed to begin at all, would not be long tolerated.[20] How,
then, in an age when railroads carried most of the freight, passengers, and mail, could a major strike be so much less critical
than today? Is it assumed that delivery of that era's freight, passengers, and mail was of no real importance, or that the movement of troops to the frontier during the Indian Wars was not
a pressing necessity? In retrospect, crises often tend to diminish
in severity, even to disappear, but few people living through

those early railway strikes regarded them as being of little consequence. More important, however mistaken newspaper editors, businessmen, and public officials, not to mention railroad managers, may have been from a present point of view, they looked upon those strikes as emergencies and acted accordingly.

Despite the simpler economic structure, the relatively lower degrees of specialization and interdependence, and the smaller proportion of the population living in urban centers, both the strikes of 1877 and the Pullman strike wrought considerable economic havoc. In 1877 the disorders swept through the major rail centers of the nation: Baltimore, Philadelphia, Pittsburgh, Buffalo, Cleveland, Toledo, Columbus, Cincinnati, Louisville, Indianapolis, Chicago, St. Louis, Kansas City, and Omaha, to name only the more important. Outside this central area there were brief flare-ups in New York City and Albany in the Northeast, in Little Rock, New Orleans, and Galveston in the South, and in San Francisco on the Pacific Slope. About two-thirds of the country's total rail mileage lay within the strike-affected area, and in those zones strikers halted most freight trains and delayed many passenger and mail trains.[21]

The disorders closed all five of the trunk lines connecting the Midwest with the cities of the Eastern seaboard. Newspapers viewed these tie-ups as a national calamity. The *New York Tribune* complained that there was "no route between the East and the West by which goods can be safely or regularly moved." It reported commerce blocked, goods—"by the hundred carloads"—destroyed or halted, merchants bankrupted, factories closed, and "thousands of industrious and order-loving men . . . out of work." So far as transportation was concerned, the *Tribune* observed the next day, "the whole country from the Hudson to the Mississippi" was held in the grip of "insurrection against the laws of the States and the Government of the United States. . . ."[22] Another newspaper lamented that "the practical effect of the embargo is as if an earthquake had opened an impassable chasm along the Alleghenies between the East and West. . . ."[23] The *New York Times* referred to the railways as "great national highways," and compared the trunk lines to "so many arteries, whose healthy action is indispensable to trade and travel." When one of them was cut or "clogged," the "interests which suffer extend across the continent"; if all of them were injured "the whole country must pay the penalty."[24] The railway network, the *Chicago Daily Tribune* declared, was "the very heart

and life of the modern system of commercial existence." Should
it be blocked, "we revert to the primitive days of stage coaches
and canal-boats," the paper asserted. "It would be like the breaking of the mainspring of a watch."[25]

Seventeen years later, the Pullman strike, which extended
over most of the United States west of the Ohio-Pennsylvania
boundary, tying up rail traffic to varying degrees throughout
that vast area, evoked similar responses from the nation's newspapers and magazines. The influential weekly, *Nation*, described
the boycott-strike as "an attempt to starve out society." The
country "subsists by the movement of trains," it continued, and
could not "exist more than a few days without such movement."[26] The *Philadelphia Times* declared that the strike was
"so perilous to public comfort and safety and so far-reaching in
its aim," that it had to be "resolutely met and overthrown." Any
temporizing would "endanger the whole industry and commerce
of the country."[27] From the center of the strike the *Chicago
Daily Tribune* observed that a paralysis of the railroads of long
duration would "throw" the nation "back into very wretched
and primitive conditions; [cut] off the supply of food and fuel
to the cities and [stop] short all their commercial and manufacturing industries, isolate the farmers from the rest of the world
. . . [and] cut down to zero the earning power of the whole
people."[28]

The editor of the *Independent* magazine regarded the impact of the strike as self-evident. "It is not required to-day to
argue how necessary railways are to our civilization," he said.
"Everyone recognizes the fact that we are dependent upon them
for our continuance in business, for our supplies of merchandise
and for food, and even for life itself, in the long run. . . ."[29]
General Nelson A. Miles, commander of the federal troops sent
to Chicago, concurred. Writing at the time of the strike, he
observed that there was "scarcely a family" in the country that
was not interested "in the peaceful and uninterrupted communication of the railways. . . ." Certainly, the nation's "producers,
farmers, manufacturers, mechanics, and men in all positions of
life" had an interest in "daily communication" and "the peaceful and certain operation, of the great lines of commerce of this
country." He noted that millions were dependent on the railroads "for their daily food," and if the lines were blocked,
"famine, pestilence, and death would overshadow thousands of
villages and cities that are now enjoying life and prosperity." He
likened such a disaster to slashing "the great arteries between

the heart and the brain of the physical system."[30] So far as these and similar statements represented current views, there was little doubt or debate but that the strikes had created national emergencies.

No one was reported to have starved because of either of the great strikes. Most cities had at least a week's supply of food on hand at the height of both of these affairs.[31] In neither instance were shortages prolonged or critical because federal intervention ended them in about two weeks' time. How severe conditions would have become without such intervention can only be surmised. At the time it was suspected, and certainly hoped, that the strikes would not last long.[32] But no one knew then (or knows today for that matter) what course the strikes might have taken or how long they might have lasted had they not been promptly checked by force.

Even so, the strikes created shortages. Supplies of staples ran low in cities across the land. Prices in some instances rose dramatically. Because few people had facilities for refrigerating foodstuffs, such items as milk, meat, fresh vegetables, and fruit had to be purchased several times a week, if not daily, during the summer months. Ordinarily there was never more than a day or two's supply of perishables on hand in any city. Inasmuch as both strikes occurred in July, these items were the first to disappear from the market stalls and the first to rise in price.[33] In some places wheat and flour, too, soon became scarce and higher priced.

For several days in 1877 the strikes cut off New York City from its usual sources of grain and meat in the Midwest. Farmers in the Middle Atlantic States helped by sending cattle and hogs to the city, but meat prices rose nonetheless. Better grades of beef, which sold for 11½¢ per pound on July 20, reached 14¢ by July 24. Within the same period good cuts of mutton went from 10¢ to 15¢ and lamb from 12½¢ to 17¢ per pound. Cheaper grades of meat, consumed by working-class people, reportedly advanced in price even more rapidly. Coarse butter from the West, selling for between 20¢ and 21¢ per pound before the embargo, rose to between 22¢ and 24¢. Eggs, chiefly from Canada and the Midwest, increased from 18¢ to 23¢ per dozen.[34]

Newspapers reported shortages of provisions, grains, and meat in other cities but gave little specific information. The *St. Louis Times* reported that the strike had materially affected the price of provisions there. "Flour has gone up to an enormous price and should the mills be stopped for a day or two longer, a good deal of suffering among the poor of the city will result from it."[35] "The price of commodities is gradually ascending," the *Chicago Post* complained. "The rioters may succeed in getting breadstuffs up to war prices." According to the *Chicago Times,* on the Monday before the strike, 1400 car loads of corn were received in Chicago. On July 27 that figure was reduced to but 94 car loads of all kinds of grain.[36] Because the area was completely dependent upon the blockaded Baltimore & Ohio for nearly all its supplies, the mining district of Allegheny County, Maryland, experienced an acute shortage of flour and other staples for several days.[37]

Coal shortages also were a problem in several communities. Because it was summer, the fuel was not needed for heating, but it was widely used for cooking. In St. Louis the strike was promptly reflected in coal prices. On Saturday, July 20, it sold for 9¢ per bushel; on Sunday, 10¢; Monday, 12¢; Tuesday, 14¢; and Wednesday, 30¢ when available, with a few families paying as much as 50¢. Two days later, thanks to a shift in the source from which the city obtained its coal, the price fell to 12½¢, with a ten bushel limit per family. Even this was 39 percent higher than the prestrike price. Baltimore, New York, Chicago, and Indianapolis all reported coal shortages and advancing prices.[38]

The impact of the Pullman strike on the supplies and prices of food and coal in major cities was similar to that of the 1877 riots. At Chicago, center of the disorders, fruit and vegetable prices rose sharply. Newspapers reported only four days' supply of potatoes on hand on July 2. By July 4 the price had risen from the usual 60¢ per bushel to 90¢. Twenty-pound packages of California peaches, 60¢ before the strike, advanced to $1.10. The greatly reduced stocks of fresh fruits and vegetables met the demands of the market only because advancing prices made them "luxuries beyond the reach of workingmen."[39]

Chicago experienced no shortages of milk, meat, or grain during the two weeks of blockade. Strikers permitted milk trains to pass and because the city was the nation's chief processing and distributing center for meat and grain, there were large stores of these items on hand. Had the strike lasted longer, however, even Chicago might have felt the pinch in these vital products. Between July 3 and 10, livestock received at the stockyards slowed to a trickle: 242 cattle, 5 calves, 19 hogs, and 8852 sheep. During the corresponding week of 1893 the Chicago yards received over 60,000 cattle, 6000 calves, 113,000 hogs, and 54,900 sheep.[40]

Eastern cities, largely dependent upon Chicago for live-stock and meat, received none and faced a shortage. New York City dealers on July 4 predicted famine unless the strike ended within two or three days. Meat prices, meanwhile, "again" went up between 2¢ and 3¢ per pound. As it turned out, farmers in nearby states had livestock enough to supply the city for perhaps two weeks. Daily consumption of beef cattle, none-theless, dropped from 15,000 to 10,000 head. Wholesale poultry prices rose by 4½¢ per pound.[41] Baltimore reported being short about 1000 head of beef cattle on July 5 and prices there went up 3¢ a pound. In Washington, D.C., beef advanced 50 percent in price between June 30 and July 4. The Associated Press reported that pork and other meat prices in New England had made "sharp advances." At Lowell there was "no meat to be had at any price."[42]

The newspapers reported spectacular rises in vegetable and fruit prices around the country: in Milwaukee prices of these items had doubled as early as June 30; in Cleveland they were 50 percent above prestrike prices by July 6. In New York City peaches that sold for $1.00 per box in June reached $3.60 by July 6.[43] Train loads of these commodities rotted unhar-vested in the fields or in box cars blocked from the markets. At Louisville 200 car loads of perishables, unable to move to Northern markets, were auctioned off. Farmers in Anna, Illinois, petitioned Governor John P. Altgeld to act to end the strike—they were losing $3000 per day because they could not ship their harvest of between thirty and forty car loads of ripe tomatoes to Chicago.[44]

The Pullman strike isolated Western communities which often were completely dependent upon the railroads for most of their foodstuffs. Faribault, Minnesota, exhausted its sugar supply by July 3 and most other staples were fast disappearing. Teams and wagons were sent to Minneapolis for relief supplies. West Superior, Wisconsin, faced a famine in meat, milk, and vegetables. Wheat, cattle, and railroad towns west of Fargo, North Dakota, were without staples excepting bread and meat. Mining towns west of Cheyenne, Wyoming, suffered shortages of all foodstuffs.[45]

A mining strike in southern Illinois had depleted coal supplies even before the railway tie-up began, and early in

July Chicago came near to running out. On July 4 the news-papers reported that soft coal was not available and that anthracite prices had risen between 50¢ and 75¢ per ton. Ice, too, became scarce. Chicago, according to the *Tribune,* used 10,000 tons of ice per day in June, July, and August. Natural ice stocks in the city were gone, none could be brought from storage in Wisconsin, and artificial ice plants turned out only about 350 tons per day.[46]

More serious than food shortages to individual health and safety was the widespread closing of industries and businesses during the strikes of 1877 and 1894. Men without jobs or in-comes could not supply their families with the necessities of life even where they were available. The strikes did not throw just railwaymen out of work. In 1877 in Chicago, St. Louis, and Toledo gangs of strikers and sympathizers paraded through the business, factory, and shipping districts, urging workmen to lay down their tools and factory managers and shopkeepers to close their businesses. Although less pressure was applied elsewhere, newspapers reported numerous sympathy strikes.[47] In cities where rioting occurred—Pittsburgh, Chicago, and St. Louis, to name but three—storekeepers and businessmen were slow to resume work. Fear of further troubles, coupled with a lack of customers and an inability to ship goods, contributed to pro-tracted closings.

Shortages of coal and other products also caused lay-offs. In Baltimore draymen, clerks, and stevedores were idle because ocean-going vessels were unable to secure cargo in some in-stances, or coal to fuel their engines in others. In Indianapolis, on July 25, a wheel works, employing 250 men, and a rolling mill, employing 240 men, closed for want of materials. A second rolling mill, the city water works, and a number of woolen, flour, and paper mills all threatened to close within a day or two because they lacked coal or raw materials. The breweries in the same city could ship no beer, and 250 drays in the Hoosier capital stood still with nothing to transport.[48]

General Winfield Scott Hancock, commander of federal forces in Pennsylvania in 1877, reported: "In a week it is said coal for manufacturing purposes will be exhausted unless freight trains can run. Machinery work will cease, the idle employee must have bread and he will be without money to purchase it. . . ."[49] Federal intervention halted the strikes before the general's grim predictions could be tested.

The Pullman strike similarly put many laborers out of work.

A "coal famine is threatened," Bradstreet's weekly report declared early in the strike, "trade with country merchants is in many instances actually stopped owing to the inability to ship goods, and factories are closing for want of fuel." The New York dry goods market was at a standstill, dealers fearing destruction of goods in transit. In Denver 1000 smeltery workers were off for lack of coal; in Chicago the Illinois Steel Company, employing 3000 men, closed for lack of coke. All but three of the flour mills in Minneapolis stopped milling, throwing 3500 men out of work. St. Paul reported 7000 idle because of the strike. In the Cheyenne area 1000 railroaders were unemployed. At the end of the first week, Bradstreet's estimated that 500,000 men were out of work because of the strike.[50]

These fragmentary opinions and reports of shortages, rising prices, and suffering were impressionistic to be sure. They represented, however, the general newspaper response to the strikes. No doubt some of the accounts exaggerated existing conditions, and it should be noted that the direst consequences were nearly always anticipated, not actually occurring. In a few instances news items would contradict the bleak reports of other items, and the New York *Chronicle* in one or two editorials dismissed the strikes of 1877 as of no real importance. The tone of the editorials, however, seemed more to be whistling in the dark than firm conviction and were belied by comments on the news pages.[51] Even allowing for error, exaggeration, and sensation-mongering, it is evident that the strikes in 1877 and 1894 created severe shortages of food and fuel and cut off the incomes of tens of thousands of workingmen.

That strikebound cities might have been supplied other than by rail proves, upon reflection, to be illusory. Existing marketing and distributing patterns depended primarily upon the regular operation of the railroads. When the trains stopped running, more was needed to supply urban areas than for nearby farmers to halt their work, load up their wagons with provisions, and haul them to market. Towns of from 10,000 to 25,000 (there were 146 in 1877 and 230 in 1894) could not live long off the countryside without some planning and organizing of the food supply. Cities ranging from 25,000 to 50,000 (there were forty-two according to the 1880 census and sixty-six by 1890) probably required more goods than their immediate areas could provide or than horse and wagon could carry to them. Even were horse-drawn vehicles equal to the task of transportation, there remained the question whether a city could obtain the variety of vital goods it needed from its own surrounding countryside.

A very considerable commerce would have been required to feed and supply cities with populations in excess of 50,000. Over a dozen of the thirty-five cities of that rank in 1877 were directly involved in the strikes and rioting.[52] Another fourteen depended on the commerce ordinarily carried by the then blocked trunk lines. Had the strikes of 1877 or 1894 continued for several weeks, it is difficult to imagine how these cities would have avoided severe food shortages. "If this striking business continues many days longer, blocking the railroads," the *Chicago Times* warned in 1877, "there is no telling when starvation about which there is so much prating by communistic orators may not come actually to the whole city. It is no child's play to supply a city of half a million of people with the wherewithal to sustain life. The quantity on hand seldom exceeds the want of a few days . . . and when the usual sources from which exhausted supplies are replenished are absolutely cut off, the crisis is, indeed serious."[53]

Prolonged strikes would have required elaborate and prompt redirecting of commerce in order to supply the larger cities. Wheat for New York City, for instance, might have been shipped by boat from Duluth or Chicago over the Great Lakes and the Erie Canal; flour for Pittsburgh might have gone down the Mississippi from St. Louis to Cairo and thence up the Ohio to its destination; pork for Baltimore and Philadelphia might have been shipped from Cincinnati or St. Louis by the Ohio and Mississippi rivers to New Orleans and from there by coastwise vessels to the Eastern port cities. These and dozens of other reroutings would have required directing and planning on a grand scale, indeed, on a scale well beyond the powers and talents of the state and federal governments as they then functioned—perhaps on a scale even beyond the powers and talents of the business community operating under the guidance of Adam Smith's "unseen hand."

Where would the barges and boats have come from to move this sudden flood of goods? Could private capital have been expected to invest in barge building on such a scale when even the most pessimistic of persons knew the railroad strikes were temporary? Who would have dredged out and reopened clogged, abandoned canals? How would the canal, river, and Great Lakes ports have received goods from the hinterland ex-

cepting by rail? And what of cities such as Indianapolis, with
75,000 persons to supply in 1877, torn by strike, and served
by no navigable waterway?

More convincing than either logic or speculation, however,
is what actually happened. When the strikes shut off food supplies, some nearby farmers did haul produce to the larger cities.
Often draymen went out with their carts to blockaded trains
and brought back goods. In one such instance at Chicago in
1894 teams hauled $1500 worth of vegetables from a halted train
into the city. The effort required twelve hours and added $50
to the cost. The produce, moreover, was so wilted by the time
it was sold that it could not command a good price. At best
these efforts were of minor significance. Many farmers who in
ordinary times hawked their produce in the cities refused to
risk life, limb, and property. The *Pittsburgh Post,* several days
after the riots there in 1877, reassured farmers that law and
order had been restored, it was safe for them to bring produce
to market, and the prices being paid for fresh vegetables would
make the trip profitable.[54]

In practice, little water transportation was substituted for
rail. At St. Louis in 1877, for example, river boatmen and
stevedores struck in sympathy with the railroad men. Great
Lakes shippers both in 1877 and 1894 found no one to load or
unload their ships during several days of disorders at Chicago.
Boatmen on the Chesapeake and Ohio Canal, which supplied
Washington and Baltimore with coal, went on strike before
the railroad troubles began in 1877 and continued on strike
throughout the crisis.[55]

Even the most successful of the canals, the Erie, enjoyed no
great increase in its business during the strikes of 1877. Weekly
toll collections showed no unusual gains, and total tolls collected
through the first week of August, 1877, fell substantially behind
similar collections in 1876 and 1878. Syracuse, located on the
canal, complained of shortages of grain and flour. "The usefulness of the Erie Canal is not yet passed," the Rochester *Union
and Advocate* commented, going on to relate the story of a
man who, when unable to leave Buffalo by rail, hit upon the
idea of going to New York City by canal. That the incident was
novel enough to be newsworthy underscores how little the canal
was used for substitute transportation.

When the *Toronto Daily Mail* suggested in an editorial
that the boatmen stood to gain from the rail strikes, the *Buffalo*

Express took it to task. "Without the railway feeders, to bring
the freight to points of accumulation, where vessels can reach
it, the great bulk of 'the year's grain crop' . . . would be left
untouched in the farmers' granaries." The canal would pick up
small local traffic, the *Express* conceded, "but every boatman on
the Erie Canal . . . knows that the amount of traffic would not
be sufficient to give profitable employment to one tenth of the
tonnage of the canal."[56]

In 1894 longshoremen at Chicago and dockworkers at
Duluth struck in sympathy with the railwaymen. "Less business
was done on the Chicago River yesterday," the *Tribune* reported
on July 4, 1894, "than for twenty years during the season of
navigation. Lake traffic was in fact more completely tied up by
the railroad strike than the railroads themselves."[57] With few
exceptions canals could not have alleviated the embargo in 1894.
Only railroads west of Pittsburgh were blocked; most of the
major canals were east of the strike area and there railroads
were still operating.

Theoretically, the nation might have turned to waterways
during railway strikes; in fact, it did not. No one expected the
railroad strikes to be permanent, however many more days or
weeks they might run. The real problem, therefore, was not to
find a substitute for railroads, but a means to keep railways
operating even during labor disputes.

The economic impact of major rail strikes was but one of
the factors that made them of concern to the federal government. The violence and civil commotion they often produced
had social and political connotations of considerable magnitude.
Frequently, law and order broke down in major rail centers
across the land; what was regarded as "domestic insurrection"
and "rebellion" took over. Millions of dollars worth of property
was destroyed, hundreds of persons were injured, and scores
killed in rioting and in pitched battles with law enforcement
officials. In 1877 there were two days of lawless looting and
pillaging in Pittsburgh; citizens in Indianapolis organized an
extralegal "committee of public safety" to protect the city from
strikers; there were brief general strikes in St. Louis, Chicago,
and Toledo, and anti-Chinese riots in California. Rioting disrupted orderly life in St. Louis and in nearby points during the
Southwest strikes of both 1885 and 1886. In 1894 widespread
lawlessness raged in Chicago even in the presence of state milita
and federal troops. Labor leaders there, in the midst of the dis-

orders, called for a general strike in support of the railwaymen.
Although it failed to materialize, public officials were properly
alarmed. The general confusion along the railways in 1894
was sufficiently disturbing to cause the Treasury Department to
suspend all money shipments between government subtrea-
suries.[58]

Neither the Hayes nor the Cleveland administrations took
the strikes of 1877 or the Pullman strike lightly. Both Presidents
met daily with their cabinets and were in almost constant contact with other advisers during the disorders. These aspects of
the strikes were noneconomic. They were, nonetheless, an integral part of the strikes and ought not to be dismissed as irrelevant.

As for the lesser railway strikes and strike-threats of the era,
the Southwest strikes, the Burlington strike, the Buffalo Switchmen's strike and the Great Northern strike, to name the more
famous, all could suddenly have erupted into full-blown crises
equal to or exceeding the strikes of 1877 and 1894 in their
seriousness. Neither government officials, the press, nor the
public could foretell in advance that these strikes would be
more limited. Few argued in favor of doing nothing during these
strikes in the hopes they would settle themselves. So far as the
press represented or influenced public opinion, it criticized the
federal government—not for acting—but for not acting more
quickly and with greater force.

From 1877 on, effective railway strikes were widely viewed as
intolerable and the necessity for ending them proved to be the
mother of federal intervention. As government officials dealt
with these affairs, the first phase of a federal railway strike policy
unfolded. Between 1877 and 1898 little of that "policy" was
formal or conscious. Inasmuch as the strikes often got out of
hand before the government was called in, the usual goal of
intervention was to halt the strikes and to restore law, order,
and regular railway service as quickly as possible. The actions
taken, born of crisis, became precedents that would guide and
justify similar interventions in the future. Only the voluntary
arbitration acts passed by Congress in 1888 and 1898 were
aimed at settling labor disputes before they reached the stage
of open hostility or at ending strikes peacefully once underway.

Apparently, this failure to deal with the labor problem
resulted directly from a belief that labor disputes, so long as
they remained orderly, lay outside the province of government.

Certainly, it was not due to a rigid application of the doctrines of laissez-faire to the railroad industry. The idea that railways were quasi-public in nature and, hence, subject to governmental regulation and control was of long standing.[59] Only a few weeks before the strikes of 1877 the United States Supreme Court ruled in the Munn case that businesses (presumably including railroads) which became clothed with a public interest were subject to regulation by the states.[60] But labor disputes, even on railways, presented something of a dilemma. On the one hand, workers could not be prohibited from "striking" (usually equated with quitting their jobs); to force men to work against their wills would be involuntary servitude. On the other hand, the government could not force the owners of private property, even of quasi-public railroads, to yield to the demands of their employees; that would be an arbitrary denial of their property rights. For the government to intervene, to rule on the issues in dispute, and to force compliance with its findings would violate both the workmen's freedom and the owners' proprietary rights. Intervention came, therefore, only after private warfare between railroads and their employees degenerated into rioting. At that point government officials could justify intervention on the side of the companies to the ends of halting domestic violence or of restoring functions of government that were blocked by the disorders.

The most obvious grounds for federal intervention in railway strikes would seem to have been the constitutional grant of authority to Congress to regulate interstate commerce. Neither before nor after 1877, however, did Congress enact laws to protect interstate commerce from obstruction during labor disputes, even though statutes outlawing strikes on interstate railways or providing machinery for settling such disputes would appear to have been within the powers of Congress. Similarly, federal responsibility for the mail would seem to have provided justification for intervention. Congress, long before 1877, made obstructing the mails a federal offense, but the law was directed against individuals who prevented mail from being delivered, not at labor disputes that blocked its passage.

Neither of these grounds was used to justify the initial intervention in 1877. Protection of interstate commerce, though often an important concern in railway strikes, did not become the official basis of federal intervention until federal judges began to use it to justify the enjoining of railway boycotts in

1888 and strikes in the 1890's. Protection of the mail, also a factor in most of the strikes, was not used as the primary justification for intervention until the Great Northern strike of 1894.

Responsibility for establishing a national strike policy and for preventing railway tie-ups rested with Congress. In general, congressmen appear to have recognized that major strikes posed a threat to the nation's health, safety, and welfare, and that such matters, because they involved the mail and interstate commerce, lay within the competency of Congress. There was, however, no agreement as how best to divert these private wars into adjudicative channels. Congress, in the end, failed to establish guidelines for the federal executive and the courts in meeting labor disputes that erupted into strikes. So far as it was able, Congress avoided the whole problem. It rarely took up labor questions unless strikes were in progress, and when the strikes ended, so did attempts to legislate. After two decades Congress could boast a handful of investigations into labor matters and two voluntary arbitration laws, neither of which proved effective.

The federal executive and the federal courts initiated the first and most meaningful measures for coping with railway strikes. The executive branch, though often hesitant about becoming involved, played a more active role than Congress. Its actions usually consisted of ad hoc responses to strikes that had reached crisis proportions. Although it intervened several times after 1877, the executive failed to work out fixed administrative procedures for meeting major disorders on the railroads. Its actions lacked consistency, varying considerably from one time to the next. Twice during major strikes the executive avoided intervention altogether; three times its intervention was anti-labor or pro-railroad—once incidentally, twice deliberately—and in one strike the administration stood neutral between railroad companies and their employees, limiting itself to protecting governmental interests.

Of the three branches, the federal judiciary pursued far and away the most decisive, inventive, and consistent course. The absence of statute law for dealing with railway strikes did not prevent the courts from acting in time of crisis. Federal judges found or created grounds for using the full powers of government to ward off threatened strikes and to halt those in progress. The judges acted boldly, displaying neither the reluctance of Congress to become involved nor the hesitancy of the executive to act. So far as a continuing federal strike policy existed during those years, it was the policy established by the federal courts.

The federal government's handling of railway strikes in the closing decades of the nineteenth century served to repress labor. In part this was due to prevailing notions of property rights and of laissez-faire government; in part it was the result of Congress' failure to deal effectively with the emerging labor problem, leaving the executive and courts to cope with strikes that had already become violent; and in part it reflected the interests and motivations of the men who made policy in the executive and judicial branches. Necessity dictated federal intervention, but not the forms that it would take. The crucial decisions were made by the officials who were bold enough to step into the various crises and act. In turn, their actions, as will be seen, were at least in part guided by their interests and convictions.

The final quarter of the nineteenth century was a critical era in the development of the federal government's policy towards labor disputes. From the experiences of that period came procedures, attitudes, and weapons that would continue to influence the handling of labor crises for decades, in some instances to the present time. These included the all-important roles of the executive and judiciary in dealing with labor disputes as contrasted with the passivity of Congress, the use of injunctions to prevent or to halt major tie-ups, and the traditional pro-management stance of the government during labor disputes.

But other ways of handling strikes on the railways were also considered, and experimented with, during those years. Some federal officials attempted to induce railroad companies, as a part of their duty to the public, to carry mail during strikes, if necessary on special trains consisting of mail cars only. A federal judge proposed that railroads in receivership (and, perhaps, all interstate railways) be required to submit their labor disputes to the courts for arbitration. A cabinet member sent to Congress the draft of a bill authorizing federal courts during railway labor disputes to enjoin striking by employees and to place the railroads in receivership pending settlement of their differences. Examination of the alternatives open to policymakers sharpens the significance of the policies that were adopted. The unused alternatives also offer suggestive insights into the continuing problem of how to cope with national emergency strikes.

By 1898 the era of great railway strikes was over. Repression of such strikes had about run its course; the problem of avoiding and ending them through negotiation became more important. Moreover, the American economy had matured considerably. By the turn of the century, rising industries had replaced the railroads "as the instigators and shapers of economic change" and as the "creator of new economic institutions."[61] The major strikes of the new century would come in the coal, steel, and automobile industries, not on the railroads. The weapons used in meeting these new threats frequently would be those developed during the railway strikes. But the government's policies after 1900 increasingly aimed at a more neutral role in major labor disputes.

• • •

CHAPTER II

First Crisis:
The Railway Strikes of 1877

THE INITIAL UPRISING of disgruntled workmen against the Baltimore & Ohio Railroad at Martinsburg, West Virginia, on July 16, 1877, gave little hint of the disorders to follow. Within a few days, however, spontaneous strikes had swept over the railway network; freight trains choked the major yards from Baltimore to St. Louis and from Buffalo to Louisville; passenger and mail service was irregular; rioting in a dozen or more centers had brought out state militias and the United States Army; and much of the country's business lay dormant. These strikes were the first labor dispute to assume national proportions; they were also the first to induce massive federal intervention.[1] By the conclusion of the brief but violent wave of disorder, it was clear to contemporaries that they had weathered a national crisis.

The origins of the strikes of 1877 lay in the depression precipitated by the Panic of 1873. In the difficult years of the 1870's, factories closed or operated only part time, industrial output fell, unemployment increased, and railroad traffic and income declined. Railroad managers, facing reduced revenues, tried to shift much, if not most, of the burden to the labor force. Economies were effected, where possible, by discharging employees. Those fortunate enough to keep their jobs experienced wage cuts, frequent layoffs, and increased work loads. Such measures were particularly galling to workers whose daily newspapers carried stories of stockwatering deals by railroad manipulators, swindles by railroad construction companies, bribery of public officials by railroad interests, and the payment of their customary 8 percent dividends by a number of railroad companies.[2]

A round of wage cuts on the Eastern lines touched off the strikes. The disorders began on the B & O at Camden Station in Baltimore and at Martinsburg on the day a 10 percent wage cut went into effect. Baltimore's mayor, Ferdinand C. Latrobe, who with his family had long been associated with the B & O, promptly ordered the police to arrest strike leaders at Camden Station.[3] A. P. Shutt, the mayor of Martinsburg, who also had close ties to the B & O, acted to put down the strike in his town but was less successful than Latrobe. After consultation with railroad officials he tried to soothe the angry trainmen who refused to move or to allow others to move freight trains through the yards. Failing to quiet the disorder in this way, Shutt ordered the arrest of the strike leaders. The pro-worker sympathies of the townspeople and the inadequacy of the local police force thwarted his efforts.[4]

Reports from Martinsburg gave no evidence of casualties or property damage. Nonetheless, John King, Jr., first vice-president of the B & O, wired Governor Henry M. Mathews of West Virginia that a "riot" was in progress which local authorities were "powerless to suppress." He requested that the militia be called out to end it. Mathews, apparently without additional information, ordered a company of volunteer militiamen from the Martinsburg area into action and instructed the officer in charge to "prevent any interference by rioters with the men at work, and prevent the obstruction of trains."[5]

The militia, poorly disciplined and bearing no hostility toward the strikers, proved unsatisfactory for strikebreaking duty. A voluntary engineer, with militia protection, attempted to run a freight train through the yards. When a striker and a militiaman exchanged shots and wounded one another—the striker fatally—the would-be strikebreaker deserted the cab of the engine. No one was found to take his place. "It is impossible for me to do anything further with my company," the officer in charge wired Mathews. "Most of them are railroad men and they will not respond. The force is too formidable for me to cope with." He thereupon dismissed his men until further notice. Mathews, however, was determined to end the disorder. "I can send, if necessary, a company in which there are no men who will be unwilling to aid in suppressing the riot and executing the law," he replied.[6]

Even before the West Virginia militia reached Martinsburg,

President John W. Garrett and other B & O officials pressed Governor Mathews to call upon the President of the United States for federal troops. "The loss of an hour," Garrett warned, "would most seriously affect us and imperil vast interests." With federal troops the rioters could be dispersed and the trains once again be moved. The governor, however, was unwilling to seek federal assistance until he had exhausted "all means within the State to suppress the riot." Believing that his forces were adequate, he sent a company of sixty-five militiamen—"none of them railroad men"—to Martinsburg. "I send arms and ammunition with them," he added, and "the force will be increased as they go on. If that force is not sufficient, I will then use other means—the riot shall be stopped." Notwithstanding Mathews' determination, Vice-President King telegraphed the Washington agent of the B & O that the governor might soon call for federal troops. The secretary of war should be informed of the situation, King suggested, so that he would be ready to respond promptly with the necessary forces.[7]

On July 17 the governor's aide, Colonel Robert M. Delaplain, apparently persuaded Mathews to change his mind about requesting federal help. His wire to the governor contained no information of new violence or disorder nor did it warn of pending riots. Delaplain noted the intensity of pro-strike sentiment in Martinsburg, however, and declared that no one could be found willing to run a locomotive even with militia protection. Although the newly arrived militiamen were "very willing" to arrest strike leaders, the aide and his "conferees" thought such a move "foolhardy." The odds, he believed, were against getting trains underway without the assistance of 200 United States Marines.[8]

By no stretch of the imagination had Mathews exhausted the powers at his command to suppress the disorders. To date one striker and one militiaman had been shot, the militia had not been ordered to clear the strikers from the railroad yards, Martinsburg had not been put in a state of emergency or under martial law, no call had been made for additional volunteers to augment the strength of the admittedly weak militia, nor had the legislature been summoned into special session to deal with the emergency. As Mathews reported to the legislature several months later, one militiaman had been wounded, one striker killed, and a total of $8,823.41 expended in the attempt to quell the strikers.[9]

Without further taxing the resources of his state, Mathews telegraphed President Hayes:

> Owing to unlawful combinations and domestic violence now existing at Martinsburg and at other points along the line of the Baltimore and Ohio Rail Road it is impossible with any force at my command to execute the laws of the State.
>
> I therefore call upon your Excellency for the assistance of the United States military to protect the law abiding people of the State against domestic violence and to maintain the supremacy of law.
>
> The Legislature is not now in session and could not be assembled in time to take any action in the emergency. A force of from two to three hundred should be sent without delay to Martinsburg where my aid Col. Delaplain will meet and confer with the officer in command.[10]

Garrett, upon hearing that federal troops had been requested, telegraphed congratulations to Mathews. To President Hayes he sent a long wire reinforcing the governor's call for assistance. The B & O, he said, could not move any freight trains because of open intimidation of its loyal employees. Unless that situation was corrected immediately, Garret anticipated "the gravest consequences," for both his railroad and all the other companies that had been "obliged to introduce measures of economy in these trying times for the preservation of the effectiveness of railway property." Only by using the Army, he informed the President, could the B & O—"this great national highway"—be again "restored for public use."[11]

Whether or not federal troops would be sent was entirely up to the President. Statute law empowered him to respond to state requests for assistance in suppressing "domestic insurrection," but it did not make granting such requests mandatory. In each instance the President was obliged to weigh the merits of the application. There were a number of pre-Civil War precedents for declining.[12]

Garret might reasonably have expected the Hayes administration to act without hesitation on the request for aid since the President and cabinet were anything but hostile to the railroad community. Secretary of State William M. Evarts, Secretary of War George W. McCrary, and Secretary of the Navy Richard

W. Thompson had very close railroad associations. Evarts and Attorney General Charles Devens, as guests of the railroads, had just completed a tour of the Pennsylvania coal regions in the private car of Tom Scott, president of the mighty Pennsylvania.[13]

Evarts was a leading New York corporation and railroad lawyer who "usually ranged on the side of capital rather than labor." He was, according to one biographer, a "typical nineteenth-century lawyer, believing in freedom of enterprise, in the rights of property, in due process of law, and in the American business man." As an attorney for some of the great Western railroads he had recently argued the "unpopular side" of the Peik and three other "Granger cases," holding that only Congress—not state legislatures—could regulate railroads operating in interstate commerce.[14] A decade later, as senator from New York, Evarts would work against passage of the federal Interstate Commerce Act. In his private practice in the famous Jacobs case, he helped to invalidate a New York law outlawing the making of cigars in tenement houses. A few days before the request for federal troops in 1877, Evart's law firm was paid a $2500 fee for legal services by the Vanderbilt-owned Lake Shore railroad.[15]

Secretary of War McCrary, although no hireling of the railroads, was far from unfriendly. It is true that he had investigated the Crédit Mobilier during his congressional career and had, as chairman of the House Committee on Canals and Railroads, reported a bill for regulating railroad rates. But on the other hand, he also was on the committee at the time generous land grants were voted to a number of Western railways, and he appears to have owed his cabinet appointment to the influence of such railroad leaders as General Grenville M. Dodge, Tom Scott, and Jay Gould. Upon leaving public service, McCrary ended his days in one of the West's leading corporate law firms serving the Atchison, Topeka & Santa Fe Railroad as general counsel.[16]

Secretary of the Navy Thompson was a long time railroad lobbyist and legal adviser. For many years chief counsel of the Terre Haute & Indianapolis, he had been appointed to the cabinet at the behest of the Indiana Republican machine. He was to leave his post under a cloud in 1880 when President Hayes "accepted" his unoffered resignation. Thompson, already a director of the Panama Railroad Company, had accepted the chairmanship of the American Committee of the Panama Canal Company at a salary of $25,000 and labored under the illusion that this would not prevent him from remaining in the cabinet.[17]

Even Hayes himself might have been expected to respond favorably to the request for troops. Only a year before, as governor of Ohio, he had ordered out the militia to suppress rioting in the coal mining area around Massillon. Operators of the mines there had appealed to the local sheriff for protection of their properties against rampaging miners; the sheriff in turn had called upon Governor Hayes for state troopers to supplement the inadequate forces at his disposal. Hayes, much to the operators' distress, at first refused, issuing instead a proclamation that warned strikers against further lawlessness. Somewhat later, after his adjutant general visited the area and recommended military intervention, Hayes sent the militia to Massillon to halt the disorders.[18] Hayes, moreover, in becoming President, had incurred some obligations to the railroad community. Tom Scott and his associates were leaders in arranging the behind-the-scene compromise that ended the disputed election of 1876 and secured the presidency for Hayes.[19]

Whatever Hayes's inclinations, Governor Mathews' request for troops reached him at a time when any move he might make could prove embarrassing. In the bitter aftermath of the disputed election many Americans regarded him as President by fraud. To order out troops against a part of the citizenry obviously could be held against him politically. On the other hand, inaction could equally well bring charges of neglect of duty. Beyond that lay the problem of the Army itself. Reduced to a peacetime total of 25,000 men, all but a skeletal force were stationed beyond the Mississippi River, guarding the Mexican border or fighting Indians. Army enlisted men, whose wages were already in arrears, were receiving no pay because Congress had adjourned without voting an Army appropriations bill for the fiscal year that began July 1.[20]

After consultation with the chief executive, the secretary of war telegraphed Mathews that the President was "averse to intervention unless it is clearly shown that the state is unable to suppress insurrection," and asked for details as to the size of the militia and the number of "insurgents." Mathews, in two separate telegrams, estimated that there were about eight hundred "rioters," and noted that West Virginia had no organized state guard. There were at his command four companies of voluntary militia, the two at Martinsburg which seemed to be in sympathy with the "rioters," one located "thirty-eight miles from railroad," and "only one company of forty men efficient [sic]." He had "no doubt" that within ten days he could organize a force of West Virginians sufficient "to suppress any Riot," but he feared, in the meantime, the destruction of "much property" and the loss of "valuable lives." "I have been reluctant to call on the President," he said, "but deemed it necessary to prevent bloodshed."[21]

It would appear that the Martinsburg railroaders, aided by their fellow-townsmen, had effected a completely successful strike. They were preventing absolutely the movement of freight trains through the town, even when the trains were offered militia protection. Vice-President King of the B & O and Governor Mathews chose to term this state of affairs "riot." Someone in Washington, apparently Secretary McCrary, upgraded the "riot" to "insurrection" in the first reply to Mathews. In his response, Mathews downgraded the "insurgents" to "rioters" once again.[22] But even as "rioters" the mob at Martinsburg was not damaging property or shedding blood. Troops were requested by Mathews not to suppress actual "insurrection," "riot," or even bloodshed, but to prevent them. Nonetheless, without further information or inquiry, and apparently satisfied that duty required that he now act, Hayes dispatched troops. He had certainly been right in not sending the Army on the basis of the information in Mathews' original telegram; he probably would have done better not to have been satisfied with the meagre response to his request for more details.

Although the Army was sent to West Virginia prematurely, a stronger case can be made for the subsequent dispatch of troops to Maryland, Pennsylvania, and other trouble spots. Undirected, unplanned, and unmanaged save by impromptu leaders, the strike spontaneously spread among railroaders across the nation. Everywhere, but especially in Baltimore, Pittsburgh, and Chicago, the striking trainmen were promptly joined by throngs of excitement-seeking adolescents, by the idle, the unemployed, the merely curious, and the malicious. Over such conglomerates of men no one exercised control or leadership, and the strikes in these cities soon took on the characteristics of riot and outright defiance of local and state authorities. As tension mounted, the militias of the various states involved were called upon to aid the local police forces. Pitched battles between rioters and the forces of law and order followed. There was wholesale destruction of property—particularly of railroad property—there was plundering, and there was considerable bloodshed on both sides.

In none of these places was the full strength of the state governments brought to bear.[23] The governors, quick to respond to calls from the railroads for force to end strikes, were reluctant to press the citizenry when they offered resistance. Once skirmishing involved bloodletting, however little, and without awaiting the outcome, the governors promptly turned to the federal government for assistance. Why is not entirely clear. Perhaps it was because in most states the militia was inadequate and poorly disciplined. Rarely did state forces command the respect of rioters when called into service and in some instances they seemed sympathetic to the strikers.[24] Beyond that, it may be the governors feared anarchy if the riots were allowed to run unchecked even for so short a time as would be required to muster more state volunteers. Perhaps they feared the political consequences of shooting voters and preferred to let federal officials assume that responsibility. Whatever their motives, they anxiously appealed to President Hayes for federal troops.

Despite the seriousness of the situation, President Hayes observed most scrupulously the proper forms whenever federal assistance was given. A governor requesting aid was obliged to declare that domestic violence or insurrection existed within his state which state forces could not suppress, that the legislature was not in session and could not be assembled in time to deal with the situation, and that federal troops were necessary to restore order.[25] As already noted, Hayes required Governor Mathews to state explicitly that West Virginia could not itself cope with the Martinsburg disorders before he would dispatch the army to that state. In Pennsylvania, where there was far less doubt as to the need for assistance, Hayes refused to move until the state's request for aid came in precisely the proper phrasing. Pennsylvania's first call for help came on July 22 in a wire from Harrisburg, over the name of Governor John F. Hartranft.

> Domestic violence existing in the State of Penna—in the city of Pittsbg and along the line Penna Rail Road & other rail Roads in said state which the authorities are unable to suppress and the legislature of Pennsylvania cannot be convened in time to meet the emergency [sic]. I have therefore to request in conformity to the Constitution the Government of the United States shall furnish me with military force sufficient to suppress Disorder and protect persons and property against Domestic violence.[26]

Governor Hartranft, however, was not in Harrisburg on July 22—indeed, he was not even in Pennsylvania. The wire had actually been sent in his name by James W. Latta, the governor's adjutant general, and Matthew S. Quay, secretary of the commonwealth.[27] Hayes ordered no troops to Pennsylvania in response to the wire from Harrisburg. At seven o'clock that evening, Hartranft personally wired the President from Creston, Wyoming Territory: "I call upon you for troops to assist in quelling mobs within the borders of the state Penna [sic]. . . ." Hayes, however, still refused to act until Hartranft, now enroute home, wired the next day from North Bend, Nebraska: "I amend my requisition from the general government by adding the words domestic insurrection exists in Pennsylvania which the state authorities are unable to suppress and the Legislature is not in session and cannot be convened in time."[28] Hayes apparently did not regard "quelling mobs" or "suppressing domestic violence" adequate grounds for intervention even though the latter was the express terminology of the Constitution. He, or perhaps Secretary McCrary, insisted on the term "domestic insurrection," probably because that was the phrase used in the pertinent section of the Revised Statutes.

For one reason or another, Hayes failed to respond directly to subsequent requests for federal assistance from the governors of Michigan, Illinois, California, Wisconsin, and Indiana. This may have been due to the faulty wording of their requests which were for aid against "the very unsettled and threatening condition of affairs," "lawlessness," "apprehended riot," "labor insurrection," and "threatened domestic violence."[29] Four of the governors, moreover, asked in effect that federal forces be put under their command or at their disposal rather than sent to their assistance. Although troops eventually were sent to Illinois, Indiana, and California, it was to enforce court orders at the request of federal judges and not to suppress domestic violence at the call of governors.

When Hayes decided to send troops in response to the calls of the governors of West Virginia, Maryland, and Pennsylvania, he, in compliance with the Revised Statutes, was careful to issue proclamations. In each he declared the existence of domestic insurrection and obstruction of the laws of the state, he warned all good citizens "against aiding, countenancing, abetting, or taking part in such unlawful proceedings," and he ordered the persons engaged in or connected with the disorders to disperse.[30]

At several meetings during the crisis, the cabinet discussed whether troops should be used in a state prior to a request for aid from the governor or before the issuance of a presidential proclamation. "Shall the troops of U.S. be used in St. Louis until Gov. calls? *No*." "Can an officer move his men ag[ain]st the mob before the Gov. calls? says Th[ompson]. Ev[arts] replies 'It will be given him in that hour what he shall do'!" "Shall the U.S. forces be used to suppress riots in Chicago, before we issue a proclamation? No, says Ev[arts]." "Discussing the propriety of allowing the U.S. forces to be used by local authorities in States where no President's proclamation has been issued. If the troops act we will justify it."[31] In each instance, Hayes and his cabinet were obviously willing to back up the Army should a local commander move without observing the forms, but they would not themselves order such action until all the proprieties had been observed.

The use of federal troops at the request of a governor to suppress domestic insurrection raised the question whether commanders of federal forces were supreme or subordinate to state authorities. The Army commanders sent to West Virginia and Maryland were ordered to report to the governors of those states. "You will act under the Governor's orders," was the instruction given one commander.[32] Shortly after federal forces moved into Pennsylvania, General Hancock, commander of the Military Division of the Atlantic, sought to clear up the question whether state or federal officials were supreme once federal forces entered the scene. In a lengthy telegram to Secretary McCrary on July 24 he discussed the matter in detail. Hancock "yielded" to the doctrine of civil supremacy over the military, he said, but was still concerned as to the relative positions of federal and state authorities. "There is a point," he wrote, "when if civil authority of the State should prove powerless, it should for the time being cease to reign, and the federal authority assume control." That point came, he asserted, when state governments "declare their inability to suppress domestic insurrection . . . and call upon the President of the U. States to intervene. . . ." When the President intervened, Hancock argued, it should not be done through the state civil authorities who had already failed, but the President himself should assume control through his own officials.[33]

"The Federal troops in Pennsylvania," McCrary replied tersely, "are to act under the orders of the Governor, as in Maryland and West Virginia." The next day, however, McCrary, at the President's order, informed Hancock that "under existing circumstances" President Hayes thought the general should take command of all military forces in Pennsylvania, both federal and state. The general government, McCrary continued, would determine in each particular instance whether the army would act under or independently of state authorities.[34]

The executive also used United States forces during the strikes to protect federal property without consulting the governors of the states where that property was located. Apparently, the administration assumed that permission of the states was not needed in such instances. In a wholly matter-of-fact fashion Hayes ordered the armed forces to secure public buildings and facilities wherever mobs threatened them. In the New York City area, for example, Army regulars and Marines were used to supplement the already armed treasury clerks who were guarding $100 million in the vaults of the subtreasury, armed forces were dispatched to protect government property in Brooklyn, and a Navy monitor was stationed in New York harbor to protect the United States customhouse. Federal arsenals, customhouses, and subtreasuries across the nation received similar protection.[35]

Federal troops had little direct contact with raging mobs during the 1877 strikes. In most instances either state militia had already broken serious resistance before the regulars arrived or the spirit of lawlessness had about run its course. Nonetheless, the federal troops had a quieting effect wherever they appeared. This was not due to the size of the forces; of necessity only small detachments could be sent to any one strike scene. But the Regular Army men were well disciplined, looked and acted as if they meant business, and conducted themselves with restraint and calm. Because they commanded the respect of the citizenry, the regulars dispersed crowds without the loss of a single soldier or the killing of a single civilian.[36]

Of itself the use of the Army to aid states in suppressing domestic insurrection created no new precedents. During Reconstruction, in particular, federal troops had repeatedly been ordered into Southern states to restore order. Those disorders, however, had grown out of political rather than capital-labor clashes, were smaller in scope, and did not require interventions on the scale of the 1877 affair. Similarly, Hayes's use of troops to protect public property in 1877 was not novel.

Of much greater significance, both to the strikes of 1877 and to subsequent federal strike policy, was the use of the Army to enforce federal court orders. Even here the federal executive was not innovating; other Presidents on other occasions had used military force to back the federal judiciary. What was new was that some federal judges, in marked contrast to the reluctance of the executive to act, were willing, even eager, to intrude themselves and their courts in labor disputes.[37]

That the federal courts became involved at all stemmed from a number of Midwestern railroads being in the hands of court-appointed receivers. Receivership was a device by which virtually bankrupted railroad companies, in their own interest and in the alleged interest of their creditors and the public, avoided liquidation. The railroad in question would be taken over and operated by receivers appointed by and answerable to the court. It was common for the receivers to be members of the regular management of the railroad involved. As a consequence, the main change wrought by receivership was that the officials, as receivers, became officers of the court and the company was in the custody of the court. As receivers, the managers operated under the full protection of the court, free from responsibility to stockholders, free from harassments of creditors and as it turned out, free from the demands of employees.[38]

The most significant legal developments of the 1877 strikes occurred in the federal courts in the Seventh Circuit which embraced the states of Illinois, Indiana, and Wisconsin. There Thomas S. Drummond, a scrupulously honest man but a domineering and somewhat imperious jurist, presided. "God rules in Israel," one attorney lamented, "but Thomas Drummond in the Seventh Circuit."[39] Before his appointment to the federal bench in 1850, Drummond had been "great among the great lawyers then in Galena [Illinois]." He listed among his clients the "bankers, merchants and best business men of the busy little town." These men regarded him as "honest, cautious, and safe."[40]

Though "devoted to justice, as he saw it," Judge Drummond was not a "conspicuous champion of popular rights," nor did he especially appreciate the "vital importance of jury trial to free institutions."[41] In 1877 he made generous use of contempt of court proceedings, which involved no juries, against strikers.

Railroads and railroad law had long interested the Illinois jurist. In the 1840's he was a promoter and director of the Galena & Chicago Union Railroad. Early in his career as judge, Drummond pioneered in the creation of federal receiverships for Midwestern railroads in financial straits. Looking upon

railways as a species of public highway, Drummond held that
the public interest required that the protecting arm of the
federal courts be extended to shield those highways from liquidation.[42] He stood ready in 1877 to protect roads in receivership against the demands of striking employees.

Equalling Drummond in zeal for protecting railroads in
the custody of the courts were Federal District Judges Walter
Q. Gresham of Indianapolis and Samuel Hubbel Treat of
Springfield. Unlike Drummond, who had had considerable business and legal experience before going to the bench, Gresham
and Treat had become judges while young men. Gresham, only
forty-six years old in 1877, had been a federal judge for nearly
eight years. Drummond was both his fatherly friend and
mentor, and the two spent much time together discussing the
law and legal matters. Upon Drummond's death in 1884,
Gresham succeeded to the seat of the "czar of the seventh circuit," and eventually spent the last two years of his life as
Grover Cleveland's secretary of state.[43] Somewhat hasty and
dramatic during the crisis of 1877, the decisive young judge
cast himself in the heroic role of defender, in Indianapolis, of
both the railroads in his charge and of Western Civilization at
large.

Judge Treat, first appointed to the Illinois state courts in
1839 at the age of twenty-nine, had since 1855 been federal judge
of the Southern District of Illinois. Scholarly and somewhat
eccentric in his habits, he was a man of inflexible beliefs who
devoted himself to his official duties to the all-but-complete
neglect of his private business affairs.[44] In 1877 Judge Treat
limited himself to thwarting strike activities against railroads
in his custody.

When, by Sunday, July 22, the great strike threatened to
sweep into the Midwestern rail centers of Indianapolis, Chicago,
and St. Louis, the federal judges in the area quickly acted, or
were induced to act, to protect railroad properties in their
charge. Whether judge or receiver should be credited with
originating the idea, Drummond was the first judge to extend
federal court protection to railroads in receivership against
strikers. When George B. Wright, receiver, under Drummond,
of the Indianapolis, Bloomington & Western, suggested that a
wage raise might stave off a strike, Drummond declared that he
would not yield to "threats or violence." It was best, he thought,
not to consider a raise until the employees proved their loyalty
by not joining in the strike. The general superintendent of the

I B & W, in relaying Drummond's views to one of the strike leaders, added an ominous warning: "A strike or other unlawful interference with the trains will be a violation of the United States law, and the court will be bound to take notice of it and enforce the penalty." On July 23 Judge Drummond instructed marshals within his jurisdiction to protect roads in receivership and to give notice that persons interfering with their operation would be summarily punished for contempt.[45] The next day he asked Attorney General Devens for federal troops to support the marshal at East St. Louis. "I took upon the property (R.R.) that is in the custody of the Court as public property for the time being & so claiming protection as such," he added in a letter July 25.[46]

Meanwhile, another receiver, apparently made of somewhat sterner stuff than Receiver Wright, was urging federal protection for the railroad he operated. James Harrison Wilson, promoter, director, vice-president, and receiver in Indiana and Illinois of the St. Louis & Southeastern, wrote Secretary of the Interior Carl Schurz: "I am managing property now in the custody of the U.S. Courts and I shall certainly not permit my employees to fix their own rate of wages, nor dictate to me in any manner what my policy shall be." In his view the fight might "just as well be made *now* as at any time," and if the general government should "be called upon to intervene in this region," he offered his services "unreservedly."[47]

A telegram next day to Judge Gresham in Indianapolis, under whom Wilson was receiver, was equally strong and only slightly more deferential. Wilson had sent many employees home, he said, and was prepared to suspend work entirely if the strike spread. "Your instructions will be observed but I am unalterably opposed to any concessions directly or indirectly to organized violence. The other railway managers here [St. Louis] concur in this programme," he concluded.[48]

Gresham, however, far from considering concessions, was organizing "reliable elements" in Indianapolis to meet the threat there. "I know what to do," he repeatedly declared as the strike fever reached Indianapolis. On July 24 he called together from eight to ten lawyers, all veteran officers of the Union Army, and outlined his plan for saving Indianapolis: a force of dependable veterans would be raised, they would be sworn in as deputy United States marshals, and would be used to preserve order and maintain railroad operations in the Hoosier capital.[49] At the same time, Gresham sought to have a detachment of federal troops brought to Indianapolis to sustain the marshal when and if the court issued writs of attachment against persons who were preventing the running of railroads in receivership. The United States marshal, Ben Spooner, wired Washington that same day asking both for troops and for blanket authorization to swear in deputies. The decision was made in Washington to send two hundred regular troopers to Indianapolis. This, added to the fact that Army reports from the scene indicated that conditions were far less serious than Gresham and Spooner portrayed them, led Devens to refuse the marshal and judge's extravagant demand for 1000 deputy marshals to suppress a mob which the same two men estimated at no more than 1000 strong.[50]

The idea that railroads in receivership were entitled to protection from the federal government quickly caught on. Acting on instructions from Judge Drummond, Gresham and Treat on July 26 issued orders to their marshals to safeguard all railroad property in the custody of their courts and to call for military assistance if civilian posses proved inadequate. That same day President Hayes and his cabinet discussed the matter and came to the conclusion that the policies of Drummond and Gresham should be urged upon federal judges in other strikebound areas. Further, it was decided, federal troops would be used to sustain the marshals whenever necessary. Judges in Tennessee, Ohio, and Pennsylvania issued such instructions to their marshals. The attorney general also authorized the swearing in of additional deputy marshals to support the courts, and a host, including many loyal railway employees, were promptly sworn in.[51]

Eventually, several strikers and strikeleaders in the Seventh Circuit were arrested and charged with contempt of court for having interfered with the operation of railroads in receivership. Judge Drummond disposed of the cases of two dozen prisoners, nine in Chicago and fifteen in Indianapolis, thereby earning the distinction of being the first federal judge to punish railway strikers for contempt of court.[52]

In his rulings, Drummond explained the role of the courts in protecting railroads, particularly those in receivership. A railroad, he observed, was not mere private property operated to serve private purposes. It fulfilled the quasi-public function of transporting persons, property, and the mails. Anyone who interfered with a railroad and prevented the performance of this function, "which affects so materially all the relations of

society, . . . commits as great an offense against the rights of
individuals and against the rights of the public, as can well be
imagined."

Federal courts in the Seventh Circuit, he continued, controlled a large number of railroads and would tolerate no interference with their operations. When a judge issued an order
directing a receiver to operate property in the name of the court,
in effect that order prohibited unauthorized persons from interfering with the receiver's possession. If there was interference,
the court was duty-bound to restore full control of the property
to the receiver "by the necessary orders or writs of assistance to
the marshal." That failing, the court could call upon the federal
government for assistance in enforcing its orders.[53]

How unsophisticated workmen were supposed to grasp the
significance of receivership, even when the companies they
worked for were in receivership, Drummond did not say. In
the case at hand, when troubles began, the marshal posted
notices that all interference would be summarily punished. To
workmen, however, the complex and technical legal relationships of the court, the receiver, and themselves were probably
not clearly understood. The court, further, did not explain how
workmen were to secure redress of their grievances in disputes
with receivers when they were denied the right to conduct an
effective strike.

Using the contempt cases as his forum, Judge Drummond
spoke out forcefully against railroad strikes in general. At
Indianapolis he lectured the prisoners on the futility of striking for higher wages. "If there is any thing that is an axiom, a
truth universally admitted to be correct," he declared, "it is
this: that we cannot by law fix the price of a bushel of wheat, or
a barrel of flour, or of a piece of domestic, or of a horse, or of
any such thing. . . . We cannot say by law that the laborer
shall have just such a price for his services." All these things,
he contended, were "regulated by the supply and demand." A
worker could not be forced to remain at a job where he
was dissatisfied with his wages, Drummond conceded, but neither could the worker force his employer to pay him more.

Although every individual had a right to leave his employment, Drummond continued, "men ought not to combine together and cause at once a strike among all railroad employes,
so as to prevent the running of trains, because the injury there
is to the public." The infinite injury to the whole community
caused by a stoppage of railways for a day, much less for a week,

was all but inconceivable to Drummond. Under such circumstances a strike was no remedy for low wages because it constituted "war upon society." And, Drummond warned, "society
will always arise . . . against those who make war upon it."[54]

To the prisoners brought before him at Chicago, Drummond asserted that strikes were antilabor in effect. Strikers, he
said, claimed the right of both refusing to work and of interfering with the labor of others. The public could have "no feeling
of respect for any such right as that," he said. "It is unlawful;
it is criminal; it affects all the relations of life, and strikes at
the root of everything in which the right of labor consists."[55]

Drummond deemed it "absolutely necessary" to impose
penalties, and not merely nominal penalties, on the offenders so
as to prevent intereference with court property in the future.
Inasmuch as most of the men before him could not pay fines,
Drummond sentenced them to from sixty to ninety days in
jail. "I dislike this mode of punishment," he confided to Attorney General Devens, "though it must be confessed, they carried
things with a high hand & it looked for a time as though men
had lost the right to use their own property as well as the
right to labor for whom they pleased and at such prices as they
pleased."[56]

That same day, in Springfield, Judge Treat was also meting
out punishment for criminal contempt of court. His views apparently coincided with Drummond's; the only reason he has not
shared credit with the Chicago jurist for developing contempt
proceedings in labor cases is that unlike Drummond, Treat did
not bother to write out his opinions so that they could be
handed down as precedents in the law reports. From newspaper
accounts of the hearing, however, it appears that Treat was
willing to go farther in punishing the strikers than his superior.
He implied that the men before him were guilty of criminal conspiracy, a much more grievous offense than mere contempt, and
hence, subject to heavier penalties.[57]

The work of Drummond, Gresham, and Treat laid the basis
for the future use of federal courts in coping with strikes, particularly on the railroads. The courts limited their activities to protecting only railroads that were in the custody of court appointed
receivers, but on those lines, for all practical purposes, strikes
were permanently outlawed. Injunctions were not yet involved.
Strikers in 1877 were punished for contempt, not in that they
had violated court orders directed at them, but in that they

had prevented the receivers from carrying out standing orders of the courts to operate railway lines in their custody.[58]

Although suppression of domestic violence, protection of federal property, and enforcement of court orders were the only grounds used to justify federal intervention in 1877, protection of the mail and of interstate commerce were given consideration. When the strikes reached their climax during the week of July 22 to 28, blockage of the mail became a matter of concern to the administration.

That the mail was frequently delayed seems to have been due more to freight-blocked yards and to railroad policy than to the intent of strikers. Throughout the disorders the strikers were reluctant to put themselves in direct conflict with the federal government by interfering with the postal service. At the same time, many of them were unwilling to allow the companies to move their passenger trains under the guise of carrying the United States mail. They, therefore, either halted only freight trains, which carried no mail, or halted all trains, offering to run specials, composed solely of mail cars, through their blockades. The respect shown mail trains probably stemmed from a desire on the part of the workers to avoid embroilment with the federal government. Perhaps they were also influenced by the case of some Boston & Maine engineers who the previous February had gone on strike, deserting their passenger trains wherever they happened to be when the strike began. Those men were arrested for obstructing the mails and were still awaiting trial in the summer of 1877.[59]

Despite the strikers' professed willingness to move mail, postal cars were blocked and delayed at many rail centers because the yards were choked with freight cars which the strikers refused to move. The railroad companies, quick to use the mails as a lever to turn the public and the government against the strikers, refused to move mail-bearing passenger trains unless all other trains were moved too. Nothing in their contracts with the government required them to run specials. "Strikers have stopped all passenger trains at East St. Louis and will permit nothing to go but the mails which we shall have also to suspend," James Wilson wired Secretary of Interior Schurz on July 24. The same day the receiver of a railroad in Indiana wired Judge Gresham for instructions. He observed that the company could not afford to run trains with mail cars only and so preferred "stopping altogether."[60] By July 27 it was reported in the *Washington Star* that "in most cases the railroad companies and not the strikers are to blame for any interruption in the mails that have taken place."[61] At least one company, the New York Central, moved its mail cars to the very end of trains to insure that if strikers cut off any cars, they would automatically cut off mail cars.[62]

Strikers in several areas sought to counter the moves of the companies by notifying the government of their willingness to run mail cars through strikebound areas if the railroads would allow this. "None of the mails have been interfered with or stopped here by parties known to strikers," a committee of engineers in Buffalo telegraphed the postmaster general on July 24. "We will furnish all engineers and firemen to pass all the mails regularly at our own expense, if the Railroad companies will permit us to," they promised. Another group of strikers wired President Hayes from Erie, Pennsylvania, that the railroad managers refused to permit mail to move east of Erie. "We would be pleased," they informed Hayes, "if you would in some way direct them to proceed with mails & also passengers."[63]

To maintain the flow of mail, the Postoffice Department sought to take advantage of the strikers' offer. T. N. Vail, general mail superintendent, wired the postmaster general from New York that trains on all roads were irregular and that there were blockades at Buffalo and Pittsburgh. But, he said, the "rioters" at Buffalo had offered to run the mail through and had indicated that strikers at other points would not interfere with the mail. "I have asked both Mr. Vanderbilt and Mr. Scott [presidents, respectively, of the New York Central and the Pennsylvania] if they will not run us with special cars on regular trains as far as they control the roads and with special trains through the riotous districts," he continued. "If they refuse this we are absolutely blocked." Postmaster General Key followed up the suggestion by himself contacting the two rail chieftains and reminding them that the United States expected the corporations to live up to their contracts in forwarding the mail.

Vanderbilt and Scott refused. "[W]e can't consent to run mail cars as specials as Mr. Vail requests through the mob who are in possession of parts of our road," Vanderbilt replied. "If our passenger trains are run, the mails will be run also." Colonel Scott went further and lectured the government on its duties. "We will do everything that is possible for the government and the public," he said, "but I fear that unless the General Government will assume such responsibilities as will enable it to enforce law and order throughout the land the anarchy which is now present with us will be made more terrible than has ever been known in the history of the world."[64] The refusal of the railroad executives to carry mail alone apparently ended the matter so far as Hayes and the cabinet were concerned. "R.R.'s refuse to carry mails alone," Hayes recorded in his brief notes of the cabinet meeting of July 25. There is no indication that the administration put further pressures on the companies.

In the days that followed, the Postoffice Department pursued an equivocal policy with regard to the movement of mail. At no point did it ask that troops be used to end blockages as the railroad companies would have liked. Officials hoped that the companies might keep mail moving as a public service, but did not compel them to carry mail on special trains as the strikers demanded. "In extra-ordinary cases, when passenger trains cannot be run," the department notified the postmaster at Indianapolis, "railroad companies, in view of the public good, ought to carry the mails temporarily without passengers."[65] On the other hand, when the postmaster at Wilkes-Barre blamed a suspension of postal service in his city on the railroad companies and asked the department to intervene, he was told that the government did not expect and could not force the companies to carry mail on any but regular trains. When companies on occasion did run specials, the department refused extra payment to cover the added expenses incurred.[66]

In Chicago, railway managers were concerned that strikers might seize trains and run the mail through without authorization. They, therefore, asked James E. White, superintendent of the railway mail service in the city, to deny recognition to the strikers and to forbid any but authorized agents of the companies to proceed with the mail. Feeling unable to give such instructions himself, White wired the department for a ruling. "I . . . believe clerks and agents should accompany these cars and distribute the mails no matter who runs the cars. Am I right?" The Postoffice Department refused to deal with hypothetical cases but promised a prompt decision should an actual case arise. "It is probable," White was told, "the Department will not, under any circumstances, encourage the strikers to the extent of recognizing their right to carry the mails on trains forcibly taken from the railroad companies."[67] The next day, his backbone stiffened by the reply, White issued a notice to "Strikers, Rioters and Other Parties Whomsoever," to the effect that all passen-

ger trains carrying mail were mail trains. If such trains were
delayed, the United States mail would be delayed and federal
postal laws violated. Any interference with mail trains "on any
pretense whatever" would be "vigorously prosecuted." This order, according to White, ended the strikers' threats to the mails
at Chicago.[68]

The position taken by the Postoffice Department and the
Hayes administration, namely that any passenger train carrying
mail was a mail train, although not openly against the strikers
or for the railroad companies, benefitted the companies more
than the strikers. A much more neutral position, suggested by
the actions of several companies, was available. During the strike
they ran one passenger-mail train each way over their lines each
day.[69] Had the federal government insisted on this being done
by all railroads, it seems probable that both the strikers and the
companies could easily have been induced to comply, the mail
would not have been long delayed or inconvenienced, and the
issue would have been neutralized.

Although the executive branch refused to use blockage of
the mails to justify federal intervention, the federal courts used
it to forge new antistrike weapons. Judge Drummond, in contempt proceedings at Indianapolis, August 1, held that strikers
had obstructed the mails because they "arrested the trains by
which they were carried."[70] In the case at Chicago he observed
that while it was true the defendants were willing to allow mail
cars to pass unmolested, "it must be borne in mind that the
mail car can only go in such a way as to enable the railroad
to transport the mail, when there are other cars accompanying
it. It is not practicable, as a general thing, for a railroad to
transport a mail car by itself, because that would be attended
by serious loss."[71] To Drummond the strike was not an extra-
ordinary circumstance requiring that mail be carried alone.

A few days later another group of strikers was tried for
obstruction of the mails in the court of Federal District Judge
John Cadwalader, in Philadelphia. According to Cadwalader's
somewhat disjointed statement of the case in his charge to the
jury, the men on trial had not physically blocked passage of a
mail train. They had, in fact, come upon the scene after a mob
had already uncoupled the mail cars and sidetracked the passenger cars of a mail train. The defendants had shouted out that
the mail should be allowed to go on alone. (On this issue
Cadwalader seems to have been confused; at one point he stated

that the men had refused to permit the mail to go on alone, in another he said that they insisted that it go on alone. He was also confused as to how long the mail was stopped. The delay, said the district attorney in correcting Cadwalader, was two or three hours, not two or three days.) After discussing the issues, Cadwalader approvingly cited Drummond's recent ruling that railroads could not be expected to carry mail cars by themselves.

The judge considered it necessary to instruct the jury on one technical point of law, to wit, under what circumstances spoken words became acts. "The rule is," he told them, "that where words constitute part of the business, rightful or wrongful, which is in question, they are acts. If, therefore, one of the crowd there said, in defining their purpose, that the mail might go on but the passenger train should not, if such words were uttered when the transaction was in progress, and as a part of it, a man who uttered those words committed a wrongful act if the jury find that such was his intention." That point made clear, the jury withdrew and subsequently returned a verdict of guilty. Other federal judges and some state courts similarly punished strikers for obstructing the mail, but rarely for spoken words in the absence of deeds.[72]

It remained for District Judge Edward Fox, in Portland, Maine, to bring to a climax the use of the mails to punish railroad strikers. Famous for his charges to juries, which were models of clarity, Fox was also noted for his partiality while on the bench. Behind the judicial black lingered the skillful advocate who for many years had successfully pleaded only his clients' side of cases. Juries could almost always tell how the outspoken, brusque, and often arbitrary judge thought a case should be decided.[73] His charge to the jury sitting in the case of Boston & Maine engineers who had gone on strike in February 1877 was no exception. When those men were finally brought to trial in November, Fox, in his charge, explained how the strikers might be found guilty of conspiracy against the United States government. By tortuous logic he held that if the jury should find that the strikers had acted collusively to break their implied contract with their employer by striking (not a federal offense), and in the course of that strike had obstructed the mail (a federal offense punishable by a fine of $100), they would be, in fact, guilty of criminal conspiracy against the government just as if they had conspired in the first place against the federal government. Criminal conspiracy against the United States government carried a fine of from $1000 to $10,000 and imprisonment not exceeding two years.[74] The men were found guilty.

The same officials who refused to carry mail alone, on the grounds that as private businesses the railroads could not be expected to render a public service at a financial loss, were eager for federal protection from strikers on the grounds that the railroads were public carriers engaged in interstate commerce. "These men," J. A. Dacus, who wrote at the time of the strikes, observed, "speaking of their private property and personal interests as a national enterprise, declared that the riot could not be quieted until the Government had enabled them to run the trains which lay blockaded. . . . And the demand was backed by the declaration that the Government was bound to see not that peace, but that the commerce was re-established in its usual channels."[75]

Not only railroad managers, but other persons as well, proposed that the federal government protect interstate commerce during strikes. General Hancock, as already noted, regarded the problem of blocked commerce of major importance and recommended that the "great routes" over which commerce flowed be "promptly opened."[76] Some of the suggestions would not have appealed to railroad officials. One anonymous Democrat, for example, wrote President Hayes, "For God's sake run the freight trains. If necessary, take control of the Roads under the Constitutional right to regulate interstate commerce. . . . Imagine," he went on, "the Commerce between these States stopped for 2 weeks. I'd rather see you fixed in the Presidential chair for 25 years; I would rather see you Emperor than to have Commerce paralyzed."[77]

Before the end of the strikes, two leading newspapers began to urge the federal government to assume responsibility for protecting interstate commerce. "The growth of rapid transportation has made the various sections of this country, and all its manifold industries and trades . . . universally interdependent," the *Chicago Daily Tribune* pointed out on July 25. Six days later the same paper observed that it was no longer possible to view the strikes as "a private business calamity or local State lawlessness." The tie-up had "abundantly demonstrated that a concerted railroad strike is a national evil. . . ." To protect the nation's credit and welfare, legislation was needed that aimed at preventing such disasters in the future, and to "provide authority for the prompt and efficient intervention of the General Government."[78]

Echoing similar sentiments, the *New York Times* declared that the hardships wrought by the railroad embargo showed that only federal authority could "be relied upon for the preservation of order in any great emergency connected with our commercial and industrial system." The question was "a wide one in its bearing upon the future of railroads," the *Times* declared, but strike conditions made it imperative to consider the government's role "in relation to the protection of life and property, and the efficient performance of the service which has grown into a national necessity."[79] Hayes and his cabinet, however, apparently saw no need for direct action to protect interstate commerce, per se, when, on other grounds, this was already being done.

Hayes's handling of the strikes in many ways deserved the praise it received. He had been obliged to act in time of crisis with few precedents to guide him and little in the way of force to execute his decisions. Even Judge Gresham, who would have preferred stronger action, admitted that Hayes had performed well. "I wish Grant had been President," he wrote a friend at the close of the strike, "yet I think President Hayes has done his duty in this emergency."[80]

Once the administration decided to intervene, the policy of sending troops only at the call of a governor or federal judge avoided technical and legal difficulties. Had troops been sent into the various troubled areas under orders to protect interstate commerce and the mails, objections might well have been raised. There were, for example, no statutes conferring such powers on the federal government, though many would argue that such powers could be inferred directly from the Constitution. Intervention on these grounds might also have branded the federal government a tool of railroad companies in breaking up the strikes. Although the end result, for all practical purposes, was the same, the administration, by acting only in response to the calls of governors and judges, was less open to charges of having allied itself with the railroads against the strikers.

Still another advantage of these grounds for intervention was that all constitutional questions were neatly avoided. The state governments had no occasion to complain that their sovereign rights were overridden as would be the case some years later when President Cleveland ordered the Army into Illinois during the Pullman strike without consulting the governor of that state.

The administration behaved with commendable restraint once the decision was made to intervene. Despite his own and his advisers' ties to the railroads, Hayes did not allow the companies to dictate policy. Pressures were brought to bear, influence was wielded, urgent requests and even demands were made, but Hayes seems to have acted consistently on his conception of the public good. At all times he appears to have been fully abreast of the progress of the disorders and in complete charge of the activities of the executive branch. Meeting daily with his cabinet during the crisis, he seems to have benefited much from their counsel. At the same time he neither allowed a drift of his power to others nor made undue delegation of responsibility or authority.

Perhaps the outstanding feature of the administration's conduct of the strike was the calm but deliberate fashion in which it acted. "Time has come," James Wilson wired from St. Louis, "when President should stamp out mob now rampant. A few resolute men can do it here. The law can be found for it after order is restored. . . ." "The whole country will soon be in anarchy and revolution unless you can save it by prompt action," Governor Hartranft urged. "I desire to earnestly press upon your immediate consideration the propriety of calling on a force of volunteers sufficient for the preservation of the peace and the protection of life and property."[81] Tom Scott demanded that a force of volunteers be summoned to clear all the railroad routes. Similarly urgent warnings and demands for action poured in from other railroad presidents, responsible statesmen and businessmen, from ordinary citizens, and from cranks. The most common plea was that Hayes call for volunteers, as Lincoln had done, to suppress insurrection.[82]

But Hayes did not see the strikes either as insurrection or the start of a communistic-anarchistic revolution. He told newspapermen, while rioting was at its worst in Pittsburgh, that the "prevailing disorders give no evidence of a spirit of communism because the attacks of the mob have not been directed against the property of the general public, but against the corporations with which the laboring element is at war."[83] Hayes's response was a far cry from Attorney General Richard

Olney's remark nearly two decades later under nearly identical circumstances, "We have been brought to the ragged edge of anarchy. . . ."

The deliberate calmness of the Hayes administration can probably be attributed to several factors. Hayes and his cabinet, for the most part, were men who had commanded troops during the Civil War or were politicians with considerable experience at leadership.[84] They had known and dealt with crises before, on the field of battle or in public office, and were not easily stampeded or panicked. Moreover, however much they may have been willing to use stronger measures, they were of necessity restrained by the smallness of armed forces at their disposal. Yet another factor may have been that strike policy was determined by the group and not by one or two individuals. If one was swayed by pressures, the others were there to redress the balance.

Finally, Hayes had a reliable, independent, and unbiased source for information during the strike. Regular Army signal corpsmen scattered across the nation kept the President abreast of conditions and frequently offset hysterical alarms rung by railway officials and others who wanted more vigorous action. A telegram from General Hancock illustrates how a military assessment counteracted that of a railroad president: "Saw Mr. Scott at Philadelphia last night at twelve. He was much impressed with the necessity of the Government calling out a sufficient body of troops to quell all disturbances along the railroad routes. He urged me to proceed to Washington at once and present the necessity for such action of the Government. The details of the present state of affairs are doubtless better known at Washington than I know them so I leave the matter with the foregoing remarks *and the assertion that everything seems quiet here at this time.*"[85] Again, between July 24 and 26, when Judge Gresham and Marshal Spooner were painting the scene at Indianapolis in the darkest hues so as to secure authorization for 1000 deputy marshals and a detachment of troops, Sergeant Wappenhans of the army signal corps was wiring from Indianapolis such messages as: ". . . strikers orderly, no indications of violence" (July 24). "Situation unchanged, strikers still prevent traffic except on two roads. . . . No signs of mob violence" (July 25); and, "During night strikers concluded not to hinder the running of passenger trains." "Not the least sign of mob violence" (July 26).[86]

The calm, restrained conduct of the Hayes administration once it became involved in the strikes, however, does not absolve it of having acted hastily in the first place or of having engaged in strikebreaking. Hayes would have done well to have used the same caution he had shown as governor of Ohio when sending troops into labor disputes. When Governor Mathews called for military assistance at Martinsburg, the administration should have questioned him closely: Was the mob at Martinsburg actually rioting? Was property being destroyed and were lives really endangered? If not, as seems to have been the case, federal authorities could have investigated before ordering out the army. Martinsburg, after all, was less than ninety miles from the capital.

Given the total strike situation in 1877, it seems unlikely that the federal government could or should have long avoided intervention. Although precipitous at Martinsburg and not sufficiently insistent that the states perform their whole duty before sending aid, the Hayes administration was right to intervene in so massive a railroad tie-up. Instead of being so scrupulous about the wordings of the various requests for aid, however, Hayes and his advisers should have been concerned about more fundamental questions. Was intervention necessary, and if so, why? What forms of intervention other than military were available? What specific purposes were to be served by intervention?

Perhaps the most serious error of the administration was allowing the governors (and in effect the railroad companies) to define the conditions of intervention. Hayes himself clearly saw that the troubles were due to a conflict between railway capital and labor, not insurrection against either state or federal governments. And yet, he sent troops at the call of the governors expressly to suppress domestic insurrection. Once federal troops moved in, they not only put down rioting and restored law and order, they also suppressed striking and restored regular railway service. Any government worthy of the name would have halted overt lawlessness and rioting, but preservation of law and order did not require that trains move on schedule. Once underway, federal intervention was more and more directed at restoring normal transportation service; the calls of the governors and federal judges for assistance in effect but served as occasions for acting.

Two considerations justified federal intervention: the calls of the governors for aid in suppressing domestic violence (not insurrection), and the halt of interstate commerce and the mail. Both should have been openly acknowledged by the administration. Troops should have been sent in to put down lawlessness only when lawlessness reigned and they should have been under strict orders in such instances to do nothing more than keep the peace. On the second issue, the blocking of interstate commerce and the mail, Hayes should have been guided by his clear understanding that the tie-up was due to grievances of workmen against their employers. This would have called for attempts to bring the warring parties to the negotiating table. Admittedly the workers' lack of leadership and organization would have handicapped such efforts, but these obstacles would not seem to have been insurmountable.

In the absence of law or precedent, it might be asked, how could the President legally have brought the parties to the conference table? The same way that in the absence of law and precedent he suppressed the strikes, that is, by conservative innovation—by stretching the old, accepted forms to cover new objectives. President John Tyler, for instance, during the Dorr Rebellion in Rhode Island in 1842, refused to send federal troops at the request of the regularly elected government to protect it from Dorr and his followers. In a private letter Tyler suggested to the governor that the difficulties might be ended if a general amnesty were proclaimed and a call were issued for a new constitutional convention to draft a more liberal frame of government.[87] Hayes, similarly, could have refused to send troops to protect railroads unless the companies agreed to rescind their recent wage cuts and establish machinery for negotiating new wages. The workers, lacking the means to carry on a long strike, and under the threat of force, probably would not have resisted the offer.

Such a proposal from the White House in 1877 would have run against the grain of railway managers and businessmen who conceded few, if any, rights to labor. To them it would have seemed well outside the constitutional prerogatives of the President to intervene in "business" matters.[88] On the other hand, most workingmen probably regarded the use of the Army to suppress the strikes as even less justified or constitutional. Cautious, unimaginative leadership in 1877 chose the easier route and suppressed the strikes under the legal form of suppressing domestic insurrection or enforcing court orders. Bolder leadership would have recognized the strikes for what they were—a capital-labor conflict—and dealt with them accordingly.

The course pursued by federal judges during the strikes, though widely praised in the newspapers and journals of the day, raised serious questions at least in the mind of Thomas M. Cooley, one of the nation's most distinguished jurists and legal writers. In an article on the general subject, "New Aspects of the Right of Trial by Jury," Cooley touched upon problems growing out of court protection of railways in receivership during strikes and the use of contempt proceedings to punish strikers who interfered with such railways. "A riot on the New York Central which interferes with the running of its trains is only a riot;" he observed, "but on the Erie Railroad it is a contempt of the Court of Chancery. In the one case only a jury can deal with it, and twelve men must agree concerning its legal bearings; in the other a single judge may administer summary punishment." This did not seem right to Cooley. "Rights and protections," he declared, "ought to be the same everywhere; the property which the receiver manages for its owners is no more sacred than that which the owners manage in person; it ought to have the same protection and no more."

Turning to the matter of summary contempt proceedings against strikers, Cooley was struck by the "great gratification" expressed in the press that the courts had been able to bring rioters summarily before them and "to inflict speedy and effectual punishment without delay or the opportunity to appeal to a popular tribunal." More important, the gratification had no regard for the fact that the property being protected was in a special category—that was thought to be only a fortuitous circumstance that afforded an opportunity for a summary remedy. What disturbed Cooley was, "the latter has been treated as a thing good in itself." The power of the courts to punish for contempt, Cooley said, "is exceedingly vague and indeterminate; its limits are uncertain; the constitutional protections which surround jury trial do not apply to it, and it is subject to few statutory regulations; for the most part the power is in the breast of a single judge without fixed rule or landmark limiting his discretion." If such broad discretionary authority was good and useful in some cases, as in the cases of the men who rioted against railways in receivership, Cooley added scornfully, it would be good in all similar cases and its exercise ought not to be dependent upon the existence of the accident of receivership. In Cooley's opinion, the expressions of approval of the summary punishment of rioters without regard for the legal basis of the punishment were "distinct admissions of belief that the restraints we impose on power are worse than useless, and they exhibit us in the aspect of abhorring unbridled authority in theory while we applaud it in practice."

Although these were among the very earliest instances in which strikers were punished for contempt by federal courts, Cooley accurately predicted that the use of such a power in time might well be subjected to restrictions. "We may be reasonably certain," he wrote, "that its frequent exercise will lead to new consideration of the logical foundations of jury trial, and perhaps also of the limitations of the power to punish as judicial contempts acts not committed in the presence of the court."[89]

In later strikes the actions of the federal courts in 1877 were the precedents that would be acted upon. Little would be remembered about the executive branch's handling of the strikes except that troops had been sent out against the strikers.

CHAPTER III

• • •

Decade of Drifting

THAT THE FEDERAL GOVERNMENT had no policy in 1877 for meeting major railway strikes was not remarkable. Until that year there had been little evidence of a need for any sort of federal labor policy. The disorders of that summer, however, served notice on the nation that a new era was beginning in labor-capital relations. They raised the spectre of widespread and violent struggle in the years ahead, and it should have been evident that the time had come to formulate a national policy for dealing with major labor disputes, at least on the railways. Such a policy, however, was not forthcoming during the relatively quiet years between 1877 and 1886. Only with the outbreak of another major railway strike did the government reluctantly take up the problem again.

The strikes of 1877 produced an immediate but short-lived demand for action. Newspaper and magazine articles agreed generally that the strikers had grievances but insisted that the men had gone about solving them in the wrong way. They further agreed that wages could not be altered by agitation because the price of labor was determined by supply and demand. Railway workmen, dissatisfied with their wages, had been within their rights to quit work but had gone too far when they attempted to prevent others from taking their places or when they obstructed the passage of trains.

There was no concensus as to what should be done to prevent such disorders in the future. The editors of *Nation* and *Harper's Weekly* thought the strikes proved conclusively the need for a larger Army.[1] Writing in *Railway Age,* former Con-

54

gressman S. A. Hurlbut called for new and stronger laws to
punish obstruction of trains. He urged that these new laws be
enforced by federal marshals "with the knowledge that the
whole power of the United States stands ready to aid, without
any circumlocution of requisition from a governor." In the same
issue of *Railway Age,* P. M. Arthur, chief of the Brotherhood of
Locomotive Engineers, called for legislation compelling the
submission of all railway labor disputes to binding arbitration.[2]

President Scott of the Pennsylvania, in a letter to the *North
American Review,* pointed out that the only railroads given
prompt federal protection during the strikes were those in receivership. He argued that railroads ought not to have to "become bankrupt in order to make secure the uninterrupted
movement of traffic over their lines, or to entitle them to the
efficient protection of the United States government. . . ." In
his opinion the laws that authorized federal courts to enjoin "so
comparatively trifling a wrong as an infringement of a patent-
right" must certainly have been intended to allow the courts
"to prevent a wrong-doing which not only destroys a particular
road, but also paralyzes the entire commerce of the country
and wastes the national wealth." The solution, he believed, was
to concentrate federal troops "at prominent points, large cities
and other great business centres," and to enact legislation giving
any interstate carrier the right to petition the courts for relief
from interference by "unlawful combinations, by threats, or
by violence." The courts, in turn, would enjoin such interference, enforcing their process by ordering the arrest of any who
disobeyed.[3]

The meaning of the strikes had not escaped the members
of the Hayes administration. At a meeting July 31, near the
end of the crisis, Hayes and the cabinet discussed the need for
a federal policy. "Sherman calls attention . . . to R.R. traffic
and its magnitude—as showing the need of National action,"
Hayes recorded in his notes. "Thompson suggests contract be-
tw[een] RRs Evarts says it is a case for govt not contract.
Secy McC[rary] says the power to regulate Commerce covers it.
Ev[arts] says the country is ready for an exertion of its power,
but it is a difficult subject. . . ."[4] Writing in his diary a few
days later, Hayes observed: "the strikes have been put down by
force; but now for the *real* remedy. Can't something [be] done
by education of the strikers, by judicious control of the capitalists, by wise general policy to end or diminish the evil?"[5] Evarts,
in a letter to Hayes on August 6, ventured the opinion that "an

attempt to probe and soothe the labor difficulties by means of a commission, under public instructions, would of itself do good. . . ."⁶ And, a few days later, Secretary McCrary confided to a friend that the strikes were "not without their useful lessons. They warn us of dangers against which we must provide for the future."⁷

Despite this obvious concern, only one recommendation for legislation was made to Congress by the executive branch. The postmaster general, in his *Annual Report,* noted the vital role of the railroads in delivering the nation's mail. He praised the "cooperation" of the companies in moving mail during the strikes but suggested that it might be well "to provide remedies" against any future disturbances in that service. Under existing law if a company and the Postoffice Department differed over terms for hauling mail, the company could refuse to handle any mail whatever. Since this easily could result in serious interruptions, he proposed that the railroads be compelled to carry mail under terms prescribed by law.⁸

The President himself made no suggestions or recommendations to Congresss respecting the need for labor or strike legislation. He did not even call attention to the proposal of the postmaster general. In his message to the special session, which met on October 15 to consider the long-delayed Army appropriations bill, he failed to mention the strikes directly. He noted only that since June 30 (the expiration date of the previous appropriations bill), the Army had been "constantly and actively employed in arduous and dangerous service. . . ." The omission was not because labor proposals would have been inappropriate to the purposes of the session; he did ask Congress to consider American participation in the Paris International Exposition and the International Prison Congress, both scheduled for 1878. In his *Annual Message* in December the President devoted a single paragraph to praising the army for the prudent manner in which it had quelled the disorders of the previous summer.⁹

Responsibility for laying down federal policy for handling future labor disputes on the railroads rested, of course, with Congress. But neither the special nor regular sessions of the Forty-fifth Congress gave attention to the labor problem. So far as the recorded proceedings of that Congress reveal what was said and done, it was almost as if the strikes had not occurred. A bill designed to "punish the forcible obstruction of interstate commerce" was introduced in each house of Congress, but never left committee. A further exception to the all-but-complete silence respecting the strikes took place during a debate on another army appropriations bill. The question was raised as to whether a provision in the bill might not make it illegal in the future to use the Army as had been done during the strikes. The brief debate on the point revealed that several senators were at least aware of the disorders of the previous summer.[10] The crisis was over, however, and before long the press of more urgent issues pushed the railway strike problem from the fore.

Nearly a full year after the strikes the House of Representatives authorized what appears to have been the first congressional investigation to touch upon labor affairs. A bill for investigating "hours of labor and the division of profits between labor and capital in the United States" had been proposed as early as March 1876 but was never brought to the floor of the House. In June 1878, however, the House set up a select committee to look into the causes of the depression which had begun five years earlier, "that labor may be restored to its just rights, [and] to the end that labor and all our varied interests may be encouraged, promoted, and protected by liberal, just and equal laws."[11]

The work of the committee came to nought. The depression had nearly run its course by the time the inquiry began. The surge of returning prosperity, in the view of many congressmen, rendered the investigation pointless. The committee, undaunted, began with the depression problem but gradually shifted its focus to the issue of Chinese immigration. Reformers appearing before the committee offered a variety of panaceas ranging from nationalization of the railroads and other major industries to prohibition and paper-money inflation. Professor William Graham Sumner, on the other hand, assured the congressmen that nothing could be done to ameliorate depression conditions save possibly to repeal existing laws that interfered with the workings of the natural economic order.[12] In all, the committee issued three reports. It reached no conclusions, however, as to causes of the depression and it offered no recommendations for "restoring labor to its just rights" except halting Chinese immigration. Nothing whatever was said of strikes on the nation's railroads.[13]

The gradual return of economic prosperity did not reduce labor agitation. Indeed, good times seemed to stimulate trouble. Labor ferment took several forms, including increased organization into unions, greater participation in third-party politics, and strikes. Trades union membership by 1883 stood at about 200,000 and during the 1880's the number of organized laborers in the United States reached a peak of almost one million. Membership in the Knights of Labor, the most important union of the 1880's, jumped from 9000 in 1879 to 52,000 in 1884. Two years later it boasted 703,000 members. Labor's interest in politics found expression chiefly in the unsuccessful Greenback-Labor Party, but workingmen in the Far West also organized politically to bar further Chinese immigration.[14] The number of men reported on strike each year grew steadily from 101,000 in 1881 to 159,000 in 1885. A peak of 407,000 was reached in 1886, setting a record that would stand until 1894, the year of the Pullman strike.[15]

The rising tide of labor unrest led the Senate in August 1882 to authorize a study of labor-capital relations. The Committee on Education and Labor, to which the task fell, was charged to investigate the general relationship of capital and labor, the wages, hours, and working conditions of American laborers as compared with their counterparts abroad, the division between capital and labor of "their joint productions," and the nature and causes of strikes. Upon completion of its investigation the committee was to report its findings and to propose legislation "to modify or remove" the causes of labor disputes and "any other legislation calculated to promote harmonious relations between capitalists and laborers, in the interests of both, by the improvement of the condition of industrial classes of the United States."[16]

The work of the committee took it to New York City, New England, and the South. The senators visited slums and factories and questioned people they met along the way. Like the House committee before it, the Senate committee took testimony and listened to the prepared statements of all sorts and conditions of men—workers, reformers, labor leaders, industrialists, and students of capital-labor problems. Fortunately for the investigation, the telegraphers' strike of 1883 broke out during the committee's stay in New York City, giving the congressmen an opportunity to observe firsthand an actual strike. A score or so telegraphers aired their side of the controversy before the committee, followed by Norvin Green, president of Western Union, and Jay Gould, financier and manipulator of stocks, bonds, railroads, and telegraph companies. Although the investigation contributed nothing to the settlement of the dispute, it elicited much information about the strike and its causes, the development of the telegraph industry, and a brief autobiographical sketch by Jay Gould.[17]

In 1885 the Senate authorized the committee to publish four thick volumes of the testimony it had collected. A fifth volume, which was to conclude the testimony and present the conclusions and recommendations of the committee, was promised but never produced.[18] The mountain of testimony and the hours of work of the committee were not a total loss. The four published volumes, like the testimony of the House committee before it, through the years have been a mine of information for historians, economists, and other students of that era.

A growing awareness of the labor problem led Congress, in 1884, to set up the United States Bureau of Labor Statistics. Several states already maintained such fact-finding agencies, that in Massachusetts, headed by Carroll D. Wright, being the best known. Beginning in 1879 congressmen regularly introduced bills calling for either a commissioner of labor or a federal bureau of labor statistics.[19] Finally, in April 1884, the House passed a bill that combined the proposals by setting up such a bureau headed by a commissioner of labor. The commissioner was given no power whatever to intervene in strikes or even to investigate labor disputes in progress. The function of the bureau was limited to gathering data, on a continuing basis, about manufacturing, labor conditions, and the like for the use of Congress. After brief debate the bill passed the Senate, and when differences in the House and Senate versions were adjusted, President Chester A. Arthur signed it into law, June 28, 1884.[20] A few days later Arthur appointed Carroll D. Wright the first federal commissioner of labor.

In 1884 and 1885 the economy dipped downward again, touching off a new wave of serious strikes. The most important involved the Knights of Labor and various properties controlled by Jay Gould. Trouble between the Knights and Gould began when the Knights struck Gould's Western Union telegraph in 1883. Gould trounced the Knights in this first encounter but his victory was not long-lived. Brief flare-ups occurred on the Gould-dominated Union Pacific in May and August 1884 when wage cuts and discrimination against union men met with defiance. Gould, already under attack from his Wall Street rivals, was obliged to retreat on both occasions.[21]

Early in 1885 trouble struck three Gould lines, the Wabash, the Missouri, Kansas & Texas, and the Missouri Pacific, again because of wage cuts. In spite of large earnings reported by the Missouri Pacific at its previous annual meeting, wages on that line were slashed below the rates paid by other Southwestern railways. The Knights went out. The strike, however, differed from most strikes of the era. The Knights acted only after deliberate and careful consideration and not on an impulsive outburst of dissatisfaction. They were well organized and seemed in full control of the strike at all times. "Every movement was directed by the executive committee," the Missouri commissioner of labor reported, "and a perfect police system maintained under which the property of the railroad company and private individuals was fully protected."[22] Supported by the four railway brotherhoods, the Knights of Labor completely tied up the freight service of Gould's Southwest system.

Public sympathy apparently lay with the striking railroaders. The governors of Kansas and Missouri sent in the militia to preserve peace, but they did not allow the troopers to be used to break the strike. Gould decided against further resistance and accepted mediation by the governors. "The railroads could not do otherwise," wrote the Harvard political economist, Frank W. Taussig, in his contemporary account. "Their traffic was annihilated, public opinion and the State Governments were against them. They accepted the terms proposed." The old wage rates were restored and future cuts were to be made only after thirty days' notice. Gould further promised that no one would be punished for having participated in the strike.[23]

The next year Gould reversed the tide running against him by crushing the final and most violent of the Knights of Labor strikes against his railroads. Almost immediately after the agreement of 1885 it became clear to his employees that Gould, or his lieutenants, were determined to run the railroads without regard for the union or the agreement. Heady from their earlier victories against Gould, the Knights were quick to seek redress of their alleged grievances. The discharge of a Knight who was a foreman on the Texas & Pacific led Martin Irons, a local leader of the union, to call out the men. "Tell the world that men of the Gould Southwest system are on strike," one union broadside proclaimed. "We strike for justice to ourselves and our fellowmen everywhere. . . . Bring in all your grievances in one bundle at once, and come out to a man, and stay out until they are all settled to your entire satisfaction. . . ."[24]

Between February 18 and mid-March the strike spread to the entire Gould railway empire in the Southwest, creating a more serious crisis than in 1885. Despite the failure of the brotherhoods to join them this time, the Knights held fast and succeeded in blockading traffic and paralyzing business at St. Louis, Kansas City, and other rail centers of the region. An attempt to settle the dispute by arbitration at the end of March ended in failure. Terence V. Powderly, grand master workman of the Knights of Labor, who disapproved of the strike, sought to end it by meeting with Jay Gould in person. Powderly left a meeting March 28 believing that the magnate had agreed to arbitration. Gould, as it turned out, had no intention of making concessions.[25]

Arbitration was not resorted to, and when the angry strikers turned to less peaceful means of persuasion, Gould met force with force. Aided by strikebreakers, Pinkerton detectives, local peace officers, the militia of several states, and federal marshals with hosts of special deputies (many of whom were loyal railway employees paid and armed by their employers but wearing the badges of federal marshals) Gould put down the strike.[26] Pitched battles in Fort Worth, Texas, Parsons, Kansas, and East St. Louis early in April resulted in a number of casualties. By the end of April, however, the railways were operating on near-normal schedules and the strike was broken. On May 4 the General Executive Board of the Knights, prodded by a congressional committee investigating the strike, ordered the men back to work. The surrender was complete and no more than one-fifth of the strikers ever again found work on Gould lines.[27]

The strikers of 1885 and 1886, like many of their counterparts in the 1877 disorders, sought to avoid conflict with the federal government by allowing mail to move freely through strikebound areas. But where the earlier strikers had offered to move mail cars through blockades only if no passenger cars were attached, the Knights during the Southwest strikes went further. They permitted all mail trains, complete with passenger cars, to proceed unmolested. Similarly, trains loaded with supplies for federal troops proceeded unhampered through the blockades.[28]

Railroad officials, like their 1877 counterparts, attempted to use mail tie-ups as well as passenger and freight blockades to win public sympathy for their cause. Taussig reported that in 1886 Gould began with virtually no public support. By careful management of the strike, that is, by letting the "effects of the strike work themselves out," Gould turned a goodly portion of the public against the strikers. "For form's sake," attempts were made to run trains, but failed. The managers threatened to suspend all passenger—hence all mail—service. As traffic lay dead, as more and more railway employees were thrown out of work, as merchants and businessmen were hurt and factories closed, as supplies ran low and prices rose, the strikers were blamed. To all offers of the strikers to run relief trains to suffering communities, Gould's agents replied that trains would run on normal schedules or not at all.

The strikers' policy of not interfering with the flow of mail might have avoided conflict with the federal government but that some of Gould's railways were in the hands of federal court receivers. Even here the strikers were cautious, interfering little with the Wabash, well known to be in receivership. On the other hand, strikers treated the Texas & Pacific, also in receivership, as if it were a part of the Missouri Pacific. Perhaps this was because for years it had been an integral part of that line and only shortly before the strike had passed into receivership.[29]

During the Southwest strikes federal judges continued to build and expand on the pioneering work begun in 1877 by Judges Drummond, Gresham, and Treat in protecting railways in receivership from strikers. The sweeping labor injunction had not yet evolved in the federal courts and no attempt was made by the judges to halt the strike per se by court action. At the same time, they did use writs of assistance, bench warrants, and contempt proceedings to harass strikers who interfered with the operation of railways in receivership.[30] One judge went farther than the others when he ruled that a peaceable but concerted work stoppage by employees of a receiver was in itself contempt of court. These new restrictions on the right of men to strike were justified on the grounds that the courts themselves stood ready to redress any grievances employees might have against receivers.

Foremost among the federal judges in these proceedings in 1885 was David J. Brewer, judge of the Eighth Circuit Court. Brewer, a strong defender of individual and property rights, was a champion of the use of injunctive powers by the courts. Believing it the function of the judiciary to protect property against both state and federal regulation, he had been the first federal judge to challenge the Supreme Court's Granger case decisions.[31]

Brewer's handling of the Wabash receivership, which only incidentally involved him with the strikers of 1885, eventually came under severe criticism in both legal and lay circles familiar with the affair. The Wabash, long in the hands of Jay Gould and his associates, was on the verge of financial collapse. Stealing the march on the creditors of the line, the Gould interests sought a receivership so as to prevent creditors from collecting the money owed them. At that time receiverships were set up on the petition of creditors, not debtors, and the federal district judge in St. Louis rejected the novel scheme. However, Brewer granted the receivership and appointed, at the petitioners' request, two managers of the Wabash to be receivers. In the view of many, the two already stood convicted of inability to operate the Wabash at a profit and by no means could be regarded as sufficiently disinterested to act as custodians of the property. Brewer took these actions "without delay, without notice to any party interested, and without chance for interested parties to be heard." He went on to authorize the receivers to place certain promissory notes, endorsed by Gould and his associates, ahead of all other indebtedness of the company and to pay some $360,000 in rebates, contracted before the receivership, to a coal company owned by the Gould group.[32]

"Some of his rulings in the Wabash Receivership case can not be supported on any theory known to lawyers," the *American Law Review* commented at the time Brewer was promoted to the Supreme Court. "Nevertheless we suppose that no judicious lawyer, acquainted with his previous character doubted his integrity in those rulings; though it is to be confessed that brokers and some of the business community did. . . . If he had been judged by those rulings exclusively, neither his appointment nor his confirmation would have been deserved."[33] Brewer's crusade to protect the sanctity of property, particularly Wabash property, found full expression in the contempt proceedings in his court during the Southwest strikes.

In March 1885 two leaders of the Missouri Pacific strike were brought before Brewer, charged with having obstructed the movement of engines and freight cars belonging to the receivers of the Wabash. Brewer accepted their plea that they had not intentionally interfered with the court or its orders. Since they had been engaged in an unlawful act that had interfered with the court's operation of the railroad, however, they would have to be punished as if the interference had been deliberate.

"Do I understand your honor to say that the act of striking—merely carrying out of a strike—was unlawful?" the attorney for the defendants asked.

"It is not the mere stopping of work themselves, but it is preventing the owners of the road from managing their own engines and running their own cars," Brewer replied. "That is where the wrong comes in. Anybody has a right to quit work, but in interfering with other persons' working, and preventing the owners of railroad trains from managing those trains as they see fit—there is where the wrong comes in." Brewer sentenced the men to sixty days in jail.[34]

Brewer's colleague in the case was one of the oldest judges then active on the federal bench, Samuel Treat of St. Louis (not to be confused with Judge Samuel Hubbel Treat of Springfield, Illinois). As a young man, Treat had settled in St. Louis, where he became an active promoter of internal improvements. In 1849 he served as a delegate to the National Railroad Convention in St. Louis, which called for federal assistance in building a railroad and telegraph line from the Missouri River to the Pacific.[35]

In the case of the Missouri Pacific strikers in 1885, Treat declared that were he sole rather than joint judge with Brewer, he would have dealt more severely with the men. He reiterated Brewer's point that no one questioned the right of the men to work or to refuse to work. But, he said, the men ought not to have resorted to "lawless measures to injure the property or the person of any other party." More particularly was this true of property in the hands of court-appointed receivers. If the workers had any just grounds for complaint, they had been free to come before the court, and it "would have instructed the receivers" with respect to the issues at controversy. Indeed, one of the primary reasons why courts so promptly punished men who interfered with receivers, Treat asserted, was that "anyone engaged in employment under them can have ample redress by applying to the court."[36]

Not long afterwards, in another strike case, Judge Brewer expanded upon these rulings. A number of employees of a Colorado railroad, dissatisfied with their wages, had quit their jobs and attempted to persuade others to do so too. All this was legal, Brewer held, but the strikers had gone further, resorting to threats of violence and intimidation to bring out the loyal employees. Brewer conceded that there had been no actual violence, but, he ruled, it was not enough to consider merely that verbal persuasion had been used. The circumstances, and the manner in which the words were spoken, and similar facts had to be taken into consideration. In this instance the strikers had overawed the other employees by means of organized demonstrations of force. Because they thus kept the receivers from operating the railroad, they were adjudged guilty of contempt.

Borrowing from Judge Treat's observations in the case of the Missouri Pacific strikers, Brewer declared that if the defendants had complaints they should have brought them before the court. "Although owning this railroad, it is not for [the company] to say who shall be employed and who not. The court has taken possession of that property, and any man connected with the administration or management of that road, I do not care who he is, whether he is doing the most humble, common work on the line of that road, has the same right as the receiver himself has, that any creditor of the road has, to come into this court and insist that any grievance which he has against the management of that road shall be considered and passed upon."[37]

From these two cases it appeared that the courts, though closely restricting the right of employees of receivers to strike, stood ready to offer judicial relief for grievances against arbitrary rulings of receivers. That workingmen in the past had failed to use this means to secure redress of grievances probably was due to ignorance of their rights. At any rate, a group of Denver & Rio Grande employees came before Brewer in May 1885 with grievances. They left disabused of the notion that they could expect a favorable reception in that quarter. The men alleged that the wages paid apprentices were not reasonably advanced as the apprentices learned their jobs, men who worked overtime were not given extra pay, others were discharged for "lack of work" when, in their opinion, there was work aplenty to do, and one of their foremen was so "blasphemous and tyrannical" as to be unfit for his position.

Brewer delivered a brief homily to the men in which he discussed how wages were determined by supply and demand and not by whim of the receiver. The company, he observed, was paying no dividends whatever to the owners of the railroad. Rather than complaining because they received no raises, the men should be grateful that they had not suffered cuts. As for the lack of overtime pay, Brewer noted that no one prevented the men from going to work for more generous employers. The other charges Brewer dismissed as "trivial." The receiver reported to Brewer that the foreman's swearing was not bad enough to warrant discharging him. He could have simply relied on the receiver's judgment, Brewer pointed out, but instead had himself investigated the matter. His information was that the foreman did not swear excessively. He was a driver and pusher of his subordinates, Brewer conceded, but he also was always fair to his men.

The judge concluded with a warning. Employees who had earlier gone on strike had made a mistake. The "evil ones" in that group could not be rehired; the misled among them would be reemployed only as needed by the receiver. Having gone on strike was not in itself sufficient grounds for not rehiring a man, Brewer declared. Of greater significance was whether the loyalties of employees were divided. Those who put loyalty to a union ahead of loyalty to their employer could scarcely expect to find favor at the hands of the receiver and might well be discharged.[38]

One other reported strike case in 1885 came before Arnold Krekel, federal judge for the Western District of Missouri. While a schoolboy in his native Prussia, Krekel had been much impressed with the state system of schools and railroads there. Later, in Missouri, he became an active advocate of state support for schools and a champion of state aid for railroad development. Elected to the Missouri Legislature in 1852, he united with others to push through a new state school law and the first appropriation made by the state for railroad purposes. In the years before 1874 Krekel served as a director of the Missouri Pacific and of the Jefferson City, Lebanon & Southwestern railways. "A terror to evildoers," Judge Krekel was a man of strong opinions who seemingly was determined "to penalize any who had ever differed with him."[39]

Strike leaders brought before Krekel in 1885 had, by "threats and intimidation," induced loyal employees of the Wabash to leave their work. This, the longtime friend of railroads ruled, was an interference with the operation of a road in receivership. The "intimidation" consisted of a letter, written by the chairman of the strike committee to a foreman: "You are requested to stay away from the shop until the present difficulty is settled," the letter stated. "Your compliance with this will command the protection of the Wabash employees. But in no case are you to consider this an intimidation." Two other letters, similar in tone and wording, were also cited. Krekel held that letters of this type came within the definition of "intimidation."

The judge went on to justify his finding by an appeal to the general welfare. When employers and employees failed to settle their differences by compromise, he said, they "must be settled by law and the courts." The general public could "not afford to tolerate conflicts, from which outside and innocent parties must suffer." How the law and courts were to settle such disputes Krekel did not indicate. In the case before him, however, only the strikers were punished for contempt. Their behavior had been inexcusable, he declared, because the courts had stood open to them had they wished to appeal the orders of the receiver.[40]

With the outbreak of the even greater strikes of 1886, the railroads turned to both state and federal courts for assistance in putting them down. Although state court judges were more active than their federal colleagues in issuing writs against strikers, one officially reported federal case was brought before Circuit Court Judge Don A. Pardee. Pardee had achieved distinction "as an admiralty judge and as a fair and able administrator of railroads" in receivership. He was a believer in "the right of property" and in "popular government," but "he would not permit himself to be driven, or moved, by popular excitement."[41] He demonstrated these traits during the strike of 1886.

Pardee added a new facet to strikes against railways in receivership when he ruled that all employees of such a line were in fact officers of the court. "As such officers," he held, "they are responsible to the court for their conduct, and if they willfully injure the property, or endanger it, or seek to cripple its operation in the hands of the receivers, they can and will be made to answer therefore."

At the same time Pardee declared that employees were entitled to "the full protection that the court can give under the laws of the land; and this, whether the grievance comes from within or without." Any employee with a complaint as to his "employment or wages or treatment" could bring the matter before the court. The court, he said, "will hear and arbitrate, and see justice done in the premises." Though officers of the court, Pardee went on, employees of a receiver were free to quit provided they did not "thereby intentionally disable the property." They must, he said, "quit peaceable and decently." On the other hand, when they combined and conspired together to quit so as to cripple the operation of the railway they were guilty of contempt. Labor organizations, although lawful and generally laudable, had no legal status or authority, and it was "preposterous that they should atttempt to issue orders that free men [were] bound to obey."

Pardee declared that none of the men before him had complained to him or to the receiver of bad treatment, insufficient wages, or other grievance. Yet, a secret organization (the Knights of Labor) had ordered the employees "to quit work, to strike, [and] to cripple the operations of a great thoroughfare for travel and commerce." From newspapers and union broadsides he had learned that this "gross contempt of court, wholly unreasonable and unjustifiable," had resulted from the firing of an employee who had been absent without leave from his job. Declaring the firing to be in violation of an agreement between the employer and the employees, the strike leaders used the incident as a pretext for taking over control of the railroad. "The real motive for the order to strike," Pardee asserted, "was to compel a recognition of a certain secret labor organization (which, by evidence, has been shown to be about as arbitrary and autocratic in dealing with labor as the famous six companies of China) as an existing power, so that its officers shall be consulted in the operation and management of railroads in which they do not own any interest, and of which they do not even pretend to be employees. . . ." Unwilling to submit to the "violence and intimidation and bulldozing" of the Knights of Labor, Pardee inflicted heavy penalties for contempt against the men before him.[42]

The federal cases arising out of the Southwest strikes reaffirmed that the courts would protect railways in receivership from strikers. The limits of strike activity against such railroads were narrowed and Judge Pardee's ruling all but outlawed men's combining and quitting the service of a receiver if the result was a crippling of the railroad. To date federal court protection was limited only to railroads in receivership.

A minor strike on the Lake Shore Railroad in June 1886, however, produced a significant portent for the future. Attorneys for that line petitioned Circuit Court Judge Gresham in Chicago for an injunction against strikers despite the fact that the company was not in receivership. They argued that the road, as a common carrier moving interstate and international commerce, was entitled to federal protection. The particular statute upon which they based their request had originally been enacted to thwart the Ku Klux Klan. It provided, among other things, that "if two or more persons conspire to injure, oppress, threaten, or intimidate any citizen in the free exercise or enjoyment of any right or privilege secured to him by the Constitution or laws of the United States," they were liable to punishment by fine or imprisonment. Gresham ruled that the right of the railroad to engage in interstate commerce derived directly from the Constitution and laws of the United States. Strikers who stopped cars and obstructed the railroad's operations deprived it of that right. It, therefore, became the duty of the court to protect the road and Gresham granted a temporary injunction to serve that purpose until a hearing on July 7. The strike ended before the hearing took place, so the order was never made permanent. Protection of interstate commerce on any railroad, whether or not in receivership, would be extended even more protection by Judge Gresham during the Burlington strike of 1888.[43]

As the Southwest strike of 1886 moved toward its climax in March and early April, Congress took cognizance of the disorders and feebly undertook to fulfill its responsibilities. One measure, a bill to incorporate national trade unions, which would empower them "to sue and be sued, to implead and be impleaded, to grant and to receive . . . property" and to use that property for purposes defined in their charters, was introduced in the Senate on March 1 and signed into law by President Cleveland on June 29. This first legislation arising from the Southwest strike never bore fruit. From its enactment till its repeal on July 22, 1932, no union ever applied for incorporation under it.[44]

The Southwest strikes also set in motion a movement in Congress to outlaw any willful obstruction of interstate commerce. During the first session of the Forty-ninth Congress (March 4, 1885–August 5, 1886) ten bills for that purpose were introduced; none emerged from committee.[45] Proponents of the measure persisted, however, and attempted to add it by amendment to the interstate commerce bill then under debate in the Senate. At least one railroad president, James C. Clarke of the Illinois Central, favored the amendment. Clarke wrote that the Southwest strike showed that "it is not only important but necessary that the Bill to regulate Interstate Commerce should have a clause making it unlawful for any conspiracy, combination of persons, Associations or Corporations impeding or preventing the passage of Interstate Commerce with reasonable dispatch from the point of shipment to the point of destination." If strikes were to be allowed to tie up railroads, he said, "let it be with Domestic Commerce within the State, and not with Interstate Commerce." Such a regulation would be "in the interest of all and to the injury of none," he concluded.[46]

Senate debate on the interstate commerce bill began on April 14, at the height of strike disorders. On May 6, Senator Morgan of Alabama proposed an amendment that would have extended federal protection to all railroads in interstate commerce. The amendment provided that if two or more persons acted together to prevent the operation of a railroad in interstate commerce, or endangered the safety of any official or employee of such a railroad, they would be guilty of unlawful conspiracy. Conviction carried a penalty for each offense of imprisonment not to exceed six months, or fine not to exceed $500, or both, at the court's discretion.

On the same day, and to the same end, Senator Joseph E. Brown of Georgia offered a more detailed and harsher amendment. It provided that anyone who "willfully and maliciously" destroyed, hurt, damaged, injured, or obstructed any railroad engaged in interstate commerce or in carrying the United States mail, or who aided, assisted, or advised others to do so, would be guilty of a felony punishable by imprisonment for from four to eight years. Any unauthorized person who turned, moved, interfered, or meddled with any switch, gate, siding, or other appurtenance of any railroad would be guilty of the same crime and subject to the same punishment. In the event someone died as a result of the commission of any of the specified unlawful acts, the offending party would be deemed guilty of murder and punished accordingly. Conviction for murder was, moreover, not to stand in the way of civil damages.[47]

Debate on the Morgan amendment took place on May 11. The brunt of the Alabama senator's argument on behalf of his proposal was that Congress should not limit its protection only to customers of the railroads. The carriers themselves were entitled to protection too. After all, he argued, the only purpose or justification of an interstate commerce law was to insure the free flow of commerce among the states. He pleaded for "even-handedness" in Congress' efforts at justice. "We want to have commerce free from trammel and without embarrassment, and free from monopoly," he said. "No set of men in the United States shall be permitted to oppress the people or to interfere with and to destroy commerce or to check it and prevent its free access to all the different parts of our country."[48]

Senators George G. Vest of Missouri and Henry M. Teller of Colorado took issue with Morgan. They sympathized with the idea of preventing a repetition of the recent disorders but thought Morgan's amendment went too far. Only the states, under the federal Constitution, had the right and duty to punish crimes against property. Teller argued that punishment for destroying property was best left to the states, all of which had laws against such crimes. It was the duty of the states to deal with disorder, to protect their lines of road, to protect their citizens, and to keep open their highways. Whenever a state was unable to perform these duties, there were constitutional methods for securing assistance from the federal government.

Morgan replied that it would be a "solecism" to assert that Congress could "make and control and fashion" contracts between shippers and carriers, regulate the terms, conditions, and prices at which freight would be delivered, and interfere with the civil rights of individuals in "all the numerous ways and by all the numerous devices" provided in the bill and yet assert that Congress had no power to punish men who obstructed commerce.[49]

Senator Henry Blair of New Hampshire, speaking against the amendment, objected that it was better suited to the criminal code than to a law regulating interstate commerce. But if strikes were to be legislated against, so ought the causes of strikes. He would propose an amendment to the amendment, he warned, providing that conspiring strikers could be punished for obstructing interstate commerce only if it could be proved in court that their employer was paying them "due and reasonable wages" and had redressed or stood ready to redress any just cause of complaint. In the absence of these conditions the penalties of the law would apply against the employer, his agents, and his managers.[50]

Satisfied that the Senate opposed this amendment to the bill he sponsored, Senator Cullom announced that he was against it because it might "embarrass the chances" for passage of any interstate commerce law. The Senate decisively tabled Morgan's motion, forty-nine to three. Brown's proposal met a similar fate immediately afterwards. No similar proposals were made during debate in the House, and in its final form the Interstate Commerce Act contained no provisions for punishing strikers who obstructed interstate commerce.[51]

Congressional response to the Southwest strikes was not limited to the incorporation of labor unions or possible laws against obstruction of interstate commerce. A rash of bills, providing in one way or another for arbitration of railway labor disputes, was introduced early in 1886. One of these, the O'Neill bill, was favorably reported to the floor of the House on March 31, just as the 1886 strike neared its violent stage. The bill provided that whenever parties to a dispute agreed to arbitrate their differences, a special three-man commission would be set up. The companies involved and their employees would each name one member and these two men in turn would choose the third. All expenses of such commissions would be borne by the federal government. No provision was made, however, for enforcing their awards.[52]

Four days of debate on the O'Neill bill in the House revealed that the Southwest strike of 1886 was forcing congressmen, however reluctantly, to consider railway labor legislation. The hardship worked on the public by the strike was condemned by both proponents and opponents of the O'Neill bill. Many spoke as if they regarded the current strike, or any other major railway tie-up, as a national crisis. "The wheels of commerce, the life of the nation, can not be blocked to meet the whim or caprice of any person or corporation, however great or strong," declared a strong supporter of the bill. An opponent of the bill took a similar stand, complaining that "The loss which has been incurred by the parties to the Southwest strike is a mere trifle, a mere begatelle, compared to that incurred by the public, whose servants the carriers are. . . ." With respect to the struggle between Gould and the Knights of Labor, he observed, many favored letting the disputants "fight it out." "But, Gentlemen," he protested, "while they are fighting it out the commerce of this country is injured and destroyed. How long," he queried, "are they to be allowed, by culpable lack of legislation, to continue a conflict that grows worse and worse as it goes on?" "When the commerce between the states is obstructed," a third congressman declared, "when passenger and freight trains on important lines of communication stand idly on the tracks for many days and thousands of workmen are unemployed; when all business depending upon interstate transportation suffers, then in this exigency the commerce clause of the Constitution clearly authorizes remedial action by Congress."[53]

Although several congressmen spoke warmly in favor of the voluntary principles of the O'Neill bill, a significant number argued that it was weak and did not go far enough to control strikes.[54] One representative, for example, wanted an impartial investigation of strikes whether or not the disputants were willing to be investigated or to submit their dispute to arbitration. Without compulsory investigation, he asserted, the weight of enlightened public opinion could not be brought to bear to end strikes. Another proposed that neither party to a dispute be allowed to invoke or receive federal assistance in coercing the other unless it was itself willing to submit to arbitration. The burden should rest more heavily on the companies than on the men, a congressman from Kansas insisted, because as public carriers they were bound to perform their duties in accord with their franchises. Only the act of God or the public enemy could excuse them from fulfilling their contractual obligations and strikes did not fall into that category. The congressman proposed that the federal courts order the railroads to fulfill their contracts or vacate their franchises. In his view, a few railroad directors placed behind bars for contempt of court would promptly end all strikes since it would force the companies to treat their employees reasonably.[55]

Those who opposed the O'Neill bill (and probably any other labor legislation) offered a variety of objections. The bill was unconstitutional because it regulated contracts, not interstate commerce, and because it proposed to set up special arbitral commissions not provided for in the Constitution. The bill was but "the cornerstone of a superstructure," "the seed of a growth" that would "hereafter give us trouble." It created "novel, uncertain and indefinite judicial tribunals." "It is a new departure," declared one congressman. "For the first time Federal interference is invoked and we ought to consider to what it must lead." The next step, he feared, would be that the federal government would commit its power to protecting all railroads and other agencies of interstate commerce. And, he warned, "behind Federal power is the Army, and how soon the bayonet may be thrust forward in support of such power no man can foresee."[56]

A few opponents of the bill argued that there were already "laws aplenty" for coping with railroad strikes and that the proposed law would but "trench upon the prerogatives of the governors of the States and of the President of the United States as well."[57] One Southern congressman openly opposed any labor legislation. "I do not believe in the power of statutory law," he declared. "We do not progress when we attempt to crystallize progress upon the statute-book," and he denied the right or the duty of the federal government to put "its hand, unhallowed and unwise," into the economic life of the country. Waxing eloquent, he pleaded for a "higher independence," a "nobler manhood," and an "ampler liberty" than that which would be "found in the leaves of a statute-book or in the chambers or the lobbies of a legislative body." Applause urged him on. ". . . I protest in the name of liberty against class legislation. We have no laborers as a class in America. Every boy born under the Star-Spangled Banner is born to glorious opportunity. He is not born to real poverty, although the winds of heaven may come through the crevices of his humble cabin, and there may be but little blanket on his limbs. He is born to boundless opportunity."[58]

This paean for laissez-faire drew great applause, but congressmen found in the strike then raging a more convincing argument for legislation. Congressman O'Neill, sponsor of the bill, observed that in five states there was "practically a revolution, all business suspended, the people of great cities suffering from the increase in the price of food and fuel from inability to obtain supplies. . . ." The time had come, he believed, to find out "how far can such disputes be regulated by law and how much can be accomplished by an appeal to public opinion."[59]

Apparently, few legislators regarded the bill as a solution to the problem of railway labor disputes. One congressman quipped that he might possibly vote for it for the same reason that he would drink a glass of water; "it might do me no good, but it certainly would do me no harm." Another called the O'Neill bill fruitless and likened it to papal bulls against comets. If passed, it would "prove a dead letter," prophesied another. Even Representative O'Neill talked of the need for compulsory arbitration if voluntary arbitration failed.[60]

In spite of the misgivings of many who supported it, the bill passed the House April 3 by a vote of 199 to 30. That same day violence broke out along the Gould lines at Fort Worth, Texas, and at Parsons, Kansas. It was with an air of urgency, therefore, that the Senate took up the measure. It was referred to committee April 5 with a recommendation for speedy consideration and put on the Senate calendar April 6. At this point action slowed down, and it was given no further attention until mid-May.[61]

Meanwhile, President Cleveland became involved in the strike. Following a day of violence in East St. Louis, Grand Master Powderly of the Knights of Labor went to Washington to confer with Congressman Andrew G. Curtin of Pennsylvania, whom he knew well. Curtin, in turn, took the labor leader to the White House and presented him to the President. Cleveland listened "patiently" to Powderly, held a private consultation with Curtin, and agreed to "intimate" to House leaders that he favored a committee to investigate the strike. Although the House had ignored earlier requests of its own members for such an investigation, on April 12 a special committee, headed by Curtin, was designated to conduct a probe of the strike.[62]

On April 22 Cleveland, his attention now fully drawn to the strike, sent Congress the first presidential message ever devoted to the labor question. "Recent events and a present condition," he said, prompted him to suggest legislation to the Congress. After noting the value of labor "as an element of national prosperity" and urging recognition that "the welfare of the laboring man should be regarded as especially entitled to legislative care," the President warned that the "real interests of labor" would not be promoted "by a resort to threats and violent manifestations." Those, he continued, who "under the pretext" of furthering labor interests "wantonly attack the rights of capital" and "sow seeds of violence" should neither be "encouraged nor conciliated." The present relationships of capital and labor, he noted, were far from satisfactory. The discontent of laborers could be traced to the "grasping and heedless exactions" of employers and to an "alleged discrimination" by government in favor of capital. On the other hand, he added, "it must be conceded that the laboring men are not always careful to avoid causeless and unjustifiable disturbances."

Whatever actions the federal government might take would have to be restricted by constitutional limitations of power, the President observed. Many grievances, moreover, could not be redressed by legislation and many undesirable conditions could not be reformed by law. What, then, could be done? Cleveland believed that voluntary arbitration offered the best solution to labor disputes. Without mentioning the O'Neill bill already passed by the House, he proceeded to castigate its main provisions. Temporary arbitrators, "chosen in the heat of conflicting claims" after disputes were already in progress, would be selected because of their bias and partisanship. Their decisions would be regarded as unfair and partisan. He recommended, therefore, that a permanent three-man commission, one member of which might well be the commissioner of labor, be set up to deal with disputes. Such a body would be stable and, as it gained experience, would grow in its ability to deal "intelligently and usefully" with labor questions. Finally, he recommended that the commission be empowered to investigate the causes of labor disputes as they occurred, whether or not submitted to the commission for arbitration.[63] Congressman William M. Springer of Illinois promptly introduced a bill embracing the President's proposals, but the House, having already passed the O'Neill bill, made no attempt to enact it.

Senate debate of the O'Neill bill began May 18 and consisted primarily of a long and forceful address by Senator Richard Coke of Texas. Coke favored adoption of the bill, he said, because it assumed that both labor and capital were "averse to conflict as disastrous and dangerous to both" and preferred harmony. The bill provided, at government expense, "the only means yet suggested" for compromising such disputes, namely, arbitration. Existing laws, as enforced by the executive and administered by the courts, were "framed to meet every conceivable case where compulsion is necessary" and adequately dealt with the effects of strikes. But courts, marshals, sheriffs, and the whole existing apparatus of government, were not adequate to prevent strikes. What was needed was a law to assist employers and employees in settling their disputes before they became warfare. The O'Neill bill was properly founded, Coke believed, on the theory that "public opinion, the great arbiter and lawmaker and executive of laws in this country" was "the only tribunal competent to deal with the contentions" of capital and labor. Once the bill became law, public opinion would be marshaled behind arbitration. Neither party to a dispute would dare to refuse to submit to arbitration or to accept the award of a commission, out of fear of public wrath. The commissions had the added advantage of recognizing both organized capital and organized labor. Regular courts, although they accepted corporations as legal entities, considered labor union members only in their individual capacities.

Coke made no direct reference to Cleveland's proposals, but he spoke against a permanent arbitration commission. Such a body would be political rather than nonpartisan, he asserted, because it would be appointed by the President and would be located in Washington. Because the capital city was "the focus and center of corporation influences and power" the commission might well become a tool of corporate interests; the blandishments and pressures of lobbies had repeatedly corrupted the Congress and other branches of the government, Coke observed. Finally, a permanent commission ran the risk of acquiring the vices, but none of the virtues, of a regular court of law. It would deprive the parties at dispute of the right of naming arbitrators of their own choosing, and, in time, he predicted, it would assume the attitude of a court in its proceedings and methods "and its bent and bias would soon become known."

Coke pressed his argument on the lines of protecting the public. "Railroad corporations are public servants and will be held to a rigid accountability for the performance of their duties as common carriers, and ought to be, strike or no strike. And those who obstruct them in the discharge of those duties by the injury or destruction of property or by unlawful violence, or threats of violence, will and ought to be sternly dealt with as criminal violators of the laws of the State. The public interest is supreme and paramount, and this requires that the flow of commerce shall be free, and shall not be obstructed either by default or design."[64]

The senator from Texas was followed, briefly, by Senator John A. Logan of Illinois, who wished to offer amendments to the bill. As too little time remained that day, further debate was "put over" to later. "Putting over" continued through the summer to the end of the session, forestalling further consideration of the bill until the assembling of the second session of the Forty-ninth Congress in December 1886.[65] Again the bill was repeatedly delayed until February 28, 1887. That day it was announced that two senators who had intended to amend the bill during the previous session would not do so; one could "no longer participate in these proceedings," and the other had decided not to press his amendment. Without further comment the bill passed. President Cleveland, receiving it at the end of the session with less than ten days' time in which to consider it, exercised a pocket-veto.[66] It would require the Burlington strike of 1888 to bring Congress and the President to agreement on legislation providing so little as even voluntary arbitration of labor disputes.

The Curtin Committee, appointed by the House April 12, 1886, to investigate the Southwest strike, did not report in time to affect the legislation of the Forty-ninth Congress which adjourned in March 1887. Apparently the first congressional committee ever assigned to investigate a strike in progress, it failed to execute its full mission. The committee questioned Gould, Powderly, and 576 other persons involved in one way or another with the strike; it traveled 4880 miles, including a considerable portion of the lines on strike; it even persuaded the executive board of the Knights of Labor to call off, officially, the strike that already was lost, but it did not make any recommendations, such as Congress had called for, for forestalling similar outbreaks in the future.[67]

Twenty-two of the twenty-five pages of the majority report were devoted to a recital of the history of the strike, tracing it back to the strike of the previous year.[68] There followed a few general observations about the rights of labor. Workmen had the right to combine together "for determining with their employers the terms of their employment," the committee declared. "Especial care" had to be taken, however, to secure "the equal rights" of workmen who desired to "keep aloof from the combination and dispose of their labor with perfect individual freedom." Combinations had to be "perfectly voluntary" with "full liberty" left to other workmen "to undertake the work which the parties combining shall refuse." Unions could no more be justified in forcing unwilling workmen to strike, the committee said, than combinations of capital could be justified in "combining to advance prices or rates of transportation. . . ." Unions also had no right to obstruct an employer from "resorting elsewhere in this country in search of a supply of labor."[69]

In assessing the specific causes of the 1886 strike, the majority report revealed that the committee had not allowed itself to be taken in by the strikers' charge that Gould and other high railroad officials had brought on the strike by a calculated disregard of the agreement ending the 1885 strike. The report admitted that there were "grievances" of which the workingmen "had just reason to complain," and that these "may have extended or enlarged the Strike." Men had been worked overtime without extra pay; their workweeks from time to time were shortened without notice, thereby reducing their earnings; the company sometimes refused to pay men for time spent traveling long distances by rail to and from work; and the Texas & Pacific maintained blacklists. These abuses, however, were not chargeable against Gould or his lieutenants, the report declared. Rather, they were "generally" the fault of unnamed "subordinates who had power over certain laborers or persons employed by the road."[70]

In rejecting labor's account of the causes of the strike, the majority report came very close to accepting management's claim that the strike was caused by the "cockiness" of the Knights of Labor following its 1885 victory and by the particular viciousness of one strike leader, Martin Irons. This man, "the leading spirit of the strike," was described as "a dangerous if not pernicious man (but for whom it is the opinion of your committee the strike would have been declared off at the request of Mr. Powderly). . . ."[71]

The committee clumsily skirted the issue of how to avert future railway strikes. Having "no doubt" but that "the concentration of wealth and power and the oppressions which have occurred . . . may have promoted the unrest of labor," it stood ready to support "whatever remedy" would give "proper protection" to railroad capital while shielding employees "from injustice and oppression." Since both companies and employees were "servants of the people of the United States," both had to be "regulated and protected by law." Noting the recent passage of the Interstate Commerce Act, the committee modestly deferred making suggestions to "an enlightened commission, soon to be appointed," whose prompt recommendations would probably resolve the whole railway labor problem.

While offering no solution of its own, the committee branded arbitration inadequate. Under existing law there was no way to bring the parties to arbitration. Moreover, it was of little practical use in restoring normal transportation quickly once a strike was under way. Finally, the committee saw no need for new laws to deal with strikes in progress. The government already had "ample power to control and regulate, so far as interstate commerce is involved, as well the rights and duties of the employers as of the employees," and that power "has been and may be further exercised."[72]

Republican Congressman James Buchanan of New Jersey submitted a minority report that severely indicted the majority for failing to do its duty. He placed the blame for the strike squarely on the companies and asserted that the failure of the "abortive efforts" of the workmen to obtain redress of their grievances produced the anger and discontent behind the strike. He believed that the police powers of the states were adequate to preserve law and order during strikes, but was concerned that the problem of railroad regulation was "rapidly outgrowing State Lines" and was "pushing to the front for recognition and solution."

Buchanan's chief complaint against the majority was its failure to use the opportunity it had to explore the strike problem as a whole. He regretted the report had not discussed "more fully and exhaustively" the questions that would occur to "any intelligent reader of the testimony."

Here was a strike [he said] which presented in one phase or another, every question which can arise in connection with this subject. The strike was unprecedented in extent and completeness. It covered, among others, a road already in the hands of the United States court. It extended to a demand for the severance of all traffic with another road in the hands of another United States court. All the roads affected were engaged in the transportation of interstate commerce. By the stoppage of traffic large quantities of interstate freight were detained, and some of it perished for want of transportation. If ever there was an occasion presented in which the whole problem of railroad transportation, the powers and duties of common carriers and their relation to the public, the power of the General Government to compel the carrier to transport interstate commerce, and the extent, if any, to which it may, in the exercise of that power, lay its hand upon the carrier, and the employees of such carrier, through Federal legislation, came up legitimately for discussion, it was the occasion in hand.[73]

But the majority report contained no such discussion, and Buchanan, after his scathing attack, declined to discuss the issues he raised.

So passed the first decade of the new era of labor-capital conflict. Except for the courts, the federal government had made little more than feeble gestures in the direction of shaping a policy for meeting large-scale railway strikes. This neglected chicken would not be long in coming home to roost.

• • •

CHAPTER IV

New Directions:
The Burlington Strike

THE OUTBREAK OF THE BURLINGTON STRIKE in February 1888 brought the nation once again face to face with the threat of a major transportation tie-up. At the time it was feared that the strike might become as widespread as, or even more extensive than, the disorders of 1877 and 1886.[1] Had railway workers on all lines fought together and effectively boycotted the Burlington, as was feebly attempted, a general railway strike might well have developed. But the affair never got beyond the serious-threat stage. It was annoying and protracted—the men refused to acknowledge defeat and harassed the company for months— but it created no transportation crisis, even in areas served by the Burlington. Public officials, having no way of knowing how the strike might develop, properly acted as if the situation were highly dangerous.

The antagonists were powerful. The conservatively managed and financed Chicago, Burlington & Quincy was a highly profitable railroad. It operated, in 1888, nearly 6000 miles of line. One of the nation's wealthiest and most important roads, it connected Chicago with the rich farm lands of Illinois and Iowa and reached westward across the Great Plains from Omaha to Denver and Cheyenne. Opposing the CB&Q were the oldest of the railway unions, the Brotherhood of Locomotive Engineers (BLE) and the more recently formed Brotherhood of Locomotive Firemen (BLF). Under the very restrained leadership of P. M. Arthur, the BLE had achieved an uncommon degree of recognition from railway managers and enjoyed considerable respect from the general public. For over ten years the engineers had scorned strikes, relying on direct negotiations to win the highest wages paid railway workmen. Believing that the generous earnings of the CB&Q were largely the product of their skill and bravery, and certain that the railroad could not be run without them, the engineers apparently felt the company was wronging them. They seemed to believe that under pressure, the Burlington's managers would accede to almost any demand they might make. The firemen, most of whom looked forward to becoming engineers, worked closely with the engineers in what they regarded as a common cause.[2]

Wage rates were the chief cause of the strike. The CB&Q paid a fixed amount for each of its runs according to the number of cars hauled, the length of the trip, and whether it was over main or branch line. Engineers and firemen were "classified" and paid on the basis of their years of service with the company. First-year men were paid two-thirds the full pay scale; second-year men, five-sixths. Only at the start of their third year did engineers and firemen receive full pay. The BLE and the BLF demanded that classification be ended and that all qualified engineers and firemen be paid full scale regardless of their years of service with the company. They also asked that a flat, per mile rate be substituted for the fixed amount per run. The proposed rates for engineers were 3½¢ per mile for passenger trains and 4¢ per mile for freights. Firemen were to receive 60 percent the amount paid engineers.

Burlington officials objected. The plan, they charged, called for substantial increases at a time when wages, if changed at all, should be cut. Moreover, if all engineers and firemen were put on full pay at the proposed scale, wages paid to Burlington employees would be higher than those paid on other roads, and the competitive position of the company would be affected. The brotherhoods replied that only after the new rates went into effect would the men earn as much as their counterparts on other lines. Without reliable statistical data, an accurate comparison of wage scales among the railroad lines was impossible. Each side, thus, could safely argue its point of view without fear of contradiction by accepted objective information.[3]

To Burlington officials, keeping absolute control of the company in their hands was as important an issue as wage rates. They saw the demands of the brotherhoods as trenching upon their prerogatives and were unwilling, as a matter of principle, to yield.[4] When local brotherhood leaders failed to reach agreement with the company, P. M. Arthur, national chief of the

BLE, and F. P. Sargent, chief of the BLF, came to Chicago to help avert a strike. The efforts of the labor leaders met brusque responses and scant courtesy from the managers. When union members voted to go on strike, Arthur and Sargent assented.[5]

Nearly all Burlington engineers and firemen, whether brotherhood members or not, left their jobs on February 27. For the next few days the company was hard put to keep its trains operating with impromptu crews. But from the beginning the lack of unity among railway laborers worked against the strikers. The Burlington's conductors, brakemen, and switchmen declined to strike. When the switchmen did go out late in March, reviving the strikers' hopes briefly, it was too late to do much good. Even among engineers and firemen, rivalries served the company well. For over a decade, official denials by labor leaders notwithstanding, unemployed engineers belonging to the BLE and to the Knights of Labor had taken over one another's jobs as strikebreakers during labor disputes. So, in 1888, Knights of Labor engineers were quite willing to man the throttles deserted by BLE engineers. The company, assisted by the Pinkerton detective agency, soon rounded up enough engineers from the East to operate on its usual schedules. Attempts of the BLE to buy off "scab" engineers were given up because of cost and an apparently unlimited supply of strikebreakers.

As it became increasingly evident that the strike was failing, the engineers turned to a relatively new weapon in railway labor disputes, the secondary boycott. At a meeting March 5, representatives of fifteen divisions of the BLE adopted resolutions calling upon their members to refuse to handle Burlington cars on any railroad, even when ordered to do so. If a member was fired for refusing to move boycotted cars, all BLE men on that line were to strike.[6]

Whether or not the strike would spread was thus left up to the managers of railways that exchanged passengers and freight with the CB&Q. Disunity within the railroad community at this point threatened to hand victory to the strikers. Most Eastern lines connecting with the Burlington continued to exchange traffic as usual; nearly all Western roads were unwilling to take a firm stand against the boycott. Alleging fear of strikes against their lines, the Western managers acquiesced in the refusal of their employees to handle the proscribed cars. One Western manager justified his company's refusal to move Burlington traffic on the ground that "it was right to avert a general strike by any and all means."[7]

Everett St. John, general manager of the Rock Island, in a letter to the general manager of the Burlington, summed up the position of many Western managers. His company stood ready to perform all duties imposed on it by law as a common carrier, he said, but would do so only when able. It would not refuse to perform those duties to all other companies simply because circumstances, for which it was not responsible, made it impossible to perform its duties to the Burlington. Nor would the Rock Island "suspend the operation of its entire line and inflict incalculable injury upon the communities dependent upon it."

Inasmuch as its engineers and firemen "positively" refused to handle traffic from or to the Burlington, St. John continued, there was little the Rock Island could do. To discharge the men for refusing to handle Burlington cars would not enable it to exchange with the Burlington and at the same time would "render it impossible to carry for anybody else." St. John could not see "how bringing about a general suspension of the operation of railways in the west can aid you in your present struggle, while I can see that it would work great injury to the country. We are not willing to attempt the impossible with the knowledge that the attempt will injure many and benefit none."[8]

The surrender of the Western managers to the boycott stemmed from more than their fear of strikes, however. The Burlington, it was later revealed in court, was unpopular with its competitors in the Chicago area. An attorney for the Rock Island referred to the Burlington as "a bully among railroads." It had, he said, "so much of the flavor of Boston about it [the company was founded, financed, directed, and managed largely by Bostonians] that it fancied all other roads were run for its own convenience." He went on to accuse the Burlington of trying to establish a gigantic Midwestern railway trust. To drive its unwilling competitors into the trust, he charged, the Burlington, in January 1888, had inaugurated a rate war that smashed existing voluntary agreements among the Chicago roads to make and maintain reasonable rates. Between January and March, Burlington tactics had driven the rates of all Chicago roads to one-third what they had been, and as a consequence a number had depleted treasuries. The managers of the Western roads, therefore, were not too distressed when the Burlington found itself in difficulties, and saw no reason for injuring themselves by going to the assistance of their headstrong competitor.[9]

To meet the threat posed by boycotts and sympathy strikes,

the Burlington turned to the federal courts. The company demanded relief in the form of injunctions forbidding connecting railroads, as common carriers of interstate commerce, to refuse to exchange traffic with it. In all, three federal judges, Walter Q. Gresham, who had been involved in such matters since 1877, Elmer S. Dundy, and James M. Love, helped by outlawing secondary boycotts against railroads carrying interstate commerce.

The first of the injunctive proceedings began March 8 when the Burlington's lawyers appeared before Judge Dundy of the Federal District Court of Nebraska. In their petition the Burlington's attorneys asked the judge to enjoin the Union Pacific, a corporation chartered by the federal government, from disregarding its obligations as a common carrier and to order it to exchange traffic with the Burlington as it did with all other connecting railways. The bill inveighed against the "secret order" of engineers, which practically controlled the motive power of most of the nation's railroads. Because of its control over nearly all skilled engineers, save those now employed by the Burlington, the BLE, through its "perfect organization," could stop, without warning, the movement of all trains and so cripple and paralyze the "social, commercial, industrial and political forces" of the entire nation as to work "immeasurable and irreparable injury and destruction" to the "property, rights and happiness" of the whole population.[10]

Judge Dundy was "one of the strangest figures that ever occupied a place on the bench, even in the West, where eccentricity is one of the open sesames to fame." In his courtroom he was absolute autocrat. When fancy moved him, he would interrupt an attorney in the midst of argument, order him to be seated, and proceed to argue the case to the jury himself. Throwing himself vigorously into the cases before him, Dundy revealed himself a man of distinct biases. A corporation, for example, had little chance in a personal injury suit brought against it by a woman. Dundy also played favorites among the lawyers who practiced before him. So notorious were his prejudices that some lawyers were known to urge their clients, when possible, to have their cases tried before other courts.

Precedent or public opinion rarely governed Dundy. He forbade the use of "oyez" in his court as "mummery" and established his own code of court etiquette. He appointed his son clerk of court and other relatives to paying positions at his disposal, seemingly oblivious to the public outcry. Just before

his death he outraged many Nebraskans by sentencing a friend
and onetime business and political associate, found guilty of
embezzling over $1 million, to a mere five-year term in prison.
In a eulogy of Dundy a friend wrote, "no man ever had a
truer friend than he, yet to those that slandered and maligned
him he could be as hard and cold as the frozen poles."[11]

In response to the bill before him in 1888, Dundy granted
a temporary but far-reaching injunction. The Union Pacific,
"its directors, officers, agents, servants and employees," twenty-
three engineers, and "their unknown confederates," whose
names would be added as soon as discovered, were to refrain
from further refusing facilities to the Burlington railroad. The
injunction ordered Union Pacific engineers to "absolutely desist and refrain from striking" or from "combining or confed-
erating for the purpose of organizing or advising" a strike
against either the CB&Q or the Union Pacific "for the purpose
of injuring" the Burlington or "interfering with its railroad
business, or in any manner violating the interstate commerce
law of the United States." The engineers as individuals and as
members of an "unlawful, unjust and wicked combination, con-
nivance and conspiracy" were ordered not to meddle or interfere with the Burlington's employees or property. They also
were not to do or refuse to do "any other act or thing" in
carrying out their "unlawful, unjust and wicked purposes" of
compelling the Burlington to discharge its employees and to
hire others in their places.

Following a hearing on March 16 and 17, Dundy made the
injunction permanent. By common law, decided cases, and
statute law, he held, railroads were common carriers. As such,
they were required to transport goods and persons, within a
reasonable time, subject to reasonable regulations, and without unreasonable discrimination. Although the constitutionality of some parts of the Interstate Commerce Act were questionable, there could be no doubt of the law's applicability to the
Union Pacific because that company was chartered by Congress
for governmental purposes and had been constructed, in part,
with the aid of federal land grants. The Interstate Commerce
Act and other federal laws required the exchange of traffic
among railroads without discrimination. To refuse to obey
these laws constituted an offense against the federal government. Respecting the engineers, Dundy pointed out that if
two or more persons combined together to disobey the federal

laws in question, they were subject to punishment for criminal conspiracy against the government of the United States.

Dundy used a loose interpretation of the Interstate Commerce Act to justify his injunction. The act provided that federal court injunctions could be used to maintain cease-and-desist orders issued by the Interstate Commerce Commission. Dundy construed this also to authorize the issuing of injunctions to enforce the general provisions of the law such as the requirement that railroads interchange traffic.[12]

Judge Dundy's order quite clearly outlawed secondary boycotts. Less certain was the right of men to strike under the order, even giving "strike" its most conservative and narrow definition: men quitting their jobs en masse. Was it lawful, under Dundy's order, for men to leave their jobs peacefully in a group, so long as they did not interfere with the company, its nonstriking employees, or the men hired to replace them if the result was injurious to the company? By implication at least the action would be conspiratorial, and hence enjoinable.

The same day that Judge Dundy was asked to move against the Union Pacific, attorneys for the Burlington requested Judge Gresham to force the Wabash railroad to interchange traffic with their client. The Wabash, in the custody of Judge Gresham's court, was operated by a receiver, General John McNulta. Both Gresham and McNulta had cause for embarrassment at the Burlington's request; Gresham was prominent among the men being considered for the Republican presidential nomination that year, and McNulta was talked of as a candidate for the governorship of Illinois. An injunction cracking down on the boycott might be regarded as antilabor; a failure to act might be interpreted as antibusiness. By skillful maneuvering Gresham succeeded in halting the boycott on the Wabash without actually issuing an injunction.

In its petition for an injunction the Burlington charged that Receiver McNulta had barred Burlington traffic from the Wabash line. The reason for this discrimination, according to the petition, was that the BLE and its chief, Arthur, had threatened to strike the Wabash if it accepted Burlington freight and passengers. This threat, the bill contended, violated the conspiracy law of Illinois and was illegal interference with the operation of a railway in receivership. The Burlington's request was threefold: that Gresham compel his receiver to exchange traffic with the Burlington, that he restrain the BLE from forbidding its members on the Wabash to handle Burlington cars, and that he require the BLE and Arthur to show cause why they should not be punished for contempt.[13]

The original hearing, scheduled for March 9, was postponed, with good effect. When Gresham handed down his ruling on March 13, he noted that the Wabash was in the hands of federal courts, operated by a receiver as a common carrier. The receiver's "rights and duties are those of a carrier," Gresham declared. "He is bound to afford to all railroad companies whose lines connect with his equal facilities for the exchange of traffic. . . . He cannot discriminate against one of the roads by maintaining a policy of non-intercourse with it."

As it turned out, McNulta had in the meantime rescinded his order, and the Wabash was accepting Burlington traffic. Gresham saw no reason, therefore, to issue new instructions. Upon questioning the receiver, Gresham learned that neither the BLE nor Chief Arthur had ordered the boycott or in any way interfered with the operation of the Wabash. Thus, there was no occasion to issue an injunction against the brotherhood or to hold it or its chief in contempt. "For the present," Gresham declared, "it is sufficient to say that the court will protect the property of the Wabash Company in its custody. The employees of the receiver cannot be obliged to remain in his service against their will, but neither they nor others will be permitted to interfere with or disturb the receiver or his subordinates in the possession and operation of the property in his custody. Lawless interference with the receiver and his employees in the discharge of their duties will not be tolerated." The injunction was kept on file "for future action should there be occasion for it."[14]

The Burlington, in two other instances during the strike, requested Judge Gresham to enjoin companies that refused to interchange freight and passengers with its lines. On March 14 an injunction was sought against the Belt Line of Chicago and was actually issued by Gresham April 3 when the switchmen's strike led to a revival of boycotting. The second instance, March 24, involved the Rock Island and led to an airing of bitternesses between that company and the Burlington growing out of the rate wars. In the end, however, the Rock Island agreed to do its duty as a common carrier, and the bill for the injunction, as in the Wabash case, was filed against being needed later.[15]

Judge Love of the Federal District Court of Southern Iowa was asked, as Dundy and Gresham had been, to enjoin the Burlington, Cedar Rapids & Northern from embargoing CB&Q

traffic. Love, who had been on the federal bench since 1855, provided a striking contrast to his colleague from Nebraska, Judge Dundy. Though a man of firm convictions, he was unfailingly courteous to everyone, including those with whom he disagreed. "A patient listener," Love had a "simplicity of manner, integrity of character, and kindness of heart" that won him wide esteem. It was his boast that in a career of thirty-six years only three of his decisions had been overturned by the Supreme Court of the United States.[16]

Love went farther than either of his colleagues in 1888 in spelling out the duties of railroads as common carriers and the powers of courts to protect railroads in carrying out their duties. In a decision handed down March 21, the Iowa jurist held that railroad corporations were quasi-public, with public duties to perform. They were not organized for "mere pecuniary profits to the owners of the property." One of the functions of government, he explained, was to provide and regulate public roads and highways because means of transportation were "indispensible to society" and because individuals were "incompetent to establish and control them" on their own. These "high duties" of government could not be delegated to individuals or to corporations so as to place them beyond the power, supervision, and control of government.

Turning to the question of interruptions in railroad service, Love declared that stoppages for "weeks and months at a time . . . inevitably [inflicted] enormous injury upon the great public for whose convenience and use railways [were] authorized." Travel was suspended, merchants and manufacturers ruined for want of transportation, property of "incalculable value" perished by the way, and whole communities suffered from a lack of fuel and the "necessaries of life." "In a word," he concluded, "mischiefs and sufferings may be inflicted upon the people which no words are adequate to express." Who, he asked rhetorically, out of consideration of their private wrongs or interests, might arbitrarily inflict such suffering on the public?

Government, Love held, had the duty to protect the public against the evil of suspensions of railway transportation. The remedy, he felt, "must rest mainly with the legislative department." The powers of courts were extremely limited. Action at law for damages clearly was no remedy; equity proceedings tended to be primarily preventive in nature; and the powers of courts to enforce performance of positive duties were narrowly circumscribed. "However grievous may be the injury inflicted upon the railway company and the public by the sudden suspension of railway service," Love continued, equity powers could not be used to prevent men from leaving their places. Similarly, strikers could not be compelled, by injunction, to return to their jobs.

Here Love drew the line, however. Once workmen left the service of a railroad the courts could enjoin them from using force, violence, intimidation, or unlawful combinations to prevent other men from taking the places they left or to interfere with the operation of railroads performing as common carriers. Love, therefore, granted an injunction compelling the Burlington, Cedar Rapids & Northern to accept Burlington traffic and issued a restraining order against BLE members, prohibiting them from interfering with the railroads.[17]

Dundy, Gresham, and Love considerably advanced the use of equity proceedings in railway labor disputes. Prior to the strike, federal courts had held strikers guilty of contempt for interfering with the operation of railways in the hands of federal receivers, but such protection had been granted only to railroads in receivership. In the Burlington strike, however, injunctions were used to protect railroads whether or not in receivership from secondary boycotts. The three judges enjoined or had stood ready to enjoin refusals to handle Burlington traffic by a land-grant railroad chartered by the federal government, a railroad in the hands of a federal court receiver, and three solvent railroads chartered by state governments.[18]

Though the three judges appeared to have dealt boycotting of interstate carriers a death blow, the practice would be revived again in the 1890's. In the absence of the new legislation called for by Love, federal courts would continue to use injunctions to protect interstate commerce against boycotts on all railroads. Indeed, the use would be developed and expanded during the 1890's. Finally, during the 1890's, some federal judges, expanding on Dundy's ruling, would enjoin striking per se, raising the questions as to whether railroad employees could quit the employ of a railroad en masse at any time, and whether they could even belong to unions that used the strike as a weapon in their battles with the railroads.

But the Burlington strike did not simply produce new and stronger judicial weapons for protecting the railroads against the depredations of strikers and boycotters. Two officials of the federal government, Postmaster General Don M. Dickinson and Thomas M. Cooley, chairman of the Interstate Commerce Commission (ICC), took actions pointing in new directions. Dickinson, seeing the need for some means to keep the mail moving regularly during railway strikes, tried to devise a policy that would insure mail delivery without involving the federal government in either crushing the strike or forcing strikers to move passengers and freight as well. Cooley saw in the strike an opportunity to strengthen the ICC while rendering a service in the area of preventing strikes or ending them fairly and peacefully once they were under way.

Dickinson was the youngest member of the Cleveland cabinet, both in length of service and in age. Forty-two years old when invited to join the administration in January 1888, Dickinson owed his appointment to his zealous efforts on behalf of the Democratic ticket in Michigan in 1884 and to his unflagging personal loyalty to the President. The postmaster general's rise in politics had been rapid, in part because of his ability and energy, and in part because few talented young lawyers went into the Democratic party in a state as solidly Republican as Michigan. Dickinson was chosen national committeeman in 1884, though only thirty-eight years old. In spite of his failure to swing Michigan to Cleveland that year, his efforts did not go unnoticed or unrewarded.[19]

The postmaster general in 1888 found that both the strikers and the railroad companies stood ready to use the mails to win governmental support to their side. When asked about mail trains, Chief Arthur explained that the BLE would not obstruct passage of the mails, and that mail trains en route to Chicago would be brought in, providing all cars other than those carrying mail were cut off. On the other hand, he continued, the brotherhood was "under no obligation to start the mails" from distribution centers. The company, however, was under contract with the government to deliver the mail, and, he suggested, if it could not fulfill its obligations, it should forfeit its contract. Inasmuch as the BLE was prepared to end the strike on a "fair and equitable basis," Arthur said, the Postoffice Department should "bring such an influence to bear on the company as to bring about a settlement."[20]

A snarling of the mails could have been of considerable value to the Burlington and other railroads involved in the strike and boycott. It might, for example, have converted the contest between themselves and the engineers into a contest between the engineers and the government. The railroads then "could have very quietly sat down and waited until the government might settle the question with the engineers for them, putting the odium of the whole matter, in case of a failure, and the hostility of the engineers upon the administration in case extreme measures had to be resorted to by the government to give the country proper mail facilities."[21] Whether or not this was the objective of the railroads, a Burlington official refused an offer of the BLE to run trains made up only of mail cars. The company's contracts obligated it only to carry mail on its regular passenger runs and those were the only trains on which the Burlington would carry mail, he said.[22]

Dickinson, though concerned about moving mail over the Burlington lines, was much more anxious about the movement of mail in the event of a general railway strike. The mail usually carried by the Burlington could be diverted over other lines. But how, if there should be a general tie-up, could the mails be moved? The postmaster general searched the law books, the pertinent cases, and the contracts between the government and the railway companies. The situation, he found, was critical. Although the law defined "all railroads and all parts of railroads which are now and hereafter may be in operation" as post roads, the term had always been construed as merely enabling the postmaster general to make contracts with the railroads. No law actually required railroad companies to carry the mails, and presumably a railroad could refuse to contract to transport mail if it chose. Moreover, the contracts under which the mails were carried provided no stronger penalty for nonperformance than the withholding of compensation. Dickinson was startled to find that if a railroad refused to contract to haul the mail the only alternative provided by law was to send it forward "by horse-express, or otherwise."[23] "In this state of things, Dickinson noted, "the government is always at a disadvantage in negotiating for improved mail facilities."[24]

Dickinson found little legal support for ordering companies to transport mail on special trains made up solely of mail cars. There was in statute law, in decided cases, and in the contracts with the companies no precise definition of the makeup of a mail train. The cases growing out of the strikes of 1877 implied that all cars of trains carrying mail were part of the mail train and as such were inviolable. But when initially made up, did a mail train have to consist of more than engine, tender, and mail cars? "As a general thing," Judge Drummond had ruled in 1877, a railroad company could not be expected to operate mail cars alone because it would result in losses to the company. Obviously, Drummond did not regard a major railroad strike as an exception to the general rule. Dickinson, in 1888, possibly relying upon his interpretation of the Act of March 3, 1879, which said: "The Postmaster General shall, in all cases, decide upon what trains and in what manner the mails shall be conveyed," disagreed.[25]

Dickinson concluded that the first obligation of the railroads was to carry the mail. He was determined, he later wrote, "to establish valuable precedents as to post-roads over railroads. We were endeavoring to lay down the principle that the railroads must carry the mails if they do no other business."[26] Lacking legal weapons to enforce this view, Dickinson, apparently without consulting President Cleveland, pursued a bold course. He decided to "risk the assertion and exercise . . . a doubtful power" and to sustain his actions by an "appeal to public sentiment."[27]

During the second week of the strike, when it appeared that the tie-up was about to spread to other lines than the Burlington, Dickinson ordered the general superintendent of the railway mail service, Thomas E. Nash, to go to Chicago. In his letter of instructions, Dickinson observed that it was unlikely that either the companies or the strikers would refuse to deliver mail over the usual routes at the customary times. If a company, however, found itself without competent men to operate the trains carrying the mail safely or if, as a matter of principle, a company refused to hire competent men who were on hand and, thus, was unable to run mail trains, Nash was ordered to request the company to put the necessary locomotives, mail cars, and other equipment at the disposal of the government. The superintendent was then to employ any competent men available to operate these special trains.

If the strikers attempted to prevent the passage of these special mail trains or if the companies refused to comply with the government's request for equipment, Nash was instructed to put the mail in the usual mail cars, place it under heavy guard, and wire for further instructions. "A sufficient force of men from the service of the United States will be placed at your disposal to carry out any instructions given you by this Department," Dickinson promised. Finally, Nash was told to call upon the representatives of the railroad companies and such "other interests" as were involved to make any necessary arrangements to prevent delay of the mail.[28]

Nash reported that it was doubted in Chicago that the strike would spread to lines other than the Burlington. The postmaster general thereupon decided that it would be "impolitic" for Nash to communicate officially with Arthur. At the same time he thought it very important that a suggestion be put in the BLE chief's mind "informally." If the companies discharged brotherhood members for refusing to move Burlington freight, Arthur would probably respond by taking all engineers and firemen, including those on passenger trains, out on strike. In this event, Dickinson suggested, "it would certainly be policy" on Arthur's part to except enough firemen and engineers from his order to move the United States mail. If this were done, "it would put the responsibility of any difficulty affecting the Department upon the companies; with whom, I think, in such case we would then have no difficulty."[29]

The postmaster general's policy was thus spelled out, but it was not put to a test so long as the strike was restricted to the Burlington. This was because much of the mail could be, and was, routed over competing parallel lines. Moreover, as already noted, the Burlington itself had little difficulty moving its trains on schedule. When the engineers and firemen on the Santa Fe line began a wildcat strike on March 15, however, it appeared that the policy might have to be implemented. Dickinson ordered Nash to transfer all through mail usually carried by the Santa Fe to other railroads.[30] Nash then called on C. W. Smith, vice-president of the company, to make arrangements to keep mail service operating in those areas where the Santa Fe had an exclusive franchise. Smith held that his company was obligated to carry mail only on its regular passenger trains and was unwilling to run specials composed of mail cars alone.[31]

Dickinson wired Nash that pressure might have to be brought to bear on the Santa Fe since it sought "clearly to manufacture public sentiment by inconveniencing the public. . . ." As soon as the Santa Fe officially refused to run mail cars as requested by the Postoffice Department, Nash was to notify him. If Nash thought it advisable, the Washington press would "have the situation" presented to it for publication. Dickinson thought the "example might be a healthy one for others. . . ."[32]

Dickinson proceeded the next day to manufacture a bit of public sentiment on his own by blasting the Santa Fe in an article in the *Washington Post*. The article stated that the postmaster general had directed Superintendent Nash to point out to both sides that good citizenship and patriotic duty required them to deliver the mail regularly despite the strike, "and this without going into the question of the right or the power of the Government in the matter." The brotherhoods had promptly and "cheerfully" agreed and had placed all the men needed for mail service at the disposal of the companies or the government. All the companies had "aquiesced in the sentiment," the postmaster general went on, "with the exception of the Atchison, Topeka & Santa Fe system." That line, though under contract to carry the mail, refused to do so unless its other business was also carried. The company would fail, Dickinson predicted, in its attempt to get the government to carry anything other than the mail. The government would not take advantage of the strikers' patriotism by urging them to haul anything but mail. The whole nation demanded regular postal service and clearly understood the attitude of the Santa Fe. Responsibility for the consequences rested wholly with the management of that company.

Dickinson then shifted his attack to include railroads in general. He reminded the carriers that the states had given them the "sovereign prerogative of eminent domain" on the ground of public necessity and that vast public aid had been granted them; "it would be well to ascertain whether there is anything in the law making railroads post roads or anything in duty obligations to the public in return for the grant of governmental powers and subsidies." He declared that he was "cognizant of the rulings and decisions" that had been made during the previous twelve years "on the question of the power of the government over railroads in such cases" and concluded, "The mail will go through."[33]

Matters came to a head before the article reached the newsstands. Late in the evening of March 17, Dickinson was summoned to the White House where he found a group of irate railroad officials protesting his ruling to the President.[34] When he arrived, the committee attempted to change his views. Dickinson adamantly insisted that the mails must be moved. About midnight a telegram arrived from Nash, reporting that the Santa Fe had surrendered. Turning to the railroad executives, Cleveland asked if anyone had "Anything further" to say.

No one did and the meeting broke up. At three o'clock the next morning the chief negotiator for the railroads wired Dickinson that the companies agreed to "move the mails tomorrow and regularly thereafter." Commenting years later, Dickinson asserted that the President's backing of his policy "broke the strike."[35]

The Santa Fe's capitulation, as reported in the *Washington Post* the day after Dickinson's threatening attack, was complete. Superintendent Nash was quoted as saying that, if necessary, trains consisting only of mail cars would go through. When mail cars were run alone, however, it was understood that the government would expect the company to run but one train daily each way.[36]

The railroad companies did not contest the administration's policy in the courts as might have been expected, probably because the strikes were so ineffective that the measures were never put into actual practice. The Santa Fe's men returned to work the very day that the company surrendered to Nash's demands, and although the strike on the Burlington continued for months, strikebreakers kept trains operating on that line at normal schedules. There was no reason for the railroads to risk court approval of Dickinson's policy so long as they did not have to comply with it in fact.

Dickinson continued his efforts to strengthen the precedents laid down for moving mail during strikes. He used his reply to a memorial from a number of railroad company presidents, seeking an authoritative definition of the Postoffice Department's policy in imposing fines and deductions for failures and delays in carrying the mails, to state again his position regarding the movement of mail during labor disputes. He declared it "the first and principal essential to an efficient mail service" that the railroad companies and the Postoffice Department "cordially cooperate . . . in affording convenient, certain, and quick transmission" of the mails. But, he went on, a "grave defect" existed in the system: "the carrying of the mails by railroads is not made compulsory by law."

Turning to the importance of the mails, the postmaster general noted that "thousands of people and thousands of interests depend or are involved in the delivery of the mails." The passengers or the freight of a single train involved but "infinitesimal interests" as compared to those of "a heavy mail." "In no case" should either be given precedence over the mails.

"[W]here delay to one or the other must occur, the mails must have the preference of expedition," he declared.

Referring to the recent troubles on the railways in the West, Dickinson stated his views most clearly:

> I do not conceive that a strike of railroad employees can afford any excuse for failure to carry the mails. There has been no case where men and facilities could not be found sufficient to carry the mails; and if cases occur where the contractors either will not, or cannot, take other business in addition, it can be no ground for refusal or failure to proceed with the Government business alone. This precedent established in March, 1888, has been generally acquiesced in by the memorialists. If a case should ever occur of a violent and unlawful obstruction to the movement of the mails, the Government will be fully able to set it aside, and so remove what might in that case otherwise constitute a valid excuse for delay.[37]

In his *Annual Report* for 1888, Dickinson did not mention his rulings regarding the movement of mail during strikes. He did, however, call attention to the "urgent need" of a law compelling the owners of railroads "to receive and carry the mails of the Republic."[38] A further effort, in the same direction, came shortly after he left office. In an article in the *North American Review*, he called public attention to the fact that railroads were not obliged by law to carry the mails and that in dealing with the companies the government was "clothed with no more authority in the premises than any private individual—*i.e.*, a right to contract if the other party will agree. . . ." This was a situation that needed correction. "With rare exceptions," he conceded, the railroads and the government had cooperated well. "But," he concluded, "the department should not, in its dealings, be in a position where it must avoid issues as to its authority, and where, in case of extremity, its only resources—as was the case in one instance in my own administration—is to risk the assertion and exercise of a doubtful power, and an appeal to public sentiment."[39]

Why Dickinson took a stand the railroads regarded as unfriendly is not easily explained. Political considerations offer a plausible explanation. 1888 was an election year. Democratic victory hopes rested upon winning the labor vote and carrying a number of the closely contested northern industrial states. Dickinson, a shrewd political manipulator, understood full well that if the Cleveland administration donned antilabor garb in March, the result could be the loss of vital votes in November. The *Railroad Gazette* may have been hinting at this in an article on the Burlington strike on March 23. "The part taken by some high officers of the Federal and state governments has also been discreditable," it editorialized. "[I]t is surprising and humiliating too, to see the officers of the Post-Office Department dickering with the strikers, for permission to move the mails. . . ."[40] Given Dickinson's fight after the election and after leaving public office for legislation to compel the railroads to carry mail, however, it may well be that his motivation was no more complicated than he professed at the time: the desire to see the mail transported efficiently, even in time of labor disorder, and without involving the government in the troubles.

Motivation aside, Dickinson's policy at best was a mere expedient aimed solely at assuring delivery of the mails. It did nothing whatever to protect the movement of interstate commerce during strikes and far less did it attempt to forestall tie-ups or to provide machinery for ending strikes once under way. However, so long as no agency of government worked to solve these larger problems, Dickinson's policy, whatever its shortcomings, had the laudable virtue of keeping the government neutral. Without aiding the cause of labor, neither did the policy throw the full weight of the federal government to the side of the railroads as had been true in earlier strikes and as would again be true in the future.

About the time Dickinson was struggling with the mails question, the Interstate Commerce Commission was wrestling with the problem of the role it should play in the Burlington strike. In March 1888 the ICC was still a young agency of government, having been created and its members appointed but a year before. Heading the commission was Thomas M. Cooley, the highly respected jurist and legal writer. For over twenty years Cooley served on the Michigan Supreme Court, and from 1859 until his death he was a professor of law at The University of Michigan. In 1868 he published one of the most influential works on constitutional law to appear in the post-Civil War era, *A Treatise on the Constitutional Limitations Which Rest Upon the Legislatures of the Several States.* In all, this work went through eight editions and made its author the nation's accepted authority on constitutional law.

Honors crowded upon Cooley excepting the highest one due him: appointment to the United States Supreme Court. His name was urged upon every President to fill every vacancy between the death of Chief Justice Salmon P. Chase and Cooley's own final illness in the 1890's. The combination of political and geographical considerations which govern such appointments, however, repeatedly ruled him out.

After 1882 Cooley began to acquire practical experience about railroads. That year the Trunk Line Executive Committee named him to a three-man commission that heard arguments regarding rate differentials to and from various Atlantic port cities. Cooley quickly demonstrated his abilities in the field and in 1886 was appointed arbitrator in a number of railroad matters. In the process he became an authority on railroad administration and late in 1886 Judge Gresham asked him to serve as receiver of all Wabash properties east of the Mississippi River. President Cleveland named Cooley to the ICC in March 1887, a post he filled until forced by illness to resign in 1892.[41]

All of Cooley's colleagues on the commission were lawyers. Two of the four had had railroad experience. Aldace F. Walker for many years was counsel for a number of railways, including the Delaware & Hudson, the Rutland, and the Vermont & Canada. A member of the Vermont Senate in 1882 and 1884, he drafted the state corporation tax law and the Vermont Railroad Commission Act. Walker was the first of the original members to leave the ICC. He resigned in 1889 to accept chairmanship of the Interstate Commerce Railway Association and its successor, the Western Traffic Association. In 1892 he became chairman of the Joint Commission of Presidents and Vice Presidents of the Trunk Line and Central Traffic Associations, in which position he was charged with carrying into effect certain "gentlemen's agreements" among the railroads. Walker left that position in 1894 to become receiver of the Santa Fe and, in 1896, its president.[42]

Walter Bragg brought experience in the area of railroad regulation to the ICC. In 1881 he had accepted the presidency of the Alabama railroad commission. From this position he conducted a long, intense, and unsuccessful battle against railroad abuses. In the process he won national recognition as an authority on the subject of railroad regulation. His testimony was influential in the shaping of the federal Interstate Commerce Act of 1887. Named to the ICC by Cleveland, Bragg served until his death in 1891.[43]

The remaining commissioners, Augustus Schoonmaker and William Ralls Morrison, were not prepared by railroad experience to serve on the ICC. Schoonmaker, a minor politico from New York, owed his appointment to his personal friendship with Cleveland. Morrison, between 1873 and 1887, had been a leading figure among Democrats in the House of Representatives. As chairman of the important Ways and Means Committee, he consistently battled for tariff reform. Defeated for reelection in 1886, he was named by Cleveland to the ICC. Morrison remained on the commission until December 31, 1897, succeeding Cooley as chairman when the latter resigned in 1892.[44]

On March 9, 1888, Chairman Cooley was approached about the Burlington strike by an attorney for the Santa Fe who sought "any opinion, suggestion or word" from the ICC that might "be made serviceable" to his company during the difficulties. After all, he urged, the strike was a matter concerning interstate commerce. Cooley was quick to agree, but pointed out that the quarrels and rate wars of the Chicago railroads also concerned interstate commerce. Were the ICC to investigate, it might well begin by going into the conditions that lay behind the strike. "In short I said very little that he will take any pleasure in reporting to his superiors," Cooley noted in his diary.[45]

A few days later the interstate commerce commissioners were in Chicago on business not connected with the strike. Railroad officials paid them court throughout their stay. Wirt Dexter, general solicitor of the Burlington, invited the commissioners to dine with him, and both he and W. C. Goudy, general counsel of the Chicago & Northwestern, offered them the use of private cars for a pending trip to Omaha. Cooley, scrupulously avoiding favors from the railroads, told Dexter that acceptance of his invitation would be reported in every newspaper in Chicago to the prejudice of the commission's work. "Though he is general solicitor of the C. B. & Q. R. Co. now in the midst of a great strike," Cooley observed, perhaps tongue-in-cheek, "this idea had not occurred to him."[46]

A tempting offer of another sort came to Cooley when D. B. Canfield, editor of the *Law Register*, offered him any sum he would name for an article on the strike. Having talked with a number of lawyers and jurists, Canfield found that all were in agreement: an article by Cooley would be "worth millions to the country" and "would settle the existing strike at once." Cooley, pleading a lack of time, declined the offer in spite of Canfield's assurance that two hours would suffice for writing it.[47]

As the boycott revived briefly at the end of March, both Cooley and his fellow commissioner, Walker, concluded that the time had come for the ICC to investigate the matter. The two also agreed that the Burlington management had been "very bad" throughout the whole affair. The next day the topic was broached at a meeting of the full commission. Cooley told his colleagues that the strike had assumed such proportions as to make it a matter of national concern. There was "great danger" that people would condemn the commission, "which had been given supervision of Interstate Commerce," if it failed to take notice of so great an interruption of that commerce as the strike. Had the commission been invited to intervene earlier, Cooley believed, it might have settled the affair with little difficulty. Although intervention at this point might be of scant value, he thought the commission should weigh the issue carefully and not "shrink" from whatever course duty dictated. At the least an investigation would enable the ICC to get to "the very bottom" of the difficulty and to "place the blame where it belonged."

Two commissioners, Morrison and Walker, agreed with Cooley: the other two, Schoonmaker and Bragg, expressed opposition "in very strong, and almost violent language." In their opinions the move would only subject the ICC to needless abuse. Cooley concluded, in the face of this opposition, to do nothing further "unless complaint should be filed which should compel the taking of action."[48]

Judge Cooley intervened informally in a strike matter a few days later when the boycott of the Burlington's traffic was ended by federal court injunctions. Cooley wired Wirt Dexter that inasmuch as the strikers now wished to be taken back to work, the company could well make concessions. The triumphant managers, however, were on their "high horses" and would yield nothing.[49]

By mid-April, the strike still unsettled, Cooley decided to spend "a couple of days" in Chicago, looking into the situation alone. This time he saw not only Wirt Dexter but also Alexander Sullivan, legal advisor of the striking enginemen. Sullivan was most anxious to have the ICC investigate and presented a petition from his clients to that effect. Cooley wrote Walker, who was in Washington with the other commissioners, telling him of his plan to return to Chicago in the near future for an investigation. He asked Walker to present his plan to the other commissioners. Cooley interpreted a wire from Washington the next day as authorization for him to set a date for the investigation. He accordingly notified the interested parties that an investigation would start May 5.[50]

Upon returning to Washington April 25, Cooley met with the full commission to discuss the investigation. To his "utter astonishment" and in spite of the telegram, both Bragg ("in strong terms and with overbearing manner") and Schoonmaker were firmly opposed to any hearings on the strike. Commissioners Morrison and Walker were hesitant because the House of Representatives was considering an investigation of its own. Schoonmaker and Bragg went on to question the authority of the ICC to investigate at all. Cooley was wroth. "In all our work up to this time I had not before been so annoyed or disgusted," he noted in his diary. He told his fellow commissioners that he had not the slightest doubt as to their authority or their duty to act. "We had no business," he told them, "to await the action of one of the houses of Congress, & to do so was belittling our functions & would justly make us contemptible. To construe the law as narrowly as Bragg & Schoonmaker seemed inclined to do, would emasculate it. It was our duty, I thought, to strengthen the law by vigorous action under it: we ought to make ourselves more felt by the railroads: be masters of the situation: be the authority in railroad matters, & by asserting authority, take leadership. Much more I said to the same effect, for I felt strongly that our office was about to be rendered ridiculous."

At Walker's request it was agreed to take up the matter again the next day. Following the meeting, Cooley worked late in his office, went home with a severe chill, and next day was seriously ill with pneumonia. By the time he was again on his feet the critical time for settling the strike question had passed.[51]

What might have followed had the work of either Dickinson or Cooley become established procedure can only be guessed. Dickinson's policy, pursued during railway strikes, might have removed the mails as an issue and kept the government neutral as between the companies and the strikers. Had Cooley not fallen ill at the critical moment in the ICC's deliberations and had he been able to persuade that body to investigate the strike, a precedent might have been set for fact-finding investigations that could have aided in the settling of railway strikes, perhaps even have led to fact-finding investigations of disputes on the railways before strikes began.

The Burlington strike had the further effect of reviving congressional interest in legislation designed to bring about the arbitration of railway labor disputes. The O'Neill bill, passed by the Forty-ninth Congress but pocket-vetoed by President Cleveland, was reintroduced with revisions. It still provided for voluntary arbitration, with no machinery for the enforcement of awards. The arbitration commissioners were still to be chosen, one each by the railroads and their employees, the third by the other two. Added to the original O'Neill bill, however, was a provision that the President, in the event of a railway labor dispute, could appoint two commissioners who, together with the commissioner of labor, would constitute a temporary three-man investigative commission. Such commission was to "examine the causes of the controversy, the conditions accompanying, and the best means for adjusting it." Commission reports were to be submitted to the President, but whether or not the recommendations were acted upon would depend upon either the force of public opinion or the actions of the President and Congress.[52]

Debate on the arbitration bill followed a pattern remarkably like that in 1886. The bill was introduced in the House where debate took place during the strike. As a result, the argument was urgent and was carried on with an eye to strike developments. The Senate procrastinated and did not take up the bill until after the strike crisis and again passed the measure with virtually no debate. The main differences between the actions of 1886 and 1888 were that in the House debate in 1888 many more representatives were insistent that a stronger measure was needed, and in 1888, the bill, when passed by Congress, was signed into law by the President.

The addition of the investigative commission to the O'Neil bill was very popular. Several House members regarded it the best feature of the revised bill. One thought it would end the Burlington strike, if adopted, and encourage arbitration of similar disputes in the future. Another representative, who wanted a permanent investigative commission instead of the proposed temporary ones, asserted that had such a body been in existence the Burlington strike would not have occurred.

Several congressmen endorsed the measure but regarded it only, as one put it, as "a short step, but a step in the right direction." Others were more vigorous in condemning the weaknesses of the measure. A New York congressman likened the addition of the investigative commissions to the "fastening of a rib into a boneless body." It would never work, he said, since one "can not attach a rib to a body where there is no spinal column. . . ." He went on, as did several other critics of the bill, to suggest stronger substitute measures. The present bill, he said, was a "mere temporary make-shift" that left all the important questions disturbing labor, transportation, and business "precisely where they have been." He called for the governmental investigation of labor disputes as they arose, accompanied by nationwide publicity of the findings. Arbitration would then be compulsory. If a railroad failed in its duty or mistreated its employees, "there should be power by law to declare such a road in default; the courts should take possession of it and compel it to serve the country." Similarly there should be power to compel workmen to continue their service until a certain time after notice of their intent to quit had been given.[53] In many respects the plan was similar to one that Attorney General Olney would propose at the close of the Pullman strike several years later.[54]

George D. Tillman of South Carolina called the bill a "fraud" and pronounced it as "void of any practical utility . . . as a balloon." He had just served on a committee that had investigated a strike on the Reading railroad, he said, and had in mind a report with specific proposals. "We mean business," he declared on behalf of his committee. "We intend to try to report something with a view to protect the public so it may have its mail, its expressage, its freight, and its travel without interruption, either by the employees of a railroad, [or] its officers and agents, engaging in strike or forcing lockouts." The report, when done, he believed, would "throw the responsibility upon this House of failing to do its duty or else provide a remedy against strikes and lock-outs as regards interstate commerce."[55]

The mood of the House, however, was neither to ignore the problem (the strike was still in progress) nor to enact strong antistrike legislation (perhaps because the elections of 1888 were near). Rather, it settled for the innocuous voluntary arbitration bill. "It is evident that it is going to pass," Tillman declared petulantly, "as anything else proposed here for labor would be sure to pass."[56]

The Senate received the bill April 19, the day following its passage in the House, and referred it to committee. Fourteen weeks later, and well after the crisis, the bill was reported favorably and without amendment to the Senate floor. There, on September 14, the sum total of debate consisted of the few remarks by Senator Wilkinson Call. "I was going to ask the Senator . . . if he did not think the Senate was rather too thin to consider so important a bill, but I will not do so as the Senator from Texas [Mr. Reagan] is anxious for its passage." The bill passed and was signed into law by President Cleveland, October 1, 1888.[57] It would be used only once during the decade it was in force.

In the meantime, the House committee referred to by Congressman Tillman, which had been appointed to investigate labor troubles in the anthracite regions of eastern Pennsylvania, published its report. The report included testimony, recommendations for federal legislation, and a draft bill for putting those proposals into law. The Tillman committee report revealed the marked preference of its authors for business conducted according to the precepts of Adam Smith. The pooling, price-fixing, production-limiting, labor-sweating practices of the anthracite operators clearly aroused the hostility of the investigators. To correct the problems of the anthracite industry and thereby end the labor troubles, the committee had four proposals which it urged Congress to adopt: interstate carriers should be prohibited from engaging in mining or manufacturing; strikes and lockouts on railroads should be outlawed; parallel or competing railroad lines should be prohibited from consolidating; and the duty on bituminous coal should be abolished or at least suspended for the present.[58]

Of the four far-reaching proposals, only the second dealt directly with the problem of railway labor disputes. The thinking of the committee with respect to the causes of and cures for railroad strikes was novel. "There is a well-grounded suspicion," the committee declared, "that a number of railway strikes and lockouts in this country have been brought about either by wanton mistreatment of employees, or by the officers of the road conspiring with outside speculators to corner some article of interstate commerce, or to wreck the securities of the road and promote stock-jobbing schemes."[59] The "best and surest preventive" of strikes, the committee suggested, "as paradoxical as it may seem to first view," was not to punish the men for striking, but to punish the "superior officers" of the railroad for "goading the men to strike." Employees would not strike, the committee asserted, unless they were grossly mistreated in some way, either by being underpaid, overworked, not promoted when deserving promotion, "ignominously treated," or "discharged without a hearing by some coarse, overbearing, money-making superior who has no regard for the feelings of the men."[60]

Congress did not have the power to outlaw strikes or lockouts in general, the committee conceded, but it did have such powers over railroads engaged in interstate commerce. The roads, "though constructed by private corporations and owned by them, are public highways," the Supreme Court had once ruled. The use of railroads was not determined by who constructed or who owned them; "no matter who is the agent, the function is that of the state. Though the ownership is private, the use is public."

Having made the point, the committee turned to a recent labor dispute in New York state for further instruction. In 1882 a railway company there had refused a three cent-per-hour raise for its employees. The men quit. No one was hired to replace them and the company suspended all service. The New York courts were appealed to for a writ of mandamus that would have compelled the railroad to run its trains as usual, notwithstanding the "strike or lockout" of its employees. To escape an unfavorable ruling, the railroad resumed service. Nonetheless, the court rendered its decision and levied all costs against the company, though it did not find it necessary to issue the writ.

In the view of the committee, the federal government would do well to follow the example suggested by the New York court. "[L]egislation ought to increase the penalties for suspending trains on account of a strike, by fining and imprisoning the controlling officers of the offending road and by placing the road itself in the hands of a receiver if necessary." Not only would such a law prevent strikes and protect the public interest, but, ultimately, it would benefit the railroads as well. Their employees would be "more faithful and efficient servants," presumably because better paid and treated, and there would be fewer "costly accidents."

The committee noted that within recent years an "almost universal demand" had arisen for federal laws regulating fares, freights, and facilities for the public on interstate railroads. "But strange to say," the report continued, "little or no agitation has been had in favor of exacting justice for the more than a million employees who carry on that interstate commerce."

The public "ought, must, and will have its mails, persons, and property carried by railroads promptly," the committee declared. How best could this be assured? Not by having the government purchase or condemn the railroads and reduce the employees to the condition of enlisted men in the armed forces. Rather, just as the railroads asserted the privilege of discharging their employees whenever they choose, without notice, so the employees ought to have equal liberty to control their labor. "As long as employees merely quit work and refrain from violence, they commit no crime and ought not to be punished for abandoning work that is disagreeable."

It was not the concern of the public or of the government whether a strike or lockout on a railroad was prevented by arbitration, profit sharing, or otherwise; that should be "an affair for exclusive consideration between a railroad and its employees." But that the railroads should be kept running was the concern of government. "If the present owners of the roads will not run them properly without strikes or other interruptions," the committee suggested, "let the Government sell them out to those who will do it."[61]

In the draft bill that accompanied the report, provision was made to carry out these recommendations. For every day that trains and cars were not run, except when prevented by the public enemy or the act of God, a railroad was to be adjudged guilty of a misdemeanor and any director, officer, receiver, trustee, or agent convicted was to be fined no less than $5000 or more than $10,000 and imprisoned for no less than thirty days or more than six months for each and every day after forty-eight hours when trains were not run as prescribed. Civil damages, carrying triple compensation, could be awarded to persons whose person or property was not carried as prescribed by law.[62]

Having already passed the arbitration bill, however, neither House nor Senate acted upon the recommendations of the Tillman committee, and the report took its place among the many other well-intentioned but soon-forgotten reports of congressional committees. In spite of the pressing need for strong legislation, evident for several years and repeatedly called for, Congress labored twice, under the pressure of major railway strikes, and brought forth at last a weak and ineffective voluntary arbitration bill. Enacted too late to settle the Burlington strike, it was used only once, when President Cleveland appointed a commission to investigate the Pullman strike after federal troops had crushed it in 1894.[63]

CHAPTER V

• • •

Appeal to the Courts

THERE WAS LITTLE LABOR PEACE in the half-dozen years immediately following the Burlington strike. The Knights of Labor, in August 1890, waged a brief, unsuccessful fight against the New York Central.[1] In 1891 and 1892 coal miners in eastern Tennessee, trying to force a halt in the use of convict labor, were suppressed by the state militia. In the silver and lead mines of the Coeur d'Alene district of Idaho in 1892, a dispute over unionization led to violence that was put down by federal troops. That same summer, striking switchmen tied up railroad traffic in the Buffalo freight yards for thirteen days until finally dispersed by the New York militia. In the Carnegie steel works at Homestead, Pennsylvania, one of the great labor battles of the late nineteenth century was fought between the Amalgamated Iron and Steel Workers' Union and the Carnegie management, assisted by Pinkerton detectives and the Pennsylvania state guard.[2]

These disturbances were, for the most part, local in character and were handled by local or state officials. The Knights of Labor were beaten without government intervention, even by New York authorities. Although the switchmen's strike involved interstate railways, the prompt action of New York officials forestalled any need for federal intervention. In the Coeur d'Alene affair federal troops were sent in and a federal court injunction was used, but only at the request of the governor, who lacked adequate forces of his own to put down "domestic insurrection."[3] In response to public reaction to the Homestead strike two congressional committees investigated the use

108

of Pinkertons in labor disputes.[4] Despite slight evidences of federal concern, however, none of the disorders contributed significantly to the development of federal policy for meeting strikes.

After 1892 matters grew worse, primarily because of the Panic of 1893 and the depression that followed. Economic stringency frayed tempers all around. Many working people, harassed by shutdowns, lockouts, layoffs, and wage cuts, felt oppressed by their employers and suspected the government of being in league with their oppressors. Employers detected rebellion, if not anarchy, in the mounting insubordination of their employees. Some capitalists saw a rising tide of red in the Populist Revolt and objected to federal "pandering of the masses" which had begun with the Interstate Commerce and Sherman Antitrust acts and was being carried forward by such laws as the Wilson-Gorman Tariff of 1894 with its income tax provisions. The continued operation of the Sherman Silver Purchase Act of 1890 seemed to a large part of the business community an invitation to runaway inflation and the collapse of the nation's currency, if not the destruction of the fabric of organized society itself.[5]

It was against this setting that a series of labor disputes again drew the federal government back to the unfinished work of coping with railway strikes. Congress, having failed to provide effective machinery for resolving disputes, now stood by while first the federal courts sought to prevent strikes and boycotts and then while both the executive and judicial branches struggled to crush labor disorders that erupted into violence and tied up the nation's transportation system.

The initial disorders on the railroads, growing out of the Panic of 1893, were minor strikes, boycotts, and threats of strike or boycott. That they came before the courts at all was again due to many railways being in receivership. The onset of the Panic had driven over two hundred companies, embracing one-fifth of the nation's total rail mileage, into the custody of the courts.[6] As the depression tightened its grip in 1893 and 1894, managers, many of whom were court-appointed receivers, economized by discharging surplus men and cutting wages. The strikes, boycotts, and threats followed. Several of these matters were brought before the federal courts on one ground or another, and the judges were asked to rule on a number of questions: Would the courts continue their ban against the boycotting of interstate carriers? Would they turn the recently adopted Sherman

Antitrust Act against labor, holding strikes to be conspiracies in restraint of interstate commerce? Would the courts review the orders of their own receivers respecting wage cuts and the discharge of employees? Would they enjoin strikes per se that were conducted against interstate railways?

The judges took up the challenge, casting about for judicial solutions to the problems before them. By no means did they agree as to what should be done. Only with respect to secondary boycotts did they speak with a single voice. The majority of those whose decisions were recorded, found solutions chiefly in the further repression of labor. These jurists construed the Sherman law to apply to labor, enjoining first the boycotting of railroads and eventually even strikes. A few judges, however, refused to use the courts against workers and tried instead to become arbiters between capital and labor.

Two recently appointed judges, Augustus J. Ricks and William Howard Taft, earned the enmity of organized labor for continuing the strong stand of the courts against boycotting. Ricks had come to the federal bench by way of court clerkships. In 1878 he was appointed clerk, first of the Federal District Court of Northern Ohio and then of the Sixth Federal Circuit Court. He was also standing master in chancery. In 1889 President Benjamin Harrison named Ricks district judge for Northern Ohio.[7]

Ricks's most important decision while on the bench was his 1893 ruling against boycotting. The railroad engineers never forgave that decision, and, in 1894, organized labor wreaked partial vengeance. The Central Labor Union of Cleveland brought charges that, at the time of his appointment to the bench, Ricks had improperly handled certain fees due him as clerk of court. An investigation by the House Judiciary Committee followed. The majority report found insufficient grounds for impeachment proceedings, but, at the same time, declared it could "not too strongly censure the practice under which Judge Ricks made up his accounts." Seven members of the committee, in a minority report, concluded that it was "impossible to reconcile" Ricks's conduct "with the rules of common honesty" and urged immediate steps toward impeachment. Ricks weathered this storm and remained on the bench until forced into retirement by poor health in 1905.[8]

Judge Taft, who was thirty-five years old in 1893, had already advanced far in the career that would eventually carry him to the White House and to chief justiceship of the United States Supreme Court. A scion of the distinguished, well-to-do Taft family of Cincinnati, he held several minor state offices, including a judgeship, before being named, in 1890, solicitor general of the United States. Two years later President Harrison appointed him a judge of the Sixth Federal Circuit Court.[9]

On both the state and the federal benches Taft was obliged to deal from time to time with labor cases. In these matters he was neither "anti-" nor "pro-" labor as such, though he was often charged, during political campaigns, with hostility toward labor. More accurately, Taft seems to have been a moderate conservative who shared many, but not all, of the prejudices then held by the well-to-do classes against organized labor. For example, he dealt harshly with sympathy strikes and boycotts. In liability suits, on the other hand, his sympathies usually lay with the injured workman. As for organized labor, Taft upheld the right of workers to belong to unions and even to strike in the interests of improving their own working conditions, providing, of course, that such strikes were conducted lawfully and without violence.[10]

The firm stands taken by Judges Gresham, Dundy, and Love against secondary boycotts in 1888 had not eliminated that weapon from the arsenal of labor unions in their continuing battles with railroad companies. Apparently convinced that a more effective boycott would have won the Burlington strike, the Brotherhood of Locomotive Engineers, at its 1889 convention, adopted "Rule 12," requiring all members, on pain of expulsion, to boycott any railroad against which a strike was authorized by the national officers. Rule 12 was brought to a practical test in the spring of 1893 when Chief Arthur authorized a strike against the Toledo, Ann Arbor & North Michigan.[11]

As had been true in the Burlington strike, managers of roads connecting with the Ann Arbor railroad allowed their employees to boycott its traffic rather than risk strikes against their own lines by resisting. The Ann Arbor, as the Burlington had done, thereupon asked the federal courts to enjoin eight companies from boycotting freight to and from its lines. Judge Ricks, on March 11, granted a temporary injunction to this effect. Employees of connecting lines were brought before him a week later, charged with having violated the injunction. "You are engaged in a service of a public character," he told them, "and the public are interested not only in the way in which you perform your duties while you continue in that service, but

are quite as much interested in the time and circumstances under which you quit that employment." If men were free to quit
whenever and wherever they pleased it was possible they might
do "irreparable damage" to their employers and "jeopardize
the lives of the traveling public." The court would not assume
the power to compel them to continue in the service of the
railroad, he said, but it would insist that they perform their
"whole duty" so long as they remained employees. The court,
moreover, would decide when that duty was fulfilled and when
the men's obligation to obey the orders of the court ceased.[12]

In a subsequent session, Ricks returned to the subject of
the special responsibilities of railway employees. The very nature of their work, involving "the custody of human life, and the
safety of millions of property," placed upon them a "higher
duty" to the public and to their employer than if their employer
were a private person. The defendants, Ricks declared, had accepted employment "with full knowledge of the exacting duties
[the company] owed to the public." They knew that a failure by
the company to fulfill its legal obligations would result in penalties and losses to it. "An implied obligation was therefore assumed by the employees," Ricks contended not only to discharge the obligations of the company faithfully but to protect
it against "irreparable losses and injuries and excessive damages
by any acts of omission on their part."

One of these implied conditions was not to leave the service of the railroad or to refuse to perform their duties when, by
neglecting them, lives would be imperiled or property destroyed. Under ordinary circumstances, employees were free to
quit the service of an employer at will. This right became "quite
different in the case of the employees of a great public corporation, charged by the law with certain great trusts and duties to
the public." Suspension of work by the engineers or firemen of
a major railroad tended to "paralyze the business of the entire
country, entailing losses, and bringing disaster to thousands of
unoffending citizens. Contracts would be broken, perishable
property destroyed, the traveling public embarrassed, injuries
sustained, too many and too vast to be enumerated." In the
case at hand, these evils were caused by a few hundred men
who, without grievance of their own against their employer,
quit his service in order to give aid to the employees of a
minor railway line who were engaged in a dispute with their
"employer. If the damage to their own employers and to" thou-

sands of the business public, who are helpless and innocent" proved to be the product of "conspiracy, combination, intimidation, or unlawful acts of organizations of employees," the court would grant such relief as it could by enjoining the defendants from committing acts of violence or intimidation, or from enforcing rules and regulations of organizations which resulted in "irremediable injuries to the employers and to the public." Those defendants who had quit their jobs outright rather than violate Rule 12 of the BLE were not punished. Judge Ricks suggested, however, that they might be sued by the company for breach of contract.[13]

Not long after, Circuit Court Judge Taft was asked to rule on another facet of the same case. Taft held that the Interstate Commerce Act obligated all interstate carriers to exchange freight with all other carriers without discrimination. Any violation of this law made the offending carrier criminally responsible. Where the carrier was a corporation, its officers, agents, and employees could be punished for willfully causing the corporation to break the law. Under this interpretation the boycotting engineers and their chief, Arthur, were criminally liable for violating the Interstate Commerce Act. They could also be charged with criminal conspiracy against the United States, Taft observed.[14]

Turning to a general discussion of the rights of labor, Judge Taft distinguished between striking and boycotting, holding the first to be legal; the second, illegal. Taft acknowledged the "inalienable right" of a man "to bestow his labor when he will and to withhold his labor as he will." But, he pointed out, that right was not absolute. A man might not use the bestowing or withholding of labor or the threat of bestowing or withholding "for the purpose of inducing, procuring, or compelling" another to commit "an unlawful or criminal act." Motivated by such a purpose, the act of bestowing or withholding labor in itself could become unlawful and criminal.

A strike was legal, Taft held, because it was by definition "for the lawful purpose of selling the labor of those who engaged in it for the highest price obtainable, and on the best terms." The "probable inconvenience or loss" that a strike imposed on an employer under ordinary circumstances was "a legitimate means available to [workmen] for inducing a compliance with their demands." A boycott, on the other hand, was illegal because it attempted to induce an employer to violate the law; in the case at hand, the Interstate Commerce Act. "Neither law nor morals can give a man the right to labor or withhold his labor for such a purpose," he declared.[15]

The injunction ordering connecting lines to interchange traffic with the Ann Arbor applied not only to the companies but with equal force to the engineers, Taft declared. This would remain true only so long as the men "assume to do the work of the defendant companies." Obedience to the injunction could be avoided, he pointed out, by quitting the companies under its ban. Once the men ceased being employees, the injunction would no longer apply to them. No court of equity had yet presumed to order men to remain in the service of an employer against their wills, Taft observed. At the same time, if the men quit in such a manner as to injure the company, they were guilty of an unlawful act and subject to both criminal and civil penalties. They were not subject, however, to court orders forcing them to work for an employer against their wishes.[16]

Judges Ricks and Taft did not set any new precedents respecting boycotting in the Ann Arbor cases; most of the same ground had been covered in the cases arising out of the Burlington strike. Judges Dundy and Love had at that time rested their findings clearly on the Interstate Commerce Act, holding boycotting illegal under that law. Judge Gresham had concluded that boycotting was illegal against interstate carriers on general constitutional grounds without reference to any specific act of Congress. Taft's one important contribution was his ruling that although boycotting by employees of an interstate carrier was illegal under the Interstate Commerce Act, strikes by employees of interstate carriers could be legal in spite of that law. It may be that this decision helped prompt the increased use of the Sherman Antitrust Act as the chief statutory weapon against strikers after 1893.[17]

The possibility that a law designed to break up monopolistic business combinations might be used against organized labor first arose during congressional debate of the Sherman Act. A number of the many antitrust proposals introduced into the Fifty-first Congress specifically exempted labor unions from their provisions; not one explicitly included unions within its scope. In Senate debate on the Sherman bill, a few members expressed fear that, if passed, it might be used against labor inasmuch as it did not exclude unions from its operations. Senator John Sherman, for whom the bill was named, declared that unions could not possibly "be included in the words or intent of the bill as now reported."[18] Nevertheless, to quiet the doubts of his colleagues, he later introduced an amendment expressly excluding from the provisions of the law combinations of labor, "made with a view of lessening the number of hours of labor or of increasing their wages." One senator arose to attack this proposed exclusion and he was promptly answered by two other senators. The Senate then passed Sherman's amendment. In the House there was no debate over the matter of excluding or including labor unions. Eight of eighteen antitrust bills introduced there, however, had specifically excluded unions from their provisions.

After a working-over in conference committee, the Sherman bill, as it finally emerged, was silent as to whether or not labor unions were exempt from its provisions. Since there was neither debate favoring nor amendments providing inclusion of unions, it seems improbable that Congress had reversed its sentiment. More likely Congress either dodged the issue, leaving it to be settled in the courts, or accepted Senator Sherman's view that since courts had already held unions, as such, to be legal, the act could not be used against them.[19]

Following passage of the Sherman Act, debate over its applicability to labor unions shifted to the federal courts. Judges weighed whether its provisions applied either to unions per se, or to strikes conducted by organized labor groups. Two of the earliest antitrust cases produced rulings which inferred that the law was not meant to be used against organized labor. Judge William L. Putnam, of the First Federal Circuit Court, in a case involving two corporations, held that the antitrust law should be interpreted in a strict, conservative way. "Careless or inept construction," he warned, "if followed out logically," might extend into very large fields of enterprise. The "inevitable result," he feared, would be that federal courts would be "compelled to apply" the law to all attempts to restrain interstate or international trade by "strikes, or boycotts and by every method of interference by way of violence or intimidation." He regarded such constructions as well beyond the intent of Congress.[20] Later that same year, Judge Edward C. Billings, of the Eastern District of Louisiana, rejected the Sherman Act as a basis for enjoining New Orleans dockworkers (at the behest of their employers) from obstructing international trade. His reason was that only the federal government could seek injunctions of that sort and that the Sherman Act had not conferred this privilege on private parties. Although he granted an injunction in the case, it was on more general grounds.[21]

Two other cases, however, resulted in rulings that supported the use of the law to break strikes. Less than two months after denying an injunction based on the antitrust act, Judge Billings became the first federal judge to apply the Sherman law against labor. In November 1892 the Workingmen's Amalgamated Council of New Orleans called a general transportation strike in support of a teamsters' strike against the use of nonunion labor. The strike tied up transportation in the Crescent City, and the United States attorney, F. B. Earhart, who in his private capacity had represented the shipowners in their earlier case, sought an injunction under the Sherman Act on behalf of the government.[22] Judge Billings granted the injunction on March 25, 1893, arguing that although congressional debates showed that the act was aimed originally at the evils of massed capital, by the time of its final adoption "the subject had so broadened in the minds of the legislators that the source of the evil in its entirety [was] dealt with. They made the interdiction include combinations of labor as well as of capital." Appeal was taken to the Circuit Court of Appeals, where Billings' ruling was upheld.[23]

The other case in which strikes were discussed in connection with the Sherman Act also occurred in the South, in the court of Judge Emory Speer of Georgia. In April 1893 the engineers of the Central of Georgia Railroad, a company in receivership, petitioned Judge Speer, asking that the working agreement between themselves and the prereceivership managers of the road be continued in force. The receivers objected to extending the contract for a number of reasons, including the fact that the BLE had an "illegal rule" as a part of its constitution. The receivers had reference to Rule 12, which provided that in the event of a strike BLE members would not handle the traffic of the railroad involved, whatever the company for whom they might be working.

Judge Speer, in his ruling in this, the Waterhouse case, held that Rule 12 was illegal under both the Interstate Commerce Act and the Sherman Antitrust Act. The contract in question, however, would be continued by the receivers, providing the engineers did not comply with Rule 12, if the question should arise. Membership in the BLE was not of itself sufficient reason for refusing a contract "so long as the rules and regulations of the order are treated [by the engineers] as subordinate to the law of the land."[24] In the course of his remarks, Speer, only a week after Judge Taft's Ann Arbor case ruling, contradicted the Ohio jurist's opinion that a strike against a railroad was legal. "In any conceivable strike upon the transportation lines of this country," he said, "whether main lines or branch roads, there will be interference with and restraint of interstate or foreign commerce." In the light of the Interstate Commerce and Sherman Antitrust laws and the "intimate interchange of commodities between people of several states of the Union," it would be "practically impossible hereafter" for men to combine together to hinder or delay the operation of a transportation company without "becoming amenable to the provisions of these statutes." It followed, therefore, he went on, "that a strike or 'boycott' . . . if it was ever effective, can be so no longer." The remedy open to organized labor when injustice was done or threatened (and apparently without regard to whether or not the company involved was in receivership) was to present strong petitions to the courts for redress against unlawful combinations and trusts wronging it. "Its membership need not doubt that their counsel will be heard, nor that speedy and exact justice will be administered wherever the courts have jurisdiction." The courts would be found competent, Speer assured labor, "to preserve the rights of the operatives, to spare them hardship, and at the same time to spare the public the unmerited hardship which it has suffered from such conflicts in the past."[25] Billings' ruling and Speer's obiter dictum in the Waterhouse case would serve as precedents for justifying use of the Sherman Act against strikers in the Pullman strike and for breaking up many other strikes for several decades.

A series of appeals to federal judges in 1893 and 1894 gave brief promise of leading to procedures for settling railway labor disputes through adjudication in the courts. Employees of railroads in receivership, in a number of instances, sought to have the courts review the orders of receivers arbitrarily lowering wages or discharging men. Had the courts been as willing to intervene as arbiters in these disputes as they were to protect railroads from strikers and boycotts by broadening the use of injunctions, the whole course of railway labor disputes and of national strike policy might have been quite different.

There were good reasons, economic and legal, for employees of receivers to avoid striking during the depression of 1893. Strikebreakers were in abundant supply, and since 1877, the courts had consistently found men who struck against receivers guilty of contempt of court. The judges on several occasions had explained that such strikes were inexcusable because all employees of receivers technically were officers of the court and had the same right as the receivers themselves to come before the court, to state their alleged grivances, and, if they proved their case, to receive relief at the judges' hands. There were, however, few reported cases of appeals from the orders of receivers prior to 1893. The outcome of the cases in 1893 and 1894, with few exceptions, did little to encourage such appeals thereafter.[26]

In the reported cases the federal judges all agreed that the special standing of employees of railways in receivership entitled them to hearings when they appealed wage cuts and other orders of receivers.[27] One receiver, whose order for a wage cut was appealed to Judge Taft, asked that his order be accepted as "conclusive of the question" and that Taft refuse to receive the petition of the employees on the grounds that it would establish a precedent involving the court in hearings "of all sorts concerning the discipline and ordinary administrative matters in the operation of the road." Taft, pointing to the special standing of the men as employees of the court itself, granted the hearing and denied that this would set a precedent for testing every other decision made by the receiver. The men, he said, had no legal right involved, but they did have the same right that the employees of any ordinary employer had to appeal to their employer's discretion to rescind the wage cut.[28]

Securing a hearing proved much easier for aggrieved workingmen than getting judges to countermand the orders of court-appointed receivers. Most of the judges, in the reported cases in 1893 and 1894, tended to give receivers very broad discretionary powers and to abide by the decisions of their appointees. The "very object" of appointing an experienced railroad manager receiver and giving him charge of a railroad in the custody of the court was to "relieve the court from the responsibility of its maintenance and management," Judge Ricks declared. Judges, "learned in the law though they may be," had little practical experience in large business undertakings. "They are not trained in those departments of railroad management which relate to the wages of employees, to the numbers necessary for the maintenance of the roadbed and for the safe operation of trains, to the tariffs for freight, and the purchases of supplies." But even if they were capable of mastering such details, Ricks continued, their time was too limited to be devoted to the actual day-to-day operation of railroads. A receiver, therefore, was named to manage the property. The instructions given him were "always general in their character," leaving him "the largest degree of discretion possible in the discharge of his duties." The determination of issues such as the one before the court "must necessarily rest with the receiver." Only when it became evident that a receiver had abused his discretion would the court intervene and then, not to overrule the receiver, but to appoint a new receiver to whom such matters could more satisfactorily be entrusted.[29]

Judge Ricks regarded wage cuts as a detail of management best left to the discretion of the receiver; Judge Cornelius Hanford of the District Court of Washington, took the same position with regard to the discharge of employees by a receiver. Hanford had risen to distinction from humble beginnings. He earned his way as a young man in a variety of ways, including carrying mail, working on a stock ranch, running a fruit store, and traveling for a soap company.[30] High-handed in his methods, Hanford, before becoming a judge, once organized a group to suppress anti-Chinese agitators in Seattle because, he said, their demonstrations drove "venture capital" away from the area. He expressed the hope at the time that a "little judicious bloodletting" might end the matter. "A tower of conservatism," his opponents charged that when cases involving the public interest were brought before him, he "invariably decided against the people."[31]

In 1894 complaint was made to Hanford by employees of a Washington railway that the receiver of the line was discharging men without cause. The judge's response was that it would be "impractical" for the court "to give such attention to matters of detail as would be necessary to justify it in overruling a receiver in the matter of selecting or discharging his subordinates." Only in matters of "general policy" could the court "give directions to a receiver."[32]

Circuit Court Judge Taft, who outranked both Ricks and Hanford, held a similar, though less extreme view than his colleagues. He stressed that as a practical matter a court could not undertake the actual operation of a railroad and had to appoint as its agent some well-known, professional railroad manager of skill and experience. At the same time, wage reductions were of such importance that even though he had approved the wage cut in question in advance of its being ordered, he would listen to an application for modification. If the receiver erred or "committed an abuse of the discretion intrusted to him," the court would intercede. "The burden of showing either must, in the nature of things," he warned, "be upon the petitioner."[33]

In a few of the cases the workers contended that the orders of the receivers were contrary to standing contracts between themselves and the prereceivership managers of the railways. Judges Dundy and Hanford held that receivers were not and could not be bound legally by such "alleged contracts." Agreements entered into before a railroad passed into receivership were not contracts of a kind binding on the receivers as successors to the previous management, Dundy argued. The receivers were under direct orders from the court to put into effect such rules, regulations, and schedules as their best judgments indicated. If an employee objected to the changes, he might petition the court to alter them, but the new rules would be regarded as *"prime facie* reasonable and just."[34]

Judge Hanford went even further. A contract of this sort, he said, would be "repugnant" to the court order placing the railroad in the hands of the receiver. "The idea that employees in the service of a railway corporation have such an interest in the railway property that effect should be given to their contracts of employment, as if they were of the same nature as covenants running with the title to real estate, and therefore binding upon those into whose hands the property may subsequently come, is fallacious. . . ." The receiver, as agent of the court, was under orders to take full charge of the property. His duties and responsibilities required that he "exercise discretion" in selecting the men to work with him. Any rule or contract to the contrary would be "incompatible" with the freedom necessary to the proper exercise of that discretion and the performance of his duties. Even were a receiver himself intentionally to enter into an agreement of this kind, thereby voluntarily limiting his control over the men serving under him, Hanford declared, that contract would be void because it would necessarily deprive him of an important part of the power vested in him by the court. "A receiver cannot lawfully thus restrict himself in the exercise of his powers," the judge ruled.[35]

Judge Taft, in the course of his decision, laid down certain considerations for guiding judges and receivers in deciding such economic questions as wage cuts. "A private employer," he noted, might "be moved by considerations of charity" when considering cuts. A court of equity, however, could not. It was limited in the exercise of its discretion, Taft held, "to such action as may be consistent with the preservation of the property and its due administration in the interests of those who own it."[36]

Standing on the opposite side of these same questions were Henry Clay Caldwell, judge of the Eighth Circuit Court, and John S. Woolson, judge of the district court for Southern Iowa. Caldwell, in 1894, had already served thirty years on the federal bench and would serve yet nine years more before retiring in 1903. During the Civil War he had risen to the rank of colonel in the Union Army and saw action in the campaign to restore federal control over the Mississippi River Valley. In June 1864 President Lincoln asked Caldwell to become federal district judge of the recently reconquered state of Arkansas. The young commander faced a difficult time, the Arkansans taking a dim view of his "getting out of the saddle and ascending the bench." But Caldwell "kept his court out of politics and administered justice with such firmness, impartiality and sound common sense" that he overcame the deep prejudices against him. In 1890 President Harrison elevated him to the circuit court bench seat left vacant when David Brewer was named to the United States Supreme Court.[37]

Caldwell, it was said, always sought to do "substantial justice" and had only contempt for those who sought to deny it by the use of legal technicalities. "His heart was as big as his brain and it always went out to the weak, the poor and the oppressed."[38] He did not regard the appointment of receivers for railroads as a matter of right, for example. Before naming a receiver for a railroad in financial difficulty, Caldwell forced the creditors to agree that unsecured claims for labor, materials, personal injuries, and the like be met before the secured debts. As he told one attorney, "If you want me to open the door, you must come to my terms." For such rulings, which the higher courts ultimately upheld, Caldwell earned a reputation for putting personal rights above property rights.[39]

Eulogists praised Judge Woolson as "the soul of honor," and referred to him as a "learned, able, diligent, and impartial judge." He was more interested in the reformation of the character of wrongdoers than in their punishment, was "unusually just," and often "tempered justice with mercy." In disposing of the work of his court he was businesslike and efficient and was distinguished for the "certainty" with which he imposed penalties "upon incorrigible transgressors. . . ."[40]

In overruling Judge Dundy in the Union Pacific case, Judge Caldwell insisted that a labor contract in existence when a receiver took over court property was valid and binding and that a judge could and should overrule a receiver when he thought it proper to do so. When a court of equity took over the operation of a railroad, Caldwell declared, all men in the employ of the road became employees of the court, were subject to its orders, and were entitled to its protection. A "sober, intelligent, experienced, and capable" labor force was essential to the safe and successful operation of a railroad, and when a court took possession of a road whose employees were conceded to have these qualities, it would not, "upon light or trivial grounds," dispense with their services or reduce their wages. Where there was a wage schedule in effect when receivers took over a railroad, especially if it were the result of long-standing mutual agreements, it would be presumed reasonable and just.

Caldwell went on to say that changes in wage schedules could not be made by the receiver alone. Not only was this a violation of a standing agreement in the case at hand, but it was a "fundamental error." Even in the absence of specific agreements, cuts should not be put into effect by receivers or courts without giving the men an opportunity to be heard. "It is fundamental in the jurisprudence of this country," he said, "that no court can rightfully make an order or render a judgment affecting the rights of one who is absent and has no notice." To the suggestion that employees could question a new schedule after it was put into effect, Caldwell scathingly replied, "The men could have small hopes of a fair and impartial hearing after the receivers had prepared new schedules behind their backs, which were declared by the receivers and the court to be '*prime facie* just and reasonable.' This was very much like first hanging a man, and trying him afterwards."

To the argument that the court should be governed by the recommendations of the majority of the receivers of the Union Pacific, Caldwell replied that four of the five receivers were "not practical railroad men." Two were lawyers residing in New York, one was a Chicago merchant, and one was a railway accountant who, though familiar with the books of the company, was not an authority on wage schedules. "These four gentlemen are eminent in the line of their professions and pursuits, and entirely capable of managing the financial affairs of this great trust for which purpose they were, doubtless, selected," Caldwell said, "but their opinions upon the subject of wage schedules are confessedly of little value." Caldwell refused to order the recommended cut.[41]

Judge Woolson took a similar position with respect to cutting wages on a railroad in his custody. The receiver ordered a wage reduction, and when workmen petitioned to have it rescinded, Woolson suggested negotiations between the receiver and the men. Direct bargaining failed and the matter was referred to a master in chancery who ordered a wage cut. It, in turn, was appealed to the judge. Woolson observed that, as a general rule, courts accepted the report of a master as conclusive as to facts. The master's findings, however, were not limited to "mere conclusions of law," but related to questions of the propriety and justice of reducing wages. In those areas, although the master's report carried great weight, the court felt obliged to reach its own conclusions, and Woolson substantially scaled down the wage cuts before ordering them into effect.[42]

Caldwell, in the course of his ruling in the Union Pacific case, like Taft, laid down suggestions for determining whether or not wage cuts should be ordered by receivers. "Sound public policy, no less than justice to the men," he said, "requires that they be paid a rate of wages that will enable them to live decently and comfortably, and school their children. Some corporations may pay their employees a less rate of wages than is here indicated, but a court of equity will not follow their bad example." The best service could not be expected of men "compelled to live in a state of pinch and want," and a court of equity would not follow so "niggardly and cheeseparing" a policy toward its employees. Although interested in the economical operation of the road and the protection of the rights of owners and bondholders, the court was unwilling to cut wages of employees "below reasonable and just compensation for their services . . . though no dividends are paid on the stock and no interest paid on the bonds."[43]

Judge Woolson shared these same sentiments. He scorned the proposition that wages should be lowered because other men stood ready to take up positions left by men who might quit if wages were cut. "The retention of faithful, intelligent, and capable employees is of greatly more importance than [a] temporary decrease in earnings, or present ability to secure other employees at reduced wages."[44] Given the conflicting results of appeals to judges over the heads of receivers, lawyers counseling laborers who were considering such appeals could safely advise but one course: be certain that the railroad company is in the custody of the right judge.

Of the jurists who listened to appeals from the decisions of receivers in 1893 and 1894, only Judge Speer seems to have seen the potential value of such proceedings in avoiding railway strikes generally. Dundy, Hanford, Ricks, and to a lesser degree Taft, all upheld their receivers and declared that, although they would hear appeals for review, the chances of their overturning receivers' orders were slight. Judges Caldwell and Woolson, on the other hand, although willing to hear appeals and to moderate or even overrule the orders of receivers, failed to see the larger, more general application that might be made of such proceedings.

Speer, however, saw the potential and raised the question: Might not such proceedings offer a solution to the problem of railway labor disputes? For the courts, "under any circumstances," to exercise control over contracts between giant corporations "engaged in the public duty of transportation" and their employees, would "doubtless appear to many as novel and dangerous," he said. "It is well, however, to consider if a proper provision, by appeal to the courts, in the frequent and destructive conflicts between organized capital and organized labor will not afford the simplest, most satisfactory, and effective method for the settlement of such controversies. Is it not," he asked, "the only method by which the public, and indeed, the parties themselves can be protected from the inevitable hardship and loss which all must endure from the frequently recurring strikes?"

Those responsible for "maintenance of public order," he warned, could no longer ignore the great changes in the relationship between employers and employees wrought by the "phenomenal development of commerce and the prevalence of labor organizations." It might be, he conceded, in spite of the scope and complexity of modern commerce and the growing strength of labor unions, that the courts would not be justified in asserting "judicial control of contracts essential to the uninterrupted transportation of the country, in which the public is so vitally concerned." But, where a railroad was in receivership, it was clear that the courts had the power to adjust employer-employee differences whenever they constituted a threat to the property.[45] The challenge which was thrown down in this, the first of the 1893–94 decisions, was ignored, if noticed at all, by those charged with the "maintenance of public order."

The remaining question before the federal courts involved the legality of railroad strikes and whether they were enjoinable. Between 1877 and 1893 there had been no question but that a strike was legal so long as it was no more than a group of men quitting their jobs together so as to put pressure on their employer to raise their pay or to better their working conditions. Men who went further, interfering with the operation of railroads or using force, violence, or intimidation to scare off strikebreakers or to force nonstriking employees to abandon their jobs, often found themselves in trouble with the courts.

The appearance of injunctions outlawing railroad strikes per se in 1893 was the product of a logical, step-by-step evolution that began in 1877. At that time federal court protection was given to railroads in receivership. Strikers were not enjoined from striking, but were punished for contempt of court when they prevented receivers from carrying out court orders to operate the railroads. Judge Gresham's temporary restraining order in the Lake Shore & Michigan Southern strike of 1886 added two new features: it appears to have been the first federal injunction specifically directed at employees, forbidding them to interfere with the operation of a railroad, and the first federal injunction used to protect the property of a company not in receivership.[46]

The injunctions issued during the Burlington strike were stronger and broader in scope than Gresham's 1886 restraining order. They were used to protect privately owned and operated railroads from boycotting by privately operated companies, by companies in receivership, or by their respective employees. The injunction handed down by Judge Dundy was the most comprehensive, enjoining both boycotting and striking that interfered with the operation of the railroad and hinting strongly that any strike whatever, including the mere combined quitting of work, would be illegal.[47]

When the tide of labor troubles began to rise again during the Panic of 1893, the legal community, both bench and bar, pondered whether the courts, in the absence of legislative action, might move to preserve peace and order on interstate railways by a still broader use of equity proceedings. Many took the position of Judge Ricks, who favored the development of equity procedures to keep pace with the mounting needs of the times.[48] Speaking with reference to this question in his Ann Arbor case ruling, he declared: "It is said the orders issued in this case are without precedent. Every just order or rule known to equity courts was born of some emergency, to meet some new conditions, and was, therefore, in its time, without a precedent. If based on sound principles, and beneficient results follow their enforcement, affording necessary relief to the one party without imposing illegal burdens on the other, new remedies and unprecedented orders are not unwelcome aids to the chancellor to meet the constantly varying demands for equitable relief."

Ricks approvingly quoted Supreme Court Justice David Brewer: ". . . the powers of a court of equity are as vast, and its processes and procedure as elastic, as all the changing emergencies of increasingly complex business relations and the protection of rights can demand." Justice Blatchford, Ricks noted, had also once asserted that "one of the most useful functions" of a court of equity was that its methods of procedure were adaptable "to the development of the interests of the public in the progress of trade and traffic by new methods of intercourse and transportation." Ricks held that the necessities growing out of the vast and rapidly multiplying interests of the expanding railroad business of the country made "new and correspondingly efficient measures of relief essential." The courts, "in the exercise of their equity jurisdiction, must meet the emergencies, as far as possible, within the limits of existing laws, until needed additional legislation can be secured."[49]

Ricks was not alone in this view. In January 1893, two months before Ricks's remarks, John H. Baker, the federal district judge of Indiana, issued a restraining order against strikers who threatened to interfere with the operation of the Lake Erie & Western, a railway not in receivership. Before becoming a federal judge, Baker had been a very successful lawyer, handling one of the largest practices in northern Indiana. In 1875 he was elected to Congress and served until 1881. His law practice was more lucrative after 1881 for his having been a congressman, and among his new clients was the Lake Shore & Michigan Southern. Baker's law partner had preceded him as counsel of the company in Indiana; Baker's son fell heir to the position when Baker was appointed judge in 1892.[50]

Among Indiana lawyers who knew him best, Baker was regarded as scholarly, stern, and a bit set in his ways. He held that all law, customary or statutory, human or divine, was "part of a mighty system whose voice [was] the harmony of the world and which should receive the homage of all mankind." Even faulty laws, of questionable purpose, enacted by incompetent legislators, were entitled to respect so long as they remained on the books, and Baker "placed the stamp of his personal and official disapproval upon all acts in defiance of law. . . ."[51]

Judge Baker, in his oral remarks at contempt proceedings against a number of strikers who violated his 1893 order, expressed sympathy for railroad workmen, their scanty wages, and their long and hard service in all kinds of weather. He recognized "the right of any man or number of men to quit the service of their employers" and the right of men "to organize if they deem it expedient to better their condition." At the same time, the preservation of society made it "absolutely indispensable that the great fundamental and God-given right of every human being, unrestrained and unintimidated, to labor and enjoy the fruits of his toil, should be protected." He saw little excuse for laborers to organize and by unlawful means attempt to subvert that basic principle.

"I do not know but that I am a little old-fashioned in my notions," he said, "but I confess I cannot look with any degree of tolerance on the false and dangerous teachings of those who actively, or by their silent acquiescence, are leading labor organizations to think that, because they are organized in associations, they have the right to seize property, or, by intimidation, to prevent well-disposed people from laboring." Certainly, such acts were no less criminal when done by associations than when done by an armed individual.

As he warmed to his subject, Baker's opening concession, that men had the right to organize, all but dissolved in a denunciation of the "secret labor organization" to which they belonged. That organization, he noted, had spread across the United States and Canada and had kindred associations by other names in Europe. "All these organizations," he declared, "have the same general aim, and that is by force, violence, and terrorism to compel their employers to submit their business, their property, and their means of livelihood to the arbitrary demands of these associations." In their "secret, oath-bound assemblies" they determined the terms under which they would work for others and then refused those who were not members of their association "the right of labor when they desired to do so." He likened the pressures that unions used to force employers to terms to the methods of a highwayman with a pistol at his victim's head. "If they compel submission, it is robbery," the jurist exclaimed, "because whoever compels me, by force or terrorism, to give up one dime of my money . . . is equally guilty whether he be the man who meets me on the streetcorner in the night time, or an organized band of strikers who take possession of my property and deprive me of its use."

Baker had no objections to laborers organizing for such purposes as learning about the principles of political economy, or the laws of supply and demand, or the effects of immigration and increased numbers of workmen on the wage market. Indeed, if workers wished to organize for any lawful purpose, including that of quitting their jobs, he said, they were within their rights. But when they "combine and confederate for the purpose of seizing other men's property, or when they undertake, by force and intimidation, to drive other men away from employment and thus deny them the right of earning a livelihood, they commit a crime . . . that this court cannot suffer to go unpunished." Baker deferred passing sentence on the men before him until he might learn more about them; "who and what they are; something about their former lives; what they have been doing; whether they have been engaged in criminal combinations before this."[52] Presumably, he placed no premium on previous union activity.

Few judges were so openly critical of organized laborers or even of strikers as was Baker. Most drafted more judicious, written opinions and forebore publishing their oral remarks. Baker's sentiments, however, were not unique on the bench and rulings against railway strikes of any sort were increasingly handed down. It was true that Judge Taft, soon after Baker's deliverance, asserted the right of men to strike. But within a week of Taft's ruling, as already noted, Judge Speer observed that in the light of the Interstate Commerce and Sherman Antitrust laws it seemed unlikely that there could be legal railroad strikes or boycotts.

Then, in January 1894, Judge Dundy specifically enjoined employees of the Union Pacific from striking. At the time that he authorized the receivers of that company to impose a wage cut, he issued, at their request, an injunction of very broad scope against strike activities on the part of the men. Dundy announced that any employees who were unhappy with his wage ruling might terminate their employment as they saw fit "so long as they did not impede, obstruct, or interfere with the business of the receivers." Those who quit, however, could not be reemployed without specific authorization from the court. Those who remained employees of the receivers were forbidden to "conspire, combine, or confederate together, or with, by, or through, any labor" organization, with the purpose of precipitating a strike or in any way hindering, impeding, obstructing, embarrassing, or injuring the receivers in the conduct of the Union Pacific's affairs. Not only were they themselves to refrain from these activities, but they were not to recommend, approve, encourage, or advise others to engage in them.[53]

Judge Caldwell, in reviewing the Union Pacific case, reversed Dundy's ruling, upholding the right of the men to organize for self-protection. They could not, he said, be enjoined from combining to protect their rights.

> In this country it is not unlawful for employees to associate, consult, and confer together with a view to maintain or increase their wages by lawful and peaceful means, any more than it was unlawful for the receivers to counsel and confer for the purpose of reducing their wages. A corporation is organized capital; it is capital consisting of money and property. Organized labor is organized capital; it is capital consisting of brains and muscle. What it is lawful for one to do it is lawful for the other to do. If it is lawful for the stockholders and officers of a corporation to associate and confer together for the purpose of reducing the wages of its employees or of devising other means of making their investments profitable, it is equally lawful for organized labor to associate, consult, and confer with a view to maintain or increase wages. Both act from the prompting of enlightened selfishness, and the action of both is lawful when no illegal or criminal means are used or threatened.

He insisted that men in all stations and walks of life had the right to associate for mutual benefit. "The legality and utility" of such organizations among laboring men could "no longer be questioned."

With respect to the use of injunctions to prevent strikes, Caldwell was conservative. An injunction might not be used to enforce "the specific performance of a contract or render personal service." There was the further objection to their use in such cases, he said, in that they were unnecessary; any interference with the operation of a railroad in receivership was contempt, with or without an injunction. The issuing of these writs only tended to lead the uninformed to think that interference with a railroad in receivership was not a crime unless previously enjoined.[54]

Caldwell's ruling did not stay the trend toward the enjoining of strikes, however. A climax in that development was reached between December 1893 and April 1894 when James G. Jenkins, judge of the Seventh Circuit Court enjoined striking per se on the Northern Pacific. Jenkins, like Judge Baker, had come to the bench from a lucrative practice that included being counsel to a major railroad company. Following admission to practice in 1857, Jenkins had moved to Milwaukee. There he married the only daughter of the federal district judge, Andrew G. Miller. He soon "enjoyed a large and profitable practice, a very large share of popularity, and the confidence and respect of his clientage." Among the more important of his clients was the Chicago & Northwestern, which he served as regular counsel in Wisconsin until his appointment to the federal bench in 1888.[55]

The full scope and meaning of Jenkins' order prohibiting employees of the Northern Pacific from striking was set forth in his final ruling in the case on April 6, 1894. According to Jenkins' recital of the facts, when receivers took possession of the Northern Pacific in August 1893, they reduced the wages of all employees between 10 and 20 percent. Continuing depressed conditions led them, late in October 1893, to order a second reduction of between 5 and 10 percent to take effect January 1, 1894.

The employees protested that their wages had been set by contract with the company prior to the receivership and were not subject to change without their consent. When the receivers rejected this argument, the employees threatened to quit, to block the hiring of strikebreakers, to sabotage trains, and to take possession of the railroad. Upon application of the receivers, Jenkins, on December 19, 1893, issued an injunction of very broad scope against the workers and instructed the United States marshal to protect all property in the hands of the receivers.

Jenkins' injunction was directed to "the officers, agents, and employees" of the receivers, "the engineers, firemen, trainmen, train dispatchers, telegraphers, conductors, switchmen, and all other employees, . . . all persons, associations, and combinations, voluntary or otherwise, whether employees of said receivers or not, and all persons generally." They were "charged and commanded" not to disable or render "in any wise unfit for convenient and immediate use" any engines, cars, or other rolling stock; not to interfere in any manner with the company's property, or "by force, threats or otherwise," to interfere with men who desired to continue in the service of the receivers or to take the place of those who quit; and not to obstruct "in any wise the operation of the railroad or any portion thereof. . . ."

To this point the injunction did not significantly differ from earlier writs of this sort. Jenkins, however, went on to add a prohibition against "combining and conspiring to quit, with or without notice," the service of the receivers "with the object and intent of crippling the property in their custody, or embarrassing the operation of the railroad." Three days later, the receivers, still unsatisfied that the injunction was inclusive enough to ward off a strike expected on January 1, 1894, asked Jenkins to enjoin workers' committees from recommending, or the national officers of the various railway brotherhoods from sanctioning, a strike. Jenkins accordingly reissued his original injunction with the additional words: "and from combining or conspiring together or with others, either jointly or severally, or as committees, or as officers of any so-called 'labor organization,' with the design or purpose of causing a strike upon the lines of railroad operated by said receivers . . . on January 1, 1894, or at any other time; and from ordering, recommending, advising, or approving by communication or instruction or otherwise, the employees of said receivers . . . to join in a strike . . . until the further order of this court." The national chieftains of the brotherhoods affected submitted a petition to Jenkins on February 14, asking that the final part of the original injunction and the portion added December 22 be stricken. Seven weeks and two days later, Jenkins, ruling on their petition, made but one slight modification which did not significantly alter the injunction.

In his decision of April 6, Jenkins disclaimed any intention of taking sides in a dispute between capital and labor. If either of these forces became a danger to the Republic it was, he said, within the "peculiar province" of Congress, not of the judiciary, to determine the necessary remedies and to declare "the general policy of the state" touching relations between them. It was the duty of the courts, however, to restrain "those warring factions" so far as their actions went against the established law of the land, "that society may not be disrupted, or its peace invaded, and that individual and corporate rights may not be infringed." Inasmuch as the threats of the Northern Pacific's employees, if put into effect, would have paralyzed the railway, thereby "stopping the commerce ebbing and flowing through seven states of the Union, working incalculable injury to the property, and causing great public privation," restraint by injunction was an appropriate remedy. Certainly, any action at law after such a strike would be worth little, he noted.

In justifying the injunction, Jenkins declared that it was no longer "open to controversy" that a court of equity might restrain "threatened trespass involving the immediate or ultimate destruction of property, working irreparable injury, and for which there would be no adequate compensation at law." Flying then in the face of the precedent, Jenkins went on to declare that "in extreme cases, where the peril is imminent, and the danger great," a court of equity could "issue mandatory injunctions requiring a particular service to be performed, or a particular direction to be given, or a particular order to be revoked, in prevention of a threatened trespass upon property or upon public rights." In other words, workers could be forced by equity proceedings to remain at their jobs and to perform specific services against their wills.

Jenkins denied that this construction in any way "derogated" the "common right" of an individual to work for whom he would at the terms he would or to leave that work as he chose. But no right was absolute, he maintained; it was always related to duty. It would be monstrous, for example, for a surgeon, appealing to the right to quit a job, to abandon his patient in the middle of an operation or for a lawyer to desert his client in the midst of a trial. Nor was the key factor the endangering of human lives, Jenkins insisted. Whether life or property rights were threatened, the fundamental principle remained the same. Under ordinary circumstances, when a railroad employee abandoned his job, the loss and the inconvenience to the company was so slight that it was "a matter of but little moment when or how he . . . quit. . . ." But this in no way altered the principle that the right was conditioned by duty. If this were true for the individual workingman, it was the more so for any large group of workmen who might suddenly quit without giving adequate notice, thereby crippling the operation of the railroad and injuring the public.

The impending strike that he had enjoined, he held, was a conspiracy to compel the receivers to accede to the demands of the workers or face a crippling of the railroad's operations. Jenkins discussed various definitions of the term "strike," and finally concluded that a strike was "a combined effort among workmen to compel the master to the concession of a certain demand, by preventing the conduct of his business until compliance with the demand. The concerted cessation of work is but one of, and the least effective of, the means to the end; the intimidation of others from engaging in the service, the interference with, and the disabling and destruction of, property, and resort to actual force and violence, when requisite to the accomplishment of the end, being the other, and more effective, means employed."

In the strongest possible terms, Jenkins ridiculed the idea that strikes could be other than violent. "It is idle to talk of a peaceable strike," he declared. "None such ever occurred. The suggestion is impeachment of intelligence. From first to last . . . force and turbulence, violence and outrage, arson and murder, have been associated with the strike as its natural and inevitable concomitants. No strike can be effective without compulsion and force. . . . It has been well said that the wit of man could not devise a legal strike, because compulsion is the leading idea of it." It was this necessary violence that made strikes illegal, he continued, and the moment violence became "an essential part of a scheme or a necessary means of effecting the purpose of a combination, that moment the combination, otherwise lawful, becomes illegal."

Although Jenkins had modified, with duty, the right of workmen to quit, he insisted upon absolute freedom for the owners of property in the conduct of their business affairs. "All combinations to interfere with perfect freedom in the proper management and control of one's lawful business, to dictate the terms upon which such business shall be conducted, by means of threats or by interference with property or traffic or with the lawful employment of others," he ruled, "are within the condemnation of the law."[56]

Even before Jenkins' harsh decision of April 6, there was a public outcry against the repressive injunctions he had issued in December. In early March the House of Representatives voted to investigate to determine whether or not the judge had "exceeded his jurisdiction in granting such writs, abused the powers or process of said court, or oppressively exercised [them], or has used his office as judge to intimidate or wrongfully restrain the employees of the Northern Pacific . . . or the officers of the labor organizations . . .," and to recommend appropriate measures to the House.[57]

The majority of the committee found itself in complete disagreement with a number of the legal conclusions of the judge and some of the procedures he had tolerated. They were surprised that Jenkins saw no impropriety in the receivers meeting with the regular managers of the road in deciding upon the wage cuts, whereas, he had not regarded it necessary to hear the views of "the other servants of the court (under the supposition that all those employed in the operation of the road were such servants) who were to be affected by the decree he was making." As for the injunctions, the committee held that the initial writ went "far beyond any heretofore rendered," that it was not sustained by either reason or authority, and that it was an unconstitutional, unlawful abuse of judicial power. The supplementary injunction it characterized as "more reprehensible than the first."

The majority report condemned Jenkin's notion that a lawful strike was impossible. If true, the laboring classes would have taken from them "the only means which they have of resisting what they may consider oppression and of calling the attention of the country to it." Should Jenkins' interpretation be upheld, the committee declared, it would strike a fatal blow at all labor organizations. The committee defended the right of laborers to organize "to procure the best rate of wages obtainable, the shortest and best hours of labor, and the greatest advantages generally for themselves." Of course, they added, if workers attempted to bar others from taking over the jobs they left, destroyed property, or interfered with the operation of their employer's business, they would be engaged in unlawful, criminal acts.

The committee found no evidence that Judge Jenkins had acted with corrupt intent and conceded that he had probably acted in accord with his interpretation of his powers. For the future, however, the committee recommended that Congress prohibit courts from "commanding performance of a labor contract or compelling involuntary servitude under any pretext," and that it define and limit the power of courts to punish for contempt. The committee offered a resolution of censure, condemning the injunctions of December 19 and 22 because they, in effect, forbade employees to quit their jobs and union officials to exercise their lawful functions. It did not, however, call for impeachment proceedings against Jenkins.[58]

A minority report was succinct and to the point. "[I]f he [Jenkins] has been corrupt, or has so wrested the law of the land that injustice has been done, so evident that it carries with it the proof of evil intent, then Congress has a plain duty to perform. But if it be a mere question of law, then the judiciary have the duty to perform and Congress, by granting a court of appeals, has ended its duty." If Jenkins' ruling upon appeal should be upheld, demonstrating the defects of existing law, Congress should then change the law. "But," the report continued, "we ought to know what the law is before we act. If it should be finally determined that Judge Jenkins was wrong, then the law may not need amendment." As for the majority recommendations, the minority thought them contradictory and confusing. "The committee think he was wrong, and yet they propose to act as if he were right." The proposed censure of the injunctions should be defeated because it confused the respective functions of the legislature and the judiciary. The House took no action whatever.[59]

Jenkins' decision outlawed the proposed strike on the Northern Pacific and severely restricted the right of men to quit the service of the company peacefully. Coupled with the various decisions proscribing boycotts, the courts appeared to be in the process of depriving labor of two of the principal weapons it used to protect itself. Jenkins' ruling was, of course, appealed. Before the ruling of the higher court was handed down in October 1894, however, the pressures of depression had driven workmen on the railroads to more desperate measures than mere threats of strike or boycott.

CHAPTER VI

Dress Rehearsal: Coxey's Army and the Great Northern Strike

THE RELATIVELY MINOR RAILWAY labor disputes that accompanied the onset of the Panic of 1893 gave way, in the second spring of the depression, to marching bands of unemployed men and to increasingly severe strikes along the nation's railways. The federal courts had been able to cope with a number of the earlier disputes, but now the executive was obliged to deal with these more serious affairs, sometimes by resorting to force. Events were moving rapidly toward the climactic labor dispute of the era, the Chicago railway boycott and strike of 1894. Just ahead of that upheaval, however, two lesser disorders, the march of the Commonweal industrial armies and the Great Northern strike, contributed significantly to the manner in which the federal government would suppress the great strike.

In handling these affairs, and the later Chicago strike, the Cleveland administration betrayed a strong predisposition in favor of capital and property rights as against the interests and rights of working men. It leaned even more heavily against labor than the Hayes administration had, possibly because business was so much more in the saddle in 1894 than it had been in 1877. The Cleveland administration also was more closely tied to the business and railroad communities than Hayes and his advisers had been.[1] The President, between his two terms, had acquired a modest fortune and a number of influential and wealthy new friends. Instead of returning to his home in Buffalo, he had practiced law in informal association with the New York City firm of Bangs, Stetson, Tracy & MacVeagh. Francis Lynde Stetson of that firm, Cleveland's friend and adviser since

1882, was an attorney for the House of Morgan.[2] E. C. Benedict, gas magnate and financier, became the former President's close friend and next-door neighbor. Not only did Benedict give the President tips on the stockmarket, he also served as Cleveland's mentor and agent in personal investments on Wall Street before, during, and after his second term. The two men also shared a joint banking account which Benedict kept solvent by generous deposits.[3] Other representatives of the New York business world close to the President included William C. Whitney and Charles S. Fairchild, members of Cleveland's first-term cabinet, and Oscar S. Straus. Whitney, a multimillionaire, invested heavily in street railways and banks; Fairchild had become one of New York's leading bankers; and Straus had made a fortune in the department store business.[4]

Almost to a man Cleveland's second-term cabinet members shared with their chief a conservative, business point of view. Secretary of State Walter Q. Gresham apparently had the fewest direct ties to the business and railroad worlds. As a federal judge, however, he had rendered conspicuous service since 1877 in protecting railroads from strikes and boycotts.[5] Secretary of War Daniel S. Lamont, like the President, had used the years between the two administrations to accumulate the beginnings of a substantial fortune. In association with William C. Whitney and Oliver Payne, Lamont had profited handsomely from street railway investments. By 1893 he was a director in no fewer than fifteen corporations including the Continental National Bank of New York and the New York Security & Trust Company.[6] Postmaster General Wilson S. Bissell, a lifelong friend of the President, was one of the leading railroad lawyers of western New York. At the time he joined the cabinet he was counsel, in Buffalo, for the Reading railroad and president of the Buffalo & Southwestern. Previously, he had been president of the Buffalo & Rochester and a director and counsel of several other railroads.[7] It is not clear whether Bissell broke these ties upon entering public office.

The one Westerner in the cabinet, Secretary of Agriculture J. Sterling Morton, had fought against Western "agrarianism" for over twenty years. In the battles over railroad rate regulation in Nebraska, the CB&Q hired Morton to use his newspaper to promote railroad interests and to oppose "granger" legislation. In the mid-1880's the same company employed him to lobby in the nation's capital against the interstate commerce bill.[8] The three Southerners in the cabinet were no more representative of the Southern view than Morton was of the Western. Hilary 'A. Herbert, the secretary of the Navy, belonged to the old "redeemer" element that had tried to bind the "New South" to the business East rather than to the agrarian West.[9] Hoke Smith, who headed the Department of the Interior, belonged to the younger generation of Southern Democrats. Though his fame as a lawyer rested on successful personal damage suits against railroad companies and his policy as editor of the Atlanta *Journal* called for strict railroad regulation, he was a business-minded conservative reformer. Atlanta friends of the Burlington's president, C. E. Perkins, regarded Smith as "a first rate man."[10] Secretary of the Treasury John G. Carlisle, in spite of an early flirtation with soft-money heresies, by the end of his term in office was called the "Judas from Kentucky" for his rigid defense of the gold standard during the Panic of 1893.[11]

The cabinet member who, more than any other, shaped strike policy was Attorney General Richard Olney. Of the group, Olney had had the longest and most intimate association with the business world. For nearly twenty years he had been one of Boston's leading railroad and corporation lawyers. He had served as a director and counsel of the Boston & Maine since 1884 and of the Boston-dominated Burlington since 1889. These were but two of the many railroad and other corporate interests that employed Olney regularly in one capacity or another.[12]

As the news columnist Alfred Henry Lewis observed, "in picking up politics, Olney [had] not mislaid any of his connections" in the business world.[13] To preserve his law practice, Olney, who had no partners or firm to handle his clients' affairs while he was in Washington, continued to serve his employers as much as his public duties allowed. With the consent of the companies involved, he continued on, while attorney general, as director and counsel of both the Boston & Maine and the Burlington and as a director of the Old Colony Trust Company. The Burlington alone paid him $10,000 per year for services rendered; the attorney generalship but $8000.[14]

Despite these intimate connections with commercial, financial, and railroad interests, Cleveland and his advisers were not pliant tools of the business community. In the first place, business as such was not a tight-knit group with a rigid, uniform point of view or set of objectives; in the second, Cleveland often was at odds with large numbers of businessmen over such issues as tariff reform and the restriction of immigration, to name but two. Rather, when issues arose between the business community and other segments of society, such as agriculture or labor, the administration understood, sympathized with, and often aided the side of business. When Cleveland and his advisers saw property interests under attack from lingering "grangerism," the free silver heresy, Populism, the Single Tax Movement, trust-busters, the income tax, and dozens of other crazes, it was not surprising that they acted to protect those interests. During the railroad strikes, Cleveland—if not all of his advisers—thought of himself as being neutral and fair and acting only to preserve the public interest. Usually, as the President and his advisers saw it, the public interest coincided with that of the railroad companies. Far from accepting labor's point of view, they simply did not comprehend it.

Widespread unemployment in the severe winter of 1893–94 lay behind the rise of the Commonweal industrial armies in April 1894. To solve the problem of unemployment, Jacob S. Coxey, a Massillon, Ohio, manufacturer-reformer, proposed a program of public works projects, sponsored by local governments and financed through interest-free federal loans, that would employ men who were out of work. When his scheme failed to find support in Congress, Coxey hit upon the notion of a "petition-in-boots" to Congress by an army of unemployed men who would lobby for the measure. Coxey left Massillon on Easter Sunday 1894, with a straggle of about one hundred men. He predicted that by the time his little band reached Washington on May Day it would swell to a hundred-thousand strong.[15]

The greatest response to Coxey's call was in the trans-Mississippi West, where large numbers of men, many of whom were railroad construction workers, had been thrown out of work when the depression halted all building. Armies of from five hundred to a thousand men sprang up under ad hoc leaders in Seattle, Portland, Tacoma, San Francisco, Butte, and as far east as Omaha. They demanded free transportation eastward from their former employers. When refused, they began to seize trains and to run them, without regard for schedules or safety, toward the nation's capital.[16]

Train stealing was not a federal offense, though it was a violation of state law in most instances. Ordinarily, these lawless acts would have been dealt with by local police agencies, or these failing, by state militias. In many of the Western trouble

spots, however, public sympathies apparently lay with the unemployed rather than with the railroad corporations. Some
states had no militia whatever, others had but inadequate forces,
and in a few states the governors refused to use the militia
against the train-stealing Coxeyites.[17]

Thanks to the Panic, the main rail lines between the Pacific
Coast and the Mississippi Valley were in the hands of federal
receivers. As property in the custody of federal courts, they were
entitled to the protection of the federal government and anyone
interfering with their operation was in contempt of court. Once
again the device of receivership drew the federal government
into a situation that ordinarily would have been regarded as
outside its province.

The Union Pacific, on Saturday, April 21, became the first
railroad to seek federal aid in protecting its properties from
Coxeyites. Both the receivers of the company and George
Hoadly, special counsel for United States government interests
in the line, wired the attorney general that an industrial army
from California, led by Charles T. Kelly, threatened the company's property in the Omaha-Council Bluffs area. The receivers asked that "a sufficient military force" be sent to the area
to protect the property of the company and, they carefully
added, "the large interests of the United States that are therein
involved."[18]

By chance, Attorney General Olney was in Boston when the
wires arrived. However, Solicitor General Lawrence Maxwell,
Jr., promptly sent the requests for aid to Secretary of War
Lamont. Lamont in turn conferred with the President and reported back that the President found "no authority for the
employment of troops in such a case except where legal process
has been issued and its execution obstructed by force, and when
such condition is made known to the President by the court
having custody of the property." This information Maxwell re-
layed in full to Hoadly the next day.[19]

When Olney returned to Washington on April 23, telegrams on his desk informed him that a critical situation was
developing on both the Union Pacific and Northern Pacific
lines. At Council Bluffs a mob had seized a Union Pacific train
and offered it to Kelly's army; at Butte another industrial army,
led by a man named Hogan, had occupied the yards of the
Northern Pacific and blocked the passage of all trains.[20] The
federal marshal at Butte, W. M. McDermott, requested instructions: should he seek aid from the state militia or the regular

Army, or should he swear in a force of deputy marshals? Olney promptly authorized the swearing in of as many deputies as might be needed "to execute any order of United States Court."[21] Inasmuch as the marshal had mentioned no court order, it would appear that Olney was laying the groundwork for intervention by the United States Army rather than relying upon state or local forces.

The crisis came next day, April 24. Counsel for the receivers of the Northern Pacific, James McNaught of New York City, telegraphed Olney that the receivers had secured "writs of injunction" from the federal courts enjoining all persons from interfering with the railroad. On April 23, he continued, the United States marshal and seven deputies attempted to execute the court order but had been prevented from doing so by a mob of Coxeyite sympathizers. A contingent of Coxeyites then took possession of the railroad yards, made up a train, boarded it, and departed for the East at forty miles per hour "with great danger to life and property." McNaught informed Olney that Federal Judge Hiram Knowles had been asked to make formal request for assistance in serving and enforcing his orders. The governor of North Dakota and Minnesota had also been asked to use the forces at their disposal to execute the court orders and, if these were inadequate, to make formal request to the President for federal assistance. Finally, McNaught said, he had fully apprised John M. Schofield, general in chief of the United States Army, of the situation.[22]

General Schofield's reply probably gave McNaught little comfort. Although he agreed to lay the matter before the President as soon as the President was not busy, it was his personal opinion that federal intervention was unwarranted. The governor of Minnesota had an adequate militia force to arrest the train stealers. "Surely," he added, "it cannot be difficult to stop the progress of that train at any point you may elect to do so, and thus detain the culprits until the State troops can arrest them." Only when it was demonstrated that state forces could not cope with the problem would a governor be justified in asking for federal assistance.[23]

Olney apparently made no direct reply to McNaught, but it was soon evident that he did not share General Schofield's views. Judge Knowles's request for federal troops, countersigned by the United States attorney for Montana, was not long in coming. In it the judge said that he had issued an order on April 20 for the arrest of Hogan at Butte because he and his followers were in contempt of court for having seized property in the hands of a court-appointed receiver. It was this order for arrest—and not an injunction as McNaught had stated—that Marshal McDermott had been unable to execute.[24] Olney responded by telling Knowles that federal troops could be employed only after the court certified to the President that the execution of a legal process was obstructed by force "not to be overcome in the ordinary manner." Judge Knowles shot back the request for aid in the specified form: "Hogan and others resist an order to arrest them . . . by force which cannot be overcome in the ordinary manner."[25]

Meanwhile, two other telegrams related to the troubles in Montana arrived at the Justice Department. Marshal McDermott, upon the advice of attorneys of the Northern Pacific, wired that he and his deputies had been unable to prevent the industrial army from stealing a train and escaping. He now requested military assistance for recapturing the train. The second telegram, from McNaught in New York, reported that a landslide near Bozeman, Montana, had halted the stolen train, and he suggested that assistance at once would prevent "great damage and probably loss of life."[26]

Armed with these telegrams, Olney went to the White House the night of April 24 to present the case for using federal troops. The attorney general argued that it was "the sole alternative left to the government;" his carefully marshaled evidence pointed to no other conclusion. The order of a federal court was being defied, and the marshal, the United States attorney, and the judge himself all certified that they had no force at their disposal for executing the order of the court. The President seemingly had no recourse but to order out the Army. Cleveland summoned General Schofield, who may have opposed the plan. After a full discussion the attorney general's recommendation was followed. Troops were dispatched to Bozeman to capture and hold the Hoganites until the marshal could catch up with them.[27] Any scruples the President may have had with regard to sending the Army into a sovereign state were satisfied next day when the governor of Montana wired for assistance, it being "impossible," he said, "for the state militia to overtake" the Hoganites.[28]

Like Hayes before him, Cleveland strained at gnats while swallowing a camel. He insisted upon all the niceties with respect to the outer forms of intervention but gave little, if any, attention to substantive questions. As General Schofield wrote to McNaught, it surely did not require the United States Army to halt a stolen train. It would seem that by simply throwing a switch and guarding it against tampering, the company could have sidetracked the Hoganites almost at will. But the railroad officials wanted more than their train back; they wanted the Hoganites taken prisoner and punished as an example to others.

Hogan and his men, meanwhile, had cleared the track at Bozeman and raced on. Stopping near Forsyth, Montana, to camp for the night of April 25, they were overtaken by the Army about midnight. Three hundred and thirty-one men were taken prisoner and about 250 others escaped in the darkness. Marshal McDermott wired Washington for further instructions. "I have been disposed to be governed by the railroad company's attorneys and the U.S. Attorney here," he said, but was concerned about taking his prisoners to Helena because of "a great deal of excitement in all towns along the line of the Northern Pacific. . . ." Such an undertaking, he believed, would necessitate the use of troops as guards along the way and at Helena.[29]

McNaught, the previous day, had advised Olney of the "necessity and right" of using troops to keep the "mob" in custody until the orders of the court were executed. He assured the attorney general that the prisoners would all be prosecuted "for contempt and also criminally."[30] Olney thereupon ordered McDermott to take all the prisoners, without exception, before the court in Helena and advised that federal troops would be provided for escorting and guarding the prisoners until they were dealt with by the court.[31]

The capture of Hogan's army did not restore peace to the railroads of the far Northwest. Other bands of restless men had formed in the major cities of Washington and Oregon and in the Coeur d'Alene district of Idaho, and were ready to march. Federal Judge Hanford of Washington informed Olney on April 24 that he had ordered the marshal in his district to protect the property of the Northern Pacific, particularly in the cities of Seattle, Tacoma, and Spokane. Olney immediately confirmed the judge's orders by authorizing the marshal, J. C. Drake, to employ as many deputies as he might need. By the 26th, Drake had sworn in a force of two hundred men. Meanwhile, on the 25th, 700 Coxeyites from Seattle and another 500 from Tacoma set out on foot for Meeker Junction, Washington. There the combined 1200, Drake believed, would probably attempt to seize a train.[32]

At about the same time that the Seattle-Tacoma industrial

armies began their march, 500 or so other Coxeyites marched out from Portland along the tracks of the Union Pacific as far as Troutdale, Oregon. On April 27 an empty freight train, with United States Marshal H. C. Grady and two deputies in the cab, was run out to the Coxeyite encampment. The apparent object was to induce the Commonwealers to commit an overt act so that action might be taken against them. The Coxeyites obliged the marshal by mobbing the train as soon as it stopped. Grady, thereupon, cut off the engine and left the scene with the Coxeyites in possession of the freight cars. In a wire to Attorney General Olney, Grady stated that the train had been seized and that he was powerless to recapture it. He did not mention his role as agent provocateur or the fact that the Commonwealers were stranded in a train without an engine.

About noon the next day the general manager of the Union Pacific arrived at Troutdale in his special train to look over the situation. The Coxeyites disconnected the engine from the special, attached it to the freight cars, and left for the East at full speed. Marshal Grady and his deputies, who were unarmed, found Troutdale full of sympathy for the Coxeyites and were unable to secure local assistance. The sheriff of the county was persuaded by Grady to request Governor Sylvester Pennoyer of Oregon to order out the state militia. When the governor refused, Grady and Federal Judge Charles B. Bellinger turned to the Justice Department, requesting that federal troops intercept the stolen train at Walla Walla.[33]

Again the Cleveland administration was called upon to make a decision, and again it would appear that there was not complete agreement as to the course to be pursued. The Army had been used in Montana to enforce a court order when state forces proved inadequate and the governor, albeit tardily, had asked for aid. In the Oregon situation, however, the governor had refused to use his own forces and had made no request for troops to the President. As for Washington state, federal officials there hinted broadly at the need for aid, not to recapture a stolen train, but to prevent the theft of a train.

The President, Secretary Lamont, Attorney General Olney, and General Schofield met the morning of April 28 to consider whether or not to use troops again in the Northwest. Olney, as earlier in the week, again presented the case for intervention. In the Hoganite affair troops had been sent under Section 5297 of the *Revised Statutes* to suppress an "insurrection" in Montana, upon the application of the governor of the state. Now the Army was to be used under Section 5298, which empowered the President to employ the militia or federal troops whenever, in his judgment, it was impracticable to enforce federal laws in the ordinary ways because of "unlawful obstructions, combinations, or assemblages of persons," or "rebellion" against federal authority.[34]

Following the meeting, General Schofield wrote to Secretary Lamont in what seems to have been a final effort to delay the use of troops. He called attention to Section 5300 of the *Revised Statutes,* which provided that when the President judged it necessary to use the Army under Section 5298, he was to issue "forthwith" a proclamation commanding the "insurgents to disperse and retire peaceably to their respective abodes within a limited time." "It has occurred to me," Schofield wrote, "that the Attorney General may possibly have overlooked this Section. . . ." The general thought a proclamation had to precede the use of troops according to law, and he recalled that such proclamations had been issued before troops were used during the strikes of 1877.[35]

The afternoon of April 28, the President and Secretary of War Lamont met and, without issuing a proclamation, ordered troops to intercept the train stolen at Troutdale.[36] Marshal Grady wired next day that the Coxeyites had been captured without injury to persons or property and that he was taking them to Portland for trial. The same day Marshal Drake wired Olney from Meeker Junction, Washington, that "railroad officials think and I concur that it would be advisable to have U.S. troops on the ground." He did not mention that three regiments of state militia were already on hand. The result was that federal troops were stationed at Spokane and alerted for action in other parts of Washington and Idaho.[37] Although there had been no requests from the governors of the states involved, the United States Army was used both to recapture trains and to guard against train thefts where mobs threatened to get out of hand.

During the next few weeks the Army, time and again, was called on to guard against train seizures and to recapture trains taken by Coxeyites.[38] By the end of April the formula for calling out the Army had become almost automatic: the receivers of a threatened railroad would go to a federal judge and secure an injunction forbidding interference with the property in their custody; when the injunction was ignored and property was taken, or when such appeared to be imminent, the judge, the marshal, and the federal attorney would wire Olney, describing the situation and requesting military assistance; Olney, in turn, would take the telegrams to the White House and secure the President's authorization for the use of the Army.

Because he knew the grounds upon which the President would allow the use of federal troops, Olney was not indiscriminate in recommending the employment of the Army despite a steady flow of requests from federal officials and from railroad attorneys. The arguments accompanying the requests were varied and at times persuasive: the government could effect tremendous savings by using the Army rather than hiring a host of deputy marshals at $5.00 each per diem; mobs were more respectful of the Army than of a marshal and his deputies; and the mere presence of the military caused industrial armies to melt away.[39] Inasmuch as none of these arguments justified the use of the Army in Cleveland's view, Olney rejected them without presenting them to the President. When a federal judge asked for troops to help capture thirty armed Coxeyites, Olney refused on the grounds that the marshal had not exhausted the ordinary resources at his command; that is, he had not sought authorization to hire a force of deputies or to raise a posse adequate to execute the orders of the court. Until these means proved ineffective, the Army could not be called into action. When troops were ordered to intervene to prevent trouble, Olney charged the federal judge of the district involved "to see to it that troops are employed only in case of exigency making such employment necessary and legally justifiable."[40]

The thwarting of the Western industrial armies by the railroads, the Justice Department, and the Army in April, converted Coxey's May Day parade up Pennsylvania Avenue into a humiliating, comic-opera rout. A scant 600 men marched on the capitol. When Coxey attempted to speak from the steps of the Capitol Building, mounted policemen chased him across the capitol grounds. With his army standing by, awestruck, Coxey was arrested and later fined for walking on the grass. His movement, though it lingered on in and around Washington for several weeks, was already dead.[41]

Concurrent with the march of the Western Coxeyites was the brief but significant strike on the Great Northern railroad west

of St. Paul. The strike was notable because it involved Eugene
V. Debs, who would later achieve considerable notoriety during
the Pullman strike, and the American Railway Union (ARU),
which he headed. More important, however, was a ruling regarding mail trains, drawn up by underlings of the Postoffice
and Justice departments and handed down during the strike.
Although it was of little consequence to the Great Northern
strike, it had the effect of putting the ARU in violation of
federal postal laws from the very outset of the union's boycott
of Pullman cars in June.

The Great Northern, like many other railways during the
depression years, brought on the strike by reducing wages.
Three times between August 1893 and March 1894 wages were
cut; three times the officers of the railway brotherhoods, to
which many of the Great Northern's employees belonged,
recommended to the men that they accept the cuts. The ARU,
however, rejected the third reduction and called for a meeting
to discuss wages with the president of the railway, James J. Hill.
Doubting that the union spoke for any significant number of his
employees, Hill refused to meet with ARU officials. The union,
thereupon, called a strike on April 13, 1894.[42]

The ARU was not yet a year old when the strike began,
but it had an energetic and resourceful leader in Debs. For
years a railway brotherhood official himself, Debs had come to
the conclusion that the brotherhoods could accomplish little
for railway employees. During strikes the brotherhoods frequently were at odds and the companies played one off against
the other, defeating them all. To halt this disunity, Debs organized the ARU on the principle that all railroad employees,
regardless of function or skill, should belong to one great union.
He hoped the organization would come to embrace so many of
the nation's railway workers that no company would be able to
resist the union's demands. Strikes, which were so costly to
working men, would no longer be necessary because the companies would yield to the union rather than risk the loss of
their entire labor force.[43]

In April 1894 the ARU was not the powerful labor combine it dreamed of becoming. It was willing, however, to strike
rather than accept another wage cut. The union gauged accurately the sentiments of the men, for not only its own members,
but many brotherhood members, joined the walkout. The strike
was conducted effectively. Debs urged his men not only to avoid

violence, which would play into the hands of Hill, but to guard property of the company. The union further agreed to move mail trains so long as no passengers or freight were transported along with the mail. The company refused to adopt this last suggestion. The strike, however, was a complete success; not one freight train moved over the line throughout the tie-up. All attempts of the company to secure men to run trains failed, even though brotherhood officials, out of fear and spite for the new union, aided in the search for recruits.[44]

After about a week, Hill, realizing the strike was succeeding, began moves to secure federal intervention. On April 19 he wired Olney that "a strike on three hours notice has occurred on our railway preventing the movement of our trains. It was instigated and is being conducted by men not in Company's employ. It is being carefully met on strictly legal grounds." This wire probably was designed to do no more than alert Olney to the situation.[45]

The next move, made April 21, was initiated by James E. White, general superintendent of the railway mail service. Whether White acted on his own or at the prompting of officials of the Great Northern is not known. White secured from the Justice Department an official opinion of the attorney general which undertook to define precisely a "mail train." Neither Congress nor the federal courts had ever defined the term, and the contracts between the companies and the Postoffice Department did not specify the exact makeup of such trains.

Superintendent White was a veteran in the wars against strikers. It was he, who, as division superintendent of the railway mail service at Chicago, in 1877, had warned strikers that any interference with mail-bearing passenger trains constituted obstruction of the mail and would be severely punished. Postmaster General Dickinson's ruling during the Burlington strike, that railroads were obliged to haul mail even if they did no other business, seemed outrageous to White. He considered that policy "unjust, shirking responsibilities, licensing lawlessness as to the other trains, and unworthy of our country."[46]

When the Democrats returned to power in 1893, White, a Republican, feared ouster from his position as division superintendent. President Perkins of the Burlington wrote Olney (then attorney for the company, but not yet attorney general of the United States), asking him to use his influence with the incoming administration to retain White in office.[47] President Cleveland, far from dismissing White, promoted him to head the railway mail service. The new general superintendent promptly set to work to have a law passed to protect the mails during strikes. Unlike Postmaster Generals Key and Dickinson, who had asked for legislation compelling railroads to deliver mail even during strikes, White urged Congress to make it a federal offense to "delay, obstruct, or prevent the passage of any train on any railroad in the United States" by which mails were being transported in order to aid a strike or for any other "malicious purpose." Postmaster General Bissell, a longtime railroad lawyer and sometime railroad executive, apparently approved White's recommendation as he submitted it to Congress in his *Annual Report* for 1893.[48] Congress, however, failed to act on the recommendation.

On April 21, 1894, White telegraphed Bissell, who was in Buffalo, for permission to seek an opinion from the attorney general respecting the stoppage of mail-carrying passenger trains of the Great Northern by strikers. Attorney General Olney was also out of town, so White, with Bissell's permission, discussed the situation with Lawrence Maxwell, the solicitor general. Maxwell, while in office, retained a number of close railroad ties. He had been counsel of the Cincinnati, Hamilton & Dayton since 1887, and in March 1895 would become a director of the company. In October 1894 he accepted election to the board of directors of the Cincinnati, New Orleans & Texas Pacific.[49] The solicitor general "astonished" White by asking him to wait a few minutes until he could prepare "the opinion of the Department." White "never waited for anything so cheerfully," and when the opinion was handed him, he found that it coincided exactly with his views. "In my judgment," White said, "the opinion was all wool and much more than a yard wide—wide enough to win the Great Northern and Chicago battles."[50] The law recommended by White, which Congress had not enacted, in a sense now became law through the opinion issued by the solicitor general in the name of the attorney general.[51]

Maxwell, referring both to statute law and to decided cases, held that it was an offense for anyone to obstruct or retard the passage of a train carrying the mail. It was no excuse that the person was willing to allow the mail car to proceed alone. The mail must be permitted to pass "in the usual and ordinary way." Strikers who had stopped mail trains, "it would seem," had already brought themselves within the provisions of the law against conspiracy and could be punished by the heavy penalties attending that crime.[52]

Pertinent parts of Maxwell's opinion and the penalties involved were then posted on the sides of Great Northern mail trains. Inasmuch as mail was regularly carried on but one through passenger train daily each way on the Great Northern, however, the strikers were able to comply with the ruling and still paralyze the freight business of the railroad.[53]

President Hill kept the administration posted on strike developments. He obviously would have been pleased had aid been given him in the form of federal troops. After a hint or two, Hill wired Cleveland on April 28 that "the authority of law & its officers are openly defied and ridiculed. The assistance of federal troops has been asked for by marshals. Any display of federal authority supported by troops will at once restore order. I hope this may be done."[54] Since the Great Northern was plagued simultaneously by train-stealing Coxeyites and strikers, it is not clear whether Hill wanted soldiers for fighting Coxeyites or for breaking the strike. He probably made no great distinction in his own mind between the two.

Attorney General Olney suspected that Hill wanted the troops for strikebreaking purposes. He cautioned Secretary Lamont against allowing troops "to be employed merely as constables to help chase and arrest particular persons charged with crime. You will notice too," Olney continued, "that on the Great Northern Railroad the present difficulties grow out of the strike between the Railroad Company and its employees. in which the employees may possibly be right. . . ." Moreover, he observed, it appeared from newspaper accounts that the strike was about to be settled. "Any unnecessary interposition of the military would, of course, aggravate matters." The next day, May 1, the strike ended when both sides accepted the ruling of a board of arbitration which was an all-but-complete victory for the union.[55]

The battle against the Coxeyites in the West produced no new legal developments. The "injunctions" issued by federal courts were simple orders to United States marshals to protect property in the custody of the court and represented no innovation whatever.[56] The contributions to federal strike policy of the Coxeyite affair were made in the executive branch of government. There, Attorney General Olney showed himself amenable to acting upon the requests, recommendations, and suggestions of railroad officials. Cleveland, in turn, again revealed his tendency to allow subordinates to shape policies for him. This had been true with respect to Postmaster General Dickinson during the Burlington strike of 1888; now it was repeated with respect to Attorney General Olney during the Coxeyite struggle. The latter affair also had the effect of conditioning the President to the use of federal troops at the call of federal judges. All these factors would reappear and be enlarged upon during the Pullman strike.

Finally, out of the Great Northern strike came the Justice Department's ruling which had the effect of putting every car of every mail-carrying train, as made up by the railroads, under the protection of the United States government. Given little attention at the time, this legal time bomb ticked quietly away, to explode, only eight weeks later, full force upon Eugene Debs and the American Railway Union.

CHAPTER VII

• • •

Climax: The Chicago Railway
Strike of 1894

THE CHICAGO RAILWAY BOYCOTT and strike of 1894, more commonly known as the Pullman strike, was the climax to nearly two decades of intermittent struggle between railroads and their employees. Because both sides were more effectively organized than ever before, the strike was one of the most intense and bitterly fought labor disputes in the country's history. Once again the federal government intervened on several fronts to halt blockage of the nation's transportation arteries.

Directing the course of the boycott and strike for labor was the American Railway Union, headed by Eugene V. Debs. Though now only a year old, the organization had already won its spurs in the fight in April against James J. Hill and the Great Northern. Following that victory, railway workers across the country (but especially in the Chicago area and in the trans-Mississippi West) flocked to its banners. By June 1894 it claimed 150,000 members and was growing rapidly.[1] To the ARU's existing strengths of bold dedicated leadership and unity when dealing with the railroads was now added the strength of numbers.

The railroads of the greater Chicago area were even more effectively organized for battle than their employees. The general managers of Chicago's twenty-four railroad companies belonged to a semisecret organization, the General Managers Association (GMA). Originally founded in 1886, the GMA worked to establish common freight and passenger rates, wage scales, and labor policies for its member companies. Some of these activities were extralegal, if not illegal, and the organization remained informal and unincorporated. In its early years the GMA had found it difficult to maintain unity. Because of rate wars and the failure to work together during the Burlington strike, it suspended activities entirely in 1889. The organization remained dormant until resurrected in January 1892. By the outbreak of the great strike in 1894, the GMA had been functioning successfully for two and a half years.

Behind the GMA was tremendous wealth, power, and prestige. Among its members were the general managers of many of the leading railroad companies in the country: the Baltimore & Ohio, the Burlington, the Chicago & Northwestern, the Erie, the Illinois Central, the Northern Pacific, the Santa Fe, the Rock Island, the Pennsylvania, and the New York Central, to name but a few. The GMA represented a total capitalization of over $2 billion; its members employed over 220,000 men, operated more than 40,000 miles of road, and had netted in excess of $100 million in profits for the year ending June 30, 1894.[2]

The decisive role in the Chicago railway strike, however, was played by neither the ARU nor the GMA. Intervention by the federal government to crush the strike determined the final outcome. President Cleveland, as oblivious to the start of this dispute as he had been to the major strikes of his first term (the Southwest in 1886 and the Burlington in 1888) and as Hayes had been to the strikes of 1877, did nothing to avert the coming clash. Even after the boycott-strike was under way he failed to use the investigative commission provided for in the Act of 1888 to attempt a peaceful settlement. Only after the strike was broken did he appoint a commission to study its causes and to recommend legislation.

Although intervention in 1894 was forced upon Cleveland by circumstances he had not shaped, federal intervention was not wholly unguided. Attorney General Olney, as he had in his war against the Coxeyites, followed the affair from its inception and was prepared to intervene quickly when occasion offered. Olney's policies, dictated to a large degree by his own predispositions in favor of the railroads, in the end became Cleveland's policies, and the actions taken, though they halted the strike, were grossly unfair to labor.

In its origins the strike of 1894 did not involve railroad companies, the ARU, or the federal government. Rather, what began as a dispute between the management and employees of the Pullman Palace Sleeping Car Company, near Chicago, escalated by stages into a general strike of the railways in and around Chicago and on westward to the Pacific Coast. The troubles began in April, in the shops and company town owned and operated by George M. Pullman, manufacturer of railway sleeping cars. Pullman, like many another businessman that spring, felt the effect of the Panic in reduced orders and less business. To offset these losses he reduced wages and staggered work schedules so as to keep most of his men employed, though for fewer hours a week. Pullman boasted of his kindness in doing everything within his power to assist "his children" (as he referred to his employees) through the difficult depression period.

The men, nonetheless, were aggrieved. Pullman, the company town, long regarded by outsiders as a model industrial community, was a flagrant example of feudalistic paternalism to those who lived under the all-pervading influence of the employer-landlord. Workmen disliked not being able to own their own homes or to participate in governing the town in which they lived. But the more immediate and practical causes of their discontent were wage rates and rents.

Not only were Pullman's employees working fewer hours at lower rates and, thus, earning substantially less than before the Panic, but the rents they paid for company housing remained unchanged. Rents in nearby communities ranged between 20 and 25 percent less. Moving to such accommodations offered no solution because it jeopardized one's job with the Pullman Company to leave its housing. Managers of the company, meanwhile, had not had their salaries cut, and the earnings of the company had declined little. There was an accumulated surplus of nearly $25 million on the company's books, and the usual 8 percent dividend had been paid on the stock in 1893.[3]

In the face of these conditions a number of Pullman employees organized and affiliated with Debs's American Railway Union. Soon after forming their union a representative delegation tried to induce the management to restore wages to the level of June 1893. If that could not be done, the delegates insisted that rents be scaled down in proportion to wage reductions. The company rejected both proposals outright, maintaining that wage rates and rents were completely unrelated. On May 10 three members of the grievance committee were dismissed from their jobs. The next day the employees went on strike and the company suspended operations.[4] Whatever may have been the rights of the company with respect to these matters, the wisdom of expecting labor to bear the brunt of the hard times was certainly open to question.

The Pullman strike was a month old when the ARU national convention met in Chicago in June. There the delegates listened to the grievances of their brethren from Pullman and determined to assist them in their struggle. The ARU delegates considered a boycott of Pullman cars but deferred so extreme a measure until efforts could be made to settle the dispute peacefully. Pullman declined to meet with a committee of ARU delegates, saying that he would not deal with men who were not employed by him. A second committee, made up of Pullman employees who belonged to the ARU, secured a hearing but were told that Pullman found nothing to arbitrate. In the light of the company's intransigency, the ARU had a choice of abandoning its members at Pullman or trying to bring pressure to bear. Newspapers at the time portrayed Debs as a power-hungry labor "dictator" who ordered his underlings to strike when, in fact, he had urged caution from the first. Precipitous action in time of widespread unemployment, he knew, would involve considerable risk for the young union. However, the ARU delegates, probably influenced by their recent victory over the Great Northern, voted unanimously to boycott all Pullman cars unless the company came to terms with its employees by noon, June 26. After that hour no ARU member was to handle Pullman cars or to move any train to which Pullman cars were attached. The convention then adjourned, leaving President Debs and the other officers of the union to conduct the boycott.[5]

In addition to the danger posed by hosts of the unemployed who stood ready to take abandoned jobs, there were other good reasons for the ARU not to stage a secondary boycott. A number of states, including Illinois, had antiboycotting statutes. Although there was no federal law against boycotting, federal courts had consistently held boycotts against railroads to be interference with interstate commerce. Boycotting had the further disadvantage of forcing ARU members to act against their employers, with whom they had no quarrel, so as to bring pressure to bear on Pullman and induce him to adjust the grievances of his employees. The railroad companies were not apt to acquiesce in such a scheme.

Overriding these objections, however, was the consideration that only a boycott seemed to hold any promise of success in forcing Pullman to terms. Moreover, it could be argued in answer to the legal objection, that a boycott of Pullman cars would not actually interfere with interstate commerce inasmuch as freight and passenger trains could continue to pass as usual so long as the railroad companies made no attempt to attach Pullman cars.

What was true of Pullman's policies respecting wage cuts was also true of the ARU's decision to boycott; although the union was wholly within its rights to test again the legality of boycotting, the wisdom of such a move was questionable. Certainly, it would be difficult to win and hold the support of the general public, which might possibly sympathize with men going on strike to redress their own grievances but would probably see little justification for a strike against innocent parties, the railroads, in order to bring pressure on Pullman to deal fairly with his employees.

Because the GMA and its member companies, as a matter of policy, refused all communications from the ARU, the union did not serve formal notice of the impending boycott. Railway officials, however, were fully aware of the embargo from notices in the newspapers and began taking counter-measures to thwart it even before it started. At a special meeting on June 25 the general managers voted to work together in resisting the boycott, and set forth reasons for resisting in a resolution issued to the public. The boycott, the managers declared, was related to matters over which they had no control and in which they had no interest. It was "confessedly not in the interest of any grievance between said railroad companies and said employees. . . ." Under these circumstances, for the companies to inconvenience the traveling public or to break existing contracts with the Pullman Company would be unjustified and unwarranted. Further, they held, it was "necessary" for the railroads to "determine for themselves" what cars they would or would not handle on their lines.[6]

Without discounting any of the stated reasons for their decision, it would appear that some factors were of considerably more importance than others in the decision to resist. The statement that to discontinue Pullman cars on passenger trains would violate existing contracts, for example, was an excuse rather than a reason for resisting the boycott. The sample contract presented to the United States Strike Commission at the close of the disorders and the testimony given by Everett St. John, general manager of the Rock Island railway and chairman of the GMA, revealed that the companies had complete discretion in the use of Pullmans. The contract made no mention of how many Pullman cars, or when, or on what classes of trains they were to be used. It simply provided that whenever sleeping cars were used they had to be leased from the Pullman Company. To the question of one of the strike commissioners, "Are you at liberty to leave Pullman cars off of any class of trains you desire?" St. John replied, "We are. We are not required to operate any of the Pullman cars upon trains where the cars are not required. It is entirely at the option of the company."[7]

Protection of managerial prerogatives and hostility toward the union which threatened those prerogatives seem to have had much to do with the decision to resist. This consideration, of course, was not among those listed in the GMA's resolution to the public. Almost from the inception of the new union the railroads had looked upon it as a potential source of trouble, and had treated it accordingly. The usual courtesies shown the brotherhoods, such as passes for officers, were never extended to the ARU or its officers. GMA Chairman St. John stated well the position of the companies with regard to the new union in his testimony before the Strike Commission: "As I understand it," he said, ". . . the American Railway Union is an effort to combine within its own order all employees of all branches of organized labor upon the various railroads as they have previously existed and I think there is no necessity for an organization of that kind. We have always gotten along comfortably well—in fact, in a very satisfactory manner—with the old orders as they exist."[8] Apparently, there was considerable concern among the railroads that the ARU, if successful, might alter existing relationships and relative strengths of management and labor which so comfortably favored the companies.[9]

When the ARU threw down its gauntlet, the railways had the choice of surrendering or accepting the challenge. To surrender, that is to make up trains without Pullman cars, might possibly have led to legal action against them by the Pullman Company and certainly would have inconvenienced their passengers. But more important, surrender would have vastly strengthened the ARU and Debs. Resistance, on the other hand, involved no legal risks whatever and promised to check, if not eliminate, the power of the ARU. The GMA decided to resist.

As the boycott got underway, action began on several fronts to counteract it. The GMA met daily to formulate policy and to assure united action by the railroads. On June 27 the man-

agers named John M. Egan, former general manager of the
Chicago & Great Western and for six years a member of the
GMA, director of resistance for the companies. As might be expected, the managers at first regarded boycotting by their
employees as primarily a disciplinary matter to be met by firm
disciplinary measures. They discussed what to do about men
who were willing to perform all their duties excepting where
Pullman cars were involved and concluded that any man refusing to do his whole duty would be dismissed. A standing committee of the GMA was authorized to begin recruiting replace-
ments for men who were discharged or who might quit. It
was further agreed that all expenses incurred in fighting the
boycott, including all costs of recruiting and maintaining new
men, would be prorated among the Chicago railroads.[10] These
decisions, as it turned out, would shortly convert the boycott
into a general railway strike.

Meanwhile, in Washington, Attorney General Olney was
moving to break the boycott on purely legal grounds. Far from
standing neutral or being reluctant to intervene, Olney from
the first was willing to throw the full weight of the federal
government into crushing the boycott. The device he initially
hit upon was protecting Pullmans by protecting the mail. Pullman cars were attached only to passenger trains; passenger trains
carried the mail; according to the *Official Opinions of the Attorneys-General* issued during the Great Northern strike in April,
every car of any train carrying mail was part of the mail train
and entitled to federal protection; hence, any ARU member
who cut off a Pullman car from a train carrying mail, or who
blocked passage of a mail train because it included Pullman cars,
was subject to punishment by the federal government.[11]

On June 23, two days after the announcement of the boycott but three days before it was to go into effect, Olney began
to marshal his forces. That day he ordered from the postmaster
general a complete set of railway postal route maps. When word
came on June 28 that mail was being delayed by the boycott, he
began issuing instructions to United States attorneys and marshals in troubled areas across the nation: "See that the passage
of regular trains carrying United States mails in the usual and
ordinary way, as contemplated by the act of Congress and
directed by the Postmaster-General, is not obstructed." He also
authorized the procuring of any necessary warrants or other
court processes and the swearing in of as many deputy marshals
or posses as might be needed to protect the mails.[12]

John W. Arnold, the United States marshal in Chicago, found himself scraping the bottom of the barrel for the men he needed to guard mail trains. To the dismay of the railroad companies, many of the men he deputized were mere "idlers" or were otherwise undesirable; some were even strikers. GMA officials, therefore, proposed to Arnold that loyal railroad employees, vouched for by the companies, be sworn in as deputy marshals. Relieved to be able to augment his forces with reliable men at no additional cost to his office, the marshal swore in 2887 railroad employees to supplement the 1589 men he had procured elsewhere. Thereafter, mail trains and other railroad property were protected by men wearing the badges of federal law officers, but who, in fact, were selected, armed, directed, and paid by the railroad companies themselves.[13]

Thomas Milchrist, the United States attorney in Chicago, read Olney's instructions to him regarding protection of the mails to the GMA the day after receiving them. Milchrist requested the railways to supply his office with the names of any persons who interfered in any way with the movement of trains carrying the mail or who cut off Pullman or other cars from mail-carrying trains. The managers saw the advantage of using the mails to protect sleeping cars and lent their full support to the plan. Some railroads reduced passenger service, and hence mail service, in an attempt to increase public sentiment in favor of federal intervention; others switched mail cars from their usual place immediately behind the coal tender to the end of the train so as to insure that if cars were cut off, the mail would be cut off too; and some were alleged to have carried mail on trains that had never carried it before.[14]

In a few instances companies stopped mail-bearing passenger trains considerable distances from Chicago, refusing to proceed farther because of "rioting" in the city. Postmaster General Bissell reminded these companies sharply of their duties as carriers of the mail. The mere anticipation of troubles in Chicago, he wrote officials of the Baltimore & Ohio, did not warrant stopping trains as far as 131 miles east of that city. The railroad companies generally found Postoffice Department officials cooperative, however. Chicago postal authorities, for example, announced June 30 that nearly all suburban passenger trains in the Chicago area would begin carrying mail after July 1 and would thereafter be under the protection of the United States government.[15]

Had the boycott remained only a boycott and not become

a full-scale strike, Olney's plan for using the mail to protect Pullman cars might have ended the affair. Official reports of postal authorities indicate that at least in the Chicago area passenger-mail trains moved freely except where blocked by abandoned freight trains. From the first, Debs and his associates feared the consequences of federal intervention. They announced that the ARU would move mail trains as it had during the Great Northern strike, provided that no Pullman cars were attached to them. The railroad companies, with the tacit acquiescence of the government, absolutely refused to move passenger-mail trains without the usual Pullman accommodations. For the most part the ARU permitted mail to pass unmolested, even when Pullman cars were carried, rather than risk trouble with the federal government.[16]

The issue of the mails might have been completely neutralized had Attorney General Olney or Postmaster General Bissell followed the precedent laid down by Postmaster General Dickinson during the Burlington strike. The government could either have taken the position that the companies were obliged to move the mail on regular passenger trains without Pullman cars or it could have demanded that the ARU allow one passenger-mail train with Pullman accommodations to pass each day each way over every line. Under either arrangement the mail would have been moved and the government could have avoided taking sides. But most of the legal precedents, the April ruling of the Justice Department regarding mail trains, and the predilections of federal officials who set policy laid with the pro-railroad position of frustrating the ARU's boycott by protecting mail trains as made up by the companies.

The boycott of Pullman cars did not long remain a mere boycott. As the general managers' policy of firing employees who refused to move sleeping cars went into effect, the embargo quickly changed into a general strike of railroads in and around Chicago and westward and southwestward to the Pacific Coast. When a man was discharged for not carrying out orders, all ARU members and sympathizers on that line promptly threw down their tools. Soon every railroad in the Chicago area was struck, and the ARU and GMA were locked in what each regarded as a life-and-death struggle. The general tie-up of all traffic became increasingly effective. Standing freights blocked the passage of nearly all trains, passenger and freight. Perishables spoiled as they stood hour after hour in the summer sun, and the early successes of the strikers threatened to undermine the morale of loyal railroad employees.[17] From the companies' point of view, something had to be done to break the ARU's strangle hold and to get both passenger and freight trains moving again.

In desperation the GMA sought further assistance from the federal government, and the eventual victory of the railroads was due to the active and open support received from that quarter. The decision to seek the alliance with Washington was made by the GMA upon the advice of a committee of its lawyers to which it had referred questions regarding legal steps to be taken against the strikers. Among the queries raised by the managers were whether they should institute proceedings against the ARU under Illinois law or federal law, whether persons interfering with interstate commerce should be prosecuted for conspiracy under the Sherman Antitrust Act, and whether or not various types of injunctions should be sought in the courts.

George R. Peck, chairman of the legal committee, reported that the lawyers believed the boycott-strike violated both state and federal laws. It was their opinion, however, that "the action which can be had under Federal laws" would be "more speedy and efficacious." The committee thought it appropriate to inaugurate proceedings under the Sherman law against the ARU and to seek injunctions to restrain the strikers. It recommended, however, that such legal matters be directed by seven lawyers from the committee. This would assure "that the laws applicable to the solution might be carefully examined and advice and assistance promptly rendered" and also that "a proper understanding may be had with the prosecuting attorney and other officers of the law controlling criminal proceedings." The GMA unanimously adopted the recommendations.[18]

That the railroad lawyers suggested applying for assistance to the federal government rather than to the state government has given rise to speculation. Did these men distrust state authorities, especially Governor John Peter Altgeld, who was known to have pro-labor sympathies and who recently had pardoned the anarchists imprisoned after the Haymarket Affair? Seemingly, any such distrust would have been offset by the well-known fact that Altgeld had repeatedly used state troops in 1893 and 1894, and at that very time was using the militia, to suppress lawlessness during strikes whenever proper application for assistance was made to him by local law enforcement officers.[19] Perhaps the railroad lawyers recommended application to the federal government because of the attractiveness of dealing with "one of their own," Attorney General Olney. Either or both of these considerations may have influenced the lawyers' decision; it is also possible, however, that the nationwide scope of the strike and the railroads' desire to restore quickly the flow of interstate commerce logically led them to turn to the federal government without regard for the personalities involved.

Once the decision was taken, approaching the United States attorney in Chicago could not have been difficult for the railroads. Even before the legal committee reported to the GMA, Milchrist called on Peck and the other lawyers to assure them of his cooperation. He told them that his instructions from Attorney General Olney "were imperative to see that mail trains were moved." Although railroad officials by then were more concerned about unclogging interstate commerce than with merely moving mail trains and Pullman cars, Milchrist's visit probably cheered and encouraged them.[20]

The attorney general also proved cooperative. On June 30, the day the GMA decided to seek federal assistance, he asked Chicago attorney Edwin Walker to act with Milchrist in conducting the legal battle against the strikers. Walker was "Nestor of the local bar," counsel for the World's Columbian Exposition, partner of A. J. Eddy (one of the members of the GMA's legal committee), solicitor since 1870 of the Chicago, Milwaukee & St. Paul in Illinois, and a corporation attorney of international reputation. As he himself later described his position, he was "counsel for the railroad companies and special counsel for the United States in the lawsuits growing out of the great railroad strike of 1894. . . ."[21]

How the attorney general came to designate a lawyer so closely tied to the railroad community to act for the government is not clear. Milchrist, the United States attorney in Chicago, apparently had nothing to do with the appointment and was not informed of it until ordered by Olney to ask Walker to act for the government. Newspaper accounts at the time reported that the GMA, lacking confidence in Milchrist, decided at its June 30 meeting to ask the attorney general to appoint a special counsel and had agreed unanimously that Walker should be named. Olney supposedly made the appointment within two hours after receiving the GMA's suggestion. Walker was on vacation when Olney's telegram offering him the job arrived. Someone, possibly his partner, accepted the position in his name, and Walker confirmed his acceptance two days later.[22]

Whether the nominee of the GMA or Olney's personal

choice, Walker was not, by any stretch of the imagination, a properly unbiased person who could conduct the government's battles with dispassionate objectivity. He was thoroughly identified with and committed to the cause of the railroads in opposition to the strike, and he acted accordingly. As Clarence Darrow, attorney for Debs and the strikers, later said, "the government might with as good grace have appointed the attorney for the American Railway Union to represent the United States."[23]

In addition to appointing Walker, Olney took other steps on June 30 to create a legal situation that would justify full federal intervention in the boycott-strike. It was the attorney general's opinion that "the President might have used the United States troops to prevent interference with the mails and with interstate commerce on his own initiative—without waiting for action by the courts and without justifying the proceeding as taken to enforce judicial decrees." But it seemed doubtful to Olney at the time "whether the President could be induced to move except in support of the judicial tribunals." Therefore, the Department of Justice, "in order to be prepared for the exigency [of using the Army], took measures to put itself in the position which had induced the President to authorize the use of troops against the Coxey movement." That is to say, Olney ordered United States attorneys in Chicago and other trouble spots to file bills in equity for federal court injunctions against the strikers.[24]

Olney's initial letter of instructions to special counsel Walker set forth clearly the attorney general's objective and his methods for achieving it. The goal was not to enforce federal laws, to move the mail or interstate commerce, or to protect federal property; it was for the United States government to assert its "rights" vigorously in Chicago, "the origin and center of the demonstration," and, thereby, make the strike "a failure everywhere else and to prevent its spread over the entire country." This would be done by means of a broad injunction protecting the mails, backed by deputy marshals and ultimately by the United States Army. The procuring of "warrants against persons actually guilty of the offense of obstructing the United States mails," Olney warned, would be inadequate. He advised instead that injunctions be obtained that would "have the effect of preventing any attempt to commit the offense." Though he authorized the hiring of as many deputy marshals as might be needed to enforce court decrees, he doubted their efficacy. ". . . I feel that the true way of dealing with the matter," he said, "is by a force which is overwhelming and prevents any attempt at resistance."[25] Olney wanted the strike crushed. The Army was the best agency for crushing it. The legal processes served the purpose of paving the way for presidential authorization to use troops.

Inasmuch as Walker had not yet returned to Chicago from his vacation, Milchrist and the railroad lawyers drafted the bill for the injunction. In their petition they asked the court to enjoin all interference with the mail, as Olney had instructed. But the bill also called for a prohibition of all interference with interstate commerce under the provisions of the Sherman Antitrust Act. The use of the Sherman Act to justify an injunction protecting interstate commerce was almost certainly the work of the railroad attorneys rather than of Milchrist or Olney. As early as June 29, it will be recalled, the general managers had asked their legal committee about the advisability of using the antitrust law to secure injunctions against interference with interstate commerce, and on June 30 the legal committee had approved such a move.

Milchrist, on the other hand, made no reference whatever to the antitrust law in his wires and letters to Olney. On June 30 he reported that he was examining the Interstate Commerce Act with a view to using certain of its provisions to justify an injunction to protect freight trains. Olney, prior to July 1, had neither mentioned protecting interstate commerce nor suggested using the Sherman Act against the strikers. His instructions to the various United States attorneys, including Milchrist on June 28, were to secure from the courts such writs as were available to prevent obstruction of the mail. Olney's first wire to Walker on June 30 read, "Want you to act for Government in proceedings to prevent obstruction of [the] United States mail. . . ." In a wire to Milchrist, June 30, Olney urged the United States attorney to push for an injunction and cited ten precedents which might be useful. Only one of the ten (Judge Speer's Waterhouse decision) made reference to using the Sherman law against strikers and that one reference was incidental and not central to the decision. Among the other cases he cited was *Hagan v. Blindell,* in which Judge Billings had granted an injunction against strikers on general grounds after denying the applicability of the Sherman Act to the case. Of the remaining cases, five were decisions relative to obstructing the mails and had nothing to do with injunctions; one was Judge Taft's Ann Arbor decision enjoining a boycott; and one was Judge Jenkins' injunction prohibiting the employees of the Northern Pacific from striking. Conspicuously absent from the attorney general's list were Judge Billings' district court decision, and the circuit court affirmation, in the case of the New Orleans dockworkers, who were enjoined from striking specifically under the terms of the Sherman Act.[26]

It was not that the idea of using the Sherman Act to protect interstate commerce against striking laborers was unknown to Olney. Rather, he was reluctant to initiate action under the law, probably because he had no wish to strengthen it through use, even against strikers. He had never approved of the law. He had fought against it as an attorney for the Whiskey Trust before becoming attorney general. Once in office and charged with enforcing the statute, he refused to push antitrust suits. When at length he brought the Sugar Trust case (*U.S.* v. *E. C. Knight, et al.*) through the courts, it was with the expectation that the case would be lost by the government.[27] In his *Annual Report* for 1893 he discussed the law at length, giving it as narrow and restricted an interpretation as possible. Olney there referred to the then recent New Orleans dockworkers' case, in which the Sherman Act had been used, and the Waterhouse decision, which held strikes to be illegal under the antitrust act, as "strikingly illustrating the perversion of the law from the real purpose of its authors."[28]

But pressures on the attorney general were mounting. The strike grew more serious, and it was soon evident that federal protection of the mails offered no hope for ending the tie-up. Determined to halt what he regarded as a reign of lawlessness on the nation's railways, Olney groped about for a weapon— almost any legal weapon—that would end the strike. There apparently was no specific law on which to base federal intervention even though the struggle transcended state lines and involved interstate commerce. At the urging of the railroad managers, the railroad lawyers, and eventually his subordinates (various United States attorneys across the country), Olney reluctantly gave way. On June 29 he is reported to have told Charles H. Tweed, general counsel of the Southern Pacific, that "the only thing which the Anti-Trust law seemed to cover was just such combinations of disaffected laborers as the American Railway Union";[29] and when the United States attorney in San Francisco asked if he might not proceed under the Sherman Act against strikers in his district, Olney replied, June 29, "Act upon *your view* of the law, which is certainly sustained by ad-

judications so far as they have gone." Finally, on July 1, when
Milchrist notified Olney that a bill for an injunction had been
drawn, based in part on the Sherman Act, and asked the attorney general's authorization to file it, Olney approved it. That
same day he wired Edwin Walker that the "advantages of bill
in equity restraining unlawful combinations against operation
federal laws, whether under interstate-commerce law, act of
July 2, 1890 [the Sherman Act], or on general grounds, are obvious and will doubtless be availed of by you, if practicable."[30]

Once Olney decided to use the Sherman Act to justify an
injunction protecting interstate commerce, his immediate concern shifted to bringing force to bear to end the strike as
quickly as possible. "Report at once if Federal process is resisted by force marshal can not overcome," he wired Milchrist.
"United States judge should join [in the report]," he added. To
Walker he wrote, ". . . immediate, vigorous measures at center
of disturbance immensely important."[31]

Olney then went to the White House to prepare the President for sending troops to Chicago to enforce the injunction.
He took with him, as he had during the Coxeyite troubles, disturbing telegrams from strike areas in New Mexico, Colorado,
and California reporting obstructed mail trains and seizures of
railroad property in the custody of federal receivers. Olney
found the President disposed to view the newspaper accounts of
the strike as "overdrawn for sensational purposes" and not planning to deal with the matter at all until the next regular meeting of the cabinet on July 3. The attorney general's "official
account" of the situation must have been effective and alarming,
for the President was immediately galvanized into action. He
ordered the Army to protect mail trains and the property of
railroads in receivership in the Far West and Southwest. The
garrison at Fort Sheridan, just north of Chicago, was alerted for
movement into the city should the need arise. But the President's declaration that the government must protect its property,
see that its business was transacted, and be ready to give prompt
assistance wherever it could legally do so, gave no clear indication that the chief executive was aware of the full scope of the
attorney general's plan, which included extending federal protection to all interstate commerce blocked by the strike.[32]
Olney's moves apparently were somewhat ahead of the President's understanding of the situation.

On Monday, July 2, Edwin Walker took command of the
government's legal position in Chicago. Thereafter, to a very

great degree, he determined the government's policies, Olney deferring to the Chicago attorney's judgments in most cases and Cleveland deferring to Olney's. Walker met with Federal Judges Peter S. Grosscup and William A. Woods, the men who were to grant the injunction, and the three carefully checked over Milchrist's bill, deciding on ways to strengthen it. Walker wanted more time for careful study of the petition, but the judges advised moving swiftly. Walker saw to it that more emphasis was put on protecting mail trains, that details of the original strike at the Pullman plant were omitted, and that references to the contracts between the railroads and the Pullman Company were deleted.[33]

Judges Grosscup and Woods apparently saw no impropriety in assisting the railroad and government attorneys in perfecting the bill for an injunction. But then, neither judge was noted for scrupulosity. Grosscup was accused repeatedly during his tenure on the bench of favoring corporate interests while personally holding extensive assets in businesses affected by his decisions. Woods, it was widely believed, owed his advancement to the circuit court less to his ability than to his partisan political rulings while district judge of Indiana.

Grosscup, who "took a moderate, conservative view of business development and business regulation and stood out against 'trust busting and labor domination,'" came under fire for a number of his rulings. He once brought down upon himself the wrath of President Theodore Roosevelt when, on appeal, he drastically reduced a $29 million fine imposed against the Standard Oil Company for violating the Sherman Antitrust Act. About the same time, he was also criticized for his rulings respecting street car lines in Chicago, Grosscup favoring a privately owned company against municipally owned lines. It was charged at the time that he had an interest in the company involved. That was never proved, but it was later revealed that he held extensive assets in, and was a director of, a streetcar company in Charleston, West Virginia. Weathering the various charges against him, Grosscup suddenly resigned in 1911 at the age of fifty-nine.[34] "He has never been what is called a 'trust buster'; he has never been the enemy of the corporation or incorporated property; has never advocated destructive methods, nor even regulation to the extent that 'regulation' would interfere with the freedom of individual initiative and energy," wrote one of the judge's contemporaries. "He has no leaning towards socialism, nor paternalism, but is an earnest individualist."[35]

Judge Woods, who rose from boyhood poverty, enjoyed almost immediate prosperity and success as a lawyer in Goshen, Indiana. In 1880 he was elected a member of the Indiana Supreme Court, and he served on that bench until his appointment as United States district judge for Indiana in 1882.[36] It was as federal district judge that Woods issued a number of rulings in election fraud cases that branded him an extremely partisan judge. After interpreting the law so as to secure the conviction of a number of Democrats accused of fraud in the 1886 elections, he completely reversed himself in 1889, thereby allowing Republicans to escape in the famous "blocks-of-five" scandal of the presidential election of 1888.[37] President Harrison, the beneficiary of the fraudulent votes, elevated Woods to a federal circuit judgeship in 1892. The Senate took 172 pages of testimony, centering around the election fraud cases, before finally voting to confirm Woods's appointment.[38]

Woods, it was said, had "a logical and discriminating mind with a turn for nice and close distinctions which sometimes approach the verge of subtlety." He was "a man of originality, depending less than the ordinary judge upon precedents and the opinions of others." He had "a genius for interpreting the law." A less friendly writer put it this way: "his strength was his weakness, for he had what lawyers call 'an acute legal mind,' and, practically, that means an ability to find a plausible reason for deciding whatever you wish."[39]

After assisting in the preparation of the bill, praying for a restraining order against the strikers, Federal Judges Grosscup and Woods mounted the bench and handed down a far-reaching injunction. Attorney General Olney characterized it as "very comprehensive," designed "to inhibit all interference with any interstate railroad running into Chicago."[40] Debs, other ARU officers, "all persons combining and conspiring with them, and all persons whosoever" were "commanded and enjoined to desist and refrain . . . from in any way or manner interfering with, hindering, obstructing, or stopping any of the business" of any of the lines named in the injunction. The order was most specific. The defendants were forbidden to interfere with "any mail trains, express trains, or other trains, whether freight or passenger, engaged in interstate commerce, or carrying passengers or freight between or among the states." They were not to interfere in any way with any "engines, cars, or rolling stock" of the companies or to injure or destroy any of the property of the railroads. They were barred from the grounds and premises of the companies. They were not to injure or destroy any part of the tracks, roadbed, switches, signals, or buildings of the companies, or to spike, lock, or fasten in any manner any switches on any of the lines. They were ordered not to uncouple any cars, engines, or parts of trains.

The judges turned from the protection of railroads to strike activities. They restrained Debs and all others from attempting to compel or induce, "by threats, intimidation, persuasion, force, or violence," any employees of the companies "to refuse or fail to perform any of their duties as employees." They were not to induce, by any of the previously mentioned means, any employee to leave or to prevent any person from entering the service of the railroads. They were enjoined from committing "any act whatever in furtherance of any conspiracy or combination to restrain" the companies "in the free and unhindered control and handling of interstate commerce" over their lines and were barred "from ordering, directing, aiding, assisting, or abetting in any manner whatever, any person or persons to commit any or either of the acts aforesaid."[41]

In spite of its comprehensive breadth, the injunction, as Judge Woods was later to observe, technically did not forbid any man to quit the service of a railroad. "[T]hough the application then made was for a writ quite as broad as that [granted by Judge Jenkins] against the employees of the receivers of the Northern Pacific," he noted, "the order proposed was so modified as to impose upon employees, individually or collectively, no restriction against quitting service, or striking, if done without direct and active interference with the operations of the roads engaged in interstate commerce and carrying the mails."[42] It is doubtful that had the strikers known of this technicality, it would have helped their cause significantly.

Not everyone was as convinced as Olney was of the value or propriety of using equity proceedings to halt the strike. Had he been on the scene earlier, Walker wrote Olney, he would have urged proceedings "upon the [criminal] side of court rather than a bill in equity." He was certain that criminal indictments against the strikers and their leaders by a federal grand jury would be more effective than the injunction in ending the strike.[43] Judge Grosscup also questioned the use of the injunction. "I am not prepossessed in favor of this injunction method of repressing violence, and hope that Congress will enact a criminal code to protect interstate commerce and the mails," he wrote Secretary of State Gresham. "It is altogether wrong," he declared, "to call Judges into the midst of such a turmoil and compel them, apparently, to take sides." Gresham, who had fought against railroad strikers since 1877 and had himself issued labor injunctions against strikes and boycotts, shared Grosscup's view. He regarded the Chicago injunction as an example of the judiciary making law by equity proceedings.[44]

Olney, however, favored the use of the injunction because he saw in it the surest and quickest way to get federal troops brought into action against the strikers. When it was issued, Olney declared to the press that the matter had passed out of his hands. "The filing of the injunction practically concluded my work," he declared, "and it is for other branches to execute such actions as the courts take." Nonetheless, his active direction of the government's side of the war against the ARU continued. When word arrived that the injunction was in force, he sent instructions to Walker and Milchrist that as soon as troops were needed, the facts were to be certified to the President by the United States attorney, the marshal, and the federal judge.[45] This was the precise formula used a few weeks earlier to induce the President to authorize the use of troops against Coxeyites.

Although the President and some of his top advisers were hesitant about using troops, Olney, Walker, and Milchrist, not to mention the railroad officials who worked closely with them, were eager to bring matters to a head. In a wire to Walker on July 3, Olney betrayed his impatience to get the Army into action. "Understand you think time for use of United States troops has not yet arrived," he noted. "If the time does come they will be used promptly and decisively."[46] Walker was not opposed to the use of troops; he repeatedly predicted that the Army would have to be employed, and at a meeting with the general managers on the morning of July 3 he stated that troops would be ordered out. He felt, however, that the strikers should be given an opportunity to obey the injunction before calling on the military to enforce the writ.[47]

The request for troops was not long delayed. Acting on the advice of his lawyers, Debs ignored the injunction and continued to send out orders to his men. Although he repeatedly warned that violence would work against union interests, there were clashes between strikers and the authorities. On the afternoon of July 3, Federal Marshal John W. Arnold wired Olney that on the previous day he had read the injunction to a jeering and hooting mob outside Chicago. The mob's response had been to drag baggage cars across the tracks, obstructing the passage of the mail. "I am unable," he reported, "to disperse the mob, clear the tracks, or arrest the men who were engaged in the acts named, and believe that no force less than the regular troops of the United States can procure the passage of the mail trains or enforce the orders of the court." He concluded his message with the statement that a general strike of tradesmen was expected the next day and that troops should be sent to Chicago "at the earliest moment." Judge Grosscup and federal attorneys Milchrist and Walker countersigned the plea.[48]

At the White House the President spent the day of July 3 discussing the use of troops in Chicago, first with the cabinet, later with an inner ring of advisers, Gresham, Lamont, Olney, and Generals John M. Schofield and Nelson A. Miles. The five advisers were not agreed as to the seriousness of the situation. Some thought it could be resolved by merely marching two hundred regulars down Michigan Avenue in Chicago. Others, including General Miles, saw the strike as far more ominous. There was danger, Miles believed, that the civil government and authority would be paralyzed if not overthrown.[49] When Olney, in midafternoon, brought Marshal Arnold's telegram to the White House, differences dissolved, and the entire garrison at Fort Sheridan was ordered to take up positions in Chicago. The urgency of the message, the fact that it was signed by the top-ranking responsible federal officials at Chicago, and the insistence of the attorney general that the use of the Army was both lawful and necessary made any other course on the President's part unlikely.

The order under which the Army went to Chicago provided that the troops were to execute the orders and processes of the United States courts, prevent the obstruction of the United States mail, and "generally to enforce the faithful execution of the laws of the United States."[50] Despite the inclusive nature of the last item, the absence of any specific reference to interstate commerce again raises the question as to whether or not President Cleveland, or the officers who drafted the order, clearly understood the conditions under which troops were being used. Cleveland's declaration at the time that "if it takes the entire army and navy of the United States to deliver a postal card in Chicago, that card will be delivered," indicates that his prime concern was still for the mail.[51] As of July 3, however, there had been no serious delays in the delivery of mail at Chicago, and the justification for using troops was that a federal court injunction, protecting not just the mail but, more im-portantly, interstate commerce, could not be enforced by civil authorities.

The arrival of troops in Chicago was met by various re-sponses. Some railroad officials, though relieved that the govern-ment had acted, had misgivings as to whether or not the Regular Army was large enough to handle the nationwide disturbances.[52] John M. Egan, official spokesman of the GMA, announced to reporters that the railroads took the position that "Pullmanism" and "railroadism" were no longer factors in the fight and that it was now "a question between the American Railway Union and the Federal Government." Strike leader Debs predicted that the first shot fired by regular soldiers at the mobs would be the signal for a new civil war.[53]

Olney told newsmen: "We have been brought to the ragged edge of anarchy and it is time to see whether the law is suffi-ciently strong to prevent this condition of affairs. If not, the sooner we know it the better that it may be changed." If Olney was trying to becloud the issue by introducing an irrelevant and emotional charge, the term "anarchy" was a happy choice. Many persons, including men in high office, feared the growth of anarchism. On the very eve of the Pullman strike the president of France had been slain by an anarchist; Governor Altgeld of Illinois, whose authority was bypassed in sending troops to Chicago, was chiefly known to the public as the man who had pardoned three of the anarchists sentenced for alleged complic-ity in the Haymarket Affair; and Chicago was regarded by many, including General Miles, as containing "more anarchists and socialists than any city on earth."[54] Whether Olney actually be-lieved that the nation stood face-to-face with anarchy cannot be known for certain. It appears more than likely, however, that he was stating his case for the use of troops in the strongest terms at his disposal.

An official protest at the uninvited presence of federal forces in Illinois was sent by Governor Altgeld to President Cleveland. In two lengthy telegrams the governor suggested that the President was being imposed upon by his advisers, and that his act was rash, unnecessary, and unconstitutional. State forces were not only able to meet any emergency which might arise in Illinois, but were ready to aid the national government else-where. The whole federal system of government, Altgeld warned, was endangered by this usurpation of authority on the part of the federal executive. In his terse replies, reportedly drafted by Olney, Cleveland asserted that his acts were constitutional. He made no attempt to answer the specific points raised by the governor. Rather, he said, "in this hour of danger and public distress," discussion might "well give way to active efforts on the part of all in authority to restore obedience to law and to protect life and property."[55] This reply for the moment precluded further debate with the governor over states' rights or the constitutionality of sending troops to Chicago.

Olney too, in his interviews with the press, dismissed Altgeld's more telling arguments by insisting that they contained "false premises" and "illogical nonsequiturs" and suggested that the governor was seeking material for his reelection campaign. "The soil of Illinois is the soil of the United States . . .," Olney declared, "and the United States is there . . . not by license or comity, but as of right. . . . The notion that the territory of any State is too sacred to permit the exercise thereon, by the United States government, of any of its legitimate functions never had any legal existence, and, as a rule of conduct, became practically extinct with the close of the Civil War."[56]

The Army was not used effectively at Chicago at first. General Miles, commander of the federal forces, was torn between sympathy for the sufferings of the working classes and fear that a bloody revolution would result if the masses were not held in check. At the White House on July 3 he had asked President Cleveland, point-blank, whether or not he was to permit his men to fire on rioters. The President, taken aback, replied that Miles would have to use his discretion when he arrived on the scene. In Chicago, Miles allowed his forces to be broken up into detachments of from ten to twenty men that were assigned to supplement police squads and marshals at scattered points in the metropolitan area.[57]

General Miles, who had anticipated great violence, was obviously pleased that the Army had no occasion to fire on rioters. "Owing to the excellent discipline and great forbearance of officers and men," he reported to Washington on July 5, "serious hostilities were avoided yesterday."[58] Olney, whom newsman A. H. Lewis described as "going into this war for the roads against the men as to a feast," was furious. Upon reading one of Miles's frequent press releases, the attorney general, according to Lewis, burst out petulantly to the effect that "if Miles would do less talking to newspapers and more shooting at strikers he would come nearer to fulfilling his mission on earth and earning his pay."[59] Orders were soon sent out from Washington

instructing Miles to concentrate his men and, after giving adequate warning to the innocent to disperse, to fire into rioting
mobs if necessary.[60]

Until the arrival of the Army on July 4, there had been
little violence in Chicago proper. Some acts of sabotage had
occurred and there had been occasional demonstrations, but
the police had effectively controlled the latter. On the 4th (contrary to Miles' optimistic report of that day's events) and the
5th, tension mounted and the mobs became more aggressive.
The climax came on July 6, when some $340,000 worth of rail-
way property, mostly empty boxcars, was put to the torch and
over 4200 state militiamen were rushed into the city to suppress
violence. The next day a skirmish between the Illinois troopers
and the mob drew blood; five militiamen were injured, four
rioters were killed, and twenty of the mob were wounded.[61]

On July 8 President Cleveland issued a proclamation calling upon the citizens of Chicago to return peaceably to their
homes. In a letter to Olney, Edwin Walker expressed the hope
that the proclamation would be but a prelude to a declaration
of martial law should the disorders continue. The attorney general, however, was of the opinion that martial law could be
declared only if Governor Altgeld called upon the President for
assistance, thus putting federal authorities in full command of
the situation.[62] Such an extreme measure did not prove necessary. The military forces in Chicago were not again seriously
challenged, and a proposed general strike of Chicago trades
unions in support of the ARU did not materialize.

From the first the rank and file of organized labor seem to
have regarded the ARU's boycott-strike sympathetically. Leaders of the labor movement, however, were divided. Some, like
James R. Sovereign, head of the dying Knights of Labor, worked
hard to bring about unity behind Debs; others, like the chiefs
of the brotherhoods, opposed the ARU and worked with the
companies to defeat it; Samuel Gompers, president of the
American Federation of Labor, stood by, cautious and doing
nothing, however strong his inner sympathies for Debs and the
ARU may have been. In Chicago the trades unions repeatedly
expressed their sympathy for the strikers and following President Cleveland's proclamation, voted a general sympathy strike
to begin July 10. By then, however, Debs was under arrest and
the cause seemed hopeless. Only about 25,000 workers responded
to the call. Meanwhile, demands from AF of L leaders in Chicago induced Gompers to call the union's executive council into

session on July 12. The council telegraphed to President Cleveland, urging him to use his influence to bring an end to the strike with fairness to both sides. The President did not reply. Debs, freed temporarily on bail, appeared before the group on invitation, and discussed strike issues. He asked Gompers to carry an offer from the ARU to the GMA, agreeing to halt the strike at once if all men were allowed to return to their former jobs without discrimination. If the railroads declined this offer, Debs suggested the AF of L call a general sympathy strike.

Debs's offer to halt the strike on such easy terms for the railroads, bore the scent of defeat. The council concluded that carrying Debs's offer to the railroads or calling a general sympathy strike would be futile. Neither move could save the ARU and might well damage the AF of L and the labor movement in general. The union leaders did agree to accompany Debs to the GMA to deliver his message, which he declined to do, and they voted a contribution to Debs's legal defense fund. They urged their followers, however, to avoid participating in any general sympathy strike. What effect a demonstration of that sort might have had earlier in the boycott-strike is debatable; the futility of one so late in the affair is generally conceded. By July 13 all rioting had ended and trains were running on schedule. On the 17th, Debs and his associates were again in custody. For all practical purposes the strike was ended.[63]

Although it was in Chicago that the main battle was fought and won against Debs and the ARU, Attorney General Olney had waged war on strikers on a dozen or more fronts from Ohio to California and from Minnesota to Texas. Olney tended to rely as much upon railway sources as upon public ones for information about strike conditions. Frequently, it was at the behest of railway officials that he authorized United States attorneys to seek injunctions against strikers. But wherever mail was obstructed or interstate commerce was blocked, Olney acted, authorizing the swearing in of deputy marshals and the seeking of injunctions such as had been issued at Chicago or requesting the President to dispatch troops to assist United States marshals in executing court orders.

The federal courts were flooded with litigation during and after the strike. The most important proceedings were those in Chicago, which will be dealt with in the next chapter. In other actions across the land, federal judges in charges to juries, rulings on petitions for injunctions, and in contempt proceedings

spoke with unusual unanimity on questions arising out of the
disorders. Although most of these rulings confirmed earlier decisions, a few reached out into uncharted regions.

In their charges to juries, grand and petit, the judges appro-
priately devoted much time to explaining legal technicalities.
The precise meaning of such terms as "conspiracy," "obstructing
the mails," and "reasonable doubt" were explicated in detail.
Little that was new was added to those terms. In California,
where feeling ran high against the railroad companies and the
sympathies of many lay with the strikers, grand jurymen seemed
more anxious to indict the companies for failure to move trains
than boycotters for cutting off Pullman cars or for refusing to
move trains with sleeping cars on them. Federal Judges Erskine
M. Ross of Los Angeles and William W. Morrow of San Francisco found it necessary to define most precisely the exact nature
of a mail train. Judge Ross instructed his grand jury that by
law the postmaster general "in all cases" decided "upon what
trains and in what manner the mails shall be conveyed." The
postmaster general had designated the Southern California and
the Southern Pacific as mail carriers. Neither company by law
was required to run any other than their regular passenger
trains for the carrying of the mails. . . ." At a later session he
further instructed the same grand jury that in making up trains
the companies, "as owners of the property, . . . are legally and
justly entitled to determine how many and what cars and
engines shall constitute their trains; and, when the composition
of trains as usually and ordinarily made up by them is reasonable and appropriate to the services required of them, the law
does not, upon the refusal of their employees to move the usual
and customary trains, require of such companies to divide the
train and run a less number of cars."[64]

Judge Morrow, in his charge, laid down rules for fixing responsibility for obstructing mail trains. He suggested that the
existing situation was "of such an extra-ordinary character" and
the tie-up of commerce and mail "so serious and long-con-
tinued" as to require the railway companies "to temporarily
waive questions concerning the makeup of regular trains . . .
and employ such resources as the company had . . . to relieve
the prevailing congestion and distress."[65] This was not, however,
the position he was to take the next April when charging a petit
jury in a criminal conspiracy case growing out of the same
strike. By then his position was not unlike that of Judge Ross.
"A mail train," Morrow said, "is a train as usually and regularly

made up, including not merely a mail car, but such other cars as are usually drawn in the train. If the train usually carries a Pullman car, then such a train, as a mail train, would include the Pullman car as a part of its regular makeup. . . . It is not for the employees of the railway company to say whether a Pullman car shall constitute a part of a mail train or not." If a train was authorized to carry mail "under the sanction of the postal authorities . . . it was a mail train in the eyes of the law."[66]

The most common question raised in the strike cases was whether or not the Sherman Antitrust Act applied to railway strikes. Unlike the rulings between 1890 and 1894 in which federal judges divided on the issue, every judge who ruled on the subject in the Pullman strike cases ruled that the law covered railway strikes. Judge Ross held that the act applied to the railway tie-up in California.[67] Judges Grosscup and Woods based their blanket injunction of July 2 in part on the antitrust law, and Judge Taft punished strikers for contempt for violating his injunction, which was also partially based on the Sherman law. In granting a preliminary injunction against strikers in St. Louis on July 6, Judge Amos Thayer declared that "a combination whose professed object is to arrest the operation of railroads whose lines extend from a great city into adjoining states, until such roads accede to certain demands made upon them, whether such demands are in themselves reasonable or unreasonable, just or unjust, is certainly an unlawful conspiracy in restraint of commerce among the states," and he cited the case of the New Orleans dockworkers in support of his contention.[68]

Circuit Court Judge John F. Philips upheld Thayer's injunction on appeal. He conceded that "the controlling, objective point, in the mind of Congress, in enacting [the Sherman Act] was to suppress what are known as 'trusts' and 'monopolies.' But," he added, "like a great many other enactments, the statute is made so comprehensive and far-reaching in its express terms as to extend to like incidents and cases clearly within the expression and spirit of the law."[69] Judge Morrow, in charging a grand jury made substantially the same points: the law, aimed primarily at preventing "the destruction of legitimate and healthy competition in interstate commerce by individuals, corporations, and trusts, grasping, engrossing, and monopolizing the markets for commodities," was in fact broad enough "to reach a combination or conspiracy that would interrupt the transportation of such commodites from one state to another. . . ." Repeating the same points in a charge to a petit jury,

Morrow added, "Pullman cars in use upon the roads are instrumentalities of commerce" and, hence, were protected by the antitrust law.[70]

It remained for Judge John H. Baker of Indiana to give a novel twist to the significance of the Sherman Act, while upholding its use against strikers. Prior to the enactment of the measure on July 2, 1890, he said, it was "entirely clear that the United States . . . had no power . . . to go into the courts of equity . . . and invoke the aid of those courts, by their restraining power, to prevent interference with the carriage of the mails or . . . of interstate commerce." The only remedy that the federal government then had was on the criminal side of the court. That is, law violators could be prosecuted after actually obstructing the mail or interfering with "the instrumentalities used in the conduct of interstate commerce. . . ." The great growth of railroad companies and unions, however, induced Congress to give the executive branch of government the right to invoke equity proceedings in railway strikes. The courts were, therefore, "clothed with the power" by the Sherman Act to restrain strikers from acts of violence without awaiting the actual commission of a crime.[71] Congressmen who participated in the debate of the Sherman Act may well have been surprised at what Baker read into their arguments, and judges, who prior to 1890 had issued processes under the Interstate Commerce Act or on general grounds, must have been somewhat jarred by Baker's ruling.

Two circuit court judges, Taft and Philips, not only upheld the use of the antitrust law to justify labor injunctions, but were also willing to go beyond that and use the broader grounds of public necessity. "The railroads," Taft declared, "have become as necessary to life and health and comfort of the people of this country as are the arteries on the human body [sic]. . . ." Yet the ARU proposed "to paralyze utterly all the traffic by which the people live . . . to starve the railroad companies and the public into compelling Pullman to do something which they had no lawful right to compel him to do. Certainly the starvation of a nation cannot be a lawful purpose of a combination, and it is utterly immaterial whether the purpose is effected by means usually lawful or otherwise," he said.[72]

Speaking along similar lines, Judge Philips declared that the business of the country had become adjusted to operations on a nationwide scale. Communities, rural and urban, had become dependent one upon the other for the "necessaries of life." If persons were free to combine together to halt the passage of trains from one community to another, these groups could "produce ruin, famine, and death in our great cities." He concluded that it "certainly ought to be permissible to the government, representing the whole people, to interpose to preserve and protect the public life and the public health."[73] Here then were clear calls for recognizing major railway strikes for what they were becoming, national emergency strikes that threatened the health and safety of the nation. Unfortunately, in coping with them the judges saw only the need for repressing the strikes, not for settling them through negotiation or arbitration, for forestalling them before they started, or for removing the causes of such strikes in the first place.

Several judges felt obliged to deal with such questions as the rights of laborers to organize and to strike. Judges Grosscup, Morrow, and Taft all agreed that railway employees had the right to organize. Grosscup declared that a workingman might join with other workers so as to cope better with his environment. He might also choose a leader, "one who observes, thinks, and wills for him," he added gratuitously.[74] Judge Morrow ruled that "the right of labor to organize for its own benefit and protection is not questioned. It has the same right in this respect as any other association, and perhaps, in some respects, its freedom is greater. The laboring man," he said, "is entitled to the highest wages and the best conditions he can command. . . ."[75]

Judge Taft spelled out the right to organize in considerable detail. He ruled that the employees of a railroad in receivership had the right to join a union "which should take joint action as to their terms of employment." It was "of benefit" both to the men and to the community at large that laborers "unite in their common interest and for lawful purposes." Having their labor to sell, he continued, "if they stand together, they are often able, all of them, to command better prices . . . than when dealing singly with rich employers, because the necessities of the single employee may compel him to accept any terms offered him." One of the legitimate functions of a union was to accumulate a fund "for the support of those who feel that the wages offered are below market prices." Unions had the right to choose officers to advise them as to "the course to be taken by them in their relations with their employer." One union might unite with other unions. Union officials "or any other person to whom they choose to listen, may advise them as to the proper course to be taken in regard to their employment, or, if they choose to repose such authority in any one, may order them, on pain of expulsion from their union, peaceably to leave the employ of their employer because any of the terms of their employment are unsatisfactory."[76]

The judges were agreed that workers had the right to quit their jobs at will. They went on, however, to hedge that right with a number of limiting conditions. Judge Ross held that "ordinarily every man has the legal right to stop work and quit his employment whenever he chooses to do so unless there be a contract that obliges him to continue for a definite time." Ross also noted that no man had a "legal or moral right, while continuing in the employment of another," to refuse to do the work he was hired to do and that he had agreed to do. When such refusal went to the extent of violating federal laws, moreover, it was the duty of public officials to step in and vindicate the law.[77]

"The individual option to work or to quit," Judge Gross-cup instructed a grand jury, "is the imperishable right of a free-man." A group of workers acting through a labor union did not have the legal right to force others to leave their posts against their will.[78] Judge Morrow declared that labor unions could not "interfere with the rights and property of others, and by force or other unlawful means seize upon the appliances of organized industry, and set at defiance the laws of the government. The right of workingmen to quit work, either singly or in a body (subject only to the civil obligations of contracts), is not denied," he continued, "provided that the abandonment of service is accomplished in a peaceful and orderly manner; and here again the privilege or freedom must be exercised without interference with the rights and property of others."[79]

In punishing ARU officials in Cincinnati for contempt, Judge Taft held that the defendants had considerably exceeded their rightful powers as union officials. Had they come to Cincinnati simply to advise the employees of the receiver to quit their jobs peacefully in order to prevent a 10 percent wage cut from going into effect, they could not have been held in contempt, "even if the strike much impeded the operation of the road." But when they advised quitting for reasons having nothing to do with the terms of their own employment, but to bring pressure on the Pullman Company, they committed lawless acts. In effect they were attempting to force the receivers to break their contract with the Pullman Company. "The breach of a contract is unlawful," Taft declared, and "a combination with that as its purpose is unlawful, and is a conspiracy." But the ARU officials were also engaged in lawless activity because they advocated what was in fact a secondary boycott, the workers having no grievance of their own against their employer. Boycotts, Taft observed, "though unaccompanied by violence or intimidation, have been pronounced unlawful in every state of the United States where the question has arisen, unless it be in Minnesota; and they are held to be unlawful in England."[80]

Three of the judges, Ross, Morrow, and Grosscup, spoke of the need for labor reforms; but changes or reform, however badly needed, they insisted, were secondary to the preservation of law and order. "It is of the first importance," Judge Ross declared, "that the law be in all things and at all times maintained. This is especially true," he said, "in times like the present, when there seems to be abroad in the land a spirit of unrest, and, in many instances, a defiance of law and order. Every man should know, and must be made to know, that whatever wrongs and grievances exist, no matter in what quarter, can only be corrected through lawful means." In supplemental remarks a few days later he continued in the same vein: "No man, no set of men, no communistic combination of men, can lawfully undertake to redress a wrong except in the way pointed out by law. Whenever men attempt to unlawfully combine themselves together for the purpose of redressing a wrong," he said, "they strike at the very foundation of those laws which give them the right of a citizen—the protection of life, of liberty, and the pursuit of happiness."[81]

Explaining that strikes must be peaceable and not interfere with the rights or property of others, Judge Morrow conceded that some might say that "this freedom accorded to the laboring man, with the restrictions named, is of no great value, since he is thereby prevented from securing the protection he ought to have for his labor, and the power to redress his grievances. This may be true and it may be conceded that the relations of labor to capital present a difficult problem for solution," he continued, "but it seems to me that the intelligence of the people ought to solve this question in a peaceful and proper manner. It certainly cannot, with the consent of the courts, be settled by violence or any unlawful means."[82]

Judge Grosscup, in a stirring appeal for law and order, told a grand jury that they were met "in an atmosphere and amid occurrences that may well cause reasonable men to ques-

tion whether the government and laws of the United States"
were yet supreme. "You doubtless feel, as I do," he went on,
"that the opportunities of life, under present conditions, are
not entirely equal, and that changes are needed to forestall some
of the dangerous tendencies of current industrial tendencies.
But neither the torch of the incendiary, nor the weapons of the
insurrectionist, nor the inflamed tongue of him who incites
the fire and sword is the instrument to bring about reforms.'
Grosscup prescribed a most conservative means for achieving
change. "To the mind of the American people, to the calm dispassionate sympathetic judgment of a race that is not afraid to
face deep changes and responsibilities," he declared, "there has,
as yet, been no appeal. Men who appear as the champions of
great changes must first submit them to discussion, discussion
that reaches not simply the parties interested, but the outer
circles of society, and must be patient as well as persevering
until the public intelligence has been reached, and a public
judgment made up. An appeal to force before that hour is a
crime, not only against government of existing laws, but against
the cause itself; for what man of any intelligence supposes that
any settlement will abide which is induced under the light of
the torch or the shadow of an overpowering threat?"[83]

Through the years and especially during the Pullman
strike, federal judges saw the necessity for new and stronger devices to protect railway property from strikers and greatly
stretched the scope of equity proceedings to meet that need. In
the face of an admitted need for labor reforms, however, the
judges stood as if blank-minded and powerless. They saw the
strike only as defiant lawlessness or insurrection on the part of
labor, not as a device in itself educative of those "outer circles
of society" that had to be convinced of the need for change. The
only solution the judges would admit of was the "restoration
of law and order," the crushing of the strike and the arrest,
punishment, and discrediting of the strike leaders. With the
ARU reduced to shambles some unspecified agency could take
up the question of labor reform with the triumphant railway
companies.

Congress was in session throughout the strike. Its role, however,
was confined almost wholly to that of spectator. An attempt was
made by a handful of Populists and Democrats to stay the
hand of the government against the strikers. The move was

doomed, however; the overwhelming majority in both houses preferred to cheer the administration's course.

Labor questions were not new to the second session of the Fifty-third Congress. In February 1894 Populist Senator William V. Allen of Nebraska, acting in response to Judge Jenkins' injunction prohibiting employees of the Northern Pacific from quitting their jobs, introduced a bill "to prevent the abuse of the writ of injunction, and other legal process. . . ." During the spring months the House Judiciary Committee investigated Jenkins and his celebrated injunctions and recommended the censure of both the judge and his writs. Soon after, bills were introduced to prohibit the use of injunctions to enforce the performance of labor contracts and to limit the power of federal judges to punish for contempt. Other bills calling for congressional investigations of labor problems, the relations of labor, capital, and agriculture, and the effects of machinery on labor were proposed. The demands of the Coxeyites that the government provide work for the idle were embraced in one bill, and on the eve of the strike in June, bills were introduced in the House calling for legislation to settle disputes between railway companies and their employees, and for the arbitration of labor disputes.[84] Excepting for the investigation of Judge Jenkins, however, none of these matters got beyond assignment to committee.

The outbreak of the boycott-strike and the legal remedies sought by the Justice Department touched off both countermoves and measures of support. On July 2, bills were filed in the House calling for an investigation of the Chicago disorders, for federal regulation of sleeping-car service, and for making all railways in the United States public postal routes. That same day, in the Senate, a bill was proposed calling for a Senate investigation of the strike. Populist Senator James H. Kyle of South Dakota offered a resolution for undoing the blanket injunction issued that day in Chicago. He proposed "that no warrant or other process, civil or criminal, shall be issued . . . out of any circuit or district court of the United States, against any person . . . for the alleged obstruction of any railroad train . . ., unless it shall appear that such person [has] . . . obstructed or hindered such train in such manner as to interfere with the safe and convenient movement of the part of such train . . . as [is] essential to the safe and convenient transportation of the mails of the United States. And the detachment of

Pullman or other parlor or sleeping coaches from any railroad train or trains shall not constitute any offense against the laws of the United States." The resolution was referred to committee.[85]

Four days later Democratic Senator James Z. George of Mississippi introduced a bill providing for the arbitration of railway labor disputes and for most of what Kyle had sought in his resolution. The bill provided that when laborers offered to arbitrate under the Act of 1888, and the employer refused, it would be unlawful for federal courts to enjoin the employees or to order United States marshals "to control, or in any manner interfere with" them. If the railroad involved was in the hands of federal receivers and the employees offered to arbitrate their differences, the receiver would accept that offer and select an arbiter with the advice of the court in the manner prescribed by law. No obstruction of any railroad growing out of a strike was to be considered as obstruction of the mails except "when said train shall have attached thereto no car on which passengers or other freight are carried or intended to be carried."

Also on July 6, the day of the severest fighting in Chicago, Senator Allen called for an investigation into the necessity and authority for government ownership and control of the railways, telegraphs, and telephones of the country and into the existing relationship of the companies and employees in the strike in Chicago to see what legislation, if any, was "necessary to prevent strikes by and lockouts of the employees thereof in the future and to bring about a more equitable, just, and permanent system of employment and wages. . . ."[86]

The Senate "radicals" continued their push when Kansas' Populist senator, William A. Peffer, offered yet another resolution, using the strike as justification for enactment of much of the Populist platform. His resolution declared that "all public functions ought to be exercised by and through public agencies," that all interstate commerce railroads "ought to be brought into one organization under control and supervision of public officers," and that railroad rates and wages should be uniform throughout the country. The resolution further declared that all coal beds ought to be owned and worked by the states or the federal government and that the wages of all miners ought to be set by law; that all money used by the people of the United States should be "supplied only by the government of the United States"; that interest rates should be uniform in all states, not exceeding the net average increase of the permanent wealth of the people; and that all revenues of the government ought to be raised by taxes on real estate.[87]

Debate on Peffer's resolution on July 10 turned into a conservative counterthrust led by Senators Cushman K. Davis, Republican of Minnesota, and John W. Daniel, Democrat from Virginia. Peffer led off with a rambling attack on capitalists and their allies, a general defense of Populist doctrines, and a specific endorsement of the strikers in Chicago. In a bitter reply to Peffer, Senator Davis defended the administration. "At a time when in the second city of the United States, and the fourth or fifth city in the civilized world, order is suspended, law is powerless, violence is supreme, life is in danger, and property is in the very arms of destruction, I am appalled to hear the trumpet of sedition blown in this Chamber to marshal the hosts of misrule to further devastation," he declared. "[T]his question does not now concern the issue between the Pullman Company and its employees. It has got beyond that. It does not concern the sympathetic strike of the American Railway Union. It has got beyond that. It does not concern any strike which may hereafter be ordered. It has gone far beyond that. . . ." Detailing the growth of the strike from a simple affair at Pullman into a boycott, Davis declared that the boycott "took the liberty of the American people by the throat, and then grew into a riot, and from thence into an insurrection which confronts this Government today with all the dormant and latent powers of revolution. . . ."

Echoing the views of the federal judges, Davis recognized that the time had come to do something about the labor problem. Not, however, until law and order were restored. Labor questions, he declared, "will not be settled as the result of any such proceedings as those against which I speak today. Something more than capital, for which I care nothing; something more than the wages of the laboring man, for whom I care much; something more than railway corporations, for whom I care nothing, is at stake here. National existence is at stake."

Davis was followed by Senator Daniel who offered a resolution endorsing "the prompt and vigorous measures adopted by the President of the United States, and the members of his administration to repulse and repress by military force the interference of lawless men with the due process of the laws of the United States, and with the transportation of the mails of the United States and with commerce among the states." The resolution was put over one day, and after an amendment to endorse the principle of arbitration was beaten off, the Senate, by voice vote, adopted the resolution as introduced.[88]

The House, five days later, debated and passed a similar vote of confidence in the administration's handling of the strike. Representative Lafayette Pence, a Colorado Populist, in the course of debate on the resolution, put forward what could and should have been embarrassing questions with regard to the government's policy.

> There may be proper time in this country, in case of dispute between striking laboring men and the corporations which employ them, for calling out the strongest arm of the Government. . . . It may be proper to issue injunctions by Federal courts. It may be proper to demand indictments by Federal grand juries. It may be proper to call out the military; but, Mr. Speaker, in my humble judgment, the American people will never believe that the Attorney-General who orders the indictments, who orders the injunctions, who orders the military, should be either the attorney for one of those corporations, a stockholder in any one of them, or a member of the board of directors of any one of them. . . . Is there a Democrat here who believes that it was the right, decent, meet, and proper thing, when the Attorney-General came to name and designate a special deputy to take charge in Chicago, that he should designate the attorney of railroad companies there? I think not. Is there a Democrat upon this floor who stands ready, of record, to say that it was the meet and proper and decent thing, calling for our praise and our congratulation, that a gentleman who has been an attorney of trusts, who was one when he was appointed, who has continued so to be for a year, and is so today . . . should be a leader in the Administration . . . in calling into force the strong arm of the Federal judiciary, the strong arm of the military?[89]

Democratic Congressman Richard P. Bland of Missouri attacked the House resolution on the grounds of states' rights. Suppression of violence and disorder was a function of the state governments and not of the federal government, he insisted. The present interference had come about in the absence of serious violence and without the invitation of the state authorities who stood ready and able to handle the situation without federal assistance.

Defenders of the resolution argued that the issue was law and order or "mobocracy" and anarchism. The chief executive, in protecting the mails and interstate commerce, was but carrying out his duties, and he was entitled to use all lawful means available to him in doing so. States' rights were in no way involved inasmuch as it was federal law that was being upheld. Congressman Thomas C. Catchings, a Democrat from Mississippi, without answering Pence's charges against the attorney general, defended Olney as "an able lawyer, a brilliant and distinguished member of the legal profession," who "could not have done less than he has done and at the same time discharged his duty to his country." The resolution was passed by voice vote, the chair estimating that two-thirds favored adoption.[90]

Once the crisis had passed, Senator Allen introduced a resolution calling upon the attorney general to furnish the Senate with all telegrams, letters, and other communications to and from the Justice Department relevant to the strike. The next day, July 26, the Senate adopted the resolution. Then suddenly, on July 27, the Senate voted to reconsider and recalled the resolution.[91] No explanation was made until December 10. On that day Senator Allen moved that the recall he rescinded and that the strike correspondence again be called for. He also wished to know, he said, why his original resolution had been so discourteously treated. Senator James L. Pugh explained. When Attorney General Olney received the resolution, he informed Democratic Senator William F. Vilas of Wisconsin that the "manifest purpose" of the resolution "was to uncover the case then pending" against Debs in the courts "and to make the facts public by a communication to the Senate." That, Olney told Vilas, would "put the government to great disadvantage" in prosecuting the cases. Olney suggested that perhaps the Senate had adopted the resolution without due consideration of its consequences. This conversation, when related to various senators, had led to the recall of the resolution.

Allen saw in all this no excuse whatever for withholding the correspondence. He asserted that nothing in the correspondence could be used as evidence in court so nothing harmful to the government's case would be revealed. Moreover, were there evidence against the defendants in the correspondence, the defense was fully entitled to view it. Several senators urged putting Allen's original resolution before the Senate Judiciary Committee, where five days earlier a similar request of Senator Peffer's for publication of the correspondence had been lodged. Allen regarded this as certain death for his proposal. Only the highly partisan Republican senator from New Hampshire, William E. Chandler, joined with Peffer in favoring the opening of the correspondence to the public.[92]

It was not until January 1897 that Congress passed a resolution asking for the full strike correspondence from the Justice Department. The task of assembling the documents fell to Judson Harmon, Olney's successor as attorney general when the latter became secretary of state. Not all the strike correspondence was published, however. Several telegrams and letters in the files of the Justice Department apparently were overlooked. Two very important letters from Edwin Walker to the attorney general were published with elisions which, if printed, would have revealed the extensive role of Federal Judges Grosscup and Woods in preparing the bill for the Chicago injunction. In the Olney papers, eventually deposited in the Library of Congress, several vital letters between Walker and Olney were preserved that properly should have been published with the strike correspondence. And from the texts of a number of the published letters it would appear that there were other letters which, if not destroyed or lost, have not yet come to light.

The intervention by the federal executive into the Chicago railway strike was the first such massive intervention by the federal government in a railway labor dispute since 1877. The similarity of the two events invites comparison of the policies pursued by the government in each. Both strikes were the product of major economic depressions, the Panics of 1873 and 1893; both began as small scale revolts against wage cuts that soon mushroomed into tie-ups of national proportions; both were marked by considerable disorder; both were ended by the combined efforts of the federal courts and Army; and both were major defeats for the railroad workers.

But here the similarities end. The strikes of 1877 were unorganized, spontaneous outbreaks in protest against employee grievances. The men struck to redress what they regarded as wrongs done them by their employers. In 1894, however, the boycott-strike was organized and planned by a labor union, the ARU, and its leader Debs. Whatever grievances the railway workers may have had against their employers, the initial cause of the difficulties was the decision of the ARU to boycott Pullman sleepers and thus redress the alleged grievance of the Pullman Company employees against their employer. Officially, the ARU members had no stated grievances against the railroads. To a large segment of the public mind the ARU was attacking innocent third parties, the railroad companies, in order to meddle in the dispute between Pullman and his workmen.

As for the manner in which the two administrations coped with their respective strikes, there were also definite differences. President Hayes, reluctant to move against the strikers, did so only when the governors of the troubled states or the federal courts asked for aid. Although President Cleveland, too, may have been reluctant to act, his attorney general was willing and eager to intervene. From the outbreak of the initial boycott on June 26 until the close of the strike in July, Olney played the dominant role, a role more important than that of the disputants.

In neither instance did the federal government seriously attempt to bring an end to the strikes by negotiations. In 1877 this would have been difficult, there being no person or group who could speak for any substantial number of the strikers. Such was not true in 1894. Debs and the ARU could have spoken for a significant number of the men on strike, and certainly the GMA could have spoken for the railroads if they could not have been represented individually. Moreover, pressure from the President might well have brought the disputants to the negotiating table. It can only be assumed that Attorney General Olney in 1894 wanted to do more than merely end the disorders; he wanted them halted by giving the railroads a complete victory over the ARU.

The Hayes administration was not charged either with favoring the railroad companies or with usurping power belonging to the states. When criticized by contemporaries, it was for being too cautious about acting against the strikers. In 1894, however, the Cleveland administration left itself wide open both to charges of partisanship and usurpation of power. Attorney General Olney's continuing ties with the railroad community, his naming of Edwin Walker to represent the government in Chicago, and his all-too-obvious willingness to work with the railroad companies tended to support the first charge. The rushing of troops to Chicago over the protests of the governor of Illinois, before violence was serious and before state or local authorities had been called upon or had been proved unwilling or unable to act effectively, bespoke usurpation of power. That the actions taken were later sustained by a unanimous Supreme Court as falling entirely within the proper sphere of federal authority did not dispel the accurate notion that there had been a bold new use of power by the federal government, however justified it may have been. From that day forward, whenever federal troops were used in a state without the call of that state, the Chicago instance served as a precedent.

The actions taken in 1894 could hardly be excused on grounds that the government was dealing with a new problem for which there were no guiding precedents. Such had been true in 1877, but by 1894 strikes were familiar and there were precedents upon which the administration could have drawn (the strikes of 1877, and the Burlington and Great Northern strikes, for instance) which would have suggested a more restrained policy. Moreover, lawlessness, rioting, and looting were far less widespread or serious in 1894 than in 1877. Only as strikers became convinced of the hopelessness of their cause did violence take on serious proportions in 1894.

That the Cleveland administration acted less impartially than the Hayes administration was not simply a matter of ties to the railway community. The Hayes administration had similar if not as extensive ties to the railroads as did the Cleveland administration. More significantly, it would seem that Hayes was master of his administration, whereas, Cleveland was not. Hayes, from the very start of the difficulties in 1877, had been in on the making of federal policy. When the governor of West Virginia first asked for assistance, it was Hayes who decided to give that assistance. In 1894, on the other hand, Cleveland appears not to have been involved in shaping federal policy until the evening of July 1, when Olney first apprised him of the seriousness of the situation in Chicago. By then Olney had already used the full powers of the Justice Department to protect mail trains, including the Pullman cars attached thereto, had appointed Walker, had ordered the seeking of the blanket injunction to protect both the mails and interstate commerce, had told Walker how important it was to use overwhelming force to end the strike, and had instructed Milchrist and Walker as to the exact wording to use in asking for federal troops.[93]

In addition to not being party to the original policy decisions taken by Olney, there is some question as to whether or not President Cleveland fully understood the basis for the actions being taken by him or in his name. Although there were regular daily meetings of the cabinet after July 1, and more frequent meetings with an inner circle of cabinet advisors, those meetings were all subsequent to the critical policy decisions save for the actual ordering of troops to Chicago. Even there Olney had carefully prepared the groundwork so that when troops finally were asked for, it would have been difficult for any chief executive to refuse the request. All too clearly Cleveland, unlike Hayes, had allowed too much power to drift to other hands, particularly into those of his aggressive attorney general. In part, as demonstrated in the Burlington and Great Northern strikes, it was Cleveland's habit to delegate broad authority to cabinet members. Another factor, however, may well have been the President's deep involvement in the struggle to lower the tariff. By chance that battle was consuming Cleveland's time and energies just as the Pullman strike began. The President's preoccupation, no doubt, allowed Olney far greater freedom of action than usual.[94]

In discussing strike issues with the press, the Hayes administration displayed far greater candor and responsibility than the Cleveland administration. President Hayes himself dispelled rumors in 1877 that the strikes were insurrectionary in nature or were led by anarchists and communists. He insisted that the rioting was essentially warfare between the railroad companies and their embittered employees. Cleveland and Olney, on the other hand, adopted the view that the strike was in effect against the government itself. And Olney, by deliberately linking the strike with anarchism, proved as willing as the most irresponsible newsman to inflame the public against Debs and the strikers he led.

With the collapse of the strike by mid-July and the prompt restoration of regular railroad service, the country had again weathered a national crisis. In suppressing the Pullman strike, both the executive and judicial branches of the federal government had found it necessary to stretch their powers to unprecedented limits. The main issues of federal intervention, raised in the welter of cases already discussed, were, for all practical purposes, subsumed in the proceedings against Debs for contempt of court. Whether or not the extraordinary exertions of federal officials fell within or exceeded the bounds of legality, remained to be determined before the highest tribunal in the land.

• • •

CHAPTER VIII

Vindication and Change

"[N]O MAN SHOULD BE ALLOWED to play the part Debs did last Summer and go unwhipped of justice," Attorney General Olney wrote Edwin Walker in January 1895. "Indeed, as I see it, no punishment he is likely to get, if he is convicted and sentenced on all the pending indictments, will be commensurate with his offense."[1] But in the weeks and months that followed the Chicago strike, Olney and Walker were more concerned with vindication of the actions they had taken than in the punishment of Debs. Not only did they seek judicial approval for what had been done, they also wanted the expedients they had devised for crushing the strike sanctified and made a part of the government's permanent arsenal for combating future railway strikes.

From the first, Walker had moved cautiously, more cautiously than Olney and other officials liked and certainly more slowly than the railroad managers desired.[2] Walker did not lack zeal—no one was more anxious than he to see Debs behind bars and the embargo on railroad traffic lifted—but his goal was to keep the government's legal position impregnable. "I have a thorough understanding with Judge Grosscup," he wrote Olney, "and while we may not proceed as rapidly as some of the impatient ones may desire, we shall be very careful to take no step in advance without sufficient evidence to support our position."[3] At the Chicago attorney's insistence, the government moved against Debs both in equity and criminal proceedings. During the early days of the strike Walker favored the criminal side as offering more long run benefits. "I firmly believe that the results of these trials, and the punishment of the leaders, will be so serious that a general strike upon any railroad will not again occur for a series of years," he wrote Olney.[4]

When the attorney general and others suggested to Walker on July 9 that he was moving too slowly, he replied that, barring miscarriage of his plans, he expected shortly to lay before the grand jury all the telegrams, records, and papers from the office of the ARU. "I have all the time been looking to final results," he said, "instead of temporary advantages." The next day Debs was arrested and his personal papers, along with the ARU's records, were seized. The seizure was somewhat highhanded, however, and at Olney's insistence Debs's papers were returned.[5]

On July 14 Walker notified Olney that the strike had "practically ended," and he outlined his proposed course of action. Debs and his associates would be brought into court to face contempt charges. Meanwhile, in a separate action, the government would bring a carefully prepared criminal indictment charging the union leaders with conspiracy against the United States. "If this course is pursued with dignity and firmness," Walker concluded, "in my opinion this is the last railway strike that will occur in this country for many years." "Your plan of procedure seems eminently judicious and is entirely approved," the attorney general replied.[6]

At the first contempt hearing on July 26, it was decided to postpone further action until September. Judge Woods could remain in Chicago only until the end of the week, leaving too little time for completion of the case. Walker complained that "the heat was really stifling, and the crowd of strikers present at the hearing made the air of the room intolerable." He had not felt well enough to proceed at once anyway. He was certain that if he had pressed for an immediate hearing, Judge Woods would have assigned the matter to a master-in-chancery for proof. "This would have been disastrous," he said, and "had such an order been made I should have dismissed the contempt proceedings." Not only would such a move have kept all involved parties in Chicago for the balance of the summer, it would also have forced him to submit substantially the same evidence at the contempt hearing that he planned to use against Debs in the criminal case. Walker did not wish to tip his hand in advance. After "a full conference with Judge Woods" he convinced the judge to hear the evidence of contempt in open court in September.

The delay would prove advantageous to the government's cause, Walker declared: "As the strike is now thoroughly broken, the American Railway Union badly demoralized, and local unions continually withdrawing, it is my opinion that by the 1st of September there will be little left of this organization." Any chance of the strike reviving in the meantime seemed unlikely, Walker thought, because Judge Woods had warned Debs that a resumption would aggravate the contempt. Walker assured the attorney general that the case would "be prosecuted to a final hearing." If the courts sustained the use of equity proceedings to restrain unions from interfering with the movement of mail and interstate commerce, he predicted an end to boycotting and "violence in aid of strikes." Thereafter, when railway employees left in a body, other employees would be able to "take their places without interference or intimidation."[7]

The delay at first had struck Olney as unfortunate. He feared that Debs and his associates would be left free to start another strike. The mere fact that they were "at large" tended "to create some apprehension and alarm" in business circles. "On the other hand," he admitted, "the advantages resulting from delay as set forth in your letter, especially as regards ultimate results, are very great. After all, the important thing is to vindicate the law and justify the preventive action taken under it. If that is accomplished the most salutory results to the community at large are, I think, sure to follow."[8]

When the hearing resumed in September, Walker was concerned that the court might not uphold that portion of the original injunction which was based on the Sherman Antitrust Act. But even if the court invalidated Section 4 of the act, authorizing the government to seek injunctions against conspiracies in restraint of trade, Walker was certain it would uphold the right of the government to use equity proceedings for restraining interference with the mail.[9]

Olney doubted that Section 4 would be held unconstitutional, and he was certain that the right of the government to invoke equity to protect the mails could not be "successfully met." He suggested, however, "a still broader ground upon which the bill . . . [could] be justified and . . . sustained," namely, the "indisputable jurisdiction of a court of equity in the case of a public nuisance." It was the "incontrovertible right" of such a court, he said, to restrain the commission of public nuisances whenever they threatened and when their commission would result in injury to the public. His argument was simple: the commonest example of a public nuisance was the obstruction of a public highway; a railroad was nothing but a "peculiar species" of public highway; as an instrument of interstate commerce an interstate railroad was, in effect, a public highway of the United States within the exclusive jurisdiction and control of the federal government; any obstruction to the use of an interstate railroad was, therefore, a public nuisance, the threat of which might be enjoined; in the case at hand the threatened obstruction was due to the "concerted, sudden and simultaneous withdrawal from service of the trained corps of expert employees necessary to the operation of such highways"; that the threatened obstruction was not physical but was "peculiar, being adapted to the peculiarities of the highways to be obstructed," was immaterial, the principle that public highways might be protected from obstruction by injunction remained unchanged; and, finally, it could not be argued that the obstruction could not be enjoined because the employees were merely quitting their work, because "the right to strike, of one man or many," alone or in concert, where the intent was unlawful (as to create a public nuisance), was enjoinable. Any act in furtherance of an unlawful intent, whether an actual quitting of work, an agreeing to quit work, or any other, was "tortious" and could be restrained by a court of equity.[10]

Walker replied on September 28, on the close of argument in the case at Chicago, that he had, on his own, arrived at the "precise points" raised by Olney. "My contention was, that independent of the Act of 1890, the Court had jurisdiction on the bill filed to restrain the American Railway Union, its officers, and others, from interrupting or hindering the transportation of interstate commerce and mail."[11]

Olney and Walker waited for several weeks while Judge Woods pondered his decision. The delay was not due to any doubts as to Debs's guilt, Walker learned from a conversation with the judge. "He realizes fully that not only your Department, but also those representing the business interests of the entire country, regard this as a most important case, and I infer from what the Judge said to me, that his opinion will be very carefully prepared, as he evidently regards this as his opportunity."[12]

Woods's forty-page decision, handed down December 14,

was not the judicial masterpiece he was bent on creating. Though studded with citations and long quotations from both American and English legal sources, it was more labored than learned, and a scattering of gratuitous remarks about Debs and the ARU belied his judicial impartiality.

The principal issue of the case involved the court's authority to issue the blanket injunction that Debs admittedly had violated. For six pages of his decision Judge Woods toyed with the argument that courts of equity were empowered to enjoin public nuisances and that the strike had been such a nuisance. In the end, he clumsily dismissed that proposition. "[W]hile the reasons to justify on the grounds considered . . . are strong, and perhaps ought to be accepted as convincing," he observed, there was no precedent for such a ruling in any previous railroad strike case.

But there was no need to create new precedents, Woods said, so long as the injunction could be upheld on the familiar grounds of the Sherman Antitrust Act. Woods noted how Congress, during debate on the measure, had considered exempting labor unions from the provisions of the statute, but, in the end, had failed to do so. He also noted that the chairman of the House Committee on the Judiciary had declared that the scope of the antitrust law would have to be left to the courts to decide. "It is therefore the privilege and duty of the court, uncontrolled by considerations drawn from other sources," Woods asserted, "to find the meaning of the statute in the terms of its provisions, interpreted by the settled rules of construction." Citing earlier cases in which the antitrust law had been declared applicable to labor, Woods held that the injunction was proper under the Sherman Act. The decision, he added, had not been easy. "I have not failed, I think, to appreciate the just force of the argument to the contrary of my opinion—it has sometimes entangled me in doubt—but my conclusion is clear that, under the act of 1890, the court had jurisdiction of the case presented in the application and that the injunction granted was not without authority of law, nor for any reason invalid."[13] Debs was sentenced to six months in jail, his confederates to three.

Woods won no particular favor with the attorney general despite his "carefully prepared and sweeping decision."[14] Olney regarded it as but a step on the way to a final decision before the Supreme Court. Woods had so long delayed his opinion that Olney was unable to make reference to it, as he had hoped to do, in his annual report to Congress. There was also danger that if the case were appealed, it would not reach the high court before the close of the current term.[15] Even the elaborately buttressed arguments of Woods's labor-of-ambition failed to please the attorney general. Some years later he characterized the ruling as "decided rightly enough but upon the wrong ground—namely the Sherman Antitrust Act."[16]

By the time Woods's decision was handed down, Olney had concluded that the injunction could be upheld without any reference whatever to the Sherman Act. Having never thought highly of the antitrust law, he had used it with considerable reluctance even against strikers. That he had in the end yielded and allowed it to be used as the basis for securing the Chicago and other injunctions was probably due to the need he felt for statutory justification in enjoining interference with interstate commerce. But the more he savored the doctrine of enjoining public nuisances, the more he was convinced that that principle could be substituted for reliance on the antitrust statute. Olney would avail himself of this argument before the Supreme Court when the Debs case was appealed.

Debs's attorneys sought to appeal Woods's decision immediately to the Supreme Court. Olney was willing to facilitate this move in order to obtain a final ruling on the basic issues, but he did not want the whole body of evidence reviewed before the high court. He would assist the appeal, he wrote Walker, "provided the questions be questions of law, clearly presented and not accompanied by cumbersome record."[17] Debs's lawyers agreed, and the case went before the Supreme Court on writs of error and habeas corpus.

The array of attorneys before the Supreme Court in the Debs case was impressive. The distinguished but aged Lyman Trumbull, and two rising lights of the Chicago bar, S. S. Gregory and Clarence S. Darrow, appeared for Debs. Olney himself, in one of his two appearances before the court while attorney general, argued the government's case, assisted by Assistant Attorney General Edward B. Whitney and Edwin Walker.

The case centered upon the authority of the federal court in Chicago to issue the original writ of injunction. Debs's lawyers contended that, for a variety of reasons, the injunction was improper. If Debs or his associates were involved in any lawless activities, they insisted, the men should be on trial on the criminal, not on the equity, side of the courts.[18] It was Olney's argument, however, that carried the day.

In presenting the government's case, Olney executed a deft sleight-of-hand. To this point the Sherman Act had been a vital part of the justification for the blanket injunction issued at Chicago. Section 4 of the act was cited as authority by the government in seeking the part of the injunction that forbade interference with interstate commerce; the court, in issuing the writ, had accepted that argument; Edwin Walker, in defense of the injunction before the circuit court, had relied partially upon the law; and Judge Woods had upheld the injunction squarely on the basis of the antitrust act. Even Assistant Attorney General Whitney devoted much of his argument before the Supreme Court to defending the injunction under the Sherman Act. When Attorney General Olney rose to deliver the final argument for the government, however, he neatly shelved the Sherman Act, declaring it unessential to the government's case.

The argument of the appellants, that the government had no right to seek the writ because it lacked a proprietary interest, Olney dismissed as untrue. The government owned the mail bags involved and had possessory rights to the mails so long as they were in transit. The argument was not vital, however, he said, because the court had based its injunction on the antitrust law and not on proprietary interests. There was not the slightest doubt, he asserted, but that Section 4 of that law gave "complete authority and justification for the bill, if statutory authority and justification be needed. . . . Nevertheless," he continued, ". . . it seems to me quite inadvisable that the jurisdiction of the court below should be thought to turn upon the government's technical relation to the mails and the mail bags, or should appear to depend upon the novel provisions of an experimental piece of legislation like the act of 1890."

Olney insisted that the government's jurisdiction rested on "other and broader grounds." Its authority, "wholly apart from its connection with the mails and quite independently of the act of 1890" derived from its general constitutional power to regulate interstate commerce. By enacting the Interstate Commerce Act in 1887, Congress had assumed full and complete authority over the nation's railroads. By this measure, "more radical and comprehensive than anything ever before attempted," control of the railroads had been "practically put in charge of a commission, which is to see to it that their duties as interstate carriers as prescribed by Congress are faithfully discharged."[19]

Federal control over the railroads was not only complete,

Olney argued, it was also exclusive. The Supreme Court, in previous decisions, had already established that state governments lacked the power to interfere with the operations of interstate railroads. How much less power, then, did ordinary citizens of a state, such as Debs and his associates, have to interfere with the flow of interstate commerce. In July, strikers had interfered on a massive scale with the railroads operating in and around Chicago, Olney continued. The state of Illinois, while it could and should have acted to protect life and property from lawless mobs, had no authority whatever to end the blockade of interstate commerce. Responsibility for ending that interference properly and exclusively rested with the federal government. The weapons available to end the tie-up included arrest and prosecution of those who obstructed the mails. They would have been useless in dealing with mobs, however, and ineffective when the object of the government was to prevent interference, not punish it. For accomplishing its purpose the precise weapon to be used was the one the government had used: the injunction. It was immaterial whether or not the government had property of its own involved at the time it sought the writ because the government was acting as "trustee of the railroads," for "as regards interstate railroad transportation, what is the United States but a trustee for all parties and interests concerned?"[20]

Clarence Darrow, who spoke last before the Court, seized upon Olney's abandonment of the Sherman Act in favor of more general grounds. He noted the rulings of Judge Baker and others that the federal government had had no power to protect interstate commerce prior to the enactment of the Sherman law. For that reason, he argued, the law had been used to secure and defend the injunction. But, he continued, everyone knew that the Sherman Act had been aimed not at labor organizations but at business combinations. For this reason Olney now sought to move to other grounds.[21]

Although the attorney general in his oral argument expressed the greatest confidence in the government's case, his behavior in the weeks that followed indicated anxiety as to the outcome. Throughout the period between September 1894 and the handing down of the Court's decision on May 27, 1895, he was careful not to prejudice his case in the eyes of the Court or of the public. He advised several United States attorneys who had indictments pending against Debs and other strike leaders to secure continuances of their cases rather than to press them. This would guarantee the good behavior of the strikers yet avoid any appearance that the government was persecuting them.[22]

When the chronic warfare between New Orleans dock-workers and their employers again broke out in October 1894 and tied up international commerce, Olney moved cautiously. He authorized a bill for an injunction under the Sherman Act, as he had at Chicago, but instructed the United States attorney to use it only if absolutely necessary. A few days later he wired the same official that the state of Louisiana was responsible for quelling any disorders. "Any interference or proceeding involving resort to military force of the United States," he warned, "is to be deprecated, and, if possible, avoided." When the trouble flared anew in March 1895, he turned a deaf ear to the pleas of shippers who wanted federal intervention of the sort that had ended the Chicago strike. A spokesman for the shippers, after conferring with the attorney general, reported that Olney had told him that the Justice Department did not wish to act further under the antitrust law until the Debs decision was rendered.[23]

Olney also showed little interest in pressing the criminal conspiracy trial of Debs and his associates in Chicago once it was halted by the illness of a juror on February 8. There was a story, denied by Walker, that when the jury was dismissed a few days later all the jurymen rushed to congratulate Debs and to tell him that so far as the trial had gone, they were convinced of his innocence. The consternation among the railroad lawyers and managers when Darrow, in a slashing counterattack, charged conspiracy between the companies and the Justice Department and demanded that the secret minutes and the correspondence of the GMA be produced in court may well have won over the jurors. Darrow's demands may even have cooled the attorney general's ardor to pursue the matter. In April, John C. Black, the new United States attorney in Chicago, after a conference with Olney, announced to the press that so long as Debs and his colleagues were before the Supreme Court on the contempt charge, the government, "moved by a spirit of eminent fairness" and unwilling to appear "in the attitude of a persecutor of any of its citizens," had decided to take no further steps until the Supreme Court had spoken.[24]

Edwin Walker repeatedly pressed the attorney general to authorize resumption of the criminal case, asserting that the government was certain to win. "Of course, we have to take our chances with the jury," he admitted, ". . . but certainly a mistrial will be better than a dismissal of the case." Olney apparently did not agree and the case was never resumed. In 1896, after Olney left the Justice Department, the case against Debs was quietly dropped.[25]

Within a week of Walker's final appeal to Olney to resume the criminal trial, the Supreme Court handed down its decision in the contempt case. Speaking for a unanimous court, Justice David J. Brewer upheld all of the contentions put forward by the attorney general. Olney observed correctly to his private secretary that Brewer had taken his arguments and turned them into the opinion of the court.[26] In its ruling the Court held that "the relations of the general government to interstate commerce and the transportation of the mails . . . are those of direct supervision, control and management." Brewer proceeded to show that the federal government had not allowed its constitutional powers over interstate commerce to lie dormant or unused and that the state governments had repeatedly been denied the right to interfere with such trade. "If a State with its recognized powers of sovereignty is impotent to obstruct interstate commerce," he asked, in a paraphrase of Olney's argument, "can it be that any mere voluntary association of individuals within the limits of that State have a power which the State itself does not possess?"

The Constitution, Brewer continued, vested full and exclusive power over interstate commerce and transmission of the mails in the national government. As a consequence, Congress properly legislated on these matters and prescribed punishments to prevent unlawful and forcible interference with either. "[T]he entire strength of the nation," moreover, might be used to enforce "in any part of the land, the full and free exercise of all national powers and the security of all rights entrusted by the Constitution to its care. The strong arm of the national government," he declared, might "be put forth to brush away all obtructions to the freedom of interstate commerce or the transportation of the mails. If the emergency arises," he continued, "the army of the Nation, and all its militia" were at the disposal of the national government "to compel obedience to its laws."

But force was not the only means available to the government. It could also turn to the courts for a "judicial determination and for the exercise of all their powers of prevention," including the use of injunctions to enjoin public nuisances.

After dismissing the various objections to the injunction as immaterial or unimportant, Brewer, in the final paragraph of the decision, discussed the applicability of the Sherman Antitrust Act. "We enter into no examination of the act of July 2, 1890 . . . upon which the Circuit Court relied mainly to sustain its jurisdiction," he said. "It must not be understood from this that we dissent from the conclusions of that court in reference to the scope of the act, but simply that we prefer to rest our judgment on the broader ground which has been discussed in this opinion, believing it of importance that the principles underlying it should be fully stated and affirmed."[27]

The course of the government was thus upheld and vindicated in every respect and on the precise grounds that Olney wished. As both Edwin Walker and Olney had predicted, it was many years before railroad employees again went on strike. For all practical purposes, despite an absence of specific legislation, the courts had outlawed strikes on interstate railways. Any labor dispute that involved interstate commerce or the mails—and what railroad strike would not—could be enjoined, and the injunction could be enforced by the full, armed might of the United States if not obeyed.

Even as judicial sanction of the government's strike policy was in preparation, forces were at work within the government, trying to devise a better solution to the railway strike problem than antilabor injunctions backed by the armed forces. Attorney General Olney himself was a leader in this movement. His motivation, in this apparent contradiction of positions, can only be guessed. It may have been, in part, his reaction to criticism of the role he had played in the strike. Although the press in general had supported his moves, a few newspapers, such as the *Chicago Times* and the New York *World,* criticized his private connections with the railroad community while fighting the strike in his public capacity.[28]

Whether thin-skinned, politically ambitious and anxious to appease labor, fearful of a public outcry at revelation of his ties to the railroads, or concerned about the rights of labor, Olney began breaking some of his connections with the railroads. In August, following receipt of his regular payment for services rendered to the Burlington, Olney asked to be removed from the payroll. He remained a director and counsel of the company, but no longer accepted pay for his services.[29] He also secured other counsel to replace him as adviser to

Benjamin P. Cheney, a director of the Santa Fe railroad. From the close of the Chicago strike to the end of his public career on March 4, 1897, Olney spent little time on the affairs of his private railroad clients.[30]

Shortly after the strike that summer, Olney also began to consider the deeper significance of the affair, especially with regard to the rights of labor. The evolution of his thinking, though slow, was marked. In a set of rough notes, apparently meant for use in drafting his *Annual Report* for 1894, Olney summarized the lessons of the disorders as he saw them at strike's end. "From this time forward," he wrote, "any strike involving the operations of inter-state commerce must count upon the United States as an important factor. Such a strike may, of course, be conducted within legal limits—in which case no interference by the United States need be apprehended." At the same time, he went on, intimidation, violence, and the terrorizing of nonstrikers would lead to punishment by the government. A second lesson, he believed, was that the sympathy strike, which had never "rested upon any rational basis," should be "wholly discredited, even in the eyes of the labor organizations themselves." A third lesson was that the strike had made advisable, if not necessary, some sort of arbitration tribunal. Although the ARU had rejected a compulsory arbitration resolution at its convention on June 12, 1894, he noted, it now appeared "that neither Mr. Debs nor the American Railway Union fairly represent the labor organizations of the country."[31]

In August the attorney general became interested in the propriety of the injunctions issued by Judge Jenkins against the employees of the Northern Pacific. Jenkins, it will be remembered, in December 1893, at the request of the Northern Pacific's receivers, had issued extremely comprehensive injunctions forbidding the employees to strike against wage cuts.[32] Justice John Marshall Harlan of the Supreme Court, on Circuit Court duty, was about to rule on an appeal from Jenkins' decision. Apparently after conversations with Olney on the subject, Harlan asked the attorney general to put his views in writing for the justice's use in preparing his decision. Olney obliged.

Olney found little fault with Jenkins' orders per se. The part of the injunction which restrained the employees "from combining and conspiring to quit, with or without notice, . . . with the object and intent of crippling the property in their custody or embarrassing the operation of said railroad," and the subsequent order prohibiting them "from so quitting . . .," as Olney saw it, were not two separate orders, one forbidding a conspiracy to quit and the other forbidding the actual quitting. They were part and parcel of the same order and should be "construed together—as a whole—as aiming at the prevention of a single specified mischief, to wit, the quitting of work pursuant to a conspiracy to that end with the express object and intent of causing the injury described in the order."

There had also been objection to the portion of Jenkins' order forbidding the heads of various labor organizations "from declaring, bringing about, or conspiring to bring about," a strike. Jenkins had justified his order on the grounds that every strike involved the use of unlawful force to make it effectual. "He practically rules, as a matter of law," Olney observed, "that unlawful force is to be a necessary ingredient of every strike." This might or might not be true, but Olney thought it "unnecessary to discuss it" because other grounds existed upon which such an order could be fully justified.

It might be argued, for example, that the injunction was justified because the intended strike was "a private wrong . . . an intentional injury to private property . . . to be inflicted by the power of confederated members." Although the isolated act of an individual quitting his job might be lawful, the "preconcerted, simultaneous, but otherwise identical acts of a great number of individuals may be oppressive to private persons and injurious to the public interests, and therefore unlawful." Again the injunction might be justified on the ground that the proposed strike would be a contempt of court. Not only the receivers, but all employees of the Northern Pacific, were officers of the court. "Could they possibly be guilty of a more flagrant contempt," Olney asked, "than by such a sudden, premeditated, and unanimous abandonment of their positions as to necessitate the shutting up of the railroad because no reasonable opportunity had been given to supply their places?"

Yet another ground for justifying the injunction, Olney suggested, was that such a strike would have created a public nuisance. It was apparently here, in August, that Olney first worked out the idea of enjoining railroad strikes as public nuisances—the point he urged upon Edwin Walker in September and still later advanced in his argument before the Supreme Court.

A railroad, Olney argued, was "only a specially contrived and improved species of public highway." Nothing had longer or "more clearly and absolutely" been settled than that an injunction could be issued to prevent the obstruction of a public highway as a nuisance. The nature of the obstruction might vary, of course, with the kind of highway involved. An ordinary highway was generally obstructed by physical objects or by damages to the roadbed; a railroad, which could be "utilized for travel and transportation only through the intervention of a corps of trained employees," could be obstructed by "the withdrawal of the expert officials and agents who operate it." Such a withdrawal, therefore, might be enjoined on the same grounds that physical obstructions to ordinary highways were enjoined.

Jenkins' injunction must stand as "unquestionably valid," Olney wrote, unless it be shown that the employees had some "peculiar right" that would justify them in creating such a public nuisance. Since they had no contract allowing them to quit on any expressly stipulated term of notice, whether or not any or all the employees could quit depended upon the effects it would have on the operation of the railroad. A single employee acting alone, Olney observed, might quit at any time so long as he did not work an injury to the property or endanger human life. On the other hand, if those who quit were so numerous as to effect serious consequences or if all employees desired to abandon service en masse, they would be "bound to give such notice of their purpose as is reasonably sufficient to procure another body of employees and thus prevent a public nuisance."[33] Obviously, Olney had not, in August, come to appreciate much of the laboring man's point of view.

Harlan, in his review of Jenkins' decision, differed with Olney. As the justice saw it, Jenkins had restrained both combining and conspiring to quit so as to work injury, and quitting work per se. Harlan held that the order was the equivalent of commanding men to remain in the active employ of the receiver and to perform their regular duties until such time as they could quit without crippling the property. A court of equity, he ruled, could not prevent a man from quitting work; there was no authority for such an order, and it would constitute an invasion of the natural liberties of the workers. Slavery and involuntary servitude, moreover, were forbidden by the Constitution. The rule, "without exception," was that equity would not "compel the actual affirmative performance by an employee of merely personal services," any more than it would force an employer to keep in his service any persons who were not acceptable to him. Harlan admitted that mass quitting, by most or all of the employees at one time, could work an injury to the property. However, "these evils, great a they are, . . . are to be met and remedied by legislation restraining alike employees and employers so far as necessary adequately to guard the rights of the public as involved in the existence, maintenance and safe management of public highways." In the absence of such legislation, the power of an employee to quit or of an employer to discharge remained absolute and beyond the authority of courts of equity. The difference between quitting, even en masse, and combining and conspiring to quit so as to work an injury, he noted, lay in the intent. Where injury was the objective and "would be irremediable at law," quitting was wrong and could be enjoined.

Harlan concluded with an admonition to judges to use restraint in issuing injunctions.

> There is no power, the exercise of which is more delicate, which requires greater caution, deliberation, and sound discretion, or is more dangerous in a doubtful case, than the issuing of an injunction. It is the strong arm of equity, that never ought to be extended, unless in cases of great injury, where courts of law cannot afford an adequate or commensurate remedy in damages. The right must be clear, the injury impending or threatened, so as to be averted only by the protecting preventive process of injunction; but that will not be awarded in doubtful cases, or new ones not coming within well-established principles, for if it issues erroneously an irreparable injury is inflicted, for which there can be no redress, it being the act of a court, not of the party who prays for it. It will be refused till the courts are satisfied that the case before them is of a right about to be destroyed, irreparably injured, or great and lasting injury about to be done by an illegal act.[34]

Olney, in writing to President Perkins of the Burlington, noted that the principal fault of Harlan's ruling was its attempt to draw a fine distinction between quitting and quitting with intent to do injury. On that point the opinion, in Olney's view, was "in conflict with the well-known rule that every man must be presumed to intend the natural consequences of his acts." In quitting the men must be presumed to know that injury to the company would follow.[35]

Sometime late in September, Edward A. Moseley, secretary

of the Interstate Commerce Commission, sought out the views of the attorney general with respect to the right of railway employees to belong to labor organizations. The receivers of the Philadelphia & Reading, citing a long-standing rule of the company, had ordered all employees belonging to labor organizations to quit their unions or be discharged. The men were considering an appeal of the order to Judge George M. Dallas of the federal circuit court in Philadelphia. After listening to Moseley's recital of the facts, Olney told the secretary that the men, in his opinion, had a just complaint. Moseley then asked Olney to talk with Stephen E. Wilkinson, grand master of the Brotherhood of Railway Trainmen (BRT). The secretary thought Olney should receive the labor leader not only with regard to the Reading case but also because, under Wilkinson's leadership, the Trainmen had refused to participate in the Chicago strike and had, thus, indirectly served the cause of both the government and of law and order. Olney granted the interview.[36]

Wilkinson related how he had worked to thwart Debs and the ARU during the great disorders by shaving off his whiskers as a partial disguise and shouldering "a musket against the rioters." When the strike ended, his brotherhood suspended or dismissed from membership thousands of its members who, contrary to orders, had joined in the strike. "Wilkinson's account interested me both during the interview and afterwards," the attorney general later wrote, "and made me keep in mind the case of his employees. The more I thought of it the more ill-advised, if not illegal, the proposed action of the [Reading's] receivers seemed. After reflection it occurred to me that, on public grounds, there would be no impropriety in my filing a brief as amicus curiae. . . ."[37]

In another version of his intervention in the Reading affair, Olney stressed his growing concern for the right of laboring men to organize. Following suppression of the Chicago strike, he said, "an opinion seemed to largely prevail that all labor organizations, since they might promote strikes and make them effectual, were in their essence illegal. Such an opinion even spread to United States judges and was made the basis of judicial action by United States courts." This view struck Olney as "so entirely unfounded and as so mischievous in its tendency and operation" that when the Reading case arose, he decided to intervene.[38]

Whether repaying a debt he felt due the Brotherhood of

Trainmen or concerned for the rights of workers, Olney took an active role in the Reading case. On October 1, he sent Moseley, for his "own use exclusively," a "hastily dictated draft of a petition" outlining the points that the employees' petition to Judge Dallas should cover. He also discussed with the secretary of the ICC the merits of various Philadelphia lawyers who might be retained by the trainmen as counsel. He then drafted "some suggestions" on the "legality and propriety of labor organizations" which, by leave of the court, he submitted to Judge Dallas for consideration.[39]

The reason for the petition before the court, Olney said, was that the receiver of the Reading had ordered members of the BRT to quite their union or be discharged. That order, he contended, if enforced, would work an unjust injury upon the petitioners. Although the regular management of the Reading, prior to the receivership, had had a rule against employees joining unions, they had never enforced it regularly. Some of the petitioners had been members of the BRT (while working for the Reading) for seven or eight years. During that time they had paid into the union, in the form of dues and assessments, "considerable sums of money" which entitled them and their families to substantial insurance benefits. If they were forced to obey the order of the receivers, the petitioners would forfeit all their insurance benefits as members of the BRT. Inasmuch as the receivers had made no complaint of the men's work, the only reason the petitioners' jobs were in jeopardy was because they belonged to a union.

Mere membership in the BRT, Olney argued, ought not to constitute grounds for discharge. The purposes of the union, as set forth in its constitution, were laudable and closely resembled those laid down by Congress in an act providing for the incorporation of labor unions. The one possible objection to the BRT's constitution might be that it authorized the calling of strikes. But even those provisions were of "an eminently conservative character," being designed to guard against any abuse of the right to strike.

"Whatever may be the customary or probable incidents or accompaniments of a strike," Olney asserted, it ought not to be ruled that "every strike must be unlawful." A strike had but three necessary elements: (1) the quitting of work, (2) by concert of two or more men, (3) simultaneously. None of these features alone or taken together was unlawful. A strike became illegal only when to these "necessary features" were added others "such as malicious intent, followed by actual injury, intimidation, violence, the creation of a public nuisance, or a breach of the peace of any sort."

Since nothing in the BRT's constitution or rules was illegal, only "business expediency" would justify the receivers in discharging men for belonging to the order. If the business reason for firing union members was that the union might possibly call a strike and disrupt service, Olney pointed out that strikes frequently occured in businesses where there were no labor organizations. "Men deeming themselves aggrieved and seeking relief or redress, though not associated in any formal way or for any general purpose, may easily unite for a single purpose of a strike." On the other hand, the strike-calling procedure of the BRT might well be regarded as working to prevent strikes. Further, so long as the Reading was in receivership, strikes could be "summarily controlled and punished through the process of contempt."

Because the Reading was in receivership, Olney noted, the question was not whether a rule laid down by the company before the receivership should be enforced, but whether the court itself was prepared to rule that mere membership in the BRT disqualified employees for service. Olney admitted that the court had the same powers as any private employer to fix the terms of employment for its employees. But he thought it would be a "curious spectacle" for a court of equity to deny laborers the right to organize for settling their differences with capital "whose right to organize is apparently not denied."

Olney suggested that a number of advantages would accrue from recognizing the right of labor to organize. First of all, it would avoid the "insidious if not illegal" proposition that a man must give up his lawful right to associate with others in order to retain his employment. Recognition further might serve to conciliate the employed classes because it would sanction their rights and indicate that no injustices were being contemplated against them. Finally, it would offer "practical proof" that "the greatest social problem of the day and the phase it has now assumed" were "fully appreciated" by the courts.

The attorney general moved to what was, for him and the times, an advanced position on the labor question. "Whatever else may remain for the future to determine," he declared, "it must now be regarded as substantially settled that the mass of wage-earners can no longer be dealt with by capital as so many isolated units. The time has passed when the individual workman is called upon to pit his feeble strength against the might of organized capital." Recognizing the inevitability of the organization of labor, Olney turned to the problem of strikes. "Organized labor now confronts organized capital . . . and the burning question of modern times is how shall the ever-recurring controversies between them be adjusted and terminated. If the combatants are left to fight out their battles between themselves by the ordinary agencies, nothing is more certain than that each will inflict incalculable injury upon the other; while, whichever may triumph, will have won a victory only less disastrous and less regrettable than defeat."

Olney pleaded that the courts step in to act as arbiters of such disputes. As yet, no better mode for settling labor-capital problems had been devised or tried than arbitration. The court, in the case at hand, could institute arbitration under the most favorable of conditions for it would stand both as employer of the laborers and arbitrator of their dispute with the receivers. Further, armed with the power to deal summarily with contempt, the court could easily enforce its own awards. Both sides to the dispute, he maintained, would have confidence in the court and in its award, and such a settlement would serve as an example for private employers.[40]

Dallas' railway background did not augur well for a decision favorable to labor. Born into a prominent Pennsylvania family, he was orphaned and left without means as a small child. Reared by relatives in Philadelphia, young Dallas was forced largely to make his own way. He could not afford a college education, so he began the study of law while working in the office of his cousin, St. George Tucker Campbell, "the most active practitioner" at the Pennsylvania bar and "the first generally recognized counsel for corporations." Dallas later worked for another relative in Pottsville and there acquired the first-hand information about anthracite mining and railroads "so important to his later career."

Dallas' reputation was that of a "sound, careful and methodical lawyer," well trained and accurate rather than brilliant. He found much work as a referee and special master for the courts.[41] For several years he was involved in the heavy litigation and proceedings growing out of the first receivership of the Philadelphia & Reading. His "broad sense of justice and capacity to deal in a practical way, with the complicated and embarrassing issues in railroad matters, gave general satisfaction," and he continued to serve the Reading. As late as April 1891, he represented that company before the Pennsylvania Supreme Court.[42] In 1892 President Benjamin Harrison named Dallas to the federal circuit court bench in Philadelphia.

As a jurist Dallas disliked "short cuts or irregular procedure." With "great skill and the utmost courtesy he kept arguments confined to the precise issue involved."[43] In deciding the Reading case he refused to consider the matter except on the narrowest of grounds, and he obviously regarded the brief of the attorney general an unwelcome intrusion.

The initial petition asking that the receivers be stopped from discharging men for belonging to the BRT, Judge Dallas noted, was signed by three men, one of whom was "personally" and "officially . . . a stranger" to the receivers. The "supposed right of interference" of that "stranger," Stephen E. Wilkinson, was "based solely" on his position as chief of the BRT. Inasmuch as there was no contract between the union and the Reading (all contracts of employment having been made directly with each individual employee), neither the association nor its chief officer "had any legal standing to be heard." Wilkinson's inclusion as a party "was not a mere misjoinder—it was without color of right." As for the other two men, one had signed the petition only a week after signing a statement, as a part of his application for employment, that he neither belonged to nor would join a labor union. Either he had lied in his application, Dallas said, or had immediately afterwards falsified it, and the receivers could not "reasonably" be expected to continue him as an employee. The receivers disclaimed any present intention of discharging the third petitioner because his yellow-dog contract had been lost in a fire.

Technically, this ended the matter, Dallas said, but two additional petitioners, in the meantime, had asked to be heard. One had been discharged as an unsatisfactory employee, not because he belonged to the BRT, and so had no case whatever. The other, hired about a year before, knew the company rule against membership in unions but had declined to sign a yellow-dog contract. A lesser agent of the receiver, nonetheless, employed him. "Without animadverting upon his participation in this equivocal means by which he secured his present employment," Dallas declared, "it may, at least, be said that his assumption that the fact that he so secured employment imposes upon the receivers an obligation to retain him in it, ought not to be sustained."

Without so much as acknowledging Olney as the source, Dallas observed that still another contention had been pressed upon the court, namely, that the general proposition under review be considered "abstractly" and "without regard to the merits of the particular cases." Ordinarily, Dallas said, an injunction was not granted "except at the suit of a party threatened with injury. . . ." He saw no reason why a court of equity should overrule or countermand an order of its receivers "at the instance of an accuser who is not interested either in the cause or in the particular subject to which his accusation relates." The practice would be unreasonable and "mischievous." If receivers were obliged to answer the charges of any "mere meddler" or "litigious busybody," their work would constantly be impeded and burdened. Even so, he said, he would answer the points raised.

Dallas' customary courtesy gave way to biting sarcasm designed to put the "meddling" attorney general in his place. Without referring to Olney directly, he brusquely disposed of his arguments. The character of the BRT was completely irrelevant, and the general ground upon which the court was urged to discuss and rule on "the good or evil influence and tendencies of such associations," he commented caustically, was "the very ground upon which [judges] should endeavor to firmly maintain a judicious reserve. . . ." Since inquiry into labor organizations involved "consideration of 'vexed and new questions,' of 'the greatest social problem of the day,' and of 'the burning question of modern times,' then surely the announcement of a 'policy of courts' concerning them should not be attempted, but avoided," he said. "The solution of social problems, and of vexed, new, and burning questions, has not been confided to the judiciary. Courts are established to administer the will of the legislature as embodied in law; and not the personal, it may be discordant, views of the judges themselves on matters of public concern."

The real question did not concern whether or not the BRT was "inimical to the general welfare" but whether the receivers should be ordered to retain BRT members in their employ in spite of the standing rule of the company and "their own unanimous judgment." There was, he said, absolutely nothing before the court warranting him to hold that the trust property would be injured by the receivers' enforcement of the rule.[44]

Judge Dallas' rebuff failed to kill the attorney general's interest in the labor question or to halt the movement for the recognition of the right of workers to organize. Hard on the heels of Olney's Reading brief (and a few days before Dallas' ruling) came support in the form of the report of the special United States Strike Commission. Cleveland had appointed the three-man body in accord with the provisions of the Arbitration Act of 1888, to investigate the causes of the Chicago strike and to recommend corrective legislation. The federal commissioner of labor, Carroll D. Wright, was chairman and John D. Kernan, a onetime member of the New York Railroad Commission, and Nicholas E. Worthington, an Illinois jurist and former congressman, completed the panel.

The commission interviewed, in all, 109 persons, including Eugene V. Debs and George W. Howard of the ARU, George M. Pullman and Thomas Wickes of the Pullman Company, and Everett St. John of the GMA. The questioning ranged far wider than the immediate strike, going into the larger issues behind labor disputes in general. Many questions were directed at the causes of strikes, the rights of workingmen, and whether or not government ownership of the railroads or compulsory arbitration of railway labor disputes offered solutions to the overall problem.

There were no heroes in the commission's account of the strike. Debs and the ARU were blamed for admitting nonrailway employees, such as the car builders at Pullman, into their union and for not foreseeing the inherent futility of the boycott-strike in a time of widespread unemployment. Pullman was damned for his stubborn refusal to deal with the union representing his employees and for not arbitrating the issues in dispute. The report disclosed in full the unsavory policies of the GMA. "It should be noted," the report said, "that until the railroads set the example a general union of railroad employees was never attempted. . . . The refusal of the General Managers' Association to recognize and deal with such a combination of labor as the American Railway Union seems arrogant and absurd when we consider [the GMA's] standing before the law, its assumptions, and its past and obviously contemplated future action. . . ." Even the Justice Department was castigated for permitting loyal railroad employees to be sworn in as deputy United States marshals at the behest of the GMA, which then proceeded to arm, feed and house, direct, and pay the men.[45] Commissioner Wright summarized the commission's conclusions well in a letter to Arthur T. Lyman: "The great trouble with the Chicago strike was that it was a pig-headed affair all around."[46]

The main thrust of the commission's report aimed less at fixing blame for the strike than at finding solutions for the strike problem on railroads in general. Writing to Henry Demarest Lloyd just after publication of the report, Wright stated that the commission had "cared nothing for persons or their character. . . . We put individuals aside, and neither Mr. Debs, Mr. St. John, nor Mr. Pullman, in their individual capacities entered into our motives. . . . It was conditions, systems, and situations that attracted us."[47]

In its conclusions the commission reported a general consensus among the witnesses that strikes, boycotts, and lockouts were "barbarisms unfit for the intelligence of this age. . . ."

> Whether [strikes are] won or lost is broadly immaterial. They are war—internecine war—and call for progress to a higher plane of education and intelligence in adjusting the relations of capital and labor. These barbarisms waste the products of both capital and labor, defy law and order, disturb society, intimidate capital, convert industrial paths where there ought to be plenty into highways of poverty and crime, bear as their fruit the arrogant flush of victory and the humiliating sting of defeat, and lead to preparations for greater and more destructive conflicts.

Could not arbitration, the report asked, offer capital and labor an alternative to "cutting each other's throats" in the settling of their differences?

The commission noted that in England labor organizations had come to be recognized and dealt with by capital and that this had, in the end, benefited both. In the United States, progress was slower. Some fifteen states had laws providing for one type of arbitration or another, and both the federal government and eleven state governments had sanctioned labor unions by law. Nonetheless, the right of labor to organize was still questioned by many. "Some of our courts . . . are still poring over the law reports of antiquity in order to construe conspiracy out of labor unions. We also have employers who obstruct progress by perverting and misapplying the law of supply and demand, and who, while insisting upon individualism for workmen, demand that they shall be let alone to combine as they please and that society and all its forces shall protect them in their resulting contentions."

The natural forces of supply and demand as regulators of the economy, the report continued, were being invalidated on every side by the concentration of power and wealth "under stimulating legislative conditions. . . ." The federal interstate commerce act and similar railroad regulation by thirty states were evidence that new means were needed to deal with the "destruction of competition by combination." But while combination was ending competition among railroad employers, competition raged unchecked among railroad employees. "In view of this progressive perversion of the laws of supply and demand by capital and changed conditions, no man can well deny the right nor dispute the wisdom of unity for legislative and protective purposes among those who supply labor." However much men differed on the "propriety and legality of labor unions," they were here to stay and would grow in power and number. Was it not the part of wisdom, then, to recognize these facts in law and try to guide these organizations, to increase their responsibility and to prevent their "follies and aggressions by conferring upon them the privileges enjoyed by corporations, with like proper restrictions and regulations?"

As for recommendations, the report noted that many proposals had been urged upon the commission, ranging from governmental ownership of railroads to the licensing of railroad employees and from the single-tax theory to the restriction of immigration and the fixing of hours of labor and wage rates by statute. Most of the proposals, of course, were not given serious consideration. The commission, however, did weigh the merits of governmental ownership of the railways. For the present, it concluded, such a plan was "too vast, manysided, and far away, if attempted, to be considered as an immediate, practical remedy." At the same time the commission urged public consideration of the question. Should the concentration of railroads into fewer and fewer hands continue, "as is by no means unlikely," the question of government ownership would be forced to the front.

The time had come, the commission believed, to establish a permanent system for investigating railway employer-employee relations. Congress did not lack power in this area. Under the interstate commerce clause it already exercised power over railroad rates, discriminations, pools, and the like and had been sustained in doing so by the courts. "In view of the

Chicago strike and its suggested dangers," the commission asserted, "the people have the same right to provide a Government commission to investigate and report upon differences between railroads and their employees, to the end that interstate commerce and public order may be less disturbed by strikes and boycotts." Just as experience had taught that public opinion of and by itself was not enough to control railroad rates, so the power to review and enforce the decisions of such a commission should be vested in the courts of law. To the argument that such laws would interfere with the private property rights of the companies, the commission replied that railroads were quasi-public corporations and did not have the "inherent rights of employers engaged in private business; they are creatures of the state, whose rights are conferred upon them for public purposes, and, hence, the right and duty of Government to compel them to do in every respect what public interest demands are clear and free from embarrassment."[48]

Specifically, the report called upon Congress to set up a permanent three-man federal strike commission with the duty and power to investigate railway labor disputes and to recommend legislation to correct the problem. Railroad companies should be compelled to obey the decisions of such a commission just as they were forced to obey decisions of the ICC. Whenever a controversy arose, the companies on one side and the unions on the other would each be required to choose a representative who would temporarily be added to the commission to hear, adjust, and determine that particular controversy.

The strike commission's report called upon the state governments to adopt systems of conciliation and arbitration and to adopt laws forbidding employers to require men, as a condition of employment to sign yellow-dog contracts. The commission further urged employers to recognize unions and to deal with them. "[E]mployers should come in closer touch with labor and should recognize that, while the interests of labor and capital were not identical, they are reciprocal." The commission suggested that employers, when possible, raise wages of workmen voluntarily. When conditions required a reduction in wages, employers should explain the causes to their employees. "If employers will consider employees as thoroughly essential to industrial success as capital, and thus take labor into consultation at proper times," the report concluded, "much of the severity of strikes can be tempered and their number reduced."[49]

The report met little favorable response save from organ-

ized labor and reformers. Debs regarded it a belated vindication
of the ARU. Henry Demarest Lloyd, among others, wrote to
congratulate the commission on its work. The *Nation,* spokesman for the respectable elements of society, condemned the
report, suggesting that it would probably serve to undermine
the use of such commissions in the future.[50] The most severe
criticisms came, as might be expected, from persons friendly to
the railroad community. "Is it not outrageous that the Strike
Commision should have submitted a report which Debs
approved?" Joseph Nimmo, chief of the Bureau of Statistics,
wrote President Perkins of the Burlington. John K. Cowen,
general counsel of the Baltimore & Ohio characterized the report as "absolutely and beyond question the most demagogic
document that ever issued from a Government Bureau."[51]

Despite the furor, two of the commissioners, Kernan and
Wright, set to work at once to bring the recommendation for a
permanent arbitration commission to reality. They worked with
members of the House Labor Committee in drafting a bill that
would replace the weak Arbitration Act of 1888.[52] Where the
earlier law had been restricted to disputes between any common
carrier engaged in interstate commerce and its employees, the
proposed new law applied to interstate railways, to companies
that owned or leased cars to such railroads, and to their respective employees. The principle of voluntary submission of disputes to arbitration remained unchanged, but where the 1888
law provided for a special three-man commission to be appointed to arbitrate each dispute as it arose, the new bill called
for a standing, five-man bipartisan commission named by the
President and confirmed by the Senate.

The 1888 law made no provision for enforcing the award
of the arbitrators. The new bill proposed that both parties had
to agree to abide by the award at the time they submitted their
dispute to arbitration. Once made, the award was to be filed
with a United States circuit court. Either party, within a stipulated period, could appeal the award to the court for a ruling
as to its reasonableness or justness. Once ruled on, the award
became final and would be enforced by the courts.

While the case was pending and for six months after the
award was handed down, no employee could be discharged except for inefficiency, violation of the law, or neglect of duty. In
turn, unions were forbidden to engage in or to aid or abet any
strikes or boycotts against the railroads during the same period.
Individual workers, following the award, could quit only after

thirty days' written notice. Charters of labor organizations covered by the law were to provide for the dismissal of workers who engaged in or who encouraged others to engage in violence during a strike or who attempted to prevent others from working.

Where railroads were in receivership the employees would be free to discuss wages, hours, and other work conditions with the court through their labor organizations. Receivers could not lawfully cut wages without notice to the men and approval of the court. Railway companies were forbidden to require yellow-dog contracts, to discharge employees for belonging to unions, to blacklist employees, or make it a condition of employment that men contribute to charitable, social, or beneficent causes.

The proposed bill, unlike the earlier law, did not empower the President to name investigative commissions to look into the causes of specific strikes. This would no longer be needed, for under the proposed law the permanent commission was authorized to inquire into the relationships between employers and employees covered by the act. It was empowered to secure from companies and unions alike such information as it needed and was to report annually to Congress. Under the new bill, moreover, whenever a dispute threatened to erupt into a strike, the commission was to bring the parties together to negotiate a peaceful settlement. At the request of any railway employee, corporation, or union, the commission would investigate a dispute and report its findings to the public, giving facts, fixing reponsibility for wrongdoing, and making recommendations.[53]

Edward Moseley, probably taking his cue from Olney's advocacy of arbitration in his letter to Judge Dallas, now sought to enlist the attorney general in the cause. In mid-December 1894 Commissioner Wright sent Olney a copy of the bill. The attorney general went to work on the proposal and, after discussing its provisions with President Cleveland, drafted a revised bill of his own. On January 17, at the request of Lawrence E. McGann, chairman of the House Labor Committee, Olney sent a lengthy critique of the original bill and his revised draft of it to the House committee.[54]

Olney wrote that he could not speak on the labor question in his official capacity but that he saw nothing wrong, "having given some attention to and feeling some interest in the subject," with his making suggestions to the House committee as an individual.[55] The attorney general's objections to the original bill ranged from trivial matters to issues of a substantial nature.

He recommended the removal of what he called the "Pullman clause," covering the manufacturers of sleeping and other railroad cars and their employees. In addition to being an obvious proviso aimed at Pullman, the clause was objectionable in that such manufacturers were not engaged in interstate commerce per se and did not become so simply by selling or leasing their cars to carriers who were.

Of greater concern was the proposed permanent standing commission. Since the act was to cover only railroads and their employees, Olney doubted that there would be enough disputes to require the establishment of "the expensive, cumbrous, and costly machinery provided for by this act." Once established, such a commission could "never be got rid of" and would certainly grow more costly to maintain through the years. He doubted also that a permanent commission could be justified on the grounds that it was to gather information on railway labor relations. The ICC and the commissioner of labor had, or could be given, the powers needed to conduct such investigations. Similarly he did not believe that the provisions for mediation and conciliation necessitated a permanent commission because Congress could empower the chairman of the ICC and the commissioner of labor to handle these activities.

The greatest portion of Olney's attention was given to the arbitration procedures established by the bill. There was, he thought, little need to discuss the desirability of arbitration. "The only alternative is industrial wars, and they are as illogical," he wrote, "as brutal, and as wasteful as the wars by which international disputes are only too often accompanied." The only questions remaining, he said, were, the tribunal for arbitration, the subjects of arbitration, the parties to arbitration, the conduct of parties pending the award of arbitration, and the remedy when arbitration was not resorted to or when the results of arbitration were not accepted.

Olney argued that ad hoc arbitration tribunals were to be preferred to a permanent commission. A permanent commission, he believed, would be a standing invitation to the parties to arbitrate or to find something to arbitrate, whereas, in his opinion, labor and management should be encouraged, so far as possible, to settle their differences between themselves. A permanent commission, moreover, would do away with one of the attractive features of arbitration: the right of each party to choose a member of the tribunal. With a permanent commission, even though one of the members would be chosen to represent railroad labor and another to represent railroad companies, the result would not be the same. In time the representatives would cease to represent. They would come to identify with the commission itself and its success rather than with the group for whom they were chosen originally to speak. A temporary three-man commission, with the government represented by perhaps the chairman of the ICC and with one representative each from the railroads and their employees, was much more to Olney's liking. Such a commission, "whatever its decisions, [would not be] so constituted as to be wholly out of sympathy with the losing party."

Turning to the subjects for arbitration, Olney accepted those provided for in the bill: wages, hours of labor, and the other terms and conditions of employment. With respect to the proper parties to arbitration, Olney thought the original bill inadequate. The object of arbitration, he said, was to settle a principle or rule "not to redress past grievances of any one or several individuals." The machinery of arbitration, therefore, ought not to be set in motion by any one or a few isolated individuals but "only at the instance of a class, [that is] of the whole body of employees performing the same service and of the same grade—that all may be represented in the proceedings and all be bound by the result." To allow each employee the right to institute arbitration proceedings "ad libitum every time he had a real or fancied grievance" would be manifestly intolerable. Similarly, such proceedings would not be binding on employees who were not parties to the arbitration. The bill, therefore, ought to recognize as parties the employer on the one hand and the labor organization representing the class of interested employees on the other. Since labor unions were now so numerous and membership so nearly universal among railway employees, such a provision would ordinarily work no hardships. Wherever there was a class of unorganized employees desiring arbitration, however, the chairman of the ICC or the commissioner of labor could work out a scheme to have the entire class represented.

Olney found no fault with the original bill's provisions for maintaining the status quo during pendency of arbitration. He was, however, concerned with the means for giving effect to the awards of arbitration commissions once decisions were handed down. An arbitration commission, he observed, was administrative, not judicial, in character and passed upon rules of business expediency and policy, not upon legal rights. The awards of arbitration commissions were, by the bill, to be subject to review and enforcement by the regular courts of law. Unlike the commissions, courts dealt with matters of legal right and were not competent to decide such policy questions as hours of labor, wage rates, and like matters. Olney believed, therefore, that the awards of arbitration commissions should be set aside by the courts only for errors of law apparent upon the record and not on substantive grounds.

Enforcement of awards involved two considerations, the length of time during which an award would be binding and the means by which an award could be enforced equally upon both parties. Olney believed that an award should be binding for at least two years. As for enforcing awards on capital and labor equally, he noted that the most difficult problem was how to force working men to abide by a decision that they did not like. Railroad companies, as public carriers, were bound by law to continue to do business no matter how displeased with an award, while employees were free to quit at will. This "one-sided operation" was inevitable, he believed. It could be mitigated by specifying that an employee ought not to quit work except upon giving three months', six months', or other appropriate notice so as to enable the company to secure a replacement. Even such a provision could not be specifically enforced upon individuals, however, and to punish quitting by fine or imprisonment would probably be inexpedient. The most to be hoped for would be compliance by employees out of "motives of expediency or of honor" because they would know what the law sanctioned.

Finally, Olney turned to the question of disputes in which parties refused to arbitrate or to abide by the award of an arbitration commission when handed down. Because the railroads were of a public nature, "paramount duty" required that they operate "at all hazards." Grievances had to be redressed with all possible speed, "but in the interim the public interests must not suffer and the business the bill is concerned with must go on with the least possible interruption." Olney urged, therefore, that the law provide that, in the event of a serious strike or strike threat, the attorney general of the United States be authorized to go into a court of equity to seek an injunction to restrain the employees from striking or obstructing the line and to call for the appointment of court receivers to take charge of the railroad company or companies involved until the controversy could be settled.

Of all the proposals in Olney's letter to McGann (and in his revised bill) this last was the most novel and controversial. Moseley, the secretary of the ICC, particularly liked it. Railroad employees, however, disliked it because the proposal would deprive them of their right to strike. Railroad managers, on the other hand, disliked the provision because it took control of their property from them whenever there was a serious strike threat.[56]

Excepting the provisions for injunctions against strikes and receiverships for railroads during disputes, Olney's revised draft was substituted for the original bill. In spite of these omissions, the attorney general worked closely with Moseley, Wright, Kernan, and McGann to secure its passage. A combination of lateness in introduction and a lack of enthusiasm conspired to defeat the bill in the lame duck session of the Fifty-third Congress. Scheduled to adjourn in early March 1895, the House did not receive the bill until January 18. Little outside pressure was applied to induce Congress to act on it. "I cannot quite understand it," Wright wrote Kernan on February 25, ". . . the officers of the brotherhoods came here and very strongly indorsed the bill as it was finally agreed upon, but other than that there is no particular interest in it, I think."[57]

House debate, which began on February 26, was neither heated nor long. Fear was expressed by one group of congressmen that the bill would deprive workers of their right to dispose of their labor as they chose. Arbitration awards, once handed down, would be enforced by injunctions and contempt proceedings for the period stipulated by law. Another group, on the other hand, was concerned that railroad companies, but not their employees, would be obliged to abide by awards inasmuch as there was no legal means to force men to labor against their wills.[58]

Some members wished to know what a new voluntary arbitration law would accomplish. The bill's manager, Contantine J. Erdman, answered that it was to be preferred to a compulsory arbitration measure because all interested parties would be behind it. Labor unions often complained that Congress ignored their wishes and passed laws they opposed; this bill was one that met labor's approval. A congressmen rose to ask who, specifically speaking for labor, endorsed the bill. Erdman named the heads of the five railway brotherhoods. A representative from New York requested the names of specific railroad managers who favored the bill. The Kansas Populist, "Sockless" Jerry Simpson, replied that he understood that the attorney general himself had drawn up part of the bill and favored it. "I understand also that he is the attorney and director of a great many railroads, which employ a great many laborers of the country. [Laughter.] That ought to be satisfactory to the gentleman." The New Yorker, undaunted, demanded that the attorney general state in writing whether or not he approved of the bill as revised.

Another representative offered additional "proof" of railroad support. "It is my opinion, based upon observation and experience in Congress, that when the railroad organizations of the country . . . are opposed to a measure pending in Congress, they manage to be heard. We generally find out something about their opinions, and it comes to us from them upon their own motion. Therefore, their silence, in my judgment, gives consent to the propriety of this measure."[59]

A few members thought it unfortunate that so important a measure should come up for vote with so little time for consideration. The managers of the bill replied, however, that the House Labor Committee had "distilled" the proposed act from between thirty and forty bills introduced in the House and had unanimously endorsed it only after consultation with the attorney general, the commissioner of labor, and the leaders of the railway brotherhoods. It was urgent, moreover, that something be done. "We are today," one congressman declared, ". . . on the very brink of what may be an industrial revolution. The committee have tried . . . to formulate some measure that would meet the threatened exigency." He pointed out that strikes were largely unnecessary; that in most instances they arose from misunderstandings which simple explanations would remove. If there were some arbiter in whom both parties could have confidence and to whom disputes could be submitted, "there would rarely if ever be an occasion for strikes." The purpose of the bill was "to provide the machinery by which such an umpire may be selected," and "to have such machinery ready before the dispute arises, that, being selected before either side becomes inflamed by passion, both may yield ready obedience to its decrees without feeling any humiliation in such submission."

A member from New York observed that "In any event, conditions can scarcely be worse than at present, when the only remedy for every slight misunderstanding seems to be the calling out of troops, with all the deplorable attendant consequences." "Strikes are too costly, and produce too much loss and misery to both employers and employees to be accepted as the best method for the adjustment of labor disputes," said an Iowa congressman. "[A]rbitrations sometimes do not accord full justice, but they are much better than war."[60]

The bill passed the House at the conclusion of debate on February 26. Although introduced in the Senate the next day, a dispute over the proper committee to consider the bill prevented any action before the close of the session on March 4. Reintroduced regularly at each new session of the Congress, the bill was not finally passed and signed into law until June 1, 1898, during the administration of William McKinley.[61]

In its final form the Erdman Act was essentially the Olney bill, though somewhat weakened. In some ways it was less strong than the Act of 1888 which it replaced. The Erdman Act covered only train service employees, the government could not initiate action during a railway labor dispute, and the investigative commissions provided for in the 1888 Act were dropped.

The Erdman Act was to be enforced by the chairman of the ICC and by the commissioner of labor, who could offer mediation services upon the motion of either party to a dispute. If that failed, they could urge arbitration by a three-man ad hoc commission consisting of a neutral member and one member each, chosen by the companies and by the employees. Arbitration awards were to be enforced by equity proceedings and were to be binding for one year. Injunctions could not be used to force individual workmen to remain in the employ of a company against their wishes. The provisions of the law most liked by the workers were those that forbade yellow-dog contracts, discrimination against union members, and the use of blacklists. These provisions, if violated, carried fines ranging from $100 to $1000.[62]

It could hardly be said that the Erdman Act revolutionized railway labor relations, despite the infrequency of railroad strikes in the years that followed its adoption. As Olney pointed out in 1908, the act had had its origins in the Chicago strike of 1894, and its purpose was "to prevent the recurrence of the evils and perils so emphatically impressed upon the public mind by that strike and its accompanying incidents." Its "presence on the statute book," he asserted on another occasion, "has had a salutary effect, though . . . I do not recall any instance in which its provisions have been actually availed of."[63]

The act was first invoked in 1899 when, at the request of conductors and trainmen in the Pittsburgh area, the chairman of the ICC and the commissioner of labor offered to mediate a dispute. The railroad managers involved regarded the offer as an intrusion on their prerogatives and rejected it out of hand. Because of the ineffectiveness of its machinery, the law remained a dead letter until revived in 1906. Between that year and the enactment of a new law, the Newlands Act of 1913, some sixty-one requests for assistance were made under the Erdman Act. Of these requests twenty-eight were settled by mediation, four by arbitration, eight by a combination of the two, and twenty-one by outside agreement after mediation had failed or one party had refused to participate. Meanwhile, the Supreme Court ruled in 1908 that the provision against yellow-dog contracts was an unconstitutional invasion of freedom of contract and, thus, invalidated that portion of the law.[64]

The great upheaval of July 1894, in the long run, proved to be broadly educative. Railway workers, convinced that major tie-ups of interstate commerce would be suppressed by the federal government, hesitated for years to engage in strikes or boycotts of any significance. At the same time, the government's use of naked force to suppress the strike at the behest of and for the benefit of the railroads seems to have won wide sympathy for the cause of labor. Increasing numbers of thoughtful men both in and out of government no longer accepted force as the ultimate answer to railway labor disputes, and the Erdman Act, weak though it was, stood as evidence of that changed attitude. To the dismay of the railroad managers, their clear-cut victory proved of little value as government officials, led by Attorney General Olney, in effect declared themselves reluctant, if not unwilling, to wield again the weapons so recently forged and burnished in the Pullman strike.

• • •

CHAPTER IX

Conclusions

BY THE 1870'S MUCH of American labor was restive. The long struggle for organization and recognition was beginning. Although the labor movement often divided over ultimate goals and the best means to reach them, working men for the most part demanded only a larger voice in determining the issues directly related to their personal well-being. They wanted to negotiate the terms of their employment, not just to accept the wages, hours, and working conditions imposed by their employers. They were concerned, too, with their dignity as men and sought security against arbitrary treatment at the hands of their bosses.

But in the 1870's, and for several decades to come, employers held the upper hand. Since at least the 1840's, businessmen in vital areas of the economy had been concentrating control of capital for large-scale enterprise, primarily through use of the corporation. The major trunk line railroad companies, by the close of the Civil War, were the greatest of these growing concentrations of economic power.

Workers, during these same years, failed completely to match the expanding power of their employers. Depressions and the Civil War had snuffed out almost all of the nation's early labor organizations. No significant union of national scope existed until the 1880's;[1] none attained power comparable to that of capital until the mid-twentieth century. Vis-àvis their employers, nearly all laborers had slipped in individual importance and bargaining power.

A considerable part of this growing gap between the bargaining positions of workers and corporate employers was in the area of law. By the 1870's the corporation was well entrenched and carefully shored up with the legal mortar of precedent. The rise of the corporation as a business form in the United States was, after all, the joint handiwork of the business and legal communities. The one furnished opportunities and economic wherewithal; the other supplied justifications and the necessary legal forms. It was not conventional reasoning, for instance, but the logic peculiar to the legal mind that defined corporations as artificial beings, distinct from the natural persons who owned and operated them, possessing legal immortality and endowed with most of the economic and legal rights of natural persons. The power of the corporate employer over its individual employees, so obvious to the workers, completely escaped the lawyers and judges, who in developing the doctrine of liberty of contract saw the two as equals. Similarly, only in the subtle contemplation of law could railroad companies conveniently change from public highways to private property and back again as necessity dictated.

No such legal legerdemain came to the assistance of working men. In the late nineteenth century, labor unions enjoyed few of the enviable legal protections afforded corporations. The right of workmen to associate freely in unions and to strike for the betterment of their working conditions, first asserted by the courts in the 1840's, was not fully conceded even in the 1890's.[2] Courts did not look upon unions as collective entities similar in nature to corporations or designed to counterbalance the power of combinations of capital. Rarely did courts recognize unions per se as parties to disputes before them. Rather, they dealt with union members as individuals or prosecuted them as conspirators.

Had unions grown apace with corporations during the three or four decades preceding 1877, much of the subsequent difficulty might have been avoided. Without the power differential in their favor, corporations would have been less tempted to increase efficiency or cut costs at the expense of labor. Attempts to do so, moreover, would have run into stiff resistance. The legal advantage of corporations also, of necessity, would not have grown so great had the two been more nearly equal. With power comparable, if not commensurate, with that of capital, labor in all likelihood would have gained tacit, if not full, legal recognition long before it did. Unable to ride roughshod over labor, employers quite possibly would have accepted some forms of collective bargaining in the late nineteenth century. And when peaceful negotiations on occasion would have given way to serious strikes, governmental intervention to protect public interests might well have been more nearly neutral between the parties.

But such were not the lines of development. By 1877 railway workmen, though poorly organized, were no longer willing to allow the terms and conditions of their employment to be set or changed arbitrarily by their employers. The companies, with equal determination, clung to their accumulated prerogatives in fixing the conditions of employment. In the absence of established machinery for peacefully resolving these differences, strikes and boycotts seemed to offer workers their only hope. When at last the troubles burst forth on the railroads in 1877, the struggle was between powerful, well-established corporations on the one hand and weak, inadequately organized workmen on the other. Wealth, power, influence, traditional privileges, and the law all tended to the side of the companies. To those considerable advantages was often added the active assistance of the federal government.

If, somehow, railroad strikes and boycotts had affected only the parties to the disputes, federal intervention would have been improbable. But by the 1870's the nation seemingly was unable and, certainly was unwilling to endure serious or protracted railway strikes. Shortages quickly developed in the necessities of life; prices advanced; large numbers of men were thrown out of work; mail was delayed; the flow of interstate commerce was halted; the public suffered great inconvenience and hardship; and, frequently, the strikes led to riot, tumult, and disorder. Under the circumstances governmental intervention in one form or another became necessary.

Ideally, the strikes should have been recognized for what they were. Following the disorders of 1877, while the problem was still fresh in the public's mind, Congress should have laid down policies for coping with similar disorders in the future. Realizing that the strikes were but symptoms of a deeper malady, Congress would then, hopefully, have moved to the problem of labor reform and the peaceful resolution of labor disputes. Unfortunately, such a course was not pursued. Rather, strikes continued to be dealt with as crises, in the heat of passion, often by officials who were strongly prejudiced to the side of the railroads.

In many ways the railway strikes of 1877 got things off on the wrong foot. By coming when they did, and in the manner they did, they established a number of precedents that thereafter stood in the way of finding more satisfactory solutions to the problem of railway labor disputes. The occasional rumblings of discontent preceding that disquieting summer had in no way prepared anyone for what followed.[3] The workers themselves, without preparation, struck in anger and frustration. They had no clearly defined objectives, only ad hoc leadership, and lacked the means to support themselves and their families during the struggle. The companies, startled at the scope and bitterness of the rebellion against them, had no formulated plans for coping with strikes on so formidable a scale. A large part of the public, uninformed as to the workers' grievances or objectives and shocked at the excesses of the mobs, had little sympathy for the strikes, whatever it may have felt toward working men in general. Least of all was the federal government prepared to deal with the disputes, labor problems until then having been almost wholly beyond its province.

For want of organization, planning, and leadership, the ill-conceived strikes of 1877 turned into undirected rioting. President Hayes, looking beyond the disorders, correctly diagnosed them as but outer manifestations of a deep-seated labor problem. Circumstances worked against treating them as such, however. Congress, the proper agency for dealing with labor reforms at the federal level, was not in session. Many people, moreover, agreed with Judges Drummond and Gresham that the strikes were a dangerous challenge to the authority of the courts and of government in general. They regarded the strikes as a species of warfare against society at large. Even President Hayes took the position that the first business before the Republic was restoration of law and order. Only after peace returned could reforms be considered. And suppression of lawlessness and riot— at least once it got beyond the powers of the states to handle— fell to the federal executive and judiciary, not to Congress. The nature of the strike, then, combined with the absence of congressional action, set the precedent that handling strikes was particularly a function of the President and of the courts.

Had Congress been in session in July 1877, there is no reason to believe that it would have moved boldly into labor reforms or even strike legislation. Certainly, the legislators took little enough notice of the strikes when next they met. This failure to act during the quiet aftermath of the July disorders only confirmed the notion that the executive and judiciary were responsible for dealing with serious strike problems. With nothing done to avert or control future strikes, when disputes again flared, the executive branch and the courts, by default, were again obliged to intervene. By chance, Congress was in session during each of the subsequent major railway strikes. In each instance it debated half-hearted measures for the voluntary arbitration of such disputes while the strikes raged. When the strikes ended, so did efforts to legislate.

Ultimately, such policy as emerged was made by the executive and judicial branches, not by Congress. Almost invariably it was policy shaped in times of crisis, when labor disputes were out of control. Few serious attempts were made by any branch of the government to remove the causes of labor friction in times of industrial peace or to encourage the peaceful settlement of disputes prior to the outbreak of hostilities. Only when strikers were actually battling their employers did the federal government intervene. Policies were then improvised on the spot and of necessity were aimed not at settling the disputes or warding off future strikes, but at suppressing riot and restoring law and order. In the fever of battle, decisions of long-range consequence were made with little or no attention to their long-term implications.

That no particular official or officials were responsible for determining federal policy during labor crises further complicated matters. When a strike situation became critical, those officials who found the problem thrust upon them, or who were willing to act, took steps to end the disorders. In 1877 it was the President and his cabinet who acted; in 1886 a congressional committee intervened; in 1888 the postmaster general and the chairman of the Interstate Commerce Commission attempted to halt a strike peacefully; during the Great Northern strike subordinate officials of the Postoffice and Justice departments made momentous policy decisions; during the Coxeyite troubles and the Chicago strike of 1894 the attorney general, assisted by railroad lawyers, determined most of the government's policies; and throughout the two decades judge-made law was probably the most important facet of the federal government's railroad strike policy.

Executive handling of the major railway strikes was often hesitant and lacking in consistency. Both Hayes and Cleveland were conscientious men who believed that the enforcement of laws should be impartial and fair to all parties. Both balked at throwing the full weight of the government nakedly to the side of the railroads. At the same time both were unwilling to accept the consequences of nonintervention. Consequently, both scrupulously insisted upon precise formulas being met that would justify intervention. At bottom their insistence upon such niceties stemmed less from their desire to avoid intervention than from their need, for consciences' sake, to cloak intervention, however thinly, in the legalistic garb of "unavoidable duty."

The willingness or unwillingness of the Presidents involved to delegate or to allow authority to drift to others had much to do with the inconsistency of policy. President Hayes, for example, exercised authority in 1877 in conjunction with his cabinet, but retained a high degree of control in his own hands. President Cleveland, on the other hand, held but loose control over his immediate subordinates. Though he himself hesitated to act during labor crises, his underlings often acted decisively, apparently without his knowledge or prior consent. During the Southwest strikes in 1885 and 1886 Cleveland did nothing more than recommend to Congress that it enact a voluntary arbitration law. Conditions existed in those strikes that would in later years have prompted a Dickinson or an Olney to intervene. But no official, not even the President, assumed responsibility for acting. In 1888 Cleveland's postmaster general, Dickinson, laid down policy with respect to the movement of mails, apparently without discussing the matter in advance with the President. During his second term Cleveland again took no important part in the struggles against Coxeyites or strikers. Attorney General Olney, Postmaster General Bissell, and a number of their subordinates, on the other hand, did act.

Executive policy lacked continuity for another reason, too. Unlike the federal judges who recorded their most important decisions in the law reports, the executive branch kept almost no records of how it handled labor problems. What past administrations did, and why, was soon forgotten. This information could be reconstructed only with difficulty, from newspapers, executive department files, and personal papers of the men involved in decision-making. When acting in time of crisis, officials had little time to reconstruct past policy from such scattered, ephemeral sources.

The federal judiciary throughout the era was more aggressive, more inventive, and more consistent than the executive in dealing with strikes. The boldness of the federal judges was probably a function of their independence from the electorate, a freedom which the other branches did not share. Judges were at liberty to act in accord with their views of the law and the felt necessities of the time. That they were creative may well be attributed to the willingness of the legal community, bench and bar alike, to build continuously on existing law and precedent; to be forever pouring new wine into old bottles. Seeing their own authority challenged by interferences with railroads in their custody and seeing the need for action to prevent the breakdown of law and order, judges refused to accept the argument that they were powerless because no statute law authorized their intervention. Assisted by a host of railroad lawyers, they sought out judicial formulas by which law and order could be restored on the nation's railways.

The consistency of the judiciary, though far from monolithic, probably was based on the system of case reporting and the sanctity of precedent. Each judge had at his fingertips the rulings of his predecessors in similar instances. These could be used as justification when a former ruling was repeated or as the basis for logical constructions that would reach out into new, uncharted regions, as needed. This combination of precedent and logic allowed for inventiveness and flexibility while seeming to preserve historical continuity.[4] No similar process was available to the Congress or to the executive.

The creativity of the judiciary in meeting the strike problem between 1877 and 1898 was heavily prejudiced to the side of the railroad companies. This predilection for the corporate side was not new; from Chief Justice John Marshall's ruling that corporation charters were contracts, through the Supreme Court's decision in 1883 that the due process clause of the Fourteenth Amendment was specifically intended to apply to corporations, the federal judiciary had done much to foster, encourage, and protect corporations.[5]

This same creative bias of the legal community had long since developed the railroad receivership. In spite of strong English precedents to the contrary, American courts of equity evolved the receivership as a means to protect railways from the consequences of economic failure. Originally, the device was a temporary expedient to provide for the operation and maintenance of insolvent railroad property until reorganized or liquidated. Through the years abuses crept in and receiverships came to enjoy longer tenure and greater power. Some receivers not only preserved the insolvent property in their charge, but with the approval of the courts proceeded to complete construction of railways, to build new lines, to rebuild old lines, and even to lease and complete the construction of other railroads, often ignoring the wishes of the owners and creditors of the company.[6]

When railway companies were threatened by strikes in 1877 and after, it was in complete harmony with past developments that the courts, step by step, built up the legal foundations for the blanket injunction that in 1894 would prohibit any interference with the operation of any railroad carrying the mail or interstate commerce. To be sure, some judges were inclined to a more neutral position or even to the side of labor. But suggestions like Judge Caldwell's, that railroads in receivership should negotiate wages with labor unions to which their employees belonged, or Judge Speer's, that courts act as arbiters of disputes between receivers and employees, received little support from their fellow jurists.

It can only be regretted that the courts' creativity failed to develop arbitration, for example, as a means for settling railway labor disputes at the time that it was developing the injunction as a device for halting strikes. Insofar as the courts were stripping workmen of the strike weapon, it would seem to have been incumbent upon them to create a substitute by which workers' rights would be protected. Just as the judges at first limited court protection by injunctions and contempt proceedings to railroads in receivership, so might they have insisted that railroads in their custody settle disputes between receivers and employees by negotiation or arbitration. And just as the courts later issued more sweeping injunctions to protect all railways carrying mail or interstate commerce, whether or not in receivership, so might they have ordered the negotiation or arbitration of all railway labor disputes on lines that sought court protection, whether or not the companies were in receivership. When receiverships were applied for, judges could have spelled out the procedures under which disputes between receivers and employees were to be resolved, before granting the request. Similarly, the petition for an injunction, which was not mandatory upon a judge, could have been granted only if the companies first attempted to negotiate their differences with their employees. The courts could even have insisted upon compulsory arbitration as a condition for making an injunction permanent.

Of course, it can be argued that the courts had never been empowered by the Constitution or the laws to force companies to recognize labor unions or to negotiate with them, or to submit their disputes to arbitration. But it is equally true that in the beginning neither the Constitution nor the laws authorized courts to create receiverships, use their powers of injunction, or punish for contempt, as was being done between 1877 and 1898. If the latter were rational and proper extensions of customary judicial powers, why not the former also? And to the argument that judges were not equipped by training to rule on questions of wage rates, hours of labor, and other terms of employment because these were economic and business rather than judicial questions, it could be maintained with equal force that for judges to have presumed to operate railways through receivers in the first place was even more an economic and business undertaking, and certainly was no easier. Judges in those instances made use of the expertese of railway managers by appointing them receivers of the property in their custody; in other areas where technical information beyond the competency of a judge was called for, the courts made use of special assistants and masters-in-chancery. They could have proceeded in a similar manner to settle labor disputes. Most preferred to assume that the receivers already appointed were fully competent to handle these questions or that the problems were outside the scope of the courts. Ultimately, it was a matter of what the judges were willing to do. Had they shown the same determination to force the settlement of railway labor disputes by peaceful means that they manifested in finding ways to suppress strikes, it is quite possible that they would have succeeded in that endeavor too.

Justice Samuel Freeman Miller of the United States Supreme Court once offered a simple explanation for the pro-railroad bias of the courts. "It is vain to contend with judges who have been at the bar, the advocates for forty years, of railroad companies, and all forms of associated capital, when they are called upon to decide cases where such interests are in contest," he said. "All their training, all their feelings are from the start in favor of those who need no such influence."[7] Certainly, many of the jurists and other public officials involved in determining railway strike policy in the late nineteenth century fitted the pattern suggested by Miller. Before becoming judges, Drummond, Hanford, Krekel, and Treat (of St. Louis) had all been active in promoting railroads in their respective communities. Several of the authors of the more stringent antilabor rulings and injunctions—Baker, Dallas, and Jenkins—had only shortly before their elevations to the bench served in the law offices of important railroad companies. The executive officers most responsible for antilabor policies—Bissell, Maxwell, Olney, and Walker—immediately before, during, and after their terms in office were directors or legal counsels of railroads. At the opposite extreme, Federal Judges Caldwell, Woolson, and Speer, and Postmaster General Dickinson, all of whom stood neutral or took a pro-labor stance, had few if any railroad connections.

It would be naïve, of course, to suggest that the policy of the government was determined solely by such influences. The prevailing views of the time, the felt needs in given situations, the concepts of justice, right, and expediency must all have played some part in the decision-making process. But to ignore the considerations of the long-term economic and professional ties of the policymakers would also be naïve. Their training, background, personalities, financial interests, and professional associations could scarcely be ruled irrelevant to the decisions they made. These men, after all, were not mere agents or pawns of the great forces at work within the society in which they lived. The tide of industrialization, the demands of free-enterprise capitalism, the needs of the era, even the elusive "spirit of the age," undoubtedly influenced them. But in the end these men, whose hands were at the levers of power, made deliberate choices. As has already been seen, some took actions that ran counter to the trends of the time. Their actions alone would seem to indicate that the forces of society were less than inexorable.

It is also probably true that these public officials responded to the crises within limits prescribed by "society" or by "public opinion." But how wide were the limits within which they acted? Would a decision by President Hayes in 1877 to have called upon the B & O to negotiate with its men instead of sending in troops have outraged public opinion? Would society have condemned the federal judges for *not* expanding the injunction into a major weapon against labor? Would there have been a great public outcry had President Cleveland refused to send troops to Chicago in 1894 until requested to do so by Governor Altgeld? Did Dickinson's ruling that the mail must be hauled alone during strikes, if necessary, cause any greater public resentment than Maxwell's finding that every car of every train carrying mail was under the protection of the federal government? Did the public note or even much care that one federal judge ordered his receivers to negotiate with their employees while another forbade his to do so?

The federal executive and judiciary chose to deal only

with the outer symptoms—the strikes themselves. The task of treating the disease that produced the strikes properly fell to the Congress. Once the other branches of government restored law and order by putting down the strikes, why did railway labor reform not become the first order of business for Congress? Why was machinery not set up for channeling railway labor disputes into courts of law or before administrative agencies or arbitration tribunals? In the first place the cumbersome procedures of Congress seemed to preclude prompt action except under the gravest circumstances. A determined minority or an apathetic or divided majority in Congress at any time could slow or even halt the grinding of the legislative mills. For Congress to undertake legislation on a new and difficult subject, as railway strikes were in that era, required both a general consensus in and out of Congress as to what should be done and active outside groups applying pressures on the lawmakers to act. So long as there was shooting in the streets, congressmen displayed an awareness of the labor problem. When a strike ended, congressmen turned to other crises or to less controversial matters. Fortunately, in one sense, but unfortunately, in another, no major strike of the era was of sufficient duration to keep Congress under pressure long enough to enact stringent labor laws. The quality of any laws Congress might have passed under duress can only be imagined.

Fully as important as the insufficient pressures on Congress to act was the absence of agreement as to what should be done if it did act. Even at the height of the most violent strikes the public did not speak with a united voice. The sympathizers of labor saw only the need for legislation to curb the power of the railroad companies and to force them to give their employees their due. Railroad officials and their friends and allies, on the other hand, called for laws restricting the right of employees to organize, strike, or picket. A very common view, moreover, was that these matters were probably best left to work themselves out without governmental interference.

The prevailing concepts of property rights also worked against the adoption of labor reform laws. It was generally accepted that the railroads, in spite of their quasi-public nature, were a species of private property. As such they were to be run by their owners or their hired managers for profit. The owners and managers of all forms of private property enjoyed wide freedom to do what they would with their property. To suggest, in a dispute over working terms for railway employees, that capital be required to sit down with labor and negotiate differences or accept settlement by adjudication or arbitration implied that workers had some rights in these matters. In the dominant view of that era, the extent of a workingman's rights was to accept or to reject employment on the terms offered. If there were any negotiations whatever, they were between the individual employee and the railroad corporation that employed him.[8]

Closely related was a widely tolerated double standard for combinations of capital as opposed to combinations of labor. The right—indeed the necessity—for capital to combine was generally accepted. How else could railroads and steel plants and oil refineries be built? Modern industry required great amounts of capital, and combination was the means by which capital was amassed for such enterprises. Within corporations the rights of individual stockholders had to give way to rule by the majority, and majority control was upheld by the courts. It was not proposed or expected that government would intervene in the affairs of a private corporation to protect the right of an individual minority stockholder to use his capital within the corporation as he chose. Similarly, not until passage of the Sherman Antitrust Act in 1890 was government expected to protect the owners of unincorporated businesses from the stifling competition of the incorporated giants in their field. Even after passage of that law the courts generally refused to apply it to mergers, holding companies, or other tight combinations prior to 1904. With respect to the development of ever larger corporations and combinations, the highly individualistic system defined by the classical economists was no longer applicable. Corporations and the amassing of capital were looked upon by the dominant groups in society as evolutionary, progressive adaptations to changing conditions and to a growing economy.[9]

The organization of workingmen into labor unions was viewed somewhat less charitably. Unions were not looked upon as labor's response to amassed capital. Rather, they were seen as collections of men with illegal designs on the property of others. Often they were linked, at least in the newspapers, with European revolutionary movements. If labor unions were not themselves illegal conspiracies, the boycotts and strikes they conducted were lawless interferences with private property, and major strikes were often compared with the rising of the Paris Commune in 1871. Even when it was accepted that laborers had freedom to associate with one another in unions, the individual freedom of each worker, whether or not a union member, was rigidly insisted upon. The rights of any one individual worker transcended the collective rights of workers combined in unions. Government *was* expected to intervene to protect the rights of the individual workingman if he chose to defy his union and to work rather than strike. Individual workers were protected from the stifling competition of organized labor. The completely free and open labor market of the classical economists was maintained, and the idea that a union, like its counterpart, the corporation, was the product of evolution, growth, and adaptation to changing conditions was forcibly denied.

The era, after all, was one of rapid industrial growth and development. Railroads and industries of all sorts were needed, and that need was universally recognized. Those who created industries, built factories, managed railroads, and owned and operated mines were the heroes of the age. The respect and admiration of the nation was grudgingly, when not enthusiastically, given the captains of industry. Ownership and managerial positions were seen as achieved and merited roles. The successful were at the top because their abilities and virtues carried them there. The ordinary workingman, by contrast, was given more sympathy than admiration. Everyone professed to believe that labor should be paid all that it rightly earned. Even among the lower ranks of society, however, few aspired to be common laborers. If the lot of the wage earner was not envied, under the prevailing set of beliefs it was presumed that he too was in the position he deserved. If he was at or near the bottom, it was because his abilities and virtues carried him no higher.[10]

Given these assumptions among the dominant groups in society, it is hardly surprising that Congress failed to act decisively in the matter of railway strikes. Apparently, voluntary arbitration was as much as Congress could agree on, despite the relative lack of success of such laws at the state level. But in their debates over the Acts of 1888 and 1898, congressmen took no notice whatever of eight different state arbitration acts adopted between 1878 and 1886. Possibly these laws were overlooked because they were relatively new; more likely they went unnoticed because they had worked so ineffectively.[11]

Passage of the Erdman Act after two decades of turmoil on the railroads marked the end of the first full phase of the development of a federal strike policy. In spite of errant strands to the contrary, the lines of policy between 1877 and the close of the Debs case in 1895 were generally in the direction of suppressing railway strikes. After the decision in the Debs case, little more could have been done along those lines short of outlawing railroad labor organizations altogether and prohibiting railway strikes and boycotts by statute. Congress was unwilling, however, to pursue the course laid down by the executive and the courts. The Erdman Act, though a direct product of the Chicago strike, bore evidence of the changes that were beginning to sweep over labor affairs in this country after 1895.

It was clear by 1898 that the federal government would not allow any railway strike of consequence to take place. There was little doubt but that injunctions, backed by the full force of the federal government, would be employed to prevent any actual blockages of the mail or of interstate commerce. At the same time, it appears that neither railway laborers nor government officials wanted to put "government by injunction" to the test. Railway workers often used strike threats to gain their objectives after 1898, but no railway labor dispute erupted into a major strike for over a quarter-century. When the strike of 1922 occurred, it was promptly met by a blanket injunction which railway labor chose not to defy.[12]

But by 1898 it was also clear to many that the mere suppression of strikes was not the answer to the railway labor problem. Repression had about reached the limits of its usefulness as a policy and so gave way to legislation designed to ward off clashes between railway labor and the federal government. Increasingly, the President and the Congress became involved in railway labor disputes before they reached crisis proportions. Federal courts, long dominant in the battles against railway strikers, had less to do with such matters after 1898. Under the new dispensation, Congress, usually at the behest of the President and with the blessings of the Supreme Court, adopted the practice of averting strikes, whenever possible, by enacting new railway labor acts.[13] The threat of a strike in 1913 led to passage of the Newlands Act. Another, in 1916, produced the Adamson Act, which established the eight-hour work day for railroad labor. The brief railway strike of 1922 caused enactment of the Railway Labor Act of 1926, which, with amendments added in 1934, maintained relative peace on the railroads until after World War II. President Harry S. Truman, angered at a strike threat in 1946, recommended that Congress provide for the drafting of striking railroaders into the Army. Although the rash proposal was not written into law, it did cause the brotherhoods to retreat.[14] In the long controversy over work rules and automation on the railways in the 1960's, executive, legislative, and even judicial intervention repeatedly postponed threatened railway strikes.

Railroad companies and railway workers led in the development of modern industrialization and in the organization of labor throughout the second half of the nineteenth century. Railway labor laws would continue to pace the nation in the development of reform legislation in the twentieth century. The Adamson Act of 1916 gave the eight-hour day to railway workers more than a decade and a half before it became general, first under the New Deal's National Industrial Recovery Act and later under the Fair Labor Standards Act. The Railway Labor Act of 1926 recognized the right of railway workers to organize and to bargain collectively with their employers through representatives chosen by the employees without "interference, influence or coercion." Under Section 7(a) of the NIRA the same rights were conferred upon labor in general in almost identical phraseology. The 1934 amendments to the Railway Labor Act prohibited company unions on the railways, the use of yellow-dog contracts, and discrimination against employees who belonged to labor organizations. These same devices were listed among the unfair labor practices prohibited to employers under the Wagner Labor Relations Act of 1935. Similarly, the rule that representatives of employees elected by majority vote would speak for the entire craft or class of employees electing them appeared first in the 1934 amendments to the Railway Labor Act. The same provision, but worded more strongly, appeared the next year in the Wagner Act. Finally, passage of the Railroad Retirement Act of 1934 marked the beginning of social security legislation during the New Deal.

The Railway Labor Act of 1926, in another area, made a contribution to the development of the national emergency strike provisions of the Taft-Hartley Act. Under the 1926 law, when negotiations and mediation failed to resolve a railway labor dispute, the President was empowered to name a board of inquiry that would investigate the points at issue and report its findings to him within thirty days. During that period and for an additional thirty days after the report was made, there could be no strike. The eighty day "cooling off" period provided for in the Taft-Hartley law was essentially similar.[15]

Despite the continued leadership of railway labor law in the field of labor legislation, the contributions of railway strikes to federal strike policy were largely over by 1895. The labor injunction, fashioned in the era of railway strikes, has remained, though modified, as a permanent part of the federal arsenal for combating major strikes in vital industries. During the twentieth century, strikes in the coal, steel, and automobile industries, and in other critical areas of the economy have filled the role once played by railway strikes. From its experiences in meeting these new crises as they have arisen, the federal government has continued to evolve a strike policy, but along new lines. As early as the anthracite strike of 1902, for example, executive intervention took the form of mediation rather than of suppression.

Today it can be argued that the major railway strikes of the late nineteenth century were precursors of the modern national emergency strike. But when, in 1947, Congress for the first time defined and provided for national emergency strikes in the Taft-Hartley Act, railway strikes were specifically excluded from the law's provisions. Obviously, this was not because railway strikes, if they occurred, would be of little consequence. Rather, their inclusion would have been a work of supererogation. They had been implicitly dealt with as national emergencies since 1877. After 1898 the Presidents, the federal courts, and Congress recognized that a paralysis of railroad traffic, calamitous though it would be, could no longer be met by crushing labor. Congress, therefore, created special machinery for avoiding railroad strikes long before the Taft-Hartley Act. It has stood ready, since 1898, to revise and redesign that machinery as often as necessary to prevent major tie-ups of the rail network.

Notes

1. W. W. Rostow, *The Process of Economic Growth,* 2d ed. (New York, 1962), pp. 302–3. Rostow's "take-off" thesis is controversial, but widely accepted. Among Rostow's severest American critics is Robert William Fogel, whose book, *Railroads and American Economic Growth: Essays in Econometric History* (Baltimore, 1964), is itself highly controversial. Fogel does not deny that railroads have been important to American economic development, but he insists that their effects have been grossly exaggerated and that whatever their contribution, they were not indispensable. He maintains that canals and natural waterways could have provided adequate transportation for the nation. He does not explain how transportation beyond the Missouri River could have developed without railways. See also Douglass C. North, *Growth and Welfare in the American Past* (Englewood Cliffs, N.J., 1966), pp. 117–21.

2. Leland H. Jenks, "Railroads as an Economic Force in American Development," *Journal of Economic History,* IV (May 1944), 13. See also: Rostow, *Process of Economic Growth,* pp. 262, 265; Alfred D. Chandler, ed., *The Railroads, The Nation's First Big Business* (New York, 1965), pp. 3–9; Robert V. Bruce, *1877, Year of Violence* (Indianapolis, 1959), pp. 30–31. For an example of the effect of railroads on commercial agriculture in four counties in Illinois, see Douglass C. North, *The Economic Growth of the United States 1790–1860* (Englewood Cliffs, N.J., 1961), pp. 147–53. Herman E. Krooss, *American Economic Development* (Englewood Cliffs, N.J., 1955), pp. 438–40, gives a succinct and impressive summary of the total impact of railways on the American economy.

3. Thomas C. Cochran and William Miller, *The Age of Enterprise, A Social History of Industrial America* (New York, 1942), pp. 67–70, 130–35, 188–89; Chandler, *The Railroads,* pp. 44–47; Wilfred Owen,

Strategy for Mobility (Washington, 1964), p. 26. See also Thomas C. Cochran's essay "The Entrepreneur in American Capital Formation," reprinted in his book, *The Inner Revolution: Essays on the Social Sciences in History* (New York, 1964), pp. 71–109.

4. Chandler, *The Railroads*, p. 22. According to statistics quoted by Douglas Alan Fisher, *The Epic of Steel* (New York, 1963), p. 125, 80 percent of all Bessemer process steel produced in the United States in 1870 and 79 percent in 1880 went for rails. John F. Stover, *American Railroads* (Chicago, 1961), p. 162, points out that the Pennsylvania withdrew the last of its wood-burning freight engines in 1862 and that other companies did soon afterwards.

5. Krooss, *American Economic Development,* pp. 34–38.

6. U.S., Dept. of Commerce, *Historical Statistics of the United States* (Washington, 1960), pp. 427–28, 711.

7. Bruce, *1877,* pp. 43–44.

8. Even Fogel, *Railroads and Economic Growth,* who argues that railways were not indispensable for American economic development from the beginning, does not suggest that once they had pulled far ahead of canals, the country could have dispensed with their services suddenly, as during a protracted railway strike, for instance.

9. Sidney L. Miller, *Inland Transportation Principles and Politics* (New York, 1933), p. 110; Stover, *American Railroads,* p. 172.

10. George Rogers Taylor, *The Transportation Revolution, 1815–1860* (New York, 1951), pp. 102–3; Stover, *American Railroads,* p. 172.

11. U.S., Dept. of Commerce, *Historical Statistics,* pp. 429, 711.

12. For example, see Thomas C. Cochran, *Railroad Leaders, 1845–1890, The Business Mind in Action* (Cambridge, 1953), pp. 189–96. The struggle of two factions for control of a New Hampshire railway is graphically recounted in Edward C. Kirkland, *Men, Cities, and Transportation* (Cambridge, 1948), II, 15–25. See also Kirkland's *Industry Comes of Age* (New York, 1961), pp. 113–14.

13. For an excellent account of the attitudes of railroad managers toward unions in this era, see Donald L. McMurry, *The Great Burlington Strike of 1888: A Case History in Labor Relations* (Cambridge, 1956), pp. 273–74.

14. Joseph G. Rayback, *A History of American Labor* (New York, 1959), p. 130.

15. McMurry, *Burlington Strike,* pp. 29–31; Bruce, *1877,* p. 47.

16. Ray Ginger, *The Bending Cross, A Biography of Eugene Victor Debs* (New Brunswick, N.J., 1949), pp. 44–50, 54–60, 64–69.

17. Donald L. McMurry, "Federation of the Railroad Brotherhoods, 1889–1894," *Industrial and Labor Relations Review, VII* (Oct. 1953), 73–92.

18. Bruce, *1877*, pp. 59, 61–63, 124–25, 305. The history of the ARU will be found in Almont Lindsey, *The Pullman Strike* (Chicago, 1942), pp. 107–20, *passim.*, and in Ginger, *The Bending Cross*, pp. 87–183.

19. Benjamin Aaron, in an essay in Industrial Relations Research Association, *Emergency Disputes and National Policy* (New York, 1955), pp. 79–80, argues that national emergency strikes were not possible until World War II. The Pullman strike, the Coeur d'Alene disturbance, the anthracite strike of 1902 and the 1919 steel strike all "attracted national attention," he says, "but this was because of the importance of the issues involved or the occurrence of violence, rather than the existence of any threat to the national health or safety." The mass-production industries in which most national emergency disputes arise were not substantially established until the 1930's, and their employees were not organized into strong unions until the 1940's. In another essay in the same book, George H. Hildebrand notes that "The concept of national emergency disputes was first applied to the railroads, in a legislative history that goes back to the Arbitration Act of 1888. It is also implicit in the no-strike-no-lockout pledge of the first world war." Fn., p. 3. See also Leonard A. Lecht, *Experience Under Railway Labor Legislation* (New York, 1955), p. 3.

President Woodrow Wilson, in an address to Congress on August 29, 1916, asked for enactment of the eight-hour day for railway workers in terms that indicate that he regarded the possibility of a railroad strike at that time as catastrophic. Should a strike occur, he said, "Cities will be cut off from their food supplies, the whole commerce of the nation will be paralyzed, men of every sort and occupation will be thrown out of employment, countless thousands will in all likelihood be brought, it may be, to the very point of starvation, and a tragical national calamity brought on . . . because no basis of accommodation or settlement has been found." *Supplement to the Messages and Papers of the President* (n.p., 1917), p. 8145.

20. The percentages are for the year 1962. U.S., Dept. of Commerce, *Statistical Abstract of the United States, 1964* (Washington, 1964), p. 570. George H. Hildebrand and Irving Bernstein, in separate essays discussing national emergency strikes, both conclude that any significant railroad strike would almost incontestably be an emergency. Industrial Relations Research Association, *Emergency Disputes,* pp. 3–45.

21. Bruce, *1877,* p. 271.

22. *New York Tribune,* July 24, 25, 1877.

23. *St. Louis Republican,* July 24, 1877.

24. *New York Times,* July 26, 1877.

25. *Chicago Daily Tribune,* July 23, 1877.

26. *Nation,* LIX (July 5, 1894), 5–6.

27. Quoted by *Washington Post,* July 3, 1877.

28. *Chicago Daily Tribune,* July 6, 1894.

29. *Independent,* XLVI (July 5, 1894), 858.

30. *North American Review,* CLIX (Aug. 1894), 183.

31. Bruce, *1877,* pp. 271–72; Lindsey, *Pullman Strike,* pp. 209–10.

32. See, for example, *Commercial & Financial Chronicle,* XXV (July 28, 1877), 1.

33. *Chicago Times,* July 26, 1877.

34. *New York Times,* July 25, 1877; *New York Tribune,* July 26, 1877.

35. *St. Louis Times,* July 26, 1877.

36. *Chicago Post,* July 25, 1877; *Chicago Times,* July 27, 1877.

37. *New York Tribune,* July 26, 27, 1877.

38. *St. Louis Times,* July 26, 27, 1877. See also *New York Tribune,* July 28, 1877; *New York Times,* July 20, 1877; *Indianapolis News,* July 26, 1877; Lindsey, *Pullman Strike,* pp. 209–10.

39. *Chicago Daily Tribune,* July 3, 4, 1894.

40. *Ibid.,* July 1, 3, 9, 11, 1894.

41. *New York Times,* July 4, 10, 1894.

42. *Chicago Daily Tribune,* July 6, 1894; *Washington Post,* July 4, 1894; AP Dispatch, *Wall Street Journal,* July 3, 1894.

43. *Chicago Daily Tribune,* July 1, 8, 1894; *New York Times,* July 6, 1894.

44. *Wall Street Journal,* July 5, 1894; *Chicago Daily Tribune,* July 3, 1894.

45. AP Dispatch, *Wall Street Journal,* July 3, 1894. See also *Chicago Daily Tribune,* July 1, 1894; *Wall Street Journal,* July 6, 1894; *New York Times,* July 9, 1894.

46. *Chicago Daily Tribune,* July 1, 4, 1894.

47. Bruce, *1877,* pp. 207–8; 239–53; 255–75. For a more detailed account of the difficulties in St. Louis, see David T. Burbank, *City*

of Little Bread: The St. Louis General Strike of 1877 (St. Louis, 1957).

48. *New York Times,* July 20, 1877; New York *World,* July 26, 1877; *Indianapolis News,* July 26, 1877.

49. Telegram, July 25, 1877, Copies of Correspondence, Reports, Orders, etc. relating to . . . Labor Disturbances . . . 1877, file #4042, Adjutant General's Office, Early Wars Branch, Record Group 94, National Archives, Washington, D.C. (hereafter cited as AGO Strike Papers).

50. Bradstreet's report quoted in *Wall Street Journal,* July 7, 1894. See also *Wall Street Journal,* July 6, 1894; *Chicago Daily Tribune,* July 8, 1894.

51. *Commercial & Financial Chronicle,* XXV (July 28, 1877), 73; (Aug. 4, 1877), 103.

52. U.S., Dept. of Commerce, *Historical Statistics,* p. 14.

53. *Chicago Times,* July 26, 1877; *Chicago Daily Tribune,* July 25, 1877.

54. *Chicago Times,* July 26, 27, 1877; *Pittsburgh Post,* July 26, 27, 1877; *Chicago Daily Tribune,* July 4, 1894.

55. Burbank, *City of Little Bread,* pp. 76, 99; *Chicago Times,* July 26, 27, 1877; Bruce, *1877,* pp. 95–96; *Nation, XXV* (July 26, 1877), 49.

56. New York, *Annual Report of the Auditor of the Canal Department* (New York, 1881), p. 416; *Syracuse Journal,* Rochester *Union & Advocate,* and *Buffalo Express,* July 25, 1877.

57. *Wall Street Journal,* July 3, 6, 1894; *Chicago Daily Tribune,* July 4, 8, 1894.

58. "The great strike in a critical industry is many-sided. It is at once an exercise in politics, in law, in history, in military policy, in public opinion (and myth making), as well as in economics." Irving Bernstein, in Industrial Relations Research Association, *Emergency Disputes,* p. 24.

59. Scattered references to the attitudes of economists, political scientists, and public and private persons will be found in Sidney Fine, *Laissez Faire and the General-Welfare State* (Ann Arbor, 1956), and in Joseph Dorfman, *The Economic Mind in American Civilization, 1606–1918* (New York, 1946–49), II.

60. *Munn* v. *Illinois,* 94 U.S. 113f. (1877).

61. Chandler, *The Railroads,* p. 211.

NOTES TO CHAPTER II

1. The federal government had previously intervened in some minor labor disputes during Jackson's administration and in the closing days of the Civil War. See Richard B. Morris, "Andrew Jackson, Strikebreaker," *American Historical Review,* LV (1949), 54f.; Rayback, *History of American Labor,* p. 110.

2. Bruce, *1877,* pp. 50–58; Walter Nelles, "A Strike and Its Legal Consequences—An Examination of the Receivership Precedent for the Labor Injunction," *Yale Law Journal,* XL (1931), 515–16; *Scribner's Monthly,* XIV (Oct. 1877), 852; Burbank, *City of Little Bread,* pp. 11–12.

3. Clifton K. Yearley, Jr., "The Baltimore and Ohio Railroad Strike of 1877," *Maryland Historical Magazine,* LI (1956), 194. For Latrobe family connections with the B & O, see Allen Johnson, ed., *The Dictionary of American Biography* (hereafter cited as DAB), 22 vols., (New York, 1957), XI, 20–28, and *The National Cyclopaedia of American Biography* (hereafter cited as *Nat'l. Cyclop.*) 55 vols. (New York, 1898–1960), IX, 427.

4. Bruce, *1877,* p. 76. Yearly, *Md. Hist. Mag.,* LI, 194, states that Shutt's son owned the Berkeley House, Martinsburg's best hotel, and depended upon the B & O for most of his business. Bruce, *1877,* p. 82, implies that Shutt himself owned the hotel.

5. King to Mathews, July 16, 1877; correspondence of Mathews and Col. C. J. Faulkner, Jr., July 16–17, 1877, *Biennial Message of Governor Henry M. Mathews with accompanying documents to the Legislature of West Virginia* (Wheeling, 1879) (hereafter cited as Mathews *Message,* or Mathews *Documents*), *Documents,* pp. 1–2.

6. Bruce, *1877,* pp. 77–79; Faulkner-Mathews correspondence, July 17, 1877, Mathews *Documents,* p. 3.

7. Garrett-Mathews correspondence, July 17, 1877, Mathews *Documents,* pp. 3–4; Bruce, *1877,* pp. 80–82.

8. Delaplain to Mathews, July 17, 1877, Mathews *Documents,* p. 4.

9. Mathews *Message,* p. 36.

10. Mathews to Hayes, July 18, 1877, AGO Strike Papers.

11. Garrett to Mathews, cited by Bruce, *1877,* p. 85; Garrett to Hayes, July 18, 1877, AGO Strike Papers.

12. U.S., *Revised Statutes,* Sec. 5297; Bennett M. Rich, *The Presidents and Civil Disorder* (Washington, 1941), pp. 51–71.

13. *New York Tribune,* July 17, 1877; Bruce, *1877,* p. 211.

14. Chester L. Barrows, *William M. Evarts, Lawyer, Diplomat, Statesman* (Chapel Hill, 1941), pp. 245, 253, 256, and 426; *Peik* v. *Chicago & Northwestern Railway Company,* 94 U.S. 164–78 (1877).

15. *Ibid.*, p. 258; Shelby M. Cullom, *Fifty Years of Public Service* (Chicago, 1911), p. 325; Benjamin R. Twiss, *Lawyers and the Constitution: How Laissez Faire came to the Supreme Court* (Princeton, 1942), pp. 93–109; Bruce, *1877*, p. 210.

16. *DAB*, XII, 3; *Nat'l. Cyclop.*, III, 201–2; Bruce, *1877*, pp. 210–11; C. Vann Woodward, *Reunion and Reaction*, 2d ed. (New York, 1956), p. 190.

17. *DAB*, XVIII, 468–69; *Nat'l. Cyclop.*, III, 202.

18. Andrew Roy, *A History of the Coal Miners of the United States*, 3d ed. (Columbus, 1907), pp. 159–64. Responding to a letter of congratulation from James A. Garfield, Hayes wrote that officials would "crush out the lawbreakers, if the courts do not fail." Thanks to the forensic skills of a rising young Canton attorney, William McKinley, only one of the twenty-three indicted "lawbreakers" was punished. Another potential power in Ohio politics, Marcus A. Hanna, then one of the coal operators, expressed his gratitude a bit later on the occasion of Hayes's nomination for the presidency. "The man who took the position as did our Gov. during our recent mining troubles at Massilon and by such action maintained the supremacy of the law giving us again the control of our property," he wrote, "Deserves [sic] to be the next President of the United States." Hayes to Garfield, May 17, 1876; Hanna to Hayes, June 16, 1876, Rutherford B. Hayes Papers, Rutherford B. Hayes Library, Fremont, Ohio (hereafter cited as Hayes Papers). See also Charles S. Olcott, *The Life of William McKinley*, 2 vols. (Boston & New York, 1916), I, 78–79.

19. Bruce, *1877*, p. 49; Woodward, *Reunion and Reaction, passim.*

20. Bruce, *1877*, pp. 87–90.

21. McCrary-Mathews correspondence, July 18, 1877, AGO Strike Papers.

22. Bruce, *1877*, pp. 90–91, calls attention to the interchanging of the terms "riot" and "insurrection." The correspondence from Washington during the strike reveals that McCrary was the only official who repeatedly referred to the strikes and strikers as "insurrection" and "insurgents." AGO Strike Papers. Hayes, in his proclamations of July 18, 21, and 23, 1877, used both "domestic violence" and "insurrection" as if he regarded the terms as interchangeable. James D. Richardson, comp., *A Compilation of the Messages and Papers of the Presidents, 1789–1897* (Washington, 1897), VII, 447–49.

23. Bruce, *1877*, pp. 100–111 and 118–83, deals with the Baltimore and Pittsburgh riots in detail.

24. For the condition of the Illinois and Indiana militias, see James W. Neilson, *Shelby M. Cullom, Prairie State Republican* (Urbana, 1962), pp. 48–50; Logan Esarey, *A History of Indiana from 1850 to 1920* (Fort Wayne, 1924), II, 1072–76.

25. Rich, *Presidents and Civil Disorder*, pp. 78–79.

26. "Hartranft" to Hayes, July 22, 1877, Hayes Papers.

27. Rich, *Presidents and Civil Disorder*, p. 74.

28. Hartranft to Hayes, July 22 and 23, 1877, Hayes Papers.

29. Lieut. Gov. [of Wisconsin] Harrison to Hayes, July 25, 1877, *ibid.* The correspondence between the governors of Michigan, Illinois, California, and Indiana and federal officials in Washington has been published in Frederick T. Wilson, *Federal Aid in Domestic Disturbances, 1787–1903*, U.S., Congress, Senate, 67th Cong., 2d sess., Senate Doc. 263 (Washington, 1922), pp. 171–73, 286–88.

30. Richardson, *Messages and Papers of the Presidents*, VII, 447–49.

31. Notes of cabinet meetings in Hayes's handwriting for July 24, 26, and 27, 1877, Hayes Papers. The President kept notes of cabinet meetings held July 24, 25, 26, 27, 28, and 31. George Frederick Howe has published those of July 24, 25, 26, and 31 in "President Hayes's Notes of Four Cabinet Meetings," *American Historical Review*, XXXVII (1932), 286–89.

32. General Thomas M. Vincent, Acting Adjutant General, to Colonel William F. Barry, Commanding Officer, Ft. McHenry, Baltimore, July 21, 1877, AGO Strike Papers.

33. Hancock to McCrary, July 24, 1877, *ibid.*

34. McCrary to Hancock, July 24 and 25, 1877, *ibid.*

35. Notes of cabinet meetings, July 24–31, 1877, *passim*, Hayes Papers.

36. Bruce, *1877*, p. 309.

37. Rich, *Presidents and Civil Disorder, passim.*

38. For a brief but excellent study of railway receiverships, see Henry H. Swain, *Economic Aspects of Railroad Receivership*, American Economic Association *Economic Studies*, 2d series, vol. 3, no. 2 (New York, April 1898), especially pp. 53–56, 71–72, and 91–100. See also *Central Law Journal*, XX (Jan. 16, 1885), 42–43, and Thomas M. Cooley, "New Aspects of the Right of Trial By Jury," *American Law Register*, XXV (Dec. 1877), 715–18.

39. Matilda Gresham, *Life of Walter Quintin Gresham, 1832–1895* (Chicago, 1919), I, 374.

40. John M. Palmer, ed., *The Bench and Bar of Illinois* (Chicago, 1899), I, 360–62.

41. Stephen Strong Gregory, "Thomas Drummond, 1809–1890," *Great American Lawyers . . . A History of the Legal Profession in America,* William Draper Lewis, ed. (Philadelphia, 1907–9), V, 506.

42. Gresham, *Gresham,* I, 366–78; *Nat'l. Cyclop.*, XX, 111–12; John Moses and Joseph Kirkland, *History of Chicago, Illinois* (Chicago, 1895), I, 416–17.

43. Gresham, *Gresham,* I, xvi, 378, and *passim*. Gustavus Myers, *History of the Supreme Court of the United States* (Chicago, 1925), p. 591, describes Gresham as "an incorruptible judge," a tribute Myers pays few other jurists in his notorious attack on the federal judiciary.

44. Frederic B. Crossley, *Courts and Lawyers of Illinois* (Chicago, 1916), I, 329; Palmer, *Bench and Bar of Illinois,* I, 34–35; *American Law Review*, XXI (May–June, 1887), 471–73.

45. Elwin W. Sigmund, "Railroad Strikers in Court, Unreported Contempt Cases in Illinois in 1877," *Journal of the Illinois State Historical Society*, XLIX (Summer 1956), 192–93.

46. Drummond to Devens, telegram, July 24 and letter, July 25, 1877, Source Chronological, Northern Illinois, General Records of the Justice Department, Record Group 60, National Archives (hereafter cited as Justice Dept. Records).

47. Bruce, *1877*, p. 255; Wilson to Schurz, July 22, 1877, Carl Schurz Papers, Library of Congress, Washington, D.C. (hereafter cited as Schurz Papers).

48. Wilson to Gresham, July 23, 1877, Walter Q. Gresham Papers, Library of Congress (hereafter cited as Gresham Papers).

49. Gresham, *Gresham,* I, 383–401; account of the strike by Capt. C. W. Smith, in manuscript in Gresham Papers. In a letter to "Tom," Aug. [1?], 1877, Gresham gave vent to his feelings. "I fear that the disturbances of the last few weeks are but the beginning of a conflict which will shake the very foundations of society itself. Our institutions are now on trial. All honest, thoughtful men know that the ballot must be restricted, and, I suppose that can be done only through blood. It is by no means clear that our revolutionary fathers did a good thing for us when they severed the ties that bound the colonies to the Mother Country. Actually they went too far with their notions of popular government. Popular government as we have it now is simply the government of the mob. The doctrines of the commune have been very successfully propagated in the citizens. . . . I confess that the future looks bloody to me. . . . An overwhelming [majority?] of the mechanics and laboring men of this city hate those who have managed to accumulate a little property. I assure you I don't overestimate the danger. . . ." Gresham Papers.

50. Telegrams of Gresham and Spooner to Devens, July 24, 25, and 26, 1877, Source Chronological, Indiana; Devens to Gresham, July 24, Judges and Clerks Book, I, Devens to Spooner, July 24–26, 1877, Instruction Book, G, Justice Dept. Records.

51. Sigmund, *Jour. Ill. State Hist. Soc.,* XLIX, 193–94; notes of the July 26 cabinet meeting, Hayes Papers.

52. Gresham, *Gresham,* I, 402f.; Drummond to Devens, Aug. 7, 1877, Source Chronological, Northern Illinois, Justice Dept. Records. Drummond tried the Indianapolis strikers for Judge Gresham who disqualified himself because of his antistrike activities.

53. *Secor* v. *Toledo P. & W. R. Co.,* 21 Fed. Cases 968f. (1877).

54. *King et al.* v. *Ohio & M. Ry. Co.,* 14 Fed. Cases 539, 541–42 (1877).

55. 21 Fed. Cases 968–69.

56. Drummond to Devens, Aug. 7, 1877, Source Chronological, Northern Illinois, Justice Dept. Records.

57. Sigmund, *Jour. Ill. State Hist. Soc.,* XLIX, 190–91, 196.

58. Ralph Henry Gabriel, *The Course of American Democratic Thought* (New York, 1940), p. 229, declares that federal court injunctions were first used in labor disputes during the Railway Strikes of 1877. The leading authorities, Felix Frankfurter and Nathan Greene, *The Labor Injunction* (New York, 1930), unfortunately, devote almost no attention whatever to injunctions preceding the Debs Case in 1895. Donald L. McMurry, in an excellent article, "The Legal Ancestry of the Pullman Strike Injunction," *Industrial and Labor Relations Review,* XIV (Jan. 1961), 236–37, traces the origins of the modern labor injunction to two early kinds of order issued by courts of equity. One, the receivership order (frequently called a "writ of assistance" during the 1870's and 1880's), was issued to a marshal and instructed him to protect property belonging to the court, and in the hands of a receiver, from damage or interference. The other kind of order, the traditional injunction, was a restraining order, directed to person or persons named, "to protect property when irreparable damage might be caused by the law's delay or when there was no adequate remedy at law." Violations of this writ were punishable as contempt of court. In 1877 it was the receivership order that the federal courts used to protect railroads in their custody. In the 1890's, receivership orders and traditional injunctions would be merged into the modern labor injunction which may be directed to persons in general and may restrain a wide variety of actions.

59. The B & M strike is described in *U.S.* v. *Stevens, et al.,* 27 Fed. Cases 1312f. (1877). Herbert G. Gutman, "Trouble on the Railroads in 1873–1874: Prelude to the 1877 Crisis?" *Labor History,* II (Spring 1961), 215–35, indicates that in a number of minor railway strikes at the onset of the depression of 1873–78, strikers consistently allowed mail to pass, sometimes, apparently, in mail cars only, other times as part of the regular passenger-train. See especially, pp 218–22, and 230.

60. Wilson to Schurz, July 24, 1877, Schurz Papers; J. P. Claypool to Gresham, July 24, 1877, Gresham Papers.

61. See also *New York Tribune,* July 26, 1877; J. A. Dacus, *Annals of the Great Strikes* (Chicago, 1877), pp. 179–80; Bruce, *1877,* pp. 205, 220–22.

62. Bruce, *1877,* p. 221.

63. *New York Tribune,* July 25, 1877; Committee to Hayes, July 24, 1877; see also Workmen's Committee, Canada Southern R.R. to Hayes, July 25, 1877, Hayes Papers.

64. Correspondence reported in the *New York Tribune,* July 25, 26, 1877.

65. *Ibid.,* July 26, 1877.

66. *Washington Star,* July 28, 1877; Drummond to Devens, July 26, 1877, Source Chronological, Northern Illinois; Devens to Drummond, July 26, 1877, Judges and Clerks Book, I, Justice Dept. Records. The Postoffice Department fined at least two railroad companies for failure to run mail trains during the strike. See Devens to Key, Jan. 20, 1878, U.S., Justice Department, *Official Opinions of the Attorneys-General of the United States,* XV, 441.

67. Correspondence quoted in Dacus, *Annals of the Great Strikes,* pp. 178–79, and in *New York Tribune,* July 27, 1877.

68. James E. White, *A Life Span and Reminiscences of Railway Mail Service* (Philadelphia, 1910), pp. 17–18.

69. In his report to President Hayes on July 26, 1877, the U.S. Army chief signal officer, General Albert J. Myer, reported that the Baltimore & Ohio, eight small railroad companies operating out of Indianapolis, and two unidentified lines passing through Pittsburgh sent one passenger-mail train each way each day. Hayes Papers. See also *New York Tribune,* July 25, 1877.

70. 14 Fed. Cases 542.

71. 21 Fed. Cases 970. This decision in effect took the position of the postmaster general's ruling and gave it legal sanction. See Devens to Drummond, July 26, 1877, Judges and Clerks Book, I, Justice Dept. Records.

72. *U.S.* v. *Clark,* 13 Philadelphia 476–79 (1877). For other cases, see *New York Times,* Nov. 8, 1877; U.S. Attorney John K. Valentine to Devens, Aug. 10, 1877, Source Chronological, Eastern Pennsylvania; Devens to U.S. Attorney Richard Crowley, Aug. 6, 1877, Instruction Book, G. Justice Dept. Records.

73. Hon. George F. Emery, "Reminiscences of Bench and Bar," *Collections and Proceedings of the Maine Historical Society,* series 2, VIII, 135–36.

74. 27 Fed. Cases 1312. For the crimes and their attendant penalties, see U.S., *Revised Statutes*, Secs. 3995 and 5440.

75. Dacus, *Annals of the Great Strikes,* p. 176.

76. Hancock to McCrary, July 25, 1877, AGO Strike Papers.

77. Anonymous to Hayes, July 1877, Hayes Papers.

78. *Chicago Daily Tribune,* July 25, 31, 1877.

79. *New York Times,* July 26, 1877. For a contrary point of view, see *Commercial & Financial Chronicle,* XXV (July 28, 1877), 73.

80. Gresham, *Gresham,* I, 408.

81. Wilson to Schurz, July 26, 1877, Schurz Papers; Hartranft to Hayes, July 25, 1877, Hayes Papers.

82. Dacus, *Annals of the Great Strikes,* p. 176; *passim,* July 21–30, 1877, Hayes Papers.

83. *Washington Star,* July 23, 1877.

84. Hayes, Devens, and Schurz were Major Generals in the Union Army, Key a Lieutenant Colonel in the Confederate Army. Sherman and McCrary held high national offices since before the Civil War, Evarts since the Civil War. *DAB,* VIII, 446–51; V, 260–62; XVI, 466–70; X, 361–62; XVII, 84–88; XII, 2–3; and VI, 215–18.

85. Italics supplied. July 22, 1877, AGO Strike Papers.

86. Official signal corps reports, Hayes Papers.

87. Rich, *Presidents and Civil Disorder,* p. 58.

88. For an editorial objecting to suggestions that the administration try to conciliate the dispute, see *Boston Daily Advertiser,* July 27, 1877.

89. *American Law Register,* XXV, 719–21.

NOTES TO CHAPTER III

1. *Nation,* XXV (Aug. 2, 30, 1877), 68, 131–32; *Harper's Weekly,* XXI (Aug. 11, 1877), 618.

2. *Railway Age, II* (Aug. 2, 1877), 1183, 1185.

3. *North American Review,* CXXV (Sept. 1877), 358–59, 361–62.

4. Notes of cabinet meeting, July 31, 1877, Hayes Papers.

5. Charles Richard Williams, ed., *Diary and Letters of Rutherford Birchard Hayes* (Columbus, 1924), III, 440, entry for Aug. 5, 1877.

6. Hayes Papers.

7. McCrary to F. L. Wood, Aug. 13, 1877, Hayes Papers. McCrary went on to say, "They call our attention to the grievances of the

working people which are no doubt real. They warn us that redress for wrongs and enforcement of rights in this country, must be sought only through the peaceful methods provided by law and executed through regular tribunals of justice, and that an appeal to violence and mob law, must inevitably bring ruin and disaster upon any cause."

8. U.S., *Annual Report of the Postmaster General of the United States . . . 1877* (Washington, 1877), p. xxxiii.

9. Richardson, *Messages and Papers of the Presidents,* VII, 452–54, 472.

10. *Congressional Record,* 45th Cong., 2d sess., pp. 374, 622, 4181, 4214, 4243.

11. *Ibid.,* 44th Cong., 1st sess., p. 2121; 45th Cong., 2d sess., p. 4754.

12. *Ibid.,* 46th Cong., 1st sess., pp. 397, 739–40, 1399, 1730; U.S. Congress, House, Select Committee, *Investigation Relative to the Causes of the General Depression in Labor and Business, etc.,* 45th Cong., 3d sess., H. Misc. Doc. No. 29 (Washington, 1879), *passim.* Sumner's testimony (pp. 181–208) was studded with negative responses to every inquiry as to whether anything could be done to improve conditions.

13. U.S. Congress, House, Select Committee, *Investigation Relative to the Causes of the General Depression in Labor and Business. Chinese Immigration,* 46th Cong. 2d sess., H. Misc. Doc. No. 5 (Washington, 1879); *Report: Chinese Immigration,* 46th Cong. 2d sess., H. Report No. 572 (Washington, 1880), p. 31.

14. Rayback, *History of American Labor,* pp. 136–42, 148, 162; Foster Rhea Dulles, *Labor in America, A History,* 2d Revised Ed. (New York, 1960), p. 183.

15. U.S. Commissioner of Labor, *10th Annual Report* (Washington, 1895), p. 1559.

16. *Cong. Rec.,* 47th Cong., 1st sess., pp. 4924, 5161, 5430, 6492; U.S. Congress, Senate, Committee on Education and Labor, *Report Upon the Relations Between Labor and Capital, and Testimony Taken by the Committee* (Washington, 1885), I, 1.

17. U.S. Cong., Sen., Comm. Edn. and Labor, *Report, Relations between Labor and Capital,* I, II, *passim.* Volume III contains testimony gathered in New England, volume IV, that gathered in the South.

18. *Cong. Rec.,* 49th Cong., 1st sess., p. 52.

19. *Ibid.,* 46th Cong., 1st sess., p. 1049; 46th Cong., 2d sess., pp. 30, 2325; 46th Cong., 3d sess., p. 30; 47th Cong., 1st sess., p. 109.

20. *Ibid.,* 48th Cong., 1st sess., pp. 3161, 4147, 4281, 4286, 4385–89, 4430.

21. Richard O'Conner, *Gould's Millions* (New York, 1962), p. 246. Julius Grodinsky, *Jay Gould: His Business Career, 1867–1892* (Philadelphia, 1957), p. 194, states that Gould was brought to the brink of financial disaster by May 1884.

22. U.S. Congress, House, Select Committee, *Investigation of Labor Troubles in Missouri, Arkansas, Kansas, Texas, and Illinois*, 49th Cong., 2d sess., H. Report No. 4174 (Washington, 1887), pp. i–xxi; F. W. Taussig, "The Southwest Strike of 1886," *Quarterly Journal of Economics*, I (Jan., 1887), 185–86; Missouri, Commissioner of Labor Statistics and Inspection, *Report in Regard to the Late Strike of Railroad Employees* (Jefferson City, 1885). For brief secondary accounts of these strikes, see Rayback, *History of American Labor*, pp. 165–66; Dulles, *Labor in America*, pp. 142–45; Philip S. Foner, *History of the Labor Movement in the United States* (New York, 1955), II, 83–86.

23. Mo., Commr. Labor Statistics, *Report in Regard to Late Strike . . .*, n.p.; Taussig, *Quart. Journ. Econ.*, I, 185; U.S. Cong., House, Select Comm., *Investigation of Labor Troubles*, p. iv.

24. Broadside quoted in Dulles, *Labor in America*, p. 143. For accounts of the 1886 strike, see Taussig, *Quart. Journ. Econ.*, I, 185–216; Missouri, Bureau of Labor Statistics, *The Official History of the Great Strike of 1886* (Jefferson City, 1886); Ruth A. Allen, *The Great Southwest Strike*, University of Texas Publication No. 4214 (Austin, 1942). Although the Knights were attacking the Gould management, the Texas & Pacific was in the hands of federal court receivers and Gould, technically, was no longer responsible for the line. One of the receivers was John C. Brown, a vice-president of the T & P since 1876 and solicitor for a half-dozen Gould lines in the Southwest, including the T & P since 1881. The Knights probably saw no distinction between Brown, solicitor for Gould, and Brown, receiver for the court. See *DAB*, III, 135–36. The various accounts of the strike agree that the men had grievances and that the Knights of Labor, and especially Martin Irons, were bidding for union recognition and power and were ready to fight on any issue. Taussig, *Quart. Journ. Econ.*, I, 186–87, places the primary blame on the union. "Their victory had been complete [in 1885]. They had taken possession of the road, controlled it for a week, violated the law, and had got what they wanted. Not a man was the worse off for having struck. Not a man was even blamed for having prevented by force the movement of trains."

25. Correspondence between Powderly and Gould is reproduced in Mo., Bureau of Labor Statistics, *Official History of the Great Strike of 1886*, pp. 64–80.

26. G. Van Hoorebeke, U.S. Attorney, Southern District, Illinois, to the Attorney General of the United States, May 8, 1886, Year

File 2914/86, Justice Dept. Records; Taussig, *Quart. Journ. Econ.*, I, 205.

27. Taussig, *Quart. Journ. Econ.*, I, 205; Dulles, *Labor in America*, p. 143; Foner, *History of Labor Movement in U.S.*, II, 85; Allan Nevins, *Grover Cleveland, A Study in Courage* (New York, 1933), p. 347.

28. Taussig, *Quart. Journ. Econ.*, I, 201; U.S. Cong., House, Select Comm., *Investigation of Labor Troubles,* p. xii; *New York Tribune*, Mar. 8, 1886.

29. Taussig, *Quart. Journ. Econ.*, I, 201–3.

30. McMurry, *Indust. & Labor Relations Rev.,* XIV, 239.

31. *DAB*, III, 22–23; obituary, *Outlook*, XCIV (Apr. 9, 1910), 785–86; Gresham, *Gresham,* II, 621; Twiss, *Lawyers and the Constitution,* p. 199; Arnold M. Paul, *Conservative Crisis and the Rule of Law* (Ithaca, 1960), pp. 70–72.

32. *American Law Review,* XXI (Jan., Feb. 1887), 141–45. See also, Gresham, *Gresham,* II, 550–52; "A Chapter of Wabash," *North American Review,* CXLVI (Feb. 1888), 178–93. Judge Gresham's ruling, dismissing the receivers appointed by Brewer from control of the portion of the Wabash in his (Gresham's) control, will be found in *Atkins and others* v. *Wabash, St. L. & P. Ry. Co. and others* and *Beers* v. *Wabash, St. L. & P. Ry. Co., and others*, 29 Fed. Rep. 161–74 (1886).

33. *American Law Review,* XXIV (Jan., Feb. 1890), 139. The same article stated that Brewer's decisions as a whole "rank well."

34. *In re Doolittle,* 23 Fed. Rep. 544, 547–48 (1885).

35. *American Law Review,* XXI (Mar., Apr. 1887), 297–302; *DAB*, XVIII, 634; *The Bench and Bar of St. Louis, Kansas City, Jefferson City, and other Missouri Cities* (St. Louis, 1884), pp. 5–6.

36. 23 Fed. Rep. 548.

37. *U.S.* v. *Kane and others,* 23 Fed. Rep. 748–57 (1885); quotation, p. 753.

38. *Frank and others* v. *Denver & R. G. Ry. Co.,* 23 Fed. Rep. 757ff. (1885).

39. *Bench & Bar of . . . Missouri Cities,* pp. 288–89; Howard I. McKee, "The School Law of 1853, Its Origin and Authors," *Missouri Historical Review,* XXXV (July 1941), 559–60; North Todd Gentry, "Some Missouri Judges I Have Known," *Mo. Hist. Rev.,* XXXIV (Apr. 1940), 342–56; Floyd C. Shoemaker, *Missouri Day by Day* (Jefferson City, 1942), I, 192–93; quotation from John F. Philips, "Administrations of Missouri Governors," *Mo. Hist. Rev.,* V (Jan. 1911), 79.

40. *In re Wabash,* 24 Fed. Rep. 217–21 (1885).

41. Memorial sketch, *Report of the 37th Annual Session of the Georgia Bar Association* (Macon, 1920), pp. 249–54; *DAB,* XIV, 201–2; *Nat'l. Cyclop.,* XVIII, 253.

42. *In re Higgins,* 27 Fed. Rep. 444–46 (1886).

43. McMurry, *Indust. & Labor Relations Rev.,* XIV, 237–39.

44. U.S., *Statutes at Large,* XXIV, 86; *Cong. Rec.,* 49th Cong., 1st sess., pp. 1900, 2985, 5447, 5565–66; Murray T. Quigg, "The Use of Injunctions in Labor Disputes," *Labor Law Journal,* III (Feb. 1952), 105n.

45. *Cong. Rec.,* 49th Cong., 1st sess., Index.

46. Clarke to Sen. Shelby M. Cullom, quoted in Cochran, *Railroad Leaders,* p. 301.

47. *Cong. Rec.,* 49th Cong., 1st sess., p. 4240.

48. *Ibid.,* p. 4351.

49. *Ibid.,* p. 4353.

50. *Ibid.,* pp. 4355–56.

51. *Ibid.,* p. 4357. House debate of the Interstate Commerce Act ran from July 21 through July 30, 1886, *passim,* pp. 7272–7775.

52. *Ibid.,* pp. 2959–60, 2980.

53. *Ibid.,* p. 3019 (Wm. Warner, Rep., Mo.); p. 2970 (John Glover, Dem., Mo.); p. 3064 (John B. Storm, Dem., Pa.).

54. Among those speaking for the bill were John J. O'Neill, Dem., Mo. (p. 2959), Warner of Mo., and William McKinley, Rep., Ohio (p. 3039).

55. *Ibid.,* pp. 2962–64 (Martin A. Foran, Dem., Ohio); pp. 2867–2968 (Charles N. Brumm, Rep.-Greenbacker, Pa.); pp. 3015–17 (John A. Anderson, Rep., Kans.). Congressmen Glover (p. 2970), Brumm (pp. 2967–68), and Thomas M. Browne, Rep., Ind. (p. 3097) all favored a compulsory arbitration law.

56. *Ibid.,* pp. 2974–75 (John H. Reagan, Dem., Texas); p. 3038 (Wm. C. P. Breckenridge, Dem., Ky.); p. 3042 (A. J. Warner, Dem., Ohio).

57. *Ibid.,* p. 2968 (John W. Daniel, Dem., Va.). See also pp. 3039–40 (Abram S. Hewitt, Dem., N.Y.).

58. *Ibid.,* p. 3038 (Breckenridge of Ky.).

59. *Ibid.,* p. 2959.

60. *Ibid.,* p. 2962 (Foran, Ohio); p. 3045 (Lewis Beach, Dem., N.Y.); p. 3062 (John H. Rogers, Dem., Ark.).

61. *Ibid.,* pp. 3066, 3107, 3139.

62. Terence V. Powderly, *The Path I Trod* (New York, 1940), p. 134; *Cong. Rec.,* 49th Cong., 1st sess., pp. 2880, 2887, 3157, 3535.

63. Richardson, *Messages and Papers of the Presidents,* VIII, 394–97. Former President Hayes, commenting on the strike of 1886 in a private letter, took the position that first law and order had to be preserved, *"instantly, with overwhelming force* and *at all hazards."* But, he went on, labor for some time had not been getting a fair share. "The Sermon on the Mount, the Golden Rule, the Declaration of Independence, all require extensive reforms to the end that labor may be so rewarded that the workingman can, with temperance, industry, and thrift, *own a home, educate his children,* and *lay up a support for old age."* Referring to Cleveland's recommendations to Congress, Hayes said "I approve heartily of President Cleveland's message and so said at the great soliders' meeting at Cleveland." Hayes to Guy [M. Bryan], May 12, 1886, Williams, ed., *Diary and Letters of Hayes,* IV, 286.

64. *Cong. Rec.,* 49th Cong., 1st sess., pp. 4618–24.

65. *Ibid.,* pp. 4624, 5449, 6649, 6677.

66. *Ibid.,* 49th Cong., 2d sess., pp. 2375–76. Nevins, *Cleveland,* p. 350, is in error in saying that Cleveland signed the bill into law. The page in the *Congressional Record* cited by Nevins states that the bill was signed by the speaker and by the president *pro tempore* of the Senate, not by the President of the United States. See also Lecht, *Experience Under Railway Labor Legislation,* p. 15.

67. *Cong. Rec.,* 49th Cong., 1st sess., p. 3391; U.S. Congress, House, Select Comm., *Investigation of Labor Troubles,* p. xxiii.

68. *Ibid.,* pp. i–xxii.

69. *Ibid.,* pp. xxiii–xxiv.

70. *Ibid.,* p. xxv.

71. *Ibid.,* p. xiv. It may have been Irons' impudence as much as his "perniciousness" that irritated the committee. In his testimony before the committee, Irons related an interview between himself and Judge Pardee just before the strike broke out. "Q. Judge [asked Irons], is the Texas and Pacific road now in the hands of the United States government?—A. Yes.
Q. Judge, if in the hands of the government, will the workmen be considered as government employees?—A. Yes.
Q. Then, Judge, if government employees, they will be subject to laws and regulations governing such, will they not, such as eight hours for a day's work?
This question rather touched to the quick, and his answer was evasive . . . [Irons observed]." Part II, 440.

72. *Ibid.,* p. xxv.

73. *Ibid.,* p. xxix. The minority report will be found pp. xxvii–xxx.

NOTES TO CHAPTER IV

1. McMurry, *Burlington Strike,* p. 70; Don M. Dickinson to Grover Cleveland, Oct. 21, 1903, Grover Cleveland Papers, Library of Congress (hereafter cited as Cleveland Papers).

2. McMurry, *Burlington Strike,* pp. 4–5, 28–33, 44.

3. *Ibid.,* pp. 38–52, 295–300, 309–10.

4. *Ibid.,* pp. 273–75.

5. Gresham, *Gresham,* I, 410–11.

6. McMurry, *Burlington Strike,* pp. 92–96, 106–9, 138–53. What in the late nineteenth century were referred to as "boycotts" were often what today are called "secondary boycotts."

7. *Washington Star,* Mar. 10, 1888.

8. St. John to Henry B. Stone, Mar. 8, 1888, quoted in McMurry, *Burlington Strike,* p. 112.

9. *Ibid.,* pp. 102–6, 130–35. Thomas M. Cooley, chairman of the ICC, seems to have blamed the rate war west of Chicago for the Burlington strike. See diary entries for Mar. 9, Apr. 1, 1888, Thomas M. Cooley Papers, Michigan Historical Collections, Ann Arbor, Mich. (hereafter cited as Cooley Papers). In correspondence with Carl Schurz, former President Hayes offered differing interpretations as to the cause of the strikes. In a letter on Mar. 21, 1888, he wrote, "Believing that the existing capital and labor troubles are mainly due to the irresponsible power of wealth on one hand, and of numbers on the other, the aim of reform should be to bring both equally under the control of laws for the general good." Williams, ed., *Hayes Diary and Letters,* IV, 378. Four days later, in a post scriptum to a second letter, Hayes took a more antirailroad position. "Do you study the 'burning question?' The trouble is not with the poor rascals. The rich rascal is the enemy to watch and control. So far the men who own or control vast wealth are wholly irresponsible, and are at the bottom of the larger part of the so-called 'Labor Troubles.' " Schurz Papers.

10. Quoted in McMurry, *Burlington Strike,* pp. 115–16.

11. Obituary, *Albany Law Journal,* LIV (Nov. 1896), 348–49; Edwin S. Towl, "Judge Elmer S. Dundy," *Proceedings and Collections of the Nebraska State Historical Society,* 2d series, V (1902), 93.

12. The case was not reported. See McMurry, *Burlington Strike,* pp. 116–17, 119–21; McMurry, *Indust. & Labor Relations Rev.,* XIV, 240–41.

13. McMurry, *Burlington Strike,* pp. 123–24.

14. *Beers et al.* v. *Wabash, St. L. & Pac. Ry. Co.,* 34 Fed. Rep. 244–48 (1888). According to Gresham, *Gresham,* I, 415–16, after reading his ruling Judge Gresham called Alexander Sullivan, attorney for the brotherhood, into his chamber and told him there should be no general strike and "urged him to give his clients good advice." Sullivan did, and there was no general strike.

15. McMurry, *Burlington Strike,* pp. 128–29, 130–35.

16. *Greenbag,* I (Sept. 1889), 392. See also *Iowa Historical Record,* VIII (Apr. 1892), 241f.; Benjamin F. Gue, *History of Iowa* (New York, 1903), IV, 170–71.

17. *Chicago, B & Q. Ry. Co.* v. *Burlington, C. R. & N. Ry. Co. et al.,* 34 Fed. Rep. 481–85 (1888); McMurry, *Indust. & Labor Relations Rev.,* XIV, 242.

18. McMurry, *Indust. & Labor Relations Rev.,* XIV, 243.

19. Arthur Pound, "Don M. Dickinson," *Michigan and the Cleveland Era,* Earl D. Babst and Lewis G. Vander Velde, eds. (Ann Arbor, 1948), pp. 109–36. Dickinson's political career in Michigan is treated extensively in Robert Bolt, "A Biography of Donald M. Dickinson" (Unpublished Ph.D. thesis, Michigan State University, 1963).

20. *Chicago Daily Tribune,* Feb. 28, 1888, quoted in McMurry, *Burlington Strike,* p. 80.

21. Congressman William L. Scott, Pennsylvania, quoted in *Detroit Free Press,* Mar. 20, 1888, scrapbooks, Don M. Dickinson Papers, Michigan Historical Collections, Ann Arbor, Mich. (hereafter cited as Dickinson Papers, Mich.).

22. McMurry, *Burlington Strike,* p. 80.

23. Don M. Dickinson, "Progress and the Post," *North American Review,* CIL (Nov. 1889), 406. The Supreme Court on four later occasions upheld the view that railroads, prior to the act of July 28, 1916, were not obliged to contract to carry mail. *Eastern Rd. Co.* v. *U.S.,* 124 U.S. 391 (1889); *Atchison, T. & S. F. Rd. Co.* v. *U.S.,* 225 U.S. 640, 650 (1912); *Delaware, Lackawanna & Western R.R. Co.* v. *U.S.,* 249 U.S. 385 (1919); and *New York, New Haven & Hartford Railroad Company* v. *U.S.,* 251 U.S. 123 (1919).

24. U.S., *Annual Report of the Postmaster General of the United States . . . 1888* (Washington, 1888), p. xxxi.

25. U.S., *Statutes at Large,* XX, 358. For Drummond's ruling, see above, p. 44.

26. Quoted in White, *A Life Span,* p. 200.

27. Dickinson, *North American Review,* CIL, 407.

28. Dickinson to Nash, Mar. 9, 1888, Letters of the Postmaster General (letter press copy books), Postoffice Department, Record Group 28, National Archives (hereafter cited as Letters, PMG, NA).

29. Dickinson to Nash, Mar. 10, 1888, *ibid.*

30. Dickinson to Nash, Mar. 17, 1888, Letters of the Postmaster General (letter press copy books), I, 859, Don M. Dickinson Papers, Library of Congress (hereafter cited as Letters, PMG, Dickinson Papers, LC). The letter press copy books of the postmaster general in the National Archives and in the Dickinson Papers, LC, though containing many of the same letters, are not identical and for a complete file, both collections must be used.

31. McMurry, *Burlington Strike,* pp. 122–23.

32. Dickinson to Nash, Mar. 17, 1888, Letters, PMG, I, 859, Dickinson Papers, LC.

33. *Washington Post,* Mar. 18, 1888.

34. I have determined the date of the meeting by the fact that during the middle of the conference the wire arrived from Chicago announcing the Santa Fe's surrender.

35. Based on an account told by Dickinson to his friend, Peter White, and quoted in Pound, "Dickinson," *Michigan and the Cleveland Era,* Babst and Vander Velde, eds., pp. 120–21; Dickinson to Cleveland, Oct. 21, 1903, Cleveland Papers.

36. *Washington Post,* Mar. 19, 1888.

37. Printed letter, *Don M. Dickinson, Postmaster General, In the Matter of the Application of the Michigan Central Railroad Company, the Pennsylvania Railroad Company, . . . dated March 1, 1888,* copy in Clarke Historical Library, Central Michigan University, Mt. Pleasant, Mich. From the context of the letter it is evident that Mar. 1, 1888, was not the actual date of writing. Apparently, it was written some time after the strike crisis in early March.

38. U.S., *Annual Report, PMG, 1888,* p. xxxi.

39. Dickinson, *North American Review,* CIL, 406–7.

40. *Railroad Gazette,* XX (Mar. 23, 1888), 192.

41. Lewis G. Vander Velde, "Thomas McIntyre Cooley," *Michigan and the Cleveland Era,* Babst and Vander Velde, eds., pp. 77–106.

42. C. A. Miller, *The Lives of the Interstate Commerce Commissioners and the Commission's Secretaries* (n.p., 1946), pp. 25–26.

43. *Ibid.,* pp. 27–28; Albert Burton Moore, *History of Alabama and Her People* (Chicago, 1927), I, 669–73.

44. Miller, *Lives of Interstate Commerce Commissioners,* pp. 21–

23; *Report of the New York State Bar Association,* 1894, pp. 530–32; *ibid., 1895,* pp. 271–75; *DAB,* XIII, 232–33.

45. Entry for Mar. 9, 1888, Cooley Papers.

46. Diary entry, Mar. 15, 1888, *ibid.*

47. Canfield also suggested that if Cooley were to open a law office in the national capital for Supreme Court business, he, Canfield, would guarantee Cooley an income of at least $25,000 per year. Diary entry, Mar. 17, 1888, *ibid.*

48. That same evening at a dinner given by Dickinson, the post-master general informed Cooley that he had prepared a telegram to send to the commissioners while they were in Chicago, demanding that they intervene to move the mails. President Cleveland held the telegram under advisement until another way out of the trouble presented itself. "Had the telegram been sent," Cooley replied, "there would have been some plain talking out there." Diary entry, April 1, 2, 1888, Cooley Papers.

49. Diary entry, Apr. 7, 1888, *ibid.*

50. Diary entries, "March" [apparently, Cooley was in error as April seems to have been the correct month] 10, 11, "April" 15, 16, and 20, 1888, *ibid.*

51. Diary entry, Apr. 26, 1888; *passim,* entries for May 1–8, 1888, *ibid.*

52. U.S., *Statutes at Large,* XXV, 501f.

53. *Cong. Rec.,* 50th Cong., 1st sess., pp. 3097, 3099, 3101, 3102, 3106, 3107.

54. See below, p. 221.

55. *Cong. Rec.,* 50th Cong., 1st sess., p. 3100.

56. *Ibid.,* p. 3108.

57. *Ibid.,* pp. 3109, 3140, 6809, 6958, 9074.

58. U.S. Congress, House, Select Committee, *Labor Troubles in the Anthracite Regions of Pennsylvania, 1887–1888,* 50th Cong., 2d sess., H. Report No. 4141 (Washington, 1889), pp. xx–xxxviii.

59. *Ibid.,* pp. xxv–xxvi.

60. *Ibid.,* p. xxx.

61. *Ibid.,* pp. xxvi–xxvii, xxix.

62. The draft bill is on pp. xxvi–xxviii of the report. See especially sections 5 and 6.

63. Lecht, *Experience Under Railway Labor Legislation,* p. 16.

NOTES TO CHAPTER V

1. *New York Tribune,* Aug. 7–13, 1890. Former President Hayes was disturbed by the strike. "The strike on the New York Central. Depew in Europe. Cause, the discharge of men because they belong to the Knights of Labor. The need for government protection involves the need of government control of railways. Protection of unwise and unjust management will never do." Williams, ed., *Diary and Letters of Hayes,* IV, 592.

2. Rayback, *History of American Labor,* pp. 195–97; Foner, *History of Labor Movement in U.S.,* II, 206–34.

3. 51 Fed. Rep. 206f.

4. U.S. Congress, 52d Cong., 2d sess., House Report No. 2447; Senate Report No. 1280.

5. Paul, *Conservative Crisis,* pp. 128–30, 163, 232–35; Donald L. McMurry, *Coxey's Army, A Study of the Industrial Army Movement of 1894* (Boston, 1929), pp. 3–11.

6. Swain, *Economic Aspects of Railroad Receiverships,* pp. 70–71.

7. Samuel P. Orth, *History of Cleveland, Ohio* (Chicago, 1910), III, 1038–39.

8. U.S. Congress, House, Judiciary Committee, 53d Cong., 3d sess., Report No. 1670.

9. *Case and Comment,* IV (Nov. 1897), 61.

10. Henry F. Pringle, *The Life and Times of William Howard Taft* (New York, 1939), I, 99–105, 126–47.

11. McMurry, *Indust. & Labor Relations Rev.,* XIV, 243.

12. *Toledo, A.A. & N.M. Ry. Co.* v. *Pennsylvania Co., et al.,* 54 Fed. Rep. 746, 747–48 (1893).

13. *Ibid.,* pp. 752–53.

14. 54 Fed. Rep. 730, 736.

15. *Ibid.,* pp. 737–38. Taft, using the terminology of his day, referred to "boycotts" which today would be termed "secondary boycotts."

16. *Ibid.,* p. 743.

17. McMurry, *Burlington Strike,* p. 281.

18. Hans Thorelli, *The Federal Antitrust Policy* (Stockholm, Sweden, 1954), p. 190.

19. *Ibid.,* pp. 172, 174, 190, 197–98, 210, 231–32.

20. *United States* v. *Patterson, et al.,* 55 Fed. Rep. 605, 641 (1893).

21. *Blindell, et al.* v. *Hagan, et al.,* 54 Fed. Rep. 40–43 (1893).

22. For Earhart's connection, see 54 Fed. Rep. 40.

23. Paul, *Conservative Crisis,* pp. 109–10.

24. *Waterhouse* v. *Comer,* 55 Fed. Rep. 149, 154 (1893).

25. *Ibid.,* pp. 157–58.

26. For an earlier instance of such an appeal, see above, pp. 65–66.

27. 55 Fed. Rep. 149–51; *Continental Trust Co. of New York* v. *Toledo, St. L. & K.C. R. Co.,* 59 Fed. Rep. 514, 517–18 (1894).

28. *Thomas* v. *Cincinnati, N.O. & T.P. Ry. Co.,* 62 Fed. Rep. 669, 670 (1894). In all the 1893 and 1894 cases save one, the judges dealt with employees as individuals. Judge Speer in the Waterhouse case permitted the Brotherhood of Locomotive Engineers (to which 211 of 250 engineers employed by the receiver belonged) to speak for the employees. This seems to have been the first instance of a federal court recognizing a labor union as spokesman for its members in a labor dispute.

29. 59 Fed. Rep. 514, 518–19, 521.

30. *Washington West of the Cascades,* 3 vols (Chicago, 1917), II, 425–39; *Who Was Who,* I, 515.

31. Robert C. Nesbit, *"He Built Seattle," A Biography of Judge Thomas Burke* (Seattle, 1961), pp. 174–75, 178, 181, 197. Hanford's friend, Judge Burke, told a congressional investigating committee in 1912 that businessmen turned to Judge Hanford's court rather than to the state courts but said that he did not know why. "You are not unaware," a congressman replied, "of the charge generally made that big interests who are nonresident bring cases to the Federal Courts because they think their interests will be better cared for than in the State courts?" p. 393n.; *Literary Digest,* XXIV (Mar. 25, 1912), 1083–84. Hanford ran into difficulties during the Progressive Era and was subjected to a congressional investigation. In 1912 he cancelled the naturalization of a man who avowed being a socialist. In the ensuing uproar—nearly a million Americans had voted the Socialist ticket in 1912— a host of accumulated grievances and charges were aired. Hanford was accused of favoritism, of allowing exorbitant fees to receivers, of drunkenness both off and on the bench, and with being "morally and temperamentally unfit" to be a judge. As damning testimony mounted against him, Hanford hastily resigned. The investigating committee, in order to save the expense of bringing witnesses to the nation's capitol for an impeachment trial, recommended that the matter be dropped. The resignation was widely regarded as proof of guilt, a conclusion supported by the facts that Hanford was not a quitter and that he continued practicing law and writing until his death in 1926. See

Joseph Borkin, *The Corrupt Judge* (New York, 1962), pp. 232–33; *Literary Digest,* XLV (Aug. 3, 1912), 173–74.

32. *In re Seattle, L.S. & E. Ry. Co. Grievance Committee of Brotherhood of Railway Trainmen, Lodge No. 196, et al. v. Brown, et al.,* 61 Fed. Rep. 541, 543 (1894).

33. *Thomas v. Cincinnati, N.O. & T.P. Ry. Co.,* 62 Fed. Rep. 23–24, 670 (1894).

34. Dundy's decision was not reported. See McMurry, *Indust. & Labor Relations Rev.,* XIV, 248–49.

35. 61 Fed. Rep. 541–43.

36. 62 Fed. Rep. 670.

37. *DAB,* III, 408; *Nat'l. Cyclop.,* XI, 478; *American Law Review,* XXX (Mar., Apr. 1896), 284.

38. *Proceedings of the Arkansas Bar Association, 1915,* pp. 150–51.

39. Quotation from Gresham, *Gresham,* II, 625. See also *Proc. Ark. Bar Ass'n., 1915,* pp. 25–26; John Hallam, *Biographical and Pictorial History of Arkansas* (Albany, ?, 1887), I, 485–86; *Amer. Law Rev.,* XXX, 282.

40. Gue, *History of Iowa,* IV, 295; *The Bench and Bar of Iowa* (Chicago, 1901), pp. 340–42; *Iowa Bar Association Report, 1900,* pp. 104–6; *Annals of Iowa,* IV, 317.

41. *Ames, et al. v. Union Pac. Ry. Co., et al.,* 62 Fed. Rep. 12–15 (1894).

42. *United States Trust Co. of New York v. Omaha & St. L. Ry. Co.,* 63 Fed. Rep. 737–43 (1894).

43. 62 Fed. Rep. 13, 15–16. Caldwell pointed out that the Union Pacific had received less than two cents on the dollar paid in on the first $36 million worth of its stock. The profits from constructing the line were represented by a bonded indebtedness of nearly $44 million. "There would seem to be no equity," he said, "in reducing the wages of employees below what is reasonable and just, in order to pay dividends on stock and interest on bonds of this character."

44. 63 Fed. Rep. 741–42.

45. 55 Fed. Rep. 152–53.

46. See above, pp. 36–41, 68–69.

47. See above, pp. 86–90.

48. Paul, *Conservative Crisis,* pp. 104–30.

49. 54 Fed. Rep. 751–53.

50. *Indiana Bar Association Report, 1916,* pp. 299, 305; *Who Was Who,* I; *Biographical Directory of the American Congress, 1774–1949* (Washington, 1950), 806. The *Indiana Reports,* 112 Indiana (1887) to 135 Indiana (1893), show Baker on briefs for the Lake Shore & Michigan Southern ten times before the Indiana Supreme Court. The dates of the last two case decisions were after Baker became judge: May 1892 and May 1893. 132 Indiana 559; 135 Indiana 363.

51. *Ind. Bar Ass'n. Report, 1916,* pp. 300–301, 307.

52. *Lake Erie & W. Ry. Co.* v. *Bailey, et al.,* 61 Fed. Rep. 494–97 (1893).

53. McMurry, *Indust. & Labor Relations Rev.,* XIV, 248–49.

54. 62 Fed. Rep. 14, 16.

55. John R. Berryman, *History of the Bench and Bar of Wisconsin,* 2 vols. (Chicago, 1898), II, 28; Parker McCobb Reed, *The Bench and Bar of Wisconsin, History and Biography* (Milwaukee, 1882), pp. 243–44; *Who Was Who,* I, 632; *Nat'l. Cyclop.,* XIX, 188; *Case & Comment,* V (Nov. 1898), 61.

56. *Farmers' Loan & Trust Co.* v. *Northern Pac. R. Co., et al.,* 60 Fed. Rep. 803–21 (1894).

57. U.S. Congress, House, Judiciary Committee, 53d Cong., 2d sess., Report No. 1049 (Washington, 1894), p. 1.

58. *Ibid.,* pp. 13–19.

59. *Ibid.,* pp. 20–22.

NOTES TO CHAPTER VI

1. See above, pp. 27–29.

2. Nevins, *Cleveland,* pp. 114, 443, 449–52; Matthew Josephson, *The Politicos 1865–1896* (New York, 1938), pp. 392, 491–93.

3. Cleveland to Benedict, Jan. 25, Oct. 30, 1894; Feb. 3, May 9, May 17, 1895; Feb. 6, 1898, Cleveland Papers (published in *Letters of Grover Cleveland, 1850–1908,* Allan Nevins, ed. [Boston and New York, 1933], pp. 345, 373, 376, 391, 392–93, 492–93).

4. Nevins, *Cleveland,* pp. 449–52.

5. See above, pp. 36–38, 68–69, 87–88.

6. Mark D. Hirsch, *William C. Whitney, Modern Warwick* (New York, 1948), pp. 466–67; *New York Times,* Mar. 5, 1893. On Feb. 24, 1893, Lamont resigned from the board of directors of the Continental National Bank and on Mar. 4 from the board of the Pennsylvania Steel Refining Co. On Mar. 30, 1893, he was notified of a meeting of the board of directors of the New York Loan & Improve-

ment Co. to be held at "Mr. Whitney's house." Daniel S. Lamont Papers, Library of Congress (hereafter cited as Lamont Papers).

7. A. A. McLeod to Richard Olney, Feb. 24, 1893, Richard Olney Papers, Library of Congress (hereafter cited as Olney Papers); *New York Times,* Feb. 19, 1893; *Boston Herald,* Feb. 13, 1893; Henry Varnum Poor and H. W. Poor, *Poor's Manual of the Railroads of the United States* (hereafter cited as *Poor's Railroad Manual*) (New York, 1895), p. 588.

8. James C. Olson, *J. Sterling Morton* (Lincoln, 1942), pp. 192, 291.

9. C. Vann Woodward, *Origins of the New South* (Baton Rouge, 1951), p. 271.

10. Perkins to Olney, Feb. 23, 1893, Olney Papers; Dewey W. Grantham, Jr., *Hoke Smith and the Politics of the New South* (Baton Rouge, 1958), pp. 14–24, 25–26, 36–37. Smith, while serving as secretary of the interior, continued to serve some private clients who were railroad bondholders. See New York *World,* Nov. 16, 1893; Smith to Cleveland, Nov. 3, 1894, Cleveland Papers.

11. Horace Samuel Merrill, *Bourbon Leader: Grover Cleveland and the Democratic Party* (Boston, 1957), p. 169. For a full account of Carlisle's life, see James A. Barnes, *John G. Carlisle: Financial Statesman* (New York, 1931).

12. Gerald G. Eggert, "Richard Olney, Corporation Lawyer and Attorney General of the United States, 1835–1895" (Unpublished Ph.D. thesis, University of Michigan, 1960), pp. 43–161.

13. Boston *Journal,* Mar. 5, 1896.

14. Eggert, "Richard Olney," pp. 175–77; Statement of Amounts Charged to Boston Office Expenses, 1891–1903, Burlington Railroad Archives, Newberry Library, Chicago, used with permission.

15. McMurry, *Coxey's Army,* pp. 21–48.

16. *Ibid.,* pp. 127–28, 149–72, 197–99.

17. Unfinished autobiographic memorandum dictated by Richard Olney to his personal secretary, A. M. Straw, Feb. 1901, Olney Papers (hereafter cited as Olney Memo). This brief sketch deals only with his attorney generalship.

18. S. H. H. Clark, Oliver W. Mink, E. Ellery Anderson, and Frederic Coudert, receivers, to the attorney general, Apr. 21, 1894; Hoadly to Olney, Apr. 21, 1894, Year File 4017/94, Justice Dept. Records (hereafter cited as Coxey File). The "interests" of the United States government in the Union Pacific consisted of a second mortgage held as security for construction loans made to the company under the Pacific Railway Acts of 1862 and 1864.

19. Acting attorney general to the secretary of war, Apr. 21, 1894,

Executive & Congressional letter copy book, XVII, 155; secretary of war to the acting attorney general, Apr. 21, 1894, Coxey File; Maxwell to Hoadly, Apr. 22, 1894, Miscellaneous letter copy book, XIV, 21, Justice Dept. Records.

20. W. J. Carroll to Jno. M. Thurston, general counsel in Washington, D.C., for the Union Pacific, Apr. 20, 1894 (received at Justice Dept. Apr. 23), Coxey File.

21. McDermott to the attorney general, Apr. 21, 1894, Coxey File; Olney to McDermott, Apr. 23, 1894, Instructions letter copy book, XXXVIII, 589, Justice Dept. Records.

22. McNaught to Olney, Apr. 23, 1894, Coxey File.

23. Schofield to McNaught, Apr. 24, 1894, Army Headquarters, Early Wars Branch, Record Group 108, National Archives (hereafter cited as Army Headquarters), Letters Sent, IV:2:452.

24. Knowles and Preston Leslie to Olney, Apr. 24, 1894, Coxey File.

25. Olney to Knowles, Apr. 24, 1894, Judges & Clerks letter copy book, VI, 102; Knowles to Olney, Apr. 24, 1894, Coxey File.

26. McDermott to Olney, McNaught to Olney, Apr. 24, 1894. McDermott told Olney that he had acted on the advice of the railroad lawyers in a subsequent letter dated May 1, 1894. Coxey File.

27. *Washington Post,* Apr. 26, 1894; Olney to McDermott, Apr. 24, 1894, Instructions letter copy book, XXXIX, 32, Justice Dept. Records.

28. Governor John E. Rickards to Cleveland, Apr. 25, 1894, Cleveland Papers.

29. McMurry, *Coxey's Army,* pp. 202–5; McDermott to Olney, Apr. 27, 1894, Coxey File.

30. McNaught to Garland, Apr. 26, 1894 (forwarded to Justice Dept. that same day), Coxey File. A. H. Garland was attorney general during Cleveland's first term.

31. Olney to McDermott, Apr. 28, 1894, Instruction letter copy book, XXXIX, 93, Justice Dept. Records.

32. Hanford to Olney, Apr. 24, 1894; Drake to Olney, Apr. 26, 1894 (two telegrams), Coxey File; Olney to Drake, Apr. 24, 1894, Instructions letter copy book, XXXIX, 39, Justice Dept. Records.

33. *New York Tribune,* Apr. 29, 1894. McMurry, *Coxey's Army,* pp. 217–18, does not mention that the freight was a dummy used to precipitate trouble. The wording of Grady's telegrams to the Justice Department seem to support rather than belie the charge in the *Tribune* article. See Grady to Olney, Apr. 27, 1894 (two telegrams); Bellinger to Olney, Apr. 28, 1894, Coxey File.

34. *Washington Star,* Apr. 26, 1894; United States, *Revised Statutes,* p. 1034. Sections 5297, 5298, and 5300 are all under "Title LXIX. Insurrection."

35. Schofield to Lamont, Apr. 28, 1894, Army Headquarters, Letters Sent, IV:2:470.

36. *New York Tribune,* Apr. 29, 1894.

37. Grady to Olney, Drake to Olney, Apr. 29, 1894, Coxey File; *New York Tribune,* Apr. 29, 1894; McMurry, *Coxey's Army,* p. 220.

38. Among other occasions, troops were sent on May 14 to Spokane to prevent the seizure of a train, on May 15 to recapture a train stolen at Montpelier, Idaho, and on May 19 to maintain order in the Coeur d'Alene district of Idaho, where there were large "combines of lawless persons." Judges & Clerks letter copy book, VI, 151; Headquarters of the Army to General Brooke, May 14, 1894, Coxey File; Army Headquarters, Letters Sent, IV:2:506-7.

39. Hanford to Olney, May 2, 1894; McNaught to Olney, May 12, 1894; McDermott to Olney, June 7, 1894; and U.S. attorney Henry V. Johnson to Olney, June 7, 1894, Coxey File.

40. Olney to Judge E. S. Dundy, June 13, 1894; to Judge Hanford, May 14, 1894; to Judge John A. Riner, May 15, 1894, Judges & Clerks letter copy book, VI, 198, 151, 153, Justice Dept. Records.

41. *Washington Post,* May 2, 1894; *Washington Star,* May 1, 2, 1894; McMurry, *Coxey's Army,* pp. 114-26.

42. Ginger, *Bending Cross,* pp. 102-7, gives a brief account of the strike.

43. McMurry, *Indust. & Labor Relations Rev.,* VIII, 73-92.

44. Minneapolis *Tribune,* Apr. 15, 1894; Ginger, *Bending Cross,* pp. 103-7.

45. Hill to Olney, Apr. 19, 1894, Coxey File. Apparently, all correspondence related to labor disputes in the spring of 1894, including the Great Northern and Illinois coal strikes, were filed by the Justice Department in the Coxey File.

46. White, *A Life Span,* pp. 17-18, 201-2.

47. Perkins to Olney, Jan. 11, 1894, Olney Papers.

48. White, *A Life Span,* pp. 202-3; U.S., *Annual Report of the Postmaster General of the United States . . . 1893* (Washington, 1893), pp. 424-26.

49. *Nat'l. Cyclop.,* XXIII, 204; *Poor's Railroad Manual, 1895,* pp. 423, 753-54. Between Nov. 1889 and May 1894 Maxwell appeared before the Indiana Supreme Court at least thirteen times by brief

on behalf of the Ohio & Mississippi Railway Co., three of these while solicitor general. See, *passim,* 122 Indiana 289 to 138 Indiana 649.

50. White, *A Life Span,* pp. 207–8. In compliance with the legal requirement that the attorney general render opinions only to the President and to cabinet members, the request for an opinion was formally sent over Bissell's name and was addressed to the attorney general. The reply was addressed to the postmaster general, not to White, and was over the attorney general's name. The original correspondence is in the Coxey File.

51. Olney held that administrative officers of the federal government should regard official opinions of the attorney general as binding "as law until withdrawn by the Attorney General or overruled by the courts . . ." U.S., Justice Department, *Official Opinions of the Attorneys-General of the United States,* XX, 654. This opinion was subsequently quoted with approval in *Smith* v. *Jackson,* 241 Fed. Rep. 747 (1917), and affirmed, 246 U.S. 388 (1918). Albert G. Langeluttig, *The Department of Justice of the United States* (Baltimore, 1927), p. 154.

52. U.S., Justice Dept., *Official Opinions of Attorneys-General,* XXI, 542–43.

53. Ginger, *Bending Cross,* p. 103; Bissell to Olney, Apr. 21, 1894, Coxey File.

54. Hill to Cleveland, Apr. 24, 1894, Cleveland Papers; Apr. 28, 1894, Coxey File.

55. Olney to Lamont, Apr. 30, 1894, Olney Papers; Ginger, *Bending Cross,* p. 104.

56. Henry James, *Richard Olney and His Public Service* (Boston and New York, 1923) p. 37n.

NOTES TO CHAPTER VII

1. United States Strike Commission, *Report on the Chicago Strike of June–July, 1894* (Washington, 1894), p. xxiii. The report stated that there were about 850,000 railway employees in the United States, 140,000 of whom belonged to the established brotherhoods.

2. *Ibid.,* pp. xxviii, xxix; Donald L. McMurry, "Labor Policies of the General Managers' Association of Chicago, 1886–1894," *Journal of Economic History,* XIII (Spring 1953), 160–78.

3. U.S. Strike Commission, *Report,* pp. xxi, xxxii–xxxvi; Lindsey, *Pullman Strike,* pp. 90–103.

4. U.S. Strike Commission, *Report,* pp. 6, xxxvii–xxxix.

5. Lindsey, *Pullman Strike,* pp. 126–31; Ginger, *Bending Cross,* pp. 117–19.

6. General Managers Association, *Minutes of Meetings* (Chicago, 1894), p. 94 (hereafter cited as GMA *Minutes*). Only twenty-five copies of these minutes were reported to have been published. Copies are located in the John Crerar Library, Chicago, and in the papers of Stuyvesant Fish, Illinois Central Railway Archives, Newberry Library, Chicago.

7. U.S. Strike Commission, *Report,* pp. 223, 547–58.

8. *Ibid.,* Debs's testimony, pp. 136–37; St. John's testimony, p. 227. St. John went on to say (p. 256) that the GMA did not deal with the ARU in part because it represented less than 25 percent of the employees of the lines. Also, in the GMA's judgment "there was no room for an organization of that kind." Chauncey M. Depew, president of the New York Central, later observed that the strike was caused "by the ambitious effort of Mr. Debs . . . to absorb all organizations of railway employees into one." Quoted by Walter B. Wines, "The Labor Troubles of 1894," *History of Chicago,* Moses and Kirkland, eds., II, 598.

9. See, for example, letters of Stuyvesant Fish to J. T. Harahan, second vice-president, Illinois Central railroad, and to James Fentress, general solicitor, June 29, 1894, Fish, out-letter file, Illinois Central Archives, used with permission.

10. GMA *Minutes,* June 26, 27, 1894, pp. 94, 101–2.

11. See above, pp. 149–50.

12. Bissell to Olney, June 29, 1894, Letters, PMG, NA; Olney to U.S. attorneys in strike areas, *passim, Appendix to the Annual Report of the Attorney-General of the United States for the Year 1896* (Washington, 1897) (hereafter cited as *Chicago Strike Correspondence).* The Appendix contains most of the official correspondence relating to the actions of the government with reference to the Chicago strike. See below, pp. 187–88.

13. U.S. Strike Commission, *Report,* pp. 227, 233; Arnold to Olney, U.S. Attorney Thomas Milchrist to Olney, Dec. 1, 1894, File 16–1–23, Justice Dept. Records (hereafter cited as Chicago Strike File); George B. Harris, vice-president of the CB&Q, to Olney, Jan. 8, 1895, Olney Papers.

14. *Chicago Daily Tribune,* June 29, 1894; GMA *Minutes,* July 1, 1894; New York *World,* July 2, 1894; *New York Times,* July 3, 1894; U.S. Strike Commission, *Report,* p. 65; Clarence Darrow, *The Story of My Life* (New York, 1932), p. 61.

15. Bissell to Charles F. Mayer, president, Baltimore & Ohio, July 10, 1894; to Joseph Wood, general manager, Pennsylvania Lines West of Pittsburgh; James McCrea, vice-president, Pennsylvania Lines West of Pittsburgh; and John Newall, president, Lake Shore &

Michigan Southern, July 11, 1894, Letters, PMG, NA; *Chicago Times,* June 30, 1894.

16. *Chicago Daily Tribune,* June 30, July 1, 1894; New York *Evening Post,* July 2, 1894; General Nelson A. Miles, commander, U.S. troops in Chicago, to commanding general of the Army, John M. Schofield, July 4, 1894, quoted in Schofield, *Forty-Six Years in the Army* (New York, 1897), p. 498. In his letter to Mayer (see note 15 above) Bissell stated that on only two days was rioting such that mail and passenger trains could not get all the way to Grand Central Station in Chicago. Letters, PMG, NA. Those two days were probably July 6 and 7, after the arrival of federal troops in Chicago. See Lindsey, *Pullman Strike,* pp. 152–53, 207–9.

17. Debs's testimony, U.S. Strike Commission, *Report,* pp. 142–43. For the impact of the strike on the economy, see above, pp. 12–15.

18. GMA *Minutes,* June 30, 1894, pp. 124–27. Quote from p. 126.

19. John Peter Altgeld, *Biennial Message to the 39th General Assembly* [of Illinois], *Jan. 9, 1895* (n.p., n.d.), pp. 40–47; Waldo R. Browne, *Altgeld of Illinois: A Record of his Life and Work* (New York, 1925), pp. 128–40; Harry Barnard, *"Eagle Forgotten," The Life of John Peter Altgeld* (Indianapolis, 1938), pp. 290–93; Harvey Wish, "The Pullman Strike: A Study in Industrial Warfare," *Journal of the Illinois State Historical Society,* XXXII (Sept. 1939), pp. 299–300.

20. GMA *Minutes,* June 30, 1894, pp. 117–23.

21. *New York Times,* July 2, 1894; *The Bench and Bar,* Vol. VI of *Industrial Chicago* (Chicago, 1896), pp. 449–52; *Who's Who in America, 1899–1900,* p. 760.

22. *Chicago Times, New York Times, Washington Post,* July 2, 1894; "Walker" to Olney, telegram, June 30, 1894, Walker to Olney, letter, July 2, 1894, *Chicago Strike Correspondence,* pp. 60, 63–64. The newspaper accounts may or may not be accurate. Other sources fail to corroborate or to contradict them. The secret GMA *Minutes* do not record either a recommendation that special counsel be appointed or that Walker be asked to assist with the case. One week after Walker's appointment, Lambert Tree, a Chicago attorney, wrote Secretary of State Gresham (July 6, 1894, Gresham Papers) that he had talked "with the rail-road managers and their attorneys" and that they "complain bitterly" over Walker's appointment. Not only was he not moving against Debs as forcefully as they would have liked, but they thought "it was a great mistake to appoint any railroad attorney to such a position" and that the fact that he was known as a railroad attorney "hurts the cause with the public." Whether the railroad officials were repenting their choice or Olney's is not clear. The charge in the July 3, 1894,

Chicago Times, that Olney knew Walker personally also is not provable. There was, for example, no correspondence whatever in the Olney Papers between the two men prior to June 30, 1894. Though Olney's clients included such Midwestern corporations as the Burlington Railroad, he himself worked in Boston. Walker, on the other hand, was located in the Chicago area. At the time he named Walker special counsel, Olney inquired of Gresham about the Chicago attorney since Gresham was from Chicago. It seems unlikely Olney would have done this had Walker been a personal acquaintance. See Gresham to Franklin MacVeagh, July 12, 1894, Gresham Papers.

23. Darrow, *Story of My Life,* p. 61.

24. Olney Memo.

25. Olney to Walker, June 30, 1894, *Chicago Strike Correspondence,* p. 60.

26. See above, p. 116; Milchrist to Olney, June 30, 1894, Olney to Walker, June 30, 1894, *Chicago Strike Correspondence,* pp. 55–59.

27. Eggert, "Richard Olney," unpublished Ph.D. thesis, pp. 281–313.

28. U.S., *Annual Report of the Attorney General of the United States . . . 1893* (Washington, 1893), pp. xxvii–xxviii.

29. Stuyvesant Fish (quoting Tweed) to James Fentress, July 2, 1894, Illinois Central Archives.

30. Charles A. Garter to Olney, June 28, 1894; Olney to Garter, June 29, 1894 (italics supplied); Olney to Milchrist, July 1, 1894; Olney to Walker, July 1, 1894, *Chicago Strike Correspondence,* pp. 17, 18, 61.

31. *Chicago Strike Correspondence,* p. 61.

32. New York *Evening Post,* July 2, 1894.

33. Walker to Olney, July 2, 1894, Chicago Strike File. This letter was published in the *Chicago Strike Correspondence,* pp. 63–64, but with elisions. All references to the role of the judges in drafting the petition for an injunction were omitted.

34. Obituary, *New York Times,* Oct. 2, 1921; *DAB,* VII, 21–22; Edgar Lee Masters, *The Tale of Chicago* (New York, 1933); pp. 297–99; Carter H. Harrison, *Stormy Years* (Indianapolis and New York, 1935), pp. 242–46.

35. *Nat'l. Cyclop.,* XV, 253.

36. *DAB,* XX, 504–5; *Nat'l. Cyclop.,* XVIII, 303–4; *Case & Comment,* IV (Jan. 1898), 85; memorial, *Indiana Bar Association Report, 1902,* pp. 223f; Palmer, ed., *Bench and Bar of Illinois,* I, 255–56; Charles W. Taylor, *Biographical Sketches and Review of the Bench and Bar of Indiana* (Indianapolis, 1895), p. 174.

37. See Jacob Piatt Dunn, *Indiana and Indianans,* 5 vols. (Chicago, 1919), II, 736–38, and Gresham, *Gresham,* II, 602–18.

38. *New York Times,* Mar. 16, 19, 1892.

39. *Ind. Bar Ass'n. Report, 1902,* p. 225; W. W. Thorton, "Supreme Court of Indiana," *Greenbag,* IV (June 1892), 267; Edward Bryant Landis, "The Influence of Tennesseeans in the Formation of Illinois," *Transactions of the Illinois State Historical Society,* XXX (1923), 147; Dunn, *Indiana,* II, 738.

40. Olney Memo.

41. *U.S. v. Debs, et al.,* 64 Fed. Rep. 724–27 (1894).

42. Woods, "Injunction in the Federal Courts," *Yale Law Journal,* VI (Apr. 1897), 248–51.

43. Walker to Olney, July 2, 1894, *Chicago Strike Correspondence,* pp. 63–64. Walker in his letter said "chancery" rather than "criminal," but from the context of the letter this appears to have been a misstatement.

44. Grosscup to Gresham, July 26, 1894, Gresham Papers; Gresham, *Gresham,* I, 419.

45. Quoted in New York *World,* July 4, 1894; Olney to Walker, Olney to Milchrist, July 3, 1894, *Chicago Strike Correspondence,* pp. 65–66.

46. *Chicago Strike Correspondence,* p. 66.

47. Walker to Olney, telegram and letter, July 2, 1894; telegram, July 3, 1894, *ibid.,* pp. 62, 63–64; GMA *Minutes,* July 3, 1894.

48. Lindsey, *Pullman Strike,* p. 275; Nevins, *Cleveland,* p. 625, discusses in detail a number of misleading statements contained in Arnold's telegram. The telegram itself is published in *Chicago Strike Correspondence,* p. 66.

49. Nevins, *Cleveland,* p. 621; Nelson A. Miles, *Serving the Republic* (New York, 1911), p. 253; Olney Memo.

50. The order is published in Schofield, *Forty-Six Years in the Army,* p. 497.

51. Quoted in Nevins, *Cleveland,* p. 628.

52. Fish to Fentress, July 2, 1894, Illinois Central Archives.

53. *Chicago Daily Tribune, Washington Post,* and *New York Times,* July 5, 1894.

54. *Boston Herald,* July 5, 1894; Nevins, *Cleveland,* p. 625; Gresham to Erskine M. Phelps, July 12, 1894, Gresham Papers; Miles to Schofield, July 18, 1894, "Chicago Strikes" document file, Office of

the Adjutant General, Early Wars Branch, Record Group 94, National Archives (hereafter cited as AG's Chicago Strike File).

55. The Altgeld-Cleveland exchange is published in *Documents of American History,* 7th ed. (New York, 1963), Henry Steele Commager, ed., pp. 609–12; Lewis, in *Chicago Times,* July 10, 1894.

56. *Washington Post,* July 7, 1894.

57. Miles claimed that the policy of scattering the troops began before he arrived in Chicago. Miles to Schofield, July 18, 1894, AG's Chicago Strike File. Accounts of Miles's conduct on July 3, and in Chicago, are given in Schofield, *Forty-Six Years in the Army,* pp. 493–505; Olney Memo.; Gresham, *Gresham,* I, 418–19; the manuscript diary of Charles S. Hamlin, Hamlin Papers, Library of Congress. Washington and Chicago newspapers carried stories that Miles was under orders not to shoot. For example, see *Chicago Times,* July 7, 1894.

58. Miles to Adjutant General, July 5, 1894, *Chicago Strike Correspondence,* p. 70.

59. *Chicago Times,* July 5, 9, 1894. In messages to his private secretary in Boston, Olney wrote, July 2, "The New War in which I am engaged has broken up all my plans for leaving Washington at present." On July 4 he wrote, "The Second War I am running is worse than the 1st." Olney Papers.

60. Schofield to Miles, July 5, 1894; General Order No. 23, July 9, 1894, published in Schofield, *Forty-Six Years in the Army,* pp. 500, 504–5.

61. Lindsey, *Pullman Strike,* pp. 205–9.

62. Richardson, *Messages and Papers of the Presidents,* XII, 5931–32;Walker to Olney, July 9, 1894; Olney to Walker, July 9, 1894, *Chicago Strike Correspondence,* p. 77.

63. Lindsey, *Pullman Strike,* pp. 222–29, 263–66; Philip Taft, *The A.F. of L. in the Time of Gompers* (New York, 1957), pp. 77–83; Ginger, *Bending Cross,* pp. 148–50.

64. *In re Grand Jury,* 62 Fed. Rep. 835, 839.

65. *In re Grand Jury,* 62 Fed. Rep. 844.

66. *U.S. v. Cassidy, et al.,* 67 Fed. Rep. 762, 780.

67. 62 Fed. Rep. 834.

68. *U.S. v. Elliott, et al.,* 62 Fed. Rep. 801–3.

69. *U.S. v. Elliott, et al.,* 64 Fed. Rep. 30.

70. 62 Fed. Rep. 842.

71. *U.S. v. Agler,* 62 Fed. Rep. 824–25.

72. *Thomas* v. *Cincinnati, N.O. & T.P. Ry. Co.,* 62 Fed. Rep. 821.

73. 64 Fed. Rep. 34.

74. 62 Fed. Rep. 832.

75. 62 Fed. Rep. 846.

76. 62 Fed. Rep. 817.

77. 62 Fed. Rep. 835.

78. 62 Fed. Rep. 832.

79. 62 Fed. Rep. 846.

80. 62 Fed. Rep. 817–18.

81. 62 Fed. Rep. 834, 836.

82. 62 Fed. Rep. 846.

83. 62 Fed. Rep. 829.

84. *Cong. Rec.,* 53d Cong., 2d sess., p. 1856, 5894, Index; U.S. Congress, House, Judiciary Committee, 53d Cong., 2d sess., H. Report No. 1049.

85. *Ibid.,* pp. 7041, 7082.

86. *Ibid.,* pp. 7155, 7156.

87. *Ibid.,* pp. 7198–99.

88. *Ibid.,* pp. 7230f., 7237, 7241, 7284.

89. *Ibid.,* p. 7544.

90. *Ibid.,* pp. 7544–56.

91. *Ibid.,* pp. 7868, 7879, 7921.

92. *Ibid.,* 53d Cong., 3d sess., pp. 153–54, 43–45.

93. New York *Evening Post,* July 2, 1894.

94. Nevins, *Cleveland,* pp. 578–88, 611.

NOTES TO CHAPTER VIII

1. Olney to Walker, Jan. 7, 1895, Olney Papers.

2. See, for example, Olney telegrams to Walker between July 1 and July 9, 1894, *Chicago Strike Correspondence,* pp. 61, 66, 74, 77; Lambert Tree to Walter Gresham, July 6, 1894, Gresham Papers.

3. Walker to Olney, July 3, 1894, *Chicago Strike Correspondence,* p. 68.

4. Walker to Olney, July 6, 1894, *ibid.,* p. 72.

5. Walker to Olney, July 9, 1894; Arnold to Olney, July 10, 1894; Walker-Olney correspondence, July 11–12, 1894, *ibid.,* pp. 77–78, 80–81.

6. Walker to Olney, Olney to Walker, July 14, 1894, *ibid.*, pp. 83–84, 85.

7. Walker to Olney (2 letters), July 26, 1894, *ibid.*, pp. 93–95.

8. Olney to Walker, July 28, 1894, Olney Papers.

9. Walker to Olney, Sept. 14, 1894, *ibid.*

10. Olney to Walker, Sept. 24, 1894, *ibid.*

11. Walker to Olney, Sept. 29, 1894, *ibid.*

12. Walker to Olney, Nov. 2, 1894, *ibid.*

13. *U.S.* v. *Debs, et al.,* 64 Fed. Rep. 724–65. See especially pp. 739–47.

14. Walker to Olney, Dec. 17, 1894, Chicago Strike File.

15. Olney to Walker, Nov. 26, 1894, Miscellaneous letter copy book, XVI, 58–59, Justice Dept. Records.

16. Olney to Cleveland, Jan. 14, 1902, Olney Papers.

17. Olney to Walker, Dec. 20, 1894, Miscellaneous letter copy book, XVI, 167–69, Justice Dept. Records.

18. Trumbull's brief is reported with the case, *In re Debs, Petitioner,* 158 U.S. 564f. A summary of the arguments of Gregory and of Darrow were reported in the *New York Times,* Mar. 26, 27, 1895.

19. Copy of Olney's argument, Olney Papers. In a private letter to C. E. Perkins, president of the Burlington Railroad, Dec. 28, 1892, Olney, referring to the ICC, wrote: "The Commission, as its functions have now been limited by the Courts, is, or can be made of great use to the railroads. It satisfies the popular clamor for a government supervision of railroads, at the same time that that supervision is almost entirely nominal. Further, the older such a commission gets to be, the more inclined it will be found to be to take the business and railroad view of things. It thus becomes a sort of barrier between the railroad corporations and the people and a sort of protection against hasty and crude legislation hostile to railroad interests. . . . The part of wisdom is not to destroy the Commission, but to utilize it. . . ." Olney Papers.

20. Olney's argument, Olney Papers.

21. *New York Times,* Mar. 27, 1895.

22. Source Chronological, Year File 12953/94, Justice Dept. Records; Olney to Earhart, Nov. 5, 1894, Instructions letter copy book, XLIV, 539 and XLV, 31, Justice Dept. Records.

23. T. McCants Stewart to Grover Cleveland, Mar. 12, 1895, Cleveland Papers; New Orleans *Picayune,* Mar. 28, 1895.

24. Ginger, *Bending Cross,* p. 166; Lindsey, *Pullman Strike,* pp. 303–

4; *Chicago Daily Tribune, Inter-Ocean,* and *Chicago Herald,* Feb. 13, 1895. Black's interview with the press was reported in the *Chicago Daily Tribune,* Apr. 28, 1895.

25. Walker to Olney, May 21, 1895; Black to Attorney General Judson Harmon, Feb. 28, 1896, Chicago Strike File. Black argued against continuation of the criminal conspiracy case because no jury could be found which would believe that Debs had not already been punished for his crimes, such a trial would add greatly to the expenses of the government, and it would be difficult to prove that the defendants had conspired to obstruct the mail. According to Black, as far as the first trial had gone, it was shown that there had been no desire on the part of the strikers to block passage of the mail and that there had been no such obstruction until mail cars were put at the very end of trains rather than in their usual place ahead of the Pullman cars.

26. Olney to A. M. Straw, May 27, [1895], Olney Papers.

27. 158 U.S. 564f., 578, 580–81, 582, 600. The impartiality of the Court left something to be desired in the Debs case. Speaking in Jan. 1893, to the New York Bar Association, Justice Brewer had denounced all strikes. "The common rule as to strikes is this:" he said, "Not merely do the employees quit the employment, and thus handicap the employer in the use of his property, and perhaps in the discharge of duties which he owes to the public, but they also forcibly prevent others from taking their places. It is useless to say they only advise. . . . It is coercion, force; it is the effort of the many, by the mere weight of numbers, to compel the one to do their bidding. It is a proceeding outside the law, in defiance of the law, and in spirit and effect an attempt to strip from one that has that which of right belongs to him, the full and undisturbed use and enjoyment of his own. . . ." Quoted in 60 Fed. Rep. 822. Justice Stephen Field, writing to his friend, Don M. Dickinson, Sept. 23, 1894, said, "However much men may differ respecting the action of Mr. Cleveland in some matters, no just man can withhold his full thanks for the bold, straight forward and courageous conduct shown by him in putting down by force the monstrous strikes. No battle of the century will reflect upon the winner greater honor." Cleveland Papers.

28. See, for example, *Chicago Times,* July 3, 8, 9 and the New York *World,* July 4, 5, 1894.

29. Joseph Nimmo, in a letter to C. E. Perkins, Nov. 19, 1894, suggested that Olney's behavior may have stemmed from growing political ambition. Perkins File, Burlington Archives. Between July 21 and Aug. 28, 1894, Congress received twenty-four petitions, mostly from labor groups, calling for Olney's impeachment. *Cong. Rec.,* 53d Cong. 2d sess., p. 7799f. Statement of Amounts Charged

to Boston Office Expenses, Jan. 1891–June 1903; Perkins to J. W. Blythe, Feb. 4, 1895, Perkins File, Burlington Archieves; Perkins to Olney, Mar. 7, 1897, Olney Papers.

30. Olney to George R. Peck, Aug. 4, 1894, Olney Papers. There was a decrease in the volume of correspondence between Olney and his Boston associates after the spring of 1895, at least so far as can be gathered from the Olney Papers. Agnes Olney Minot, Olney's daughter, who lived with him in Washington, declared that after a year or so in the cabinet, Olney did relatively little for his former clients. A. M. Straw to Henry James, Mar. 2, 1922, Olney Papers.

31. Olney Papers. The ideas contained in these notes were not used in the final draft of the attorney general's *Annual Report*.

32. See above, pp. 130–33.

33. Olney to Harlan, Aug. 26, 1894, Olney Papers.

34. *Arthur, et al.* v. *Oakes, et al.,* 63 Fed. Rep. 310–29 (1894).

35. Olney to Perkins, Oct. 4, 1894, Olney Papers.

36. Olney to Charles S. Hamlin, Aug. 10, 1899, Olney Papers.

37. Olney Memo.

38. Olney to A. C. Griscom, Jr., May 16, 1898, Olney Papers.

39. Olney to Moseley, Oct. 1, 3, 1894; Olney to Dallas, Oct. 6, asking leave to file the brief; Oct. 11, to say that he had changed his mind and would not file it; and, finally, Nov. 3, 1894, saying he had again changed his mind and would file the brief. *Ibid.*

40. Olney, *Legality and Propriety of Labor Organizations, Some Suggestions Submitted by Richard Olney, esq. as amicus curiae . . .* (n.p., 1894), copy in Olney Papers.

41. J. W. F. White, "The Judiciary of Allegheny County," *Pennsylvania Magazine of History and Biography,* VIII (1883), 143–93; obituary, *Legal Intelligencer,* LXXIV (Mar. 9, 1917), 157–58; obituary, *Pennsylvania Bar Association Report,* 1917, p. 77.

42. *University of Pennsylvania Law Review,* LXV (Mar. 1917), 470–72; quotation from *Pa. Bar Ass'n. Report,* 1917, pp. 77–78; 141 Pennsylvania 484 (Mar., Apr. 1891).

43. *Legal Intelligencer,* LXXIV, 158.

44. *Platt* v. *Philadelphia & R. Rd. Co., et al.,* 65 Fed. Rep. 659–67 (1894).

45. U.S. Strike Commission, *Report,* p. xv, and *passim,* xxiii–xxviii, xxxii–xxxix, xxxi, xlv. Olney was taken aback to learn that the charge was true. He had ordered that all such deputies be paid by the Justice Department. He seems to have been shocked only

that the men were paid by the railroads, not that the GMA had recruited, supplied, armed, and supervised them. So far as he could, Olney had the railroads reimbursed from government funds for the money they paid their employees who acted as deputy United States marshals. Olney to Milchrist and Walker, Nov. 26, 1894, Miscellaneous letter copy book, XVI, 54–55, 58–59; Olney to Walker, Dec. 31, 1894, Olney Papers; Olney to various United States attorneys, ordering repayment to the railroads, Instructions letter book, XLIII, Justice Dept. Records.

46. Wright to Lyman, Dec. 31, 1894, Letters, U.S. Strike Commission, I, 459–60, Record Group 13, Labor and Transportation Branch, National Archives (hereafter cited as Letters, U.S. Strike Commission).

47. Wright to Lloyd, Nov. 19, 1894, *ibid.,* I, 325–26.

48. U.S. Strike Commission, *Report,* pp. xlvi–li. The commission had planned to endorse outright government operation of the Union Pacific. Charles Francis Adams, however, advised the commissioners that the government would be obliged to buy up much of the line which was not covered by the government's second mortgage and that twenty years of litigation would follow any attempted purchase. He advised the "guarded statement" which was substituted. Professor F. W. Taussig agreed with Adams and helped to sway the commission on the point. Carroll D. Wright to John D. Kernan, Sept. 5, 15, 1894, Letters, U.S. Strike Commission, I, 148–50, 180–81.

49. U.S. Strike Commission, *Report,* pp. lii–liv.

50. *Passim,* Letters, U.S. Strike Commission; Lindsey, *Pullman Strike,* pp. 357–59.

51. Nimmo to Perkins, Nov. 17, 1894, Perkins File, Burlington Archives; Cowen to Secretary of War Lamont, Nov. 20, 1894, Lamont Papers.

52. Wright to Sarah K. Bolton, Oct. 25, 1895, Letters, U.S. Strike Commission, II, 106–7.

53. U.S., *Statutes at Large,* XXV, 501; H.R. 8259, copy in Olney Papers.

54. James Morgan, *The Life Work of Edward A. Moseley in the Service of Humanity* (New York, 1913), p. 149; Olney Memo.; copy of H.R. 8259, with comments in the hand of Grover Cleveland; Olney to Straw, Jan. 2, 1895; McGann to Olney, Jan. 14, 1895; Olney to McGann, Jan. 17, 1895, Olney Papers.

55. Olney to McGann, Jan. 17, 1895, Olney Papers. The discussion that follows is based on the same letter.

56. Olney Memo.

57. Letters, U.S. Strike Commission, II, 46–47. Gompers opposed the bill, but not too actively, because the railway brotherhoods favored it. Samuel Gompers, *Seventy Years of Life and Labor* (New York, 1925), II. 135–40.

58. *Cong. Rec.*, 53d Cong., 3d sess., p. 2789.

59. *Ibid.*, pp. 2789, 2793, 2794, 2796.

60. *Ibid.*, pp. 2795–96, 2803.

61. *Ibid.*, pp. 2789–2805, 2819, 2881, 2961–62, 3075; 54th Cong., 1st sess., pp. 49, 3463; 54th Cong., 2d sess., pp. 2387–90, 2403; 55th Cong., 2d sess., pp. 72, 4638–49, 4842–58, 5046–53, 5566.

62. Lecht, *Experience Under Railroad Labor Legislation*, pp. 17–18.

63. Olney, "Discrimination vs. Union Labor—Legal?" *American Law Review*, XLII (Mar., Apr. 1908), 162–63; Olney Memo.

64. Lecht, *Experience Under Railroad Labor Legislation*, pp. 18–19.

NOTES TO CHAPTER IX

1. Norman J. Ware, *The Labor Movement in the United States 1860–1895: A Study in Democracy* (New York, 1929), p. 1.

2. *Commonwealth* v. *Hunt,* Massachusetts Reports, 4 Metcalf 45 (1842), was the first instance of a state supreme court denying that the common law doctrine of conspiracy applied to a labor union. The decision also upheld the right of workers to strike to improve their own working conditions.

3. Gutman, *Labor History*, II; 215–35.

4. Jerome Frank, *Law and the Modern Mind* (New York, 1949), provides a lengthy discussion of judge and lawyer-made law and the psychology of decision-making.

5. Twiss, *Lawyers and the Constitution,* pp. 42–62 and *passim.*

6. Cooley, *Amer. Law Reg.*, XXV, 715–18; Swain, *Economic Aspects of Railroad Receiverships,* pp. 53–56; Lawrence Godkin, "The Courts as Railway Managers," *Albany Law Journal,* XXXII (July 18, 1885), 45–47.

7. Charles Fairman, "Justice Samuel F. Miller," *Political Science Quarterly,* L (Mar. 1935), 43.

8. For an excellent discussion of the respective views of railway management and railway labor in 1888, see McMurry, *Burlington Strike,* pp. 273–77.

9. U.S. Strike Commission, *Report,* pp. xlvii–xlviii, provides a contemporary (1894) recognition of this double standard.

10. Fine, *Laissez Faire and the General-Welfare State,* pp. 96–101, discusses the "cult of success" and its basic tenets.

11. The states that passed such laws were Maryland (1878), New Jersey (1880), Pennsylvania (1883), Ohio (1885), and New York, Massachusetts, Kansas, and Iowa (1886). The Massachusetts State Arbitration Board, which was the most successful, between 1887 and 1900, settled 109 out of 1458 strikes or lockouts. In New York, between 1887 and 1900, of 402 cases acted upon (345 by the board's initiative) only 19 disputes were adjusted without a strike or lockout taking place. Ting Tsz Ko, *Governmental Methods of Adjusting Labor Disputes in North America and Australia* (New York, 1926), pp. 19, 25, and 54.

12. Lecht, *Experience Under Railway Labor Legislation,* pp. 18–43; Irving Bernstein, *A History of the American Worker, 1920–1933, The Lean Years* (Boston, 1960), pp. 211–12.

13. For example, see presidential messages to Congress: Wilson, Aug. 29, 1916, *Messages and Papers of the Presidents, Supplement* (Washington, 1917), pp. 8144–49; Truman, May 25, 1946, *Public Papers of the President of the United States: Harry S. Truman . . . 1946* (Washington, 1962), pp. 277–80; and Kennedy, July 22, 1963, *Public Papers of the President of the United States: John F. Kennedy . . . 1963* (Washington, 1964), pp. 586–94. For examples of the Supreme Court's sanctioning of the right of Congress to intervene legislatively to avoid railroad strikes, see *Wilson* v. *New,* 243 U.S. 322 (1917); *Virginian Railway Co.* v. *System Federation No. 40,* 300 U.S. 515 (1937); and *Order of Telegraphers* v. *Chicago & N.W. Rwy. Co.,* 362 U.S. 330 (1960).

14. Lecht, *Experience Under Railway Labor Legislation,* pp. 25, 28–29, 47, 195–97.

15. U.S., *Statutes at Large,* XLIV, 577 (Railway Labor Act, 1926); XLVIII, 198–99 (N.I.R.A., Sec. 7a); XLVIII, 1186–88 (Amendments, Railway Labor Act, 1934); XLIX, 452–53 (Wagner Act, Secs. 7 and 8); LXI, part 1, pp. 155–56 (Taft-Hartley Act, national emergency strike provisions). For the relationship of the Railway Labor Act of 1926 to Sec. 7 (a) of the N.I.R.A., see Irving Bernstein, *The New Deal Collective Bargaining Policy* (Berkeley and Los Angeles, 1950), pp. 18–23, 32–33. For the relationship of the 1934 Amendments to the Railway Labor Act to the Wagner Act, see the same work, *passim,* especially pp. 56–57, 134–35.

Bibliography

PRIMARY SOURCES

Manuscript Materials

Grover Cleveland Papers. Library of Congress.

Thomas McIntyre Cooley Papers. Michigan Historical Collections, University of Michigan.

Don M. Dickinson Papers. Library of Congress.
————. Michigan Historical Collections, University of Michigan.

1877 Strike Papers; Chicago Strike Papers. Adjutant General's Office, Record Group 94, Early Wars Branch, National Archives.

Stuyvesant Fish Papers. Illinois Central Archives, Newberry Library, Chicago.

Walter Q. Gresham Papers. Library of Congress.

Charles S. Hamlin Papers. Library of Congress.

Rutherford B. Hayes Papers. Rutherford B. Hayes Library, Fremont, Ohio.

Justice Department General Records. Record Group 60, Justice and Executive Branch, National Archives.

Daniel S. Lamont Papers. Library of Congress.

Letters of the Postmaster General. Postoffice Department, Record Group 28, Business Economics Branch, National Archives.

Letters of the United States Strike Commission. Record Group 13, Labor and Transportation Branch, National Archives.

Letters Sent File. Army Headquarters, Record Group 108, Early Wars Branch, National Archives.

Richard Olney Papers. Library of Congress.

Charles E. Perkins Papers. Burlington Archives, Newberry Library, Chicago.

Carl Schurz Papers. Library of Congress.

United States Documents

Biographical Directory of the American Congress, 1774–1949. Washington, 1950.

Congressional Record.

Public Papers of the Presidents of the United States: John F. Kennedy . . . 1963. Washington, 1964.
———: *Harry S. Truman . . . 1946.* Washington, 1962.

Richardson, James D., comp. *A Compilation of the Messages and Papers of the Presidents, 1789–1897.* Washington, 1897.

Supplement to the Messages and Papers of the Presidents: Woodrow Wilson. Washington, 1917.

United States. *Federal Cases.*
———. *Federal Reporter.*
———. *Reports.*
———. *Revised Statutes.* Washington, 1875.
———. *Statutes at Large.*

United States Commissioner of Labor. *Tenth Annual Report.* Washington, 1895.

United States Congress. House. Judiciary Committee. *Report on the Receivership of the Northern Pacific Railroad Company.* 53d Cong., 2d sess., H. Report No. 1049. Washington, 1894.
———. ———. ———. *Report to Accompany Memorial of Central Labor Union of Cleveland, Ohio, Preferring Charges Against Augustus J. Ricks . . .* 53d Cong., 3d sess., H. Report No. 1670. Washington, 1894.
———. ———. Select Committee. *Investigation of Labor Troubles in Missouri, Arkanasas, Kansas, Texas and Illinois.* 49th Cong., 2d sess., H. Report No. 4174. Washington, 1887.
———. ———. ———. *Investigation Relative to the Causes of the General Depression in Labor and Business, etc.* 45th Cong., 3d sess., H. Misc. Doc. No. 29; 46th Cong., 2d sess., H. Misc. Doc. No. 5. Washington, 1879.

——. ——. ——. *Labor Troubles in the Anthracite Regions of Pennsylvania, 1887–1888.* 50th Cong., 2d sess., H. Report No. 4141. Washington, 1889.

——. ——. ——. *Report: Chinese Immigration.* 46th Cong., 2d sess., H. Report No. 572. Washington, 1879.

——. Senate. Committee on Education and Labor. *Report Upon the Relations between Labor and Capital, and Testimony Taken by the Committee.* Washington, 1885. 4 vols.

United States Department of Commerce. *Historical Statistics of the United States, Colonial Times to 1957.* Washington, 1960.

——. *Statistical Abstract of the United States, 1964.* Washington, 1964.

United States Department of Justice. *Annual Report of the Attorney General of the United States for the Year . . . 1893; 1894; Appendix, 1896.*

——. *Official Opinions of the Attorneys-General of the United States.*

United States Postoffice Department. *Annual Report of the Postmaster General of the United States for the Year . . . 1877; 1888; 1893; 1894.*

United States Strike Commission. *Report on the Chicago Strike of June–July, 1894.* Washington, 1894.

Wilson, Frederick T. *Federal Aid in Domestic Disturbances 1787–1903.* 67th Cong., 2d sess., Senate Doc. 263. Washington, 1922.

State Documents

Illinois. Governor John Peter Altgeld. *Biennial Message to the 39th General Assembly, Jan. 9, 1895.* n.p., n.d.

Indiana. *Indiana Reports.*

Massachusetts. *Massachusetts Reports.*

Missouri. Adjutant-General. *Report in Regard to the Late Strike of Railroad Employees.* Jefferson City, 1885.

——. Bureau of Labor Statistics. *The Official History of the Great Strike of 1886.* Jefferson City, 1886.

——. Commissioner of Labor Statistics and Inspection. *Report in Regard to the Late Strike of Railroad Employees.* Jefferson City, 1885.

New York. *Annual Report of the Auditor of the Canal Department.* New York, 1881.

Pennsylvania. *Pennsylvania Reports.*

West Virginia. Governor Henry M. Mathews. *Biennial Message with Accompanying Documents to the Legislature of West Virginia, Session of 1879.* Wheeling, 1879.

Wisconsin. *Wisconsin Reports.*

Other Primary Sources

Cullom, Shelby M. *Fifty Years of Public Service.* Chicago, 1911.

Darrow, Clarence. *The Story of My Life.* New York, 1932.

Dickinson, Don M. "Progress and the Post," *North American Review,* CIL (Nov. 1889), 399–411.

General Managers Association. *Minutes of Meetings.* Chicago, 1894.

Gompers, Samuel. *Seventy Years of Life and Labor.* New York, 1926. 2 vols.

Howe, George Frederick. "President Hayes's Notes of Four Cabinet Meetings," *American Historical Review,* XXXVII (Jan. 1932), 286–89.

Miles, Nelson A. *Serving the Republic.* New York, 1911.

Nevins, Allan, ed. *Letters of Grover Cleveland, 1850–1908.* Boston and New York, 1933.

Olney, Richard. "Discrimination vs. Union Labor—Legal?" *American Law Review,* XLII (Mar. Apr. 1908), 162–63.
———. *Legality and Propriety of Labor Organizations, Some Suggestions* . . . n.p., 1894.

Powderly, Terence V. *The Path I Trod: The Autobiography of Terence V. Powderly.* New York, 1940.

Schofield, John M. *Forty-Six Years in the Army.* New York, 1897.

White, James E. *A Life Span and Reminiscences of Railway Mail Service.* Philadelphia, 1910.

Williams, Charles Richard, ed. *Diary and Letters of Rutherford Birchard Hayes.* Columbus, 1924. 6 vols.

Woods, William A. "Injunction in the Federal Courts," *Yale Law Journal,* VI (Apr. 1897), 248–51.

SECONDARY SOURCES

Allen, Ruth A. *The Great Southwest Strike* (The University of Texas Publication No. 4214). Austin, 1942.

Babst, Earl D. and Lewis G. Vander Velde, eds. *Michigan and the Cleveland Era: Sketches of University of Michigan Staff Members and Alumni Who Served the Cleveland Administrations, 1885–1889, 1893–1897*. Ann Arbor, 1948.

Barnard, Harry. *"Eagle Forgotten," The Life of John Peter Altgeld.* Indianapolis, 1938.

Barnes, James A. *John G. Carlisle: Financial Statesman.* New York, 1931.

Barrows, Chester L. *William M. Evarts: Lawyer, Diplomat, Statesman.* Chapel Hill, 1941.

Bench and Bar (Industrial Chicago, Vol. VI). Chicago, 1896.

The Bench and Bar of Iowa. Chicago and New York, 1901.

The Bench and Bar of St. Louis, Kansas City, Jefferson City, and Other Missouri Cities. St. Louis, 1884.

Bernstein, Irving. *A History of the American Worker, 1920–1933: The Lean Years.* Boston, 1960.
———. *The New Deal Collective Bargaining Policy.* Berkeley and Los Angeles, 1950.

Berryman, John R. *History of the Bench and Bar of Wisconsin.* Chicago, 1898. 2 vols.

Bolt, Robert. "A Biography of Donald M. Dickinson." Unpublished Ph.D. Thesis, Michigan State University, 1963.

Borkin, Joseph. *The Corrupt Judge: An Inquiry into bribery and other high crimes and misdemeanors in the federal courts.* New York, 1962.

Browne, Waldo R. *Altgeld of Illinois: A Record of his Life and Work.* New York, 1925.

Bruce, Robert V. *1877: Year of Violence.* Indianapolis and New York, 1959.

Burbank, David T. *City of Little Bread: The St. Louis General Strike of 1877.* St. Louis, 1957 (microcard).

Chandler, Alfred D., ed. *The Railroads, The Nation's First Big Business.* New York, 1965.

"A Chapter of Wabash." *North American Review,* CXLVI (Feb. 1888), 178–93.

Cochran, Thomas C. "The Entrepreneur in American Capital Formation." *The Inner Revolution: Essays on the Social Sciences in History.* New York, 1964.
———. *Railroad Leaders, 1845–1890, The Business Mind in Action.* Cambridge, 1953.
——— and William Miller. *The Age of Enterprise: A Social History of Industrial America.* New York, 1942.

Cooley, Thomas M. "New Aspects of the Right of Trial by Jury." *American Law Register,* XXV (Dec. 1877), 705–21.

Crossley, Frederic B. *Courts and Lawyers of Illinois.* Chicago, 1916.

Dacus, J. A. *Annals of the Great Strikes.* Chicago, 1877.

Dictionary of American Biography. Allen Johnson, ed. New York, 1957. 22 vols.

Documents of American History, 7th edn. Henry Steele Commager, ed. New York, 1963.

Dorfman, Joseph. *The Economic Mind in American Civilization, 1606–1918.* New York, 1946–49. 3 vols.

Dulles, Foster Rhea. *Labor in America, A History.* New York, 1960. 2d revised ed.

Dunn, Jacob Piatt. *Indiana and Indianans.* Chicago, 1919. 5 vols.

Eggert, Gerald G. "Richard Olney, Corporation Lawyer and Attorney General of the United States, 1835–1895." Unpublished Ph.D. Thesis, University of Michigan, 1960.

Emery, George F. "Reminiscenses of Bench and Bar." *Collections and Proceedings of the Maine Historical Society,* series 2, VIII, 135–36.

Esarey, Logan. *A History of Indiana from 1850 to 1920.* Fort Wayne, 1924. 2 vols.

Fairman, Charles. "Justice Samuel F. Miller." *Political Science Quarterly,* L (Mar. 1935), 43 ff.

Fine, Sidney. *Laissez Faire and the General-Welfare State, A Study of Conflict in American Thought, 1865–1901.* Ann Arbor, 1956.

Fisher, Douglas Alan. *The Epic of Steel.* New York, 1963.

Fogel, Robert William. *Railroads and American Economic Growth: Essays in Econometric History.* Baltimore, 1964.

Foner, Philip S. *History of the Labor Movement in the United States.* New York, 1947, 1955. 2 vols.

Frank, Jerome. *Law and the Modern Mind.* New York, 1949.

Frankfurter, Felix and Nathan Greene. *The Labor Injunction.* New York, 1930.

Gabriel, Ralph Henry. *The Course of American Democratic Thought.* New York, 1940.

Gentry, North Todd. "Some Missouri Judges I Have Known." *Missouri Historical Review,* XXXIV (Apr. 1940), 342–56.

Ginger, Ray. *The Bending Cross: A Biography of Eugene Victor Debs.* New Brunswick, 1949.

Godkin, Lawrence, Jr. "The Courts as Railway Managers." *Albany Law Journal,* XXXII (July 18, 1885), 45–47.

Grantham, Dewey W., Jr. *Hoke Smith and the Politics of the New South.* Baton Rouge, 1958.

Gregory, Stephen Strong. "Thomas Drummond. 1809–1890." *Great American Lawyers . . . A History of the Legal Profession in America.* William Draper Lewis, ed. 8 vols. Philadelphia, 1907–9. V, 506 f.

Gresham, Matilda. *Life of Walter Quintin Gresham, 1832–1895.* Chicago, 1919. 2 vols.

Grodinsky, Julius. *Jay Gould: His Business Career, 1867–1892.* Philadelphia, 1957.

Gue, Benjamin F. *History of Iowa.* New York, 1903. 4 vols.

Gutman, Herbert G. "Trouble on the Railroads in 1873–1874: Prelude to the 1877 Crisis?" *Labor History,* II (Spring 1961), 215–35.

Hallam, John. *Biographical and Pictorial History of Arkansas.* Albany, 1887.

Harrison, Carter H. *Stormy Years: The Autobiography of Carter H. Harrison.* Indianapolis and New York, 1935.

Hirsch, Mark D. *William C. Whitney, Modern Warwick.* New York, 1948.

Industrial Relations Research Association. *Emergency Disputes and National Policy.* New York, 1955.

James, Henry. *Richard Olney and His Public Service*. Boston and New York, 1923.

Jenks, Leland H. "Railroads as an Economic Force in American Development." *Journal of Economic History*, IV (May 1944), 1–20.

Josephson, Matthew. *The Politicos, 1865–1896*. New York, 1938.

Kirkland, Edward C. *Industry Comes of Age*. New York, 1961.
———. *Men, Cities, and Transportation*. Cambridge, 1948. 2 vols.

Ko, Ting Tsz. *Governmental Methods of Adjusting Labor Disputes in North America and Australia*. New York, 1926.

Krooss, Herman E. *American Economic Development*. Englewood Cliffs, N.J., 1955.

Landis, Edward Bryant. "The Influence of Tennesseeans in the Formation of Illinois." *Transactions of the Illinois State Historical Society*, XXX (1923), 133–53.

Langeluttig, Albert G. *The Department of Justice of the United States*. Baltimore, 1927.

Lecht, Leonard A. *Experience Under Railway Labor Legislation*. New York, 1955.

Lindsey, Almont. *The Pullman Strike: The Story of a Unique Experiment and of a Great Labor Upheaval*. Chicago, 1942.

McKee, Howard I. "The School Law of 1853, Its origin and Authors." *Missouri Historical Review*, XXXV (July 1941), 539–61.

McMurry, Donald L. *Coxey's Army: A Study of the Industrial Army Movement of 1894*. Boston, 1929.
———. "Federation of the Railroad Brotherhoods, 1889–1894." *Industrial and Labor Relations Review*, VII (Oct. 1953), 74–92.
———. *The Great Burlington Strike of 1888: A Case History in Labor Relations*. Cambridge, 1956.
———. "Labor Policies of the General Managers' Association of Chicago, 1886–1894." *Journal of Economic History*, XIII (Spring 1953), 160–78.
———. "The Legal Ancestry of the Pullman Strike Injunction." *Industrial and Labor Relations Review*, XIV (Jan. 1961), 235–56.

Masters, Edgar Lee. *The Tale of Chicago.* New York, 1933.

Merrill, Horace Samuel. *Bourbon Leader: Grover Cleveland and the Democratic Party.* Boston, 1957.

Miller, C. A. *The Lives of the Interstate Commerce Commissioners and the Commission's Secretaries.* n.p., 1946.

Miller, Sidney L. *Inland Transportation Principles and Politics.* New York, 1933.

Moore, Albert Burton. *History of Alabama and Her People.* Chicago and New York, 1927. 3 vols.

Morgan, James. *The Life Work of Edward A. Moseley in the Service of Humanity.* New York, 1913.

Morris, Richard B. "Andrew Jackson, Strikebreaker." *American Historical Review,* LV (1949), 54 ff.

Moses, John and Joseph Kirkland. *History of Chicago, Illinois.* Chicago, 1895. 2 vols.

Myers, Gustavus. *History of the Supreme Court of the United States.* Chicago, 1925.

National Cyclopaedia of American Biography. New York, 1891–1960. 55 vols.

Neilson, James W. *Shelby M. Cullom, Prairie State Republican.* Urbana, 1962.

Nelles, Walter. "A Strike and Its Legal Consequences—An Examination of the Receivership Precedent for the Labor Injunction." *Yale Law Journal,* XL (Feb. 1931), 507–54.

Nesbit, Robert C. *"He Built Seattle;" A Biography of Judge Thomas Burke.* Seattle, 1961.

Nevins, Allan. *Grover Cleveland: A Study in Courage.* New York, 1933.

North, Douglass C. *The Economic Growth of the United States, 1790–1860.* Englewood Cliffs, N.J., 1961.
———. *Growth and Welfare in the American Past: A New Economic History.* Englewood Cliffs, N.J., 1966.

O'Connor, Richard. *Gould's Millions.* New York, 1962.

Olcott, Charles S. *The Life of William McKinley.* Boston and New York, 1916. 2 vols.

Olson, James C. *J. Sterling Morton.* Lincoln, Nebraska, 1942.

Orth, Samuel P. *A History of Cleveland, Ohio.* Chicago, 1910. 3 vols.

Owen, Wilfred. *Strategy for Mobility.* Washington, 1964.

Palmer, John M., ed. *The Bench and Bar of Illinois.* Chicago, 1899. 2 vols.

Paul, Arnold M. *Conservative Crisis and the Rule of Law: Attitudes of Bar and Bench, 1887–1895.* Ithaca, 1960.

Philips, John F. "Administrations of Missouri Governors." *Missouri Historical Review,* V (Jan. 1911), 79 ff.

Poor, Henry Varnum and H. W. Poor. *Poor's Manual of the Railroads of the United States, 1895.* New York, 1895.

Pound, Arthur. "Don M. Dickinson." *Michigan and the Cleveland Era.* Earl D. Babst and Lewis G. Vander Velde, eds. Ann Arbor, 1948. pp. 107–36.

Pringle, Henry F. *The Life and Times of William Howard Taft.* New York, 1939. 2 vols.

Quigg, Murray T. "The Use of Injunctions in Labor Disputes." *Labor Law Journal,* III (Feb. 1952), 105–13.

Rayback, Joseph G. *A History of American Labor.* New York, 1959.

Reed, Parker McCobb. *The Bench and Bar of Wisconsin, History and Biography.* Milwaukee, 1882.

Rich, Bennett M. *The Presidents and Civil Disorder.* Washington, 1941.

Rostow, W. W. *The Process of Economic Growth,* 2d edn. New York, 1962.

Roy, Andrew. *A History of the Coal Miners of the United States,* 3d edn. Columbus, 1907.

Shoemaker, Floyd C. *Missouri Day by Day.* Jefferson City, 1942.

Sigmund, Elwin W. "Railroad Strikers in Court: Unreported Contempt Cases in Illinois in 1877." *Journal of the Illinois State Historical Society,* XLIX (Summer 1956), 190–209.

Stover, John F. *American Railroads.* Chicago, 1961.

Swain, Henry H. *Economic Aspects of Railroad Receiverships* (American Economic Association, *Economic Studies,* 2d series, vol. 3, no. 2). New York, April 1898.

Taft, Philip. *The A.F. of L. in the Time of Gompers.* New York, 1957.

Taussig, F. W. "The Southwest Strike of 1886." *Quarterly Journal of Economics*, I (Jan. 1887), 185–216.

Taylor, Charles W. *Biographical Sketches and Review of the Bench and Bar of Indiana*. Indianapolis, 1895.

Taylor, George Rogers. *The Transportation Revolution, 1815–1860*. New York, 1951.

Thorelli, Hans. *The Federal Antitrust Policy*. Stockholm, 1954.

Thorton, W. W. "Supreme Court of Indiana." *Greenbag*, IV (June 1892), 267.

Towl, Edwin S. "Judge Elmer S. Dundy." *Proceedings and Collections of the Nebraska State Historical Society*, 2d series, V (1902), 93.

Twiss, Benjamin. *Lawyers and the Constitution: How Laissez Faire Came to the Supreme Court*. Princeton, 1942.

Usher, Ellis Baker. *Wisconsin: Its Story and Biography, 1848–1913*. Chicago and New York, 1914. 8 vols.

Vander Velde, Lewis G. "Thomas McIntyre Cooley." *Michigan and the Cleveland Era*. Earl D. Babst and Lewis G. Vander Velde, eds. Ann Arbor, 1948. pp. 76–106.

Ware, Norman J. *The Labor Movement in the United States 1860–1895: A Study in Democracy*. New York, 1929.

Washington West of the Cascades. Chicago, 1917. 3 vols.

White, J. W. F. "The Judiciary of Allegheny County." *The Pennsylvania Magazine of History and Biography*, VII (1883), 143 ff.

Wines, Walter B. "The Labor Troubles of 1894." *History of Chicago*. John Moses and Joseph Kirkland, eds. 2 vols. Chicago, 1895. II, 598 ff.

Wish, Harvey. "The Pullman Strike: A Study in Industrial Warfare." *Journal of the Illinois State Historical Society*, XXXII (Sept. 1939), 299 ff.

Witte, Edwin. "Early American Labor Cases." *Yale Law Journal*, XXXV (1926), 832–35.

Woodward, C. Vann. *Origins of the New South, 1877–1913*. Baton Rouge, 1951.

———. *Reunion and Reaction*, 2d edn. New York, 1956.

Yearley, Clifton K., Jr. "The Baltimore and Ohio Railroad Strike of 1877." *Maryland Historical Magazine*, LI (1956), 188–211.

Index

Adamson Act, 239–40
Alabama Railroad Commission, 99
Allen, William V., 183
Altgeld, John Peter, 13, 161, 172–74, 235
Amalgamated Iron and Steel Workers' Union, 108
American Federation of Labor, 174–75
American Railway Union (ARU): origin, 147; Great Northern strike, 147–50; Chicago railway strike, 152–57, 160–61, 168–69, 174–75; Chicago strike cases, 178, 180–82, 193–96; mentioned, 7, 151, 178, 185, 188–89, 203, 213, 217; *see also* Chicago railway strike; Debs, Eugene V.; *Debs, in re;* Great Northern strike; Pullman, strike at; railroad brotherhoods; strikers and the mail; United States courts; United States Strike Commission; *United States* v. *Debs*
anarchy, 31, 43, 48–49, 109, 161, 172, 187, 191
Ann Arbor case, see *Toledo, A.A. & N.M. Ry. Co.* v. *Pennsylvania Co., et al.*
arbitration, 22, 61, 71, 79, 150, 183–86, 210, 214, 216; compulsory, 74, 104, 203, 213; voluntary, 2, 19, 21, 238; *see also* Arbitration Act of 1888, Erdman Act, O'Neill bill, United States Strike Commission
Arbitration Act of 1888: modified

O'Neill bill, 103; House debate, 103–4; Senate action, 104–5; signed by President, 105; used after Chicago railway strike, 213; mentioned, 184, 217, 224, 238; *see also* Erdman Act, O'Neill bill, United States Strike Commission
arbitration commission: temporary, 72, 103, 224; permanent, 75, 103, 217; temporary v. permanent, 75–76; 219–20
Army: called for by states, 1877, 26–27; appropriations, 29, 56–57; condition, 1877, 29; called for by courts, 1877, 37–38; troops sent, 30; dispatched to West Virginia too soon, 30; dispatched elsewhere properly, 30; effectiveness, 34; demands for larger Army, 54–55; praised by Hayes, 56; called for against Commonwealers, 141; not needed, 143; ordered out, 142, 144–46; refused in Great Northern strike, 150; ordered into Chicago railway strike, 171; role in Chicago strike, 171–75; refused in New Orleans dockworkers' strike, 200; Supreme Court upholds use at Chicago, 201; reluctance to use after Chicago strike, 202, 239; *see also* executive branch intervention
Army, formula for calling out: Hayes, 31–33, 231; Cleveland, 140, 142, 145–46, 163, 170, 231
Army officers' reluctance to intervene, 49, 141–42, 145, 171, 173–74

Arnold, John W., 159, 170–71
Arthur, Chester Allen, 59
Arthur, P. M., 55, 81–82, 87–88, 91, 94, 111, 113; *see also* Brotherhood of Locomotive Engineers
Atchison, Topeka & Santa Fe Railroad, 28, 94–96, 99, 100, 153, 203
Atlanta *Journal*, 138
attorney general, *Annual Report of, 1893*, 165; *1894*, 197, 203
attorney general of the United States, *see* Devens, Charles; Justice Department; *Official Opinions of the Attorneys-General of the United States;* Olney, Richard

Baker, John H., enjoins strike, 126–28; discusses Sherman Act, 178; mentioned, 130, 199, 234
Baltimore, 9, 12–14, 16–17, 24–25, 30
Baltimore & Ohio Railroad: 1877 strikes, 25–26, 29–30; mentioned, 12, 24, 27, 153, 159, 217, 235
Bangs, Stetson, Tracy & MacVeagh, 136
bargaining power, 226
Bellinger, Charles B., 144
Belt Line of Chicago, 88
Benedict, E. C., 137
Billings, Edward C., 115, 117, 164–65
Bissell, Wilson S.: ties to railroads, 137; criticizes railroads, 159; mentioned, 149, 160, 231, 235
Black, John C., 200
blacklist, 78, 218
Blair, Henry, 71
Bland, Richard P., 186
Blatchford, Samuel, 126
Boston, 84
Boston & Maine Railroad, 41, 45, 138
Boston & Maine strike, 41, 45–46
boycott, 1, 101; of Burlington, 81, 83; enjoined, 84–90; "Rule 12" adopted, 111; courts rule against, 1893–94, 111–14; illegal under Sherman Act, 115, 117; of Pullman cars, 155–59; *see also*

Burlington strike, secondary boycott, United States courts
Bozeman, Montana, 142–43
Bragg, Walter, 99–102
Brewer, David J.: Southwest strike cases, 62–66; quoted, 126; decision, Debs case, 201–2; quoted, 278; mentioned, 121
Brotherhood of Locomotive Engineers (BLE): early history, 6–7; in Burlington strike, 81–83; 85–92, 94; in Ann Arbor strike, 111–14; before Judge Speer, 1893, 116–17; *see also* Arthur, P. M.; railroad brotherhoods; "Rule 12" of BLE
Brotherhood of Locomotive Firemen (BLF), 6; in Burlington strike, 81–83, 94; *see also* railroad brotherhoods
Brotherhood of Railway Trainmen (BRT): Reading case, 207–9, 211–12; *see also* railroad brotherhoods
Brown, Joseph E., 70
Buchanan, James, 79–80
Buffalo, 9, 17, 24, 42; Switchmen's strike, 1892, 19, 108
Buffalo & Rochester Railroad, 137
Buffalo & Southwestern Railroad, 137
Buffalo Switchmen's strike, 19, 108
Bureau of Labor Statistics, 59, 217
Burlington, Cedar Rapids & Northern Railroad, 88, 90
Burlington Railroad, *see* Chicago, Burlington & Quincy Railroad
Burlington strike of 1888: causes, 82–83, 100; boycott, 83–84; boycott enjoined, 84–90; problem of mail, 90–98; role of ICC, 98–103; congressional reaction, 103–5; mentioned, 19, 69, 77, 107–8, 111, 114, 148, 151, 191; *see also* Arbitration Act of 1888; Arthur, P. M.; Cooley, Thomas M.; Dickinson, Don M.; executive branch; railroad brotherhoods; United States courts
Butte, Montana, 139–41

Cadwalader, John, 44–45

Caldwell, Henry Clay: background, 121; holds labor contracts binding on receivers, 122; wages to be negotiated, 122; overrules receivers, 122–23; prescribes guide for wages, 123; upholds right to organize, 129; conservative use of injunctions, 129–30; mentioned, 233, 235

California: anti-Chinese riots, 18; requests troops, 1877, 32; Commonweal army from, 140; trouble during Chicago railway strike, 166; strike cases, 175–77; *see also* Morrow, William W.; Ross, Erskine M.

Call, Wilkinson, 105

Campbell, St. George Tucker, 210

canals, 3, 5; as substitutes for railroads, 8, 16–18

Canfield, D. B., 100–101

Carlisle, John G., 138

Carnegie Steel Company, 108

Catchings, Thomas C., 187

causes of strikes (general), 105–6 213; *see also* particular strikes by name

Central Labor Union of Cleveland, 110

Central of Georgia Railroad, 116

Chandler, William E., 188

Chase, Salmon P., 99

Cheney, Benjamin P., 203

Chesapeake and Ohio Canal, 17

Chicago: impact of major strikes, 12–18 *passim;* mail problem in 1877, 43–44; troops asked for, 1894, 170–71; strike violence, 174; proposed general strike, 174–75; *see also* Burlington strike, Chicago railway strike

Chicago & Great Western Railroad, 158

Chicago & Northwestern Railroad, 100, 130, 153

Chicago, Burlington & Quincy Railroad: condition in 1888, 81; rivalry with other railroads, 83–84; seeks injunctions against boycott, 84–85, 87–88; mentioned, 100–101,

111, 137–38, 202; *see also* Burlington strike; Olney, Richard; Perkins, Charles E.

Chicago, Milwaukee & St. Paul Railroad, 162

Chicago railway (Pullman) strike of 1894: seen as national emergency, 10–14; sympathy strikes, 18; precedents for government's policy, 117, 147, 150–51; the antagonists, 152–53; origin at Pullman, 153–55; ARU intervention, 155–56; GMA reaction, 156–58; Olney protects Pullman cars via mail, 158–60; boycott becomes general railway strike, 160–61; GMA fights strike, 161–62; Olney acts to break strike, 162–64; dcision to use Sherman Act, 164–66; troops readied, 166; blanket injunction, 166–70; Army used, 170, 172; Altgeld's protest, 172–73; strike crushed, 173–75; labor support of ARU, 174–75; Chicago strike litigation, 175–82; Congress's reaction, 182–88; policy compared with 1877, 188–91; punishment of Debs, 192–94; contempt proceedings, 194–97, 201–2; conspiracy trial, 200–201; United States Strike Commission, 213–17; leads to Erdman Act, 217–25; mentioned, 207; *see also* American Railway Union; Army; Chicago; Cleveland, Grover; Debs, Eugene V.; executive branch intervention; General Managers Association; injunctions; mail; mail trains; Pullman, George M.; Pullman Palace Sleeping Car Co.; Pullman, strike at; Olney, Richard; St. John, Everett; United States courts; United States marshals; Walker, Edwin

Chinese immigration, 57–58

Cincinnati, Hamilton & Dayton Railroad, 149

Cincinnati, New Orleans & Texas Pacific Railroad, 149

Clarke, James C., 69

Cleveland, Grover: urges investigation of Southwest strike, 74–75; calls for arbitration, 75–76; pocket-vetoes O'Neill bill, 77; not consulted in Burlington strike, 93; backs Dickinson's mail policy, 95–96; ties with business and railroad communities, 136–37; battles Commonwealers, 142, 144–46; formula for calling out Army, 142, 145, 163, 170, 231; promotes James White, 148–49; allows Olney to set policy, 153, 167; seems not to understand policy, 166, 171–72; hesitates to use Army, 140, 170, 189; controversy with Altgeld, 172–73; issues proclamation, 174; policy compared with Hayes's, 142, 188–91; appoints Chicago Strike Commission, 213; discusses arbitration bill, 218; evaluated, 230–31; mentioned, 36, 48, 69, 99–100, 107, 138–39, 151, 235; *see also* Burlington strike; Chicago railway strike; executive branch intervention; Olney, Richard; Southwest strike of 1886

Cleveland administration: ties with railroads, 136–39; not tool of business, 138–39; battles Commonwealers, 142, 144–46; compared with Hayes administration, 142, 188–91; mentioned, 19, 98

coal strikes: east Tennessee, 1891–92, 108; Massillon, Ohio, 29; southern Illinois, 1894, 13

Coeur d'Alene, 143

Coke, Richard, 76–77

collective bargaining, 2, 6, 228, 240

commissioner of labor, 59, 75, 219, 223–24

Commonweal industrial armies : Coxey's scheme, 139; response, 139; march on Washington, 139; Westerners steal trains, 139–40; sympathy for, 140; railroads in receivership, 140; calls for troops, 140; crisis on Northern Pacific and Union Pacific, 141; General

Schofield sees no need for troops, 141; Olney prepares to intervene, 141–42; troops ordered out, 142–43; Hogan's army captured, 143; troops sent to Pacific Northwest, 144–46; Schofield opposed plan, 145; Olney uses Army judiciously, 146; precedents for Chicago railway strike, 150–51, 163, 170; *see also* Army, United States courts, United States marshals

Congress: policy-making responsibility, 21, 56; reaction to 1877 strikes, 56–57; investigates depression, labor problems, 57–59; reaction to Southwest strike of 1886, 69–80; debates Interstate Commerce Act, 70–71; reaction to Burlington strike, 103–7; passes Arbitration Act of 1888, 105; debates Sherman Act, 114–15; 178, 196; reaction to Chicago railway strike, 182–88; supports Cleveland's strike policy, 185–86; evaluation of role, 1877–98, 228–30, 236–39; labor legislation since 1900, 240–41; *see also* congressional investigations, legislation recommended

congressional investigations: causes of depression, 57; capital-labor relations, 57; Southwest strike, 1886, 61, 74–75; anthracite labor troubles, 105–7; Pinkerton detectives, 108–9; Judge Ricks, 110; Judge Jenkins' injunctions, 133–35; proposed strike investigations, 102, 183

conspiracy: charged in 1877, 40, 45–46; Southwest strikes, 67; Lake Shore strike, 68; attempts to outlaw in interstate commerce, 69–71; injunctions against, 86–87, 128–29, 131–33, 169; Debs's trial for, 200–201; mentioned, 150, 214; *see also* United States Courts

constitutional authority: for sending Army to aid states, 32; for protecting interstate commerce, 47, 69, 71–72, 201 contempt of court: used against 1877 strikers, 37–40; Cooley's view of, 52–53; in Southwest strikes, 62, 65, 67–68; proposed limitation of, 134; against Commonwealers, 140, 142–43; in Chicago railway strike, 175, 177, 180; Debs charged with, 193–94; mentioned, 73, 88, 204, 209, 233; *see also* Brewer, David J.; Drummond, Thomas S.; Dundy, Elmer S.; Gresham, Walter Q.; Treat, Samuel H.; United States courts

Continental National Bank of New York, 137

contracts: breach of, 113, 180–81; prereceivership contracts binding on receiver, 116–17, 122; not binding on receiver, 120; between Pullman Co. and railroads, 156–57, 167

Cooley, Thomas M.: on use of injunctions, 52–53; chairman, ICC, 91; background, 98–99; colleagues on ICC, 99–100; courted by railroads, 100–101; proposed investigation of Burlington strike, 101; ICC opposes inquiry, 101; Cooley believes ICC approves inquiry, 101–2; heated debate with ICC, 102; Cooley falls ill, 102–3; quoted, 262

corporations, 227–28, 232, 237

courts, *see* United States courts

Cowen, John K., 217

Coxey, Jacob S., 139, 146; *see also* Commonweal industrial armies

Coxey's army, Coxeyites, *see* Commonweal industrial armies

Crédit Mobilier, 28

Cullom, Shelby M., 71

Curtin, Andrew G., 74–75

Curtin Committee, 74–75, 77–80; *see also* Southwest strike of 1886

Dacus, J. A., 46

Dallas, George M., background, 210–11; decision in Reading case, 211–12; mentioned, 207–8, 218,

234; see also *Platt v. Philadelphia & R. Rd. Co., et al.;* Olney, Richard

Daniel, John W., 185

Darrow, Clarence S., 163, 199–200

Davis, Cushman K., 185

Debs, Eugene V.: founds ARU, 147; conducts Great Northern strike, 147–48, 150; cautions against boycotting, 155; leads Chicago railway strike, 155; allows mail to pass, 160; enjoined, 168–69; disobeys injunction, 170; pleads for labor support, 174–75; contempt trial, 193, 196; sentenced, 196; appeal to Supreme Court, 197–99, 201–2; conspiracy trial, 200–201; criticized by United States Strike Commission, 213; mentioned, 151–52, 157, 172, 189, 203, 207, 217; *see also* American Railway Union, Chicago railway strike, Great Northern strike

Debs, in re: preparation of case, 192–95; circuit court decision, 195–97; arguments before Supreme Court, 197–99; decision, 201–2; 238; see also *United States v. Debs*

Delaplain, Robert M., 26–27

Delaware & Hudson Railroad, 99

Denver & Rio Grande Railroad, 65

depressions, *see* Panics of 1873, 1893

Devens, Charles, 28, 37–38, 40

Dexter, Wirt, 100–101

Dickinson, Don M.: appointed postmaster general, 91; concern for mail, Burlington strike, 92–93; orders railroads to carry mail alone, 93; attacks railroad refusal, 94–95; backed by Cleveland, 95–96; fights for law forcing railroads to carry mail, 96–98; neutralizes mail issue, 102; criticized by James White, 148; mentioned, 151, 160, 231, 235; *see also* Burlington strike; Cleveland, Grover

discrimination against union members, 240

Dodge, Grenville M., 28
"domestic insurrection," 18, 30, 32, 34, 108; see also "domestic violence"
"domestic violence," 27, 31–32, 41, 51; see also "domestic insurrection"
Dorr Rebellion, 51
Drake, J. C., 143, 145
Drummond, Thomas S.: background, 35–36; protects railroads in receivership, 37–40; ruling on mail trains, 44; mentioned, 45, 93, 229, 234; see also railway strikes of 1877
Dundy, Elmer S.: background, 85–86; enjoins boycott of Burlington, 86–87; rules labor contracts not binding on receivers, 120; overruled, 122; enjoins strike on Union Pacific, 128–29; overruled, 129; mentioned, 90, 111, 114, 124

Earhart, F. B., 116
East St. Louis, 37, 41; violence during Southwest strikes, 61, 74
Eddy, A. J., 162
Egan, John M., 158, 172
eight-hour day, 239
election: disputed presidential, 1876, 29; presidential, 1888, 168; "block of five" scandals, 168
eminent domain, 95
employees of receivers, 39; declared "officers of court," 67, 118, 204; cannot be compelled to work, 88; special standing, 118; declared "employees of court," 122; may be compelled to work, 132; bill to allow arbitration of disputes with receivers, 184; see also injunctions, receiverships
enjoining, see injunctions
Erdman, Constantine J., 222
Erdman Act: Wright-Kernan draft bill compared with Arbitration Act of 1888, 217–18; Olney revisions, 218–21; debate in Congress, 222–24; passed, 224; in operation, 224–25; mentioned, 2, 238–39; see also Arbitration Act of 1888, O'Neill bill
Erie Canal, 4, 16–18
Erie Railroad, 4, 52, 153
Evarts, William M., 27; ties to railroads, 28; cabinet discussions, 33, 55
executive branch: view of role, 20–21; role in 1877 strikes, 27–35, 41–44, 46–47; 1877 role evaluated, 47–52; lack of leadership after 1877 strikes, 55–56; role in Southwest strikes, 74–76; role in Burlington strike, 90–98; role against Commonwealers, 140–46; role in Great Northern strike, 148–50; role in Chicago railway strike, 158–67, 170–75; Chicago strike policy evaluated, 188–91; punishes Debs, 192–93; promotes Erdman Act, 218–24; evaluation of executive role overall, 230–31
executive branch intervention: to enforce federal court orders, 34–35, 38, 140–46, 171–75; to protect interstate commerce, refused, 46–47; to protect mail, 41–44 (refused), 90–98, 148–50, 158–60; to protect federal property, 34; to suppress domestic insurrection, 29–34

Fair Labor Standards Act, 240
Fairchild, Charles S., 137
federal courts, see United States courts
federal executive, see executive branch, Justice Department, Postoffice Department
federal judiciary, see United States courts
federal property, see executive branch intervention
federal troops, see Army
federal v. state authority, 33–34, 47–48, 70–71, 73, 161, 172–73, 186–87, 189–90
Forbes, John Murray, 3
Fox, Edward, 45
France, president of, 172

freedom of contract, 225, 227
free-silver movement, 139

Galena & Chicago Union Railroad, 35
Garrett, John W., 26–27
General Managers Association (GMA): founded, 152; purposes, 152; disunity, 153; strength in 1894, 153; reaction to Pullman boycott, 156–57; daily meetings, 157; choose director, 158; offer to supply deputy marshals, 159; federal assistance sought, 161; legal committee, 161–62, 164; secret minutes called for, 200; criticized by United States Strike Commission, 213; mentioned, 189; *see also* Chicago railway strike
general railway strike, 81, 92, 153, 158, 160, 193
general strike, 19, 175; proposed to support Debs and ARU, 171, 174
George, James Z., 184
Gompers, Samuel, 174–75
Goudy, W. C., 100
Gould, Jay: testifies to congressional committee, 58–59; role in Southwest strikes, 61–63; mentioned, 3, 28, 72, 77–78
government, *see* United States government
Grady, H. C., 144–45
"granger" cases, 28, 62
"grangerism," 139
Grant, Ulysses S., 47
Great Northern Railroad: cuts wages, 147; strike against, 146–50; arbitrates, 150; mentioned, 152; *see also* Great Northern strike; American Railway Union; Debs, Eugene V.; Hill, James J.
Great Northern strike, 1894: causes, 146–47; protection of mail, 148–50; arbitrated, 150; mentioned, 7, 19, 21, 136, 152, 155, 158, 190–91, 230; *see also* American Railway Union; Debs, Eugene V.; Hill, James J.; Maxwell, Lawrence Jr.; *Official Opinions of the Attorneys-General of the United States;* White, James E.

Green, Norvin, 58
Greenback-Labor party, 58
Gregory, S. S., 197
Gresham, Walter Q., role in 1877 strikes, 36; defends Indianapolis, 37; calls for troops, 38; evaluates Hayes, 47; enjoins strike on Lake Shore Railroad, 68–69; enjoins boycott of Burlington, 87–88; names Cooley receiver of Wabash Railroad, 99; Cleveland's Secretary of state, 137; objects to blanket injunction, 169–70; quoted, 250, 260, 263; mentioned, 40, 49, 62, 90, 111, 114, 125, 229; *see also* Burlington strike; Lake Shore strike, 1886; railway strikes of 1877; United States courts
Grosscup, Peter S.: sketch, 167; helps draft bill for injunction, 167; terms of blanket-injunction, 168–69; questions use of injunction, 169–70; signs call for troops, 171; quoted on right to organize, 179; on right to quit work, 180; on law, order, and reform, 181–82; mentioned, 177, 188, 192; *see also* Chicago railway strike, United States courts

Hancock, Winfield Scott: quoted on strike of 1877, 14; discusses federal v. state authority, 33; calls for protection of interstate commerce, 46, 49
Hanford, Cornelius: sketch, 119; refuses to overrule receiver, 120; holds labor contract not binding on receiver, 120; mentioned, 124, 143, 234
Harlan, John Marshall, 203, 205–6
Harmon, Judson, 188
Harrison, Benjamin, 110–11, 121, 168, 211
Hartranft, John F.: calls for federal troops, 1877, 31–32; mentioned, 48
Hayes, Rutherford B.: called upon for troops by West Virginia, 27; by Pennsylvania, 31; by other

states, 32; as governor of Ohio used militia to break strike, 29; ties to railroads, 29; reluctant to send troops, 29, 189; sends troops to West Virginia, 30; to Pennsylvania, 32; insists upon correct form, 31–33; is urged to protect interstate commerce, 46–47; policy evaluated, 47–52; fails to call for legislation, 55–56; compared with Cleveland, 142, 188–91; quoted on later strikes, 248, 258–59; mentioned, 19, 42, 153, 230–31, 235; see also executive branch intervention; McCrary, George W.; railway strikes of 1877

Hayes administration: ties to railroads, 27–29, 136, 190; decides to back courts with troops, 38; policy regarding mail, 42–44; evaluation of policies, 47–52; discusses labor reforms, 55–56; compared with Cleveland administration, 142, 188–91

Haymarket Affair, 161, 172

Herbert, Hilary A., 138

Hill, James J., 147–48, 150, 152; see also Great Northern strike

Hoadly, George, 140

Hogan's army: occupies train yards, 140; warrant issued for arrest, 141–42; steals train, 142; captured and punished, 143; mentioned, 144

hours and wages legislation, 215

Howard, George W., 213

Hurlbut, S. A., 55

Illinois: calls for aid, 1877, 32; antiboycott law, 155; militia used in strikes, 161, 174; duty to protect life and property, 199; mentioned, 161, 173

Illinois Central Railroad, 69, 153

immigration restrictions, 215

impeachment, 110

income tax, 109, 139

incorporation of labor unions, 69, 71, 208

Indiana: asks for federal troops, 1877, 32; Supreme Court, 168

Indianapolis: men idled by 1877 strikes, 14; "committee of public safety" organized, 18; impact of strikes of 1877, 36–39; Army signal corps reports from, 49

Indianapolis, Bloomington & Western Railroad, 36–37

Indian wars, 8

inflation, 57, 109

injunctions: not used in 1877, 40; not used in Southwest strikes, 62; used in Lake Shore strike, 68–69; used in Burlington strike, 85–90; Coeur d'Alene, 108; Ann Arbor boycott, 111, 114; based on Sherman Act, 115–17; forbidding strikes, 125–33; antistriking injunctions condemned, 134; used against Commonwealers, 141, 145–46; in Chicago railway strike, 163–69, 175; questioned, 169–70; court upholds Sherman Act injunction against labor, 177–78, 194–96; Supreme Court upholds Chicago injunction, 201–2; Olney discusses Jenkins' injunction, 203–5; Harlan modifies Jenkins' injunction, 205–6; Olney proposes injunction to prevent railway strikes, 221; limits on injunctions, 89–90, 114, 206; cannot be used to command performance, 114, 129, 205, 224; can be used to command performance, 132; "government by injunction," 239; mentioned, 233–35, 239, 241; see also United States courts

insurrection, 48

interest-free federal loans, 139

interstate commerce: blocking of: in 1877, 11–12; in 1886, 61; in 1894, 13–14, 160–61; mentioned, 51, 228; protection of: 20–21; considered in 1877, 46–47; proposals to amend interstate commerce act to protect commerce, 69–71; by injunction, 1886, 68–69; Burlington strike, 85;

Chicago railway strike, 164, 166, 168–69; mentioned, 41, 98, 163, 171, 187, 203, 233, 239; regulation of: ICC Act, 69–70; mentioned, 20, 28, 55, 101, 106; *see also* executive branch intervention, United States courts

Interstate Commerce Act: bill under debate, 69; amendments proposed to protect against strikes, 69–71; as justification for enjoining boycotts, 86–87; strikes illegal under, 116; mentioned, 28, 79, 109, 113–14, 164, 166, 178, 198, 215

Interstate Commerce Commission, chairman: power under Erdman Act, 224–25; mentioned, 91, 219, 230; *see also* Cooley, Thomas M.

Interstate Commerce Commission (ICC): members, 98–100; role in Burlington strike, 100–3; mentioned, 216, 219

intimidation by strikers: charged in 1877, 27; written, 66; enjoined, 90, 113, 169; characteristic of strikes, 133; not characteristic, 203; mentioned, 68, 115, 125, 127, 181, 194, 209

investigative commissions: proposed in 1877, 56; proposed by O'Neill bill, 75–76; added to Arbitration Act of 1888, 103–4; not used during Chicago railway strike, 153; appointed after Chicago strike, 213; United States Strike Commission proposes permanent commission, 215–16; not included in Erdman Act, 218, 224; *see also* Arbitration Act of 1888; O'Neill bill, United States Strike Commission

investment banking, 3

Irons, Martin, 60, 78–79; quoted, 258

Jacobs, in re, 28

Jefferson City, Lebanon & Southwestern Railroad, 66

Jenkins, James G.: background, 130; enjoins strike on Northern Pacific 130–34; investigated by Congress, 134–35, 183; injunction discussed by Olney, 203–5; Harlan modifies Jenkins' injunction, 205–6; mentioned, 164–65, 169, 234

Justice Department: and Commonwealers, 140–42, 145–46; role in Great Northern strike, 149–50; role in Chicago railway strike, 158, 162–63, 190, criticized, 213; Chicago strike correspondence, 187–88; mentioned, 160, 200, 230; *see also* Olney, Richard

Kelly, Charles T., 140

Kelly's army, 140

Kernan, John D., 213, 217, 222

Key, David M., 42, 56, 149

King, John Jr., 25–26, 30

Knights of Labor, 7, 58, 174; strikes against Gould, 59–61, 68, 72, 74, 78; "scab" against BLE, 83

Knowles, Hiram, 141–42

Krekel, Arnold, 66–67, 234

Ku Klux Klan, 68

Kyle, James H., 183–84

labor: agitation in 1880's, 57–58; restiveness after 1870, 226; lack of organization and consequences, 226–28; *see also* railway workers

laborers' rights: to work or not to work (and limitations), 39, 78, 113–14, 180, 237; to quit work (and limitations), 54, 64, 90, 107, 112, 127–28, 132, 179–80, 205; to strike (and limitations), 65, 78, 111, 113–14; 128, 195, 227; to organize, belong to unions (and limitations), 78, 111, 127, 129, 134, 179, 207, 209, 227, 237, 240; to bargain collectively, 240; to choose representatives for bargaining, 240

labor reforms: Hayes talks of, 55; federal judges discuss, 180–82; mentioned, 185, 228–29, 236, 240; *see also* United States government labor policy

labor union recognition: BLE and BLF, 81–82; called for by United

306 RAILROAD LABOR DISPUTES

States Strike Commission, 214–16;
called for by Olney, 209–10;
denied, 7, 227, 237
labor unions: membership, 1880's,
58; sympathy of for Debs and
ARU, 174–75; "inevitable," 210,
215; wiped out by Civil War and
depressions, 226; failure to keep
pace with corporations, 227–28;
see also railway labor unions
laissez-faire, 1, 20, 22, 74
Lake Erie & Western Railroad, 126
Lake Shore & Michigan Southern
Railroad, 28; strike in 1886,
68–69, 125–26
Lake Shore strike, 1886, 68–69,
125–26
Lamont, Daniel S., 137, 140, 144–45,
150
Latrobe, Ferdinand C., 25
Latta, James W., 32
law and order, 214, 230, 232;
precedence over reforms, 181,
185, 229
law reports, 40, 214, 231–32
lawyers: employed by railroads, 5–6;
members of ICC, 99; court ICC's
favor, 100; receivers of Union
Pacific, 122; advise U.S. attorney,
142; GMA's legal committee,
161–62, 164; help create the
corporation, 227; assist judges in
suppressing strikes, 232
legislation recommended: following
1877 strikes, 54–56; to protect
railroads from boycotting, 89;
to require railroads to carry mail,
97; compulsory arbitration of
railway labor disputes, 104; by
Tillman committee, 105–6; to
resolve capital-labor differences,
131, 169, 206; that contempt
proceedings be restricted, 134; to
protect railroads from strikes, 149;
prolabor bills during Chicago
railway strike, 183–84; United
States Strike Commission
proposals, 215–16
legislature: West Virginia, 27;
Pennsylvania, 31–32;
Missouri, 66

Lewis, Alfred Henry, 138, 173
Lincoln, Abraham, 48, 121
Lloyd, Henry Demarest, 214, 217
Logan, John A., 77
Love, James M., 85, 88–90, 111, 114
Lyman, Arthur T., 214

mail: grounds for federal intervention, 20–21; Boston & Maine
strike, 41, 45–46; railway strikes of
1877, 41–45; courts punish
obstruction of, 44–46; Southwest
strikes no problem, 61–62;
Burlington strike, 91–98; Great
Northern strike, 148–50; Chicago
railway strike, 158–60, 166, 171;
courts enjoin interference with,
164; used by railroads to win
support, 41, 61–62, 91, 159; used
by strikers to win support, 42, 91;
neutralizing as a strike issue, 44,
98, 102, 160; see also railroad
companies and the mail
mail trains: special, 22; definition,
43–45, 92–93, 149, 151, 158,
176–77, 184, 235; inviolable, 92;
mentioned, 147, 150, 162, 168, 190
Marshall, John, 232
marshals, see United States marshals
martial law, 26, 174
Martinsburg, West Virginia: strike
in 1877, 25–26, 29–30
Massillon coal strike, 1876, 29
Mathews, Henry W.: calls out
militia, 25–26; requests federal
troops, 27; mentioned, 29–31, 50
Maxwell, Lawrence Jr., 140; ties to
railroads, 149; defines mail train,
149–50, 235
McCrary, George W., 27; ties to
railroads, 28; mentioned, 29–30,
32–34, 55–56; quoted, 253–54
McDermott, W. M., 140, 142–43
McGann, Lawrence E., 218, 222
McKinley, William, 224
McNaught, James, 141–43
McNulta, John, 87–88
mediation: of Southwest strike of
1885, 60; see also President of the
United States, as strike mediator

Milchrist, Thomas, 159, 162, 164–65, 170–71, 190
Miles, Nelson A., 10, 171–74
militia, 145, 201; inadequacy, 31; West Virginia, 25; prolabor sympathies, 25–26; inadequacy, 26, 29; in Southwest strikes, 60; New York, 108; Pennsylvania, 108; Oregon, 144; Illinois, 18, 161, 174; against Commonwealers, 139–40; inadequate, 140–41
Miller, Andrew G., 130
Miller, Samuel Freeman, 234
Missouri Commissioner of Labor, 60
Missouri, Kansas & Texas Railroad, 59
Missouri Pacific Railroad, 62, 66
Missouri Pacific strike, 1885, 59, 63–65
Morgan, House of, 137
Morgan, John T., 70–71
Morrison, William Ralls, 101–102
Morrow, William W., 176–81
Morton, J. Sterling, 137–38
Moseley, Edward A., 206–7, 218, 222
Munn v. *Illinois*, 20, 246

Nash, Thomas E., 93–96
national emergency strike, 1, 7–8, 21, 23, 179, 191, 241
National Industrial Recovery Act (NIRA), 240
nationalization of railroads, *see* railroads, government ownership
Newlands Act, 1913, 225, 239
newspaper reaction to major rail strikes, 9–12, 15, 46–47
New Orleans dockworkers' strikes, 116, 165, 177, 200
New York Central Railroad, 4, 42, 52, 153
New York City: impact of 1877 and 1894 strikes, 11–14
New York Railroad Commission, 213
New York Security & Trust Co., 137
Nimmo, Joseph, 217
Northern Pacific Railroad: Jenkins enjoins strike against, 130–33; harassed by Hogan's army, 140–43; mentioned, 153

Official Opinions of the Attorneys-General of the United States, 148, 158, 160
Old Colony Trust Co., 138
Olney, Richard: background, 138; battles Commonwealers, 140–46; role in Great Northern strike, 148–50; opposes troops for Great Northern, 150; decides to protect Pullman cars via mail cars, 158–60; appoints Edwin Walker, 162–63; instructions to Walker, 163–64; avoids use of Sherman Act, 165–66; approves bill for injunction based on Sherman Act, 166; lays ground for using troops, 163, 170; troops sent to Chicago, 171–72; country brought "to ragged edge of anarchy," 172; answers Altgeld, 173; attacked in Congress, 186; defended, 187; Debs case, 192–202; appointed secretary of state, 201; breaks ties with railroads, 202–3; favors compulsory arbitration, 203; discusses Jenkins' injunction, 203–5; defends Reading BRT members, 208–10; defines strike, 208–9; role in Erdman Act, 218–24; quoted, 275; quoted on ICC, 277; mentioned, 48–49, 104, 151, 153, 161, 189, 191, 231, 235; *see also* Cleveland, Grover
O'Neill bill: provisions, 71–72; House debate, 72–74; Senate debate, 76–77; passed, 77; pocket-vetoed, 77; revived, 103; *see also* Arbitration Act of 1888
Order of Railway Conductors, 6
Panic of 1873, 4, 6, 24, 57, 188
Panic of 1893, 4, 109, 117, 125, 136, 138, 140, 154, 188
Pardee, Don A., 67–68
Payne, Oliver, 137
Peck, George R., 161–62
Peffer, William A., 184–85; 187–88
Peik v. *Chicago & Northwestern R.R.,* 28
Pence, Lafayette, 186–87
Pennoyer, Sylvester, 144

Pennsylvania: 1877 strikes, 30–34;
call for federal troops, 31–32;
coal fields, 28, 105; Homestead,
108
Pennsylvania Railroad, 4, 5, 28, 31,
42, 55, 153
Perkins, Charles E., 138, 148, 206,
217
Philadelphia & Reading Railroad,
104, 137; case involving men
belonging to BRT, 207–12
Philips, John F., 177–78
Pinkerton detectives, 61, 83, 108–9
Pittsburgh: 1877 riots, 30–31;
mentioned, 9, 14, 16–18, 42, 48,
224
Platt v. *Philadelphia & R. Rd. Co.
et al.,* 206–12; Olney's brief,
208–10; decision, 210–12
police: inadequacy, 25; local, 139,
174
Populists, 109, 139, 182–86
postmaster general, 158, 230;
Annual Report of, 1877, 56;
1888, 97; *1893,* 149; *see also*
Bissell, Wilson; Dickinson,
Don M.
Postoffice Department: role in 1877
strikes, 42–44; Burlington strike,
91–98; Great Northern strike,
148–50; criticizes railroads during
Chicago strike, 159; assists
railroads during Chicago strike,
159; *see also* Bissel, Wilson,
Dickinson, Don M.; mail
Powderly, Terence V., 61, 74, 77, 79
precedents (legal), 85, 96, 126, 160,
164, 196, 229, 232
presidential messages: Hayes, 1877,
56; Cleveland, 1886, 75–76
presidential proclamations: Hayes,
32–33; Cleveland, 145, 174
President of the United States:
authority to assist states, 27; other
courses available, 51; as strike
mediator, 50–52, 175, 189, 240–41;
see also Cleveland, Grover;
executive branch; Hayes,
Rutherford B.
prices, 74, 228; 1877, 11–12;
1886, 62; 1894, 12–14

prolabor sympathies of public, 25,
140, 176, 225
public opinion, 81, 85, 94–95, 216,
229, 235
Pugh, James L., 187
Pullman, George M., 154–57, 178,
189, 213–14
Pullman, strike at, 154–55, 213
Pullman cars: boycotted, 155–56;
contracts regarding, 157;
protected by mail cars, 160; cut
off, 176; part of mail train, 177
Pullman employees: complaints,
154; organize, 154; strike, 154;
seek ARU support, 155; criticized
by United States Strike
Commission, 213
Pullman Palace Sleeping Car Co.,
153–57; 180, 185, 188, 213
Pullman strike, *see* Chicago railway
strike, 1894
Putnam, William L., 115

Quay, Matthew S., 32

railroad brotherhoods: attempts to
federate, 6–7; support Southwest
strike of 1885, 60; do not support
Southwest strike of 1886, 61; agree
to run special mail trains, 95;
officers enjoined from sanctioning
strike, 131; agree to Great
Northern wage cuts, 147; officers,
fight ARU, 148; Chicago railroad
companies prefer to ARU, 157;
oppose ARU in Chicago strike,
174; cited as favoring Erdman
Act, 222–23; back down from
strike in 1946, 239; *see also*
brotherhoods (by name)
railroad companies: abuses, 5, 24;
switch mail cars to ends of trains,
42, 159; allow employees to
boycott other companies, 83, 111;
cooperation among, 157; disunity,
83–84, 153; rivalry, 84; rate wars,
84, 100; receiverships used to
prevent strikes, 104, 221–22
railroad companies and the mail:
agree to carry mail cars only,
41–42; refuse to carry mail cars

only, 42–43, 92–95, 148; refuse to run mail trains without other trains, 41–42; refuse to run mail trains without Pullman cars, 160; required to run one mail train daily each way, 44, 96, 150, 160; required (or not required) by law to carry mail, 56, 92–93, 96–97; required (or not) to carry mail on special trains, 43–45, 92–93, 148, 176, 235; *see also* mail

Railroad Retirement Act of 1934, 240

railroads: basis of industrial society, 3; bellwether of economy, 3–4; bonded debt, 4–5; capital formation, 3; consumers of iron and coal, 3; depression economies, 24, 109, 147; dividends, 1877, 24–25; employees of, 5; federal assistance to, 64; first "big-businesses," 2; given eminent domain, 95; governmental owner-ship and operation, 57, 184, 213, 215; growth, 1877–94, 5; indispen-sibility, 4, 9–11, 46–47, 89, 112, 178–79; investment, 3–5; land grants, 5, 28, 86, 90, 95; led to urbanization, 3; mileage, 4–5; net income, 4–5; opened west, 2–3; pacesetters of industrialization, 2; political influence of, 5; regula-tion, 20, 28, 62, 106, 137–38; statistics, 4–5; surpass canals, 4–5; *see also* railroad companies, rail-way workmen

railroads referred to as: "quasi-public in function," 20, 38–39, 89, 112, 216; "post-roads," 92, 95, 183; "private property," 227; "public highways," 9, 27, 36–37, 68, 195, 204, 227; "public (or court) property," 37–38; "public servants," 77, 89

Railway Labor Act of 1926 and Amendments of 1934, 239–40

railway labor unions, 6–7; attempts to federate, 7; failure to work together, 7; during Southwest strike of 1886, 61; during Burlington strike, 83; during

Great Northern strike, 148; during Chicago railway strike, 174–75, 207; *see also* American Railway Union; Brotherhood of Locomotive Engineres; Brother-hood of Locomotive Firemen; Brotherhood of Railway Trainmen; Knights of Labor, Trainmen's Union

railway mail service, 43, 93, 148–49; *see also* mail

railway strike of 1922, 239

railway strikes: Boston & Maine, 1877, 41, 45–46; of 1877, 9–12, 15, 24–53; Union Pacific, 1885, 59; Southwest, 1885, 59–60; Southwest, 1886, 60–61; Lake Shore, 1886, 68–69; Burlington, 1888, 81–105; Buffalo switchmen's, 1892, 108; New York Central, 1890, 108; Great Northern, 1894, 146–51; Chicago railway (Pull-man), 1894, 152–75; of 1922, 239; *see also* separate entry for each

railway strikes as: national emergencies, 1–2, 7–8, 50, 179; in 1877, 9–12, 15–19; in 1886, 72; Chicago railway strike, 10–15; public nuisances, 194–97, 201, 204–5

railway strikes of 1877: as a national emergency, 9–12, 15, 19; origins, 24; outbreak at Martinsburg, 25–26, 29–30; at Pittsburgh, 30–31; courts protect receivership property, 35–41; problem of the mail, 41–46; problem of interstate commerce, 46–47; aftermath, 54–57; mentioned, 1, 7, 81, 92, 153, 188, 190, 230

railway strike threat of 1946, 239

railway workmen: brakemen, 83; conductors, 83, 130; engineers, 82–84; 86, 91–92, 94, 100, 112–14, 116, 130; firemen, 82–84, 94, 112, 130; switchmen, 18, 83, 88, 130; telegraphers, 130; train dispatch-ers, 130; trainmen, 130, 207–9, 211–12; weaknesses, 6; attempts to organize, 7; special responsi-

bilities, 111–12; licensing of 215;
see also Brotherhood of Locomotive Engineers, Brotherhood of
Locomotive Firemen, Brotherhood of Railway Trainmen,
labor, railroad brotherhoods,
railway labor unions
Reading case, see *Platt* v. *Philadelphia & R. R.R. Co., et al.*
Reading Railroad, *see* Philadelphia
& Reading Railroad
Reagan, John H., 105
receivers: decisions appealed to
judges, 64–68, 117–25, 207–12;
discretion great, 118–20;
discretion limited, 122–23, 218;
not bound by prereceivership
labor contracts, 120; bound by
prereceivership labor contracts,
121–23
receiverships, 35, 109, 232, 234;
property protected against
strikers, 1877, 35–38; Southwest
strikes, 62–68; 1893–94, 127–33;
against Commonwealers, 140–46;
abuses of, 25, 62, 232–33;
proposed to forestall strikes, 22,
104, 221; mentioned, 39, 80
Revised Statutes, 32, 144–45
Ricks, Augustus J., background, 110;
Ann Arbor case ruling, 112–14,
118–19; mentioned, 124, 126
Rock Island Railroad, 84, 88, 153,
156
Roosevelt, Theodore, 167
Ross, Erskine M., 176–77, 180–81
"Rule 12" of Brotherhood of
Locomotive Engineers, 83, 111–14,
116
Rutland Railroad, 99

St. John, Everett, 84, 156–57, 213–14
St. Louis: impact of 1877 strikes, 4,
9, 12, 14, 17–18; impact of Southwest strikes, 61, 63–64; mentioned,
16, 24, 36
St. Louis & Southeastern Railroad,
37
Santa Fe Railroad, *see* Atchison,
Topeka & Santa Fe Railroad

Sargent, F. P., 83
"scabbing," 7, 83
Schofield, John M., 141–42, 144–45,
171
Schoonmaker, Augustus, 100–102
Schurz, Carl, 37, 41
Scott, Thomas, 28, 42, 48–49, 55
secondary boycott: outlawed by
courts, 87, 181; antiboycotting
statute, 155; mentioned, 83, 85,
90, 110–11, 155; *see also* boycott
Sherman, John, 55, 114
Sherman Antitrust Act: Congress
debates applicability to labor,
114–15; courts consider applicability to labor, 115–17; GMA
lawyers decide law covers Chicago
strike, 161–62; used in bill for
injunction, 164; Olney hesitates
to use, 164–66; courts apply to
Chicago strike, 177–78; Walker
and Olney discuss section 4 as
basis for injunction, 194–95;
Judge Woods upholds injunction
on basis of, 195–96; Olney prefers
not to use, 197–99; Olney shelves
act, 200; Supreme Court sidesteps
issue, 202; mentioned, 109–10,
167, 237
shortages of food and fuel, 74, 228;
in 1877, 11–12; in 1886, 62;
in 1894, 12–14
Shutt, A. P., 25
Simpson, "Sockless" Jerry, 222–23
single-tax movement, 139, 215
Smith, Adam, 16, 105
Smith, C. W., 94
Smith, Hoke, 138
social security legislation, 240
solicitor general, 111; *see also*
Maxwell, Lawrence Jr.
Southern California Railroad, 176
Southern Pacific Railroad, 165, 176
Southwest strikes, 19, 61–62, 231; of
1885: 59–60, cases, 63–67;
mentioned, 18, 78; of 1886: 60–61,
cases, 67–68, congressional response, 69–80, mentioned, 18, 81,
153, 230
Sovereign, James R., 174

special counsel for the United States, *see,* Walker, Edwin

Speer, Emory: Waterhouse decision, 116–17, 124–25; mentioned, 128, 164, 233, 235

Spooner, Ben, 38, 49

Springer, William M., 76

state v. federal authority, 33–34, 47–48, 70–71, 73, 161, 172–73, 186–87, 189–90

Stetson, Francis Lynde, 136

strikebreakers, 61, 83, 96, 117, 125, 130, 158

strike investigations: proposed for 1877 strikes, 56; proposed for Southwest strike, 74–75; Southwest strike investigated, 77–80; ICC proposes study of Burlington strike, 101–2; proposed for Chicago railway strike, 183; conducted by United States Strike Commission, 213–16

strikers: fear federal intervention, 41, 61, 148, 160; punished for conspiracy against United States government: 45–46; punished for contempt, 38–40, 63–68, 112–13, 127, 196; punished for obstructing mail, 44–45

strikers and the mail: offer to run mail trains, 41–42; offer to run trains with mail cars only, 41–42, 95, 148; offer to run passenger trains, 42, 61; offer to run troop and emergency supply trains, 61–62; refuse to start new mail trains, 91; offer to run mail trains without Pullman cars, 160

strikes: called "warfare," 214, 229; courts declare illegal, 117, 128, 132; courts declare legal, 113–14, 117, 128; defined, 113, 133, 208–9; enjoinable, 125–35; enjoined, 90, 110, 125, 183, 203; number of men on strike, 58; outlawed by Congress, 239; outlawed by Sherman Act, 115–17, 128; outlawed in interstate commerce, 68–69, 87, 125, 127–28, 202; outlawed on railways in receivership, 40, 63,

68, 135; sympathy strikes, 14, 17, 84, 111, 203; *see also* United States government strike policy

strikes other than railway: anthracite coal, 1902, 241; Coeur d'Alene, 1892, 108; Homestead, 1892, 108–9; telegraphers', 1883, 58–59; Tennessee miners', 1891–92, 108

strikes outlawed: by courts, 86–87, 125–35, 167–69; by Congress, 69–71, 105

strike violence, 18; at Martinsburg, 25–26; elsewhere in 1877, 30–31; in Southwest strikes, 61, 74; impact on congressional debate, 74; in Chicago railway strike, 170–71, 174; Judge Grosscup on, 182; Jenkins rules strikes violent by nature, 133, 204; Olney disagrees, 208–9

Sugar Trust case, 165

Sullivan, Alexander, 101

Sumner, William Graham, 57

supply and demand, 214–15

Supreme Court, *see* United States Supreme Court

Taft, William Howard: background, 110–11; holds strikes legal, boycotts illegal, 113–14; agrees to hear appeals from receivers' orders, 118–21; mentioned, 117, 123–24, 128, 164, 177–79, 180–81

Taft-Hartley Act, 240–41

Taussig, Frank W., 60–61

telegraphers' strike of 1883, 58–59

Teller, Henry M., 70–71

Terre Haute & Indianapolis Railroad, 28

Texas & Pacific Railroad, 60, 62, 78

Thayer, Amos, 177

third-party politics, 57–58

Thompson, Richard W., 27; ties to railroads, 28–29; 55

Tillman, George D., 104

Tillman committee report, 105–7

Toledo, A.A. & N.M. Ry. Co. v. *Pennsylvania Co., et al.,* 111–14, 126, 164

Toledo, Ann Arbor & North
 Michigan Railroad, 111, 114
Trainmen's Union, 7
train theft, 139, 142, 144–45, 150
Treat, Samuel, 64–65, 234
Treat, Samuel Hubbel, 36, 38, 40, 62
Truman, Harry S., 239
Trumbull, Lyman, 197
Tweed, Charles H., 165
Tyler, John, 51

unemployment, 14–15, 139–40, 155,
 213
Union Pacific case, 122–23, 129
Union Pacific Railroad, 59, 85–87,
 122, 128–29, 140, 144
Union Pacific strikes of 1884, 59
United States courts, 21–22; eager to
 intervene in 1877, 35; protect
 railways in receivership, 35–41;
 view of strikes, 39–40; punish
 obstruction of the mail, 44–46;
 construe obstruction of mail into
 conspiracy against U.S., 45–46;
 role in Southwest strikes, 62–69;
 outlaw Burlington boycott, 85–90;
 continue to outlaw boycotting,
 111–14; rule on applicability of
 Sherman Act to labor, 115–17;
 hear appeals from receivers,
 117–25; enjoin strikes, 125–33;
 battle Commonwealers, 140–44;
 role in Chicago railway strike,
 166–70, 175–82; punish Debs,
 193–99, 200–202; Reading case,
 207–12; evaluation, 231–35;
 creative in suppressing strikes,
 176, 182, 231–32; not creative in
 avoiding strikes, 182
United States courts, as arbiters:
 when railways in receivership: 62,
 124–25, 210; when railways not
 in receivership, 124–25, 233
United States government: national
 debt, 4–5; receipts, 4–5;
 employees, 5; strike policy, 1,
 21–22, 80, 117, 202–5, 230;
 labor policy, 1, 19–20, 54–56
United States marshals (and
 deputies): ordered to protect railways in receivership, 37, 130;

Civil War veterans as deputies,
 37; Indianapolis requests 1000
 deputies, 38, 49; resisted by
 Commonwealers, 141; unable to
 prevent train thefts, 142;
 encourage train theft, 144; follow
 railroad attorneys' advice, 143;
 cost of deputies, 146; ordered to
 protect mail, 158; Olney
 authorizes deputies, 141, 163, 175;
 railroad employees used as
 deputies, 38, 61, 159, 213;
 companies repaid cost of deputies,
 279–80 n. 45
United States Strike Commission:
 cited, 156–57; appointed, 213;
 report of, 213–16; reaction to
 report, 216–17
United States Supreme Court:
 Munn case, 20; Debs case,
 197–202; uphold yellow-dog
 contracts, 225; fostered
 corporations, 232; encouraged
 railroad legislation to avoid
 strikes, 239
United States v. Debs, 168–69,
 195–96
United States v. E. C. Knight Co.,
 165

Vanderbilt, William, 28, 42
Vermont & Canada Railroad, 99
Vermont Railroad Commission Act,
 99
Vest, George G., 70
Vilas, William F., 187
violence, see strike violence

Wabash Railroad, 59, 62–63, 66,
 87–88, 99
wage–: cuts, 25, 59–60, 65, 109,
 117–20, 122–23, 128–29, 134, 147,
 154, 156, 180, 188, 203, 216, 218;
 raises, 36, 129, 216; rates, 82, 152,
 234
wages: set by supply and demand,
 39 65; by law, 184
Wagner Labor Relations Act, 240
Walker, Aldace F., 99, 101–2
Walker, Edwin: appointed special
 counsel, 162–63; takes charge of

government's policy, 166–67; helps draft bill for blanket injunction, 167; signs request for troops, 170–71; wants martial law, 174; moves cautiously, 192–93; discusses section 4 of Sherman Act, 194; Debs case, 192–98, 200–202; urges resumption of criminal case, 201; mentioned, 164, 186, 188–90, 204, 235; *see also* Chicago railway strike; Olney, Richard

Wappenhans, Sergeant, 49

Waterhouse v. *Comer,* 116–18, 124, 164–65

Western Union Telegraph, 58

Whiskey Trust, 165

White, James E., 43–44, 148–49

Whitney, Edward B., 197–98

Whitney, William C., 137

Wickes, Thomas, 213

Wilkinson, Stephen E., 207, 211

Wilson, James Harrison, 37, 41, 48

Wilson-Gorman Tariff of 1894, 109

Woods, William A.: helps draft bill for injunction, 167; background, 168; hands down blanket injunction, 168–69; initial contempt hearing, 193–94; sees ruling as "his opportunity," 195; ruling in Debs case, 195–97; mentioned, 177, 188, 198; *see also* Grosscup, Peter S.

Woolson, John S., 121, 123–24, 235

Workingmen's Amalgamated Council of New Orleans, *see* New Orleans dockworkers' strikes

Worthington, Nicholas E., 213

Wright, Carroll D., 59, 213, 217–18, 222

Wright, George B., 36–37

yellow-dog contracts, 211, 216, 218, 224–25, 240